THE FRUITS AND FRUIT TREES
OF MONTICELLO

THE FRUITS AND FRUIT TREES OF

Monticello

PETER J. HATCH

UNIVERSITY OF VIRGINIA PRESS

Charlottesville and London

This book was made possible in part by a gift from Luella and Martin Davis.

University of Virginia Press
© 1998 by the Thomas Jefferson Memorial Foundation
Printed in Canada on acid-free paper

First published 1998
First paperback edition published 2007

2 4 6 8 9 7 5 3 1

Frontispiece: see figure 21.

The Library of Congress has cataloged the hardcover edition as follows:
Library of Congress Cataloging-in-publication Data
Hatch, Peter J., 1949–
The fruits and fruit trees of Monticello / Peter J. Hatch.
p.   cm.
Includes bibliographical references and index.
ISBN 0-8139-1746-8 (alk. paper)
1. Monticello (Va.)   2. Jefferson, Thomas, 1743–1826—Homes and
haunts—Virginia.   3. Orchards—Virginia.   4. Gardens—Virginia.
I. Title.
E322.74.H38   1998   97-10088
978.5'482—dc21   CIP

ISBN-13: 978-0-8139-2691-9

To
Ro Ro, Oh Oh,
Lu Lu,
and
More More

Contents

List of Illustrations   viii

Preface   xi

Introduction   1

Part I

The Farm Orchard and the Fruit Garden   13

Fruit-Tree Culture at Monticello   20

The South Orchard   42

Part II

Apples: "Our Democratic Fruit"   59

The Luxury of the Peach   79

Cherries: For Use or Delight   93

Pears: Leisure-Class Fruit   100

Plums of the Old World and New   107

Apricots: Precious but Precarious   117

Nectarines: The "Artificial Plant"   122

Almonds: A Futile Experiment   125

Quinces: Humble and Forgotten   127

Part III

Grapes: The Species of Utopia   131

Figs: "Vulgar" Fruit or "Wholesome Delicacy"   161

Strawberries: Arcadian Dainties   167

Currants, Gooseberries, and Raspberries   175

Appendix: Fruit Varieties Grown
by Thomas Jefferson at Monticello   183

Notes   189

Bibliography   207

List of Credits   215

Index   217

Illustrations

Aerial view of Monticello . . . . frontispiece

Archaeological excavations of south orchard xii

Restored fruitery xv

FIGURES

1. Andrew Jackson Downing 1

2. Title page of Downing's *Fruits and Fruit Trees of America* 2

3. Thomas Jefferson 3

4. Jefferson's plan for an ornamental farm on the hillside of Monticello 3

5. William Prince nursery broadside, 1790 4

6. Jefferson's fruit and vegetable gardens 7

7. Monticello fruit garden with vineyard, vegetable garden wall, and garden pavilion 8

8. St. George Tucker 15

9. George Washington's Mount Vernon fruit garden. 16

10. Upper Bremo, the home of John Hartwell Cocke 17

11. Recess cottage at Bremo. 18

12. Title page of Batty Langley's *Pomona* 21

13. Frontispiece of Philip Miller's *Gardener's Dictionary*, 8th ed., 1768 22

14. William Cobbett 22

15. A Green Gage plum "headed down" according to William Forsyth's *Treatise on the Culture and Management of Fruit Trees*, 2d ed., 1803 23

16. Assumed portrait of Bernard McMahon. 23

17. Re-created "old nursery" 25

18. Budding and grafting techniques from Forsyth's *Treatise* 26

19. Re-created paling fence 28

20. Re-created ha-ha ditch 28

21. Monticello and its southeastern slope 30

22. John Custis. 31

23. "Heading down" a pear tree as illustrated in Forsyth's *Treatise* 34

24. Tent caterpillars 36

25. Insect pests of the pear 37

26. Apple varieties from Langley's *Pomona* 40

27. Garden Book page from 1769 with early fruit-planting plans. 43

28. Jefferson's 1778 orchard plan 44

29. Jefferson's notes for 1778 orchard plan 45

30. Jefferson's notes on nurseries and "Directions Oct. 1783". 46

31. Jefferson's planting memorandum for William Prince order in 1791 48

32. Jefferson's 1806 plan for the top of Monticello mountain 50

33. Garden Book from 1810 52

34. Jefferson's chart reflecting the state of the south orchard in 1811. 53

35. 1811 orchard plan 54

36. Planting record from 1812 Garden Book 54

37. Albemarle, or Newtown, Pippin harvest in 1910. . . 60

38. Apples from Langley's *Pomona* 61

39. Old World apples from Langley's *Pomona* 62

40. Advertisement for William Smith nursery, 1755 63

41. Father Abraham apple 64

42. Jefferson's drawing of an apple mill and press. 65

43. Fire blight 67

44. Cedar-apple rust 68

45. Carolina parrot 69

46. Ralls Genet apple. 70

47. Green and yellow forms of Newtown Pippin. . . 71

48. Harvest time in central Virginia Pippin orchard 72

49. Esopus Spitzenburg apple 73
50. Hewes Crab apple 74
51. White Calville apple 76
52. Calville Blanc d'Hiver 76
53. Early, or Prince's, Harvest apple 77
54. English Codling apple 77
55. English peaches from Langley's *Pomona* 80
56. Directions for peach pruning in
    William Cobbett's *American Gardener* 82
57. Late Heath peach 87
58. Large Yellow Pineapple, or
    Lemon Cling, peach 88
59. Bloody, or Indian Blood Cling, peach 89
60. Teton de Venere peach from
    Langley's *Pomona* 89
61. Teton de Venus from Henri Louis Duhamel
    Du Monceau, *Traité des arbres fruitiers* 89
62. Teton de Venus from William Coxe's
    View of the Cultivation of Fruit Trees 90
63. Alberges peach 90
64. October peaches ripening in
    the south orchard 92
65. Cherry tree on the border of
    the kitchen garden 94
66. Cherries discovered by archaeologists
    at Monticello in 1981 95
67. Cherries from Langley's *Pomona* 96
68. Kentish cherry 98
69. May Duke cherry 99
70. Pear varieties from Langley's *Pomona* 101
71. Seckel pear 102
72. Beurré Gris from Langley's *Pomona* 103
73. Beurré Gris from Duhamel's *Traité* 103
74. Crassane from Langley's *Pomona* 104
75. Crassane from Duhamel's *Traité* 104
76. St. Germaine from Langley's *Pomona* 105
77. St. Germaine from Duhamel's *Traité* 105
78. Virgouleuse from Langley's *Pomona* 106
79. Virgouleuse from Duhamel's *Traité* 106
80. Chickasaw plum in the south orchard 107

81. Plums from Langley's *Pomona* 109
82. Green Gage plum from Coxe's *View* 110
83. Green Gage plum from Langley's *Pomona* . . . 110
84. Plum varieties from Langley's *Pomona* 113
85. Blue Imperatrice plum 114
86. Mirabelle plum 115
87. Apricot varieties from Langley's *Pomona* 118
88. Nectarine varieties from Langley's *Pomona* . . . 123
89. Portugal Apple quince 128
90. Restored northeast and
    southwest vineyards 132
91. Detail of the first Monticello vineyard
    and berry squares from 1778 orchard plan 133
92. Philip Mazzei 133
93. March 25, 1807, vineyard plan 136
94. Wild grapes, *Vitis vulpina* 141
95. Pruning techniques from copy of
    Robert Bolling's "Sketch of Vine Culture" . . . 144
96. John Adlum 146
97. Catawba grape 147
98. Vine-training systems from John James Dufour's
    American Vine Dresser's Guide 148
99. Grape training, from S. W. Johnson's
    Rural Economy 149
100. Vineyard espalier system at Monticello 150
101. Pruning techniques from Bolling's
     "Sketch of Vine Culture" 150
102. Black rot on grapes 151
103. Phylloxera attack on grape leaves 151
104. Alexander grape 153
105. White Frontinac, or Muscat Blanc,
     from Langley's *Pomona* 155
106. Muscat Blanc from Duhamel's *Traité* 155
107. Cornichon Blanc 156
108. Muscat of Alexandria 157
109. Norton's Virginia, or Norton's Seedling 159
110. White, or Marseilles, fig 162
111. Figs growing in the submural beds
     at Monticello 165
112. Detail of White, or Marseilles, fig 166

113. Wood strawberry, *Fragaria vesca* 168

114. Pine strawberries in the vegetable garden. . . . 169

115. Alpine strawberry 172

116. Chili strawberry 173

117. Gooseberries 177

COLOR PLATES

following page 62

1. Newtown, or Albemarle, Pippin from William Coxe's unpublished second edition of "A View"

2. Newtown Pippins from the south orchard

3. Esopus Spitzenburg apples from the south orchard

4. Esopus Spitzenburg from Coxe's "View"

5. Hewes Crab and Roan's White Crab

6. English Codling

following page 78

7. Newtown Pippin from George Brookshaw's *Horticultural Repository*

8. Winesap apple

9. White Calville, or Calville Blanc d'Hiver

10. Golden Pearmain

11. Pomme Gris in the south orchard

12. Hewes Crab in the south orchard

13. Breast of Venus, or Poppa di Venere, peach

14. Alberges peach

15. Pesca Mela, or Apple, peach

16. Vaga Loggia peach

following page 94

17. Lemon Cling and Indian Blood Cling peaches

18. Heath Cling peach

19. Heath Cling peach ripening in the south orchard

20. Oldmixon Cling peach

21. Oldmixon Free peaches

22. May Duke cherry

23. Carnation and White Heart cherries

24. Red Heart, White Heart, and Black Heart cherries

25. Kentish, English Bearer, and Carnation cherries

26. Seckel pear in the south orchard

27. Seckel pear from Coxe's "View"

28. Beurré Gris, or Brown Beurré, pear

29. Crassane pear

following page 110

30. Plums from Coxe's "View"

31. Green Gage plum from William Hooker's *Pomona Londinensis*

32. Green Gage plums in the south orchard

33. Moor Park apricot

34. German, or Peach, apricot

35. Violet Hative nectarine

following page 142

36. Lachrima dolce grape, possibly Jefferson's "Lachrima Christi"

37. Colorino grape

38. Picolit grape, possibly Jefferson's "Abrostine White"

39. Aleatico grape

40. Seralamanna grape

41. Muscat Blanc grapes ripening in the northeast vineyard

42. Sangiovese grape from Giorgio Gallesio's *Pomona italiana*

43. Sangiovese grapes in the southwest vineyard

following page 158

44. "Fico Albo," or Marseilles, fig from Gallesio's *Pomona*

45. Fig harvest at Monticello in 1991

46. Strawberries

47. White Antwerp raspberry

48. White Dutch currant

49. *Ribes aureum*, the yellow-flowering currant

Preface

Thomas Jefferson's fruit plantings — his orchards, vineyards, berry squares, and nursery —have been re-created at Monticello through the efforts of the Thomas Jefferson Memorial Foundation. Today, visitors to Monticello can observe the restored south orchard (first planted in 1982), the submural beds with plantings of the Marseilles fig (1984), the northeast vineyard (1985), berry squares of currants, raspberries, gooseberries, and figs (1986), the north orchard of Hewes Crab apple trees (1991), a sample of the paling fence (1992), the southwest vineyard of Sangiovese grapes (1993), and the nursery exhibit (1994). Jefferson's favorite fruits — from the Alpine strawberry to Chasselas Rosé grape; from the Albemarle Pippin to the Esopus Spitzenburg apple; from the Green Gage plum and Moor Park apricot to the Seckel pear, Oldmixon Free peach, and Carnation cherry — have been brought back to Monticello. They are regularly sampled in summer fruit tastings and autumn apple tastings, educational outreach programs that are part of Monticello's Saturdays in the Garden series. Fruit is harvested throughout the growing season and distributed to Monticello employees or else, when in overwhelming abundance, passed on to a local charitable organization.

The re-creation of Jefferson's Fruitery was the result of a commitment, beginning in the mid-1970s, to restore all of the missing landscape features within the second roundabout at Monticello. Architectural historian William Beiswanger spearheaded and coordinated many landscape restoration projects through the 1970s and 1980s and prepared plans for the restoration of the Monticello orchards and vineyards in 1979. As a horticulturist, I had been hired in 1977 to be superintendent of grounds, and archaeologist William Kelso was engaged in 1979 to initiate an archaeological program di-

rected toward the restoration of the fruit and vegetable garden. Using the disciplines of geology, horticulture, architecture, landscape architecture, and archaeology, we strove to re-create Jefferson's garden and orchards with an unusual dedication to historical accuracy.

Between 1979 and 1981 archaeological excavations attempted to confirm the documentary evidence about the south orchard and vegetable garden. Archaeologists discovered the entrance gate to the garden, enabling the garden squares to be laid out according to Jefferson's specifications. They also uncovered the remnants of the original 1,000-foot-long rock wall and the foundations of the garden pavilion, a prerequisite for the re-creation of this sprawling seven-acre complex on the southern slope of Monticello mountain. Horticultural activity—digging, planting, the decay of roots —often leaves distinct soil stains in terms of color or texture, a lasting archaeological legacy. By carefully troweling away topsoil, archaeologists were able to decipher stains of about fifty of the original fruit trees in the south orchard. The stains, some caused by planting holes, others by the decay of the trunks and roots, presented a pattern that conformed fairly closely to Jefferson's 1778 and 1811 orchard plans. Soil stains for the black locust posts for the paling fence also were uncovered, revealing a very specific ten-foot spacing. A 125-foot sample of this ten-foot-high fence was restored in 1992 above the vegetable garden along Monticello's Mulberry Row.

In conjunction with the archaeologically discovered soil stains, Jefferson's 1811 plan for the south orchard was used to stake tree locations for replanting. The 1811 date corresponds to the Monticello era the Thomas Jefferson Memorial Foundation has traditionally sought to re-create. Using this plan meant that the orchard would not represent the collection of

Archaeological excavations of south orchard in 1980. Newspaper was placed over tree (*center*) and posthole (*left*) stains, which conform to Jefferson's 1778 and 1811 grid maps.

150 fruit tree varieties Jefferson had assembled over his lifetime but rather presents the mature Monticello orchard after forty-two years of growing successes and cultural failures. For example, although Jefferson planted twenty-four plum varieties during his fruit-gardening career, by 1811 the orchard contained only two plum trees. Approximately thirty Jefferson varieties of ten species of fruit trees were replanted in the south orchard. In a few cases, where the Jefferson variety was unavailable, nineteenth-century fruit varieties were substituted. Violet Hative, the oldest nectarine variety still in cultivation, dating from around 1830, was planted as a substitute for the Jefferson varieties (Red Roman, Yellow Roman),

which are extinct today. Trees for the restoration were obtained from a variety of sources—commercial nurseries, private collectors of old apple varieties, experimental research stations throughout the United States and Europe — and planting began in 1982.

The pomological lessons learned by Thomas Jefferson became readily apparent to restorers 180 years later. Peaches, figs, and grapes thrive in the microclimate of the south orchard, while currants, gooseberries, pears, and to some extent apples suffer in the withering heat and blistering sun of the south-facing Monticello hillside. Fruit-killing frost is rarely a problem because of the way warm air drains upward during spring and fall nights. Barriers and fences are imperative to fend off indigenous pests: groundhogs, rabbits, and especially the eastern white-tailed deer, whose populations have expanded with suburban sprawl and the resultant alterations to the native forest. Today, deer are the worst fruit pest at Monticello, grazing the foliage and fruit of apples and grapes and girdling young trees with their early autumn rutting. Other serious Jefferson-era pests still confound Monticello gardeners, whether peach tree borers, plum curculio, or the black rot and downy mildew that surely plagued Jefferson's grape-growing endeavors. Other pests are of more recent introduction, such as cedar-apple rust, Johnsongrass, or the Japanese beetle.

Locating Jefferson's favorite fancy fruits has been a singular challenge for restorers. Many varieties apparently have become extinct, including many of the Italian peaches from Philip Mazzei that were Jefferson introductions into North America, such as Vaga Loggia, Alberges, and Mela, or Apple, peach. The English Codling apple, which Philip Miller said was "too well known to describe" in 1768, and the Medlar Russetin apple, apparently an uncommon and distinct Virginia variety, have disappeared from cultivation. Monticello's mystery apple, the Taliaferro, which Jefferson said was "the most juicy apple I have ever known," probably is extinct. William Kenrick in *The New American Orchardist*, 1845, described the fruit as "the size of a grape shot, or from one to two inches in diameter; of white color, streaked with red; with a sprightly acid [taste]." Such a historical description of the Taliaferro is so incomplete that even if one were to locate an apple called Taliaferro, it would be very difficult to verify. Other Jefferson varieties now apparently lost include the Virginia White apple, the colony's first named horticultural variety; the famed Alexander grape, a hybrid which held great promise to pioneer American viticulturists; and the much-sought-after Hudson strawberry, whose lineage is still a question.

The challenge of locating Jefferson varieties often involved deciphering his personal names for plants. For example, the "Carolina Canada" peach Jefferson received from Timothy Matlack was undoubtedly Kennedy's Carolina, named for a New Yorker, Robert Kennedy, who brought this peach north from Charleston, South Carolina, and popularized it. Later this peach became known as Lemon Cling, which Monticello gardeners located in 1982. The "Calvit" apple sent to Monticello by John Armstrong in 1804 was surely Calville Blanc d'Hiver, still known to apple connoisseurs, and the "Bursé" pear Jefferson ordered from the William Prince nursery in 1791 was unquestionably the French pear Beurré Gris, available in some fruit collections today. Other names, particularly of peach varieties, will never be deciphered: we will never know the true identity of the "fine white, red, & yellow plum peaches from Balyal's [a Monticello workman]," or the "ox-eye-striped" apple that Jefferson obtained from John Armstrong of Cincinnati in 1804.

One problem that has challenged gardeners since the beginnings of commercial horticulture is ascertaining that varieties are true to name. We obtained apple trees labeled Albemarle Pippin from a nursery source and planted them in 1982, but when they began bearing in 1988 it was obvious the apples were not Pippins. Eighteen trees had to be removed and replanted. Although unknown in the United States, the Poppa di Venere peach was available in 1982 from an Italian fruit research station. The staff responded to Monticello's request for scion wood and seemed to understand the elaborate procedure for importation: unless a plant or bud stick can be certified virus-free, it must be quarantined by the U.S. Department of Agriculture. Only a limited number of commercial varieties are so certified, and the Breast of Venus required a quarantine period in the department's Beltsville, Maryland, nurseries.

Unfortunately, the initial shipment of budwood was addressed to Monticello rather than the USDA. The package arrived in New York City, and a customs officer soon called to announce that the scion wood was to be incinerated. The following year, 1983, a French nurseryman forwarded Teton de Venere scions to Beltsville for Monticello's south orchard. This time, the scions arrived in May, after the station's rootstock had all been used, and so again, the plant material was destroyed. It was the third year, 1984, when all the procedures went smoothly: the forms arrived from Beltsville announcing first delivery, then propagation, and finally that the young trees were established in the quarantine nursery. Nine years passed until the quarantine on the Breast of Venus peach was lifted (the delay was attributed to government budget problems), and in the summer of 1993 Monticello gardeners retrieved scion wood and propagated the plants. In 1995 these trees began bearing; after fourteen years of searching and waiting, the fruit proved not to be the Breast of Venus. Gardeners at Monticello not only commiserated with Jefferson's own problems with stocking his orchards but learned the two great lessons of gardening—persistence and patience. The search, however, continues.

Other Jefferson fruit trees have been more successfully retrieved. The Hewes Crab survived the decline of cider production by functioning as a rootstock upon which to graft less vigorous or hardy dessert apples in a Shenandoah Valley state experimental fruit station. This fine cider apple, described as "ambrosia" by some, was the basis for Monticello's north orchard re-creation in 1992. Old peach varieties have not survived like apples, but the Monticello collection is noteworthy and includes Heath Cling, the first named American peach; Oldmixon Free, the favorite for dessert for its candy-sweet flavor; Indian Blood Cling, a curiosity yet excellent to eat out of hand; Lemon Cling, an early peach with an unusual lemony taste and plumlike texture; and "October" peaches that hang on the trees until almost Thanksgiving. Jefferson's favorite pear, apricot, and plum—respectively, the Seckel, Moor Park, and Green Gage—were easily retrieved from commercial sources. His favorite cherry, the Carnation, was more elusive, but eventually was found, along with the May Duke cherry, at the New York State Experimental Fruit Station in New York. The Beurré Gris pear came from the National Fruit Trial Station at Faversham in Kent, England. Sources for Jefferson's collection of fruit trees are as diverse as the collection itself.

The northeast vineyard was restored in 1985, based on the 1807 Jefferson planting plan, perhaps the most detailed documented grape planting in America before 1830. In addition, archaeologists had surveyed the site of this vineyard in the early 1980s, but except for a suggestion of postholes, their findings were inconclusive. Although Jefferson had written instructions for one of his workers to "espalier" the grapes, the training methods and possible espalier structure used at Monticello were a matter of speculation. Ultimately, we adapted a method and structure from the writings of Edward Antill, in the 1771 edition of the *Transactions* of the American Philosophical Society. Antill's system specified what was also called a "Roman frame": a four-rail fence with posts four feet apart, and the horizontal rails at three, four, five, and six feet above the ground.

Most of the *vinifera* cultivars planted in 1807 were of ancient origin, and retrieving them was a matter of resolving the nomenclature issues: to find modern synonyms for what Jefferson called the "Queen's grape" or the "Great July" or what was sent to him as the "Black cluster" or "Brick-coloured." Twenty-one varieties were planted in 1985; such diversity reflected Jefferson the experimenter rather than Jefferson the wine maker. Most of the grape collection was assembled from the Foundation Plant Materials Service at the University of California, Davis. An exception was the Scuppernong vines, which came from John Hartwell Cocke's Bremo, where extant vines survive from early nineteenth-century plantings. The quality and the amount of the harvests have depended on the nature of the growing season and the diligence of pesticide applications. In 1990, 300 bottles of dry white wine were made from this vineyard after combining as many as nine different grape varieties. The northeast vineyard represents an unusual collection of Italian varieties —from the fingerlike table grape Olivette Blanche to the Aleatico, which produces a very sweet, muscat-flavored wine. In contrast, the larger southwest vineyard was replanted in 1993 entirely with the Sangiovese grape, a variety documented by Jefferson in 1807 and the principal ingredient of Chianti. The goal of this re-creation is to create a Chianti-style wine, for either private use or for sale, and the initial harvest of 1995 produced 300 bottles.

The Monticello berry squares were laid off, terraced into seventeen levels, and replanted in 1986. Restored varieties have included the Red Dutch currant, the oldest named currant cultivar still in cultivation, and the yellow flowering currant, *Ribes aureum*, collected by Lewis and Clark; nineteenth-century gooseberries; a modern variety of raspberry; and Angelica and Marseilles figs. The older European gooseberries suffered from the heat, humidity, and disease and were

Restored fruitery

replaced in 1990 with a modern cultivar that contains American gooseberry bloodlines. Although probably still in cultivation outside the United States, the White and Red Antwerp raspberries so far have eluded us. A portion of the submural ("below the wall") beds were restored in 1984 with plantings of six varieties of fig, including Marseilles, Brunswick, Green Ischia, and Angelica. As long as winter temperatures stay above 15 degrees, figs thrive in the microclimate of the Monticello fruitery. In the late 1980s and early 1990s, thousands of figs were harvested from these plants with little attention given to winter protection. Jefferson's favorite, Marseilles, has proved to be especially hardy and cold resistant.

The fruits and fruit trees of Monticello are regarded as part of a museum collection, and efforts are made to document and care for these plants with the same amount of attention as is given to indoor museum collections. New plants for the collection — from the Peach apricot to the Red Antwerp raspberry — continue to be sought, and fruit gardeners at Monticello experiment with new techniques of keeping Jefferson's collection healthy and alive. The horticultural challenge of upholding and clarifying the Jefferson vision is substantial; the rewards, however, of sampling his "precious refreshment" are enduring. The search for the fruits and fruit trees of Monticello, the documentation of Thomas Jefferson's 170 varieties, and the quest for true-to-name specimens inspired this book.

I want to thank the Thomas Jefferson Memorial Foundation for their support of this project, particularly President Dan Jordan and Douglas Wilson, Director of the International Center for Jefferson Studies. Cinder Stanton provided assistance with the Italian fruit varieties, and C. Allen Brown led me to the John Hartwell Cocke papers dealing with fruit. I also want to salute our staff of gardeners and groundskeepers, who cared for the gardens and landscape while I was at the library looking at microfilm.

THE FRUITS AND FRUIT TREES
OF MONTICELLO

Introduction

The title of this work is inspired by Andrew Jackson Downing's *Fruits and Fruit Trees of America*, first published in 1845 and the standard pomological authority by the "fairest name in American horticultural literature" (figs. 1, 2). Downing's *Fruits* is a technical work that in the ninth edition of 1849 described 894 varieties of the finest fancy fruit known at the time. The mid-nineteenth century was the golden age of pomology in the United States, a period when public interest in the cultivation and development of connoisseur fruit was unequaled; when apples, pears, and peaches were critically reviewed and competitively rated with the fervor we now reserve for leisure-time activities like Hollywood movies and popular music. Downing's impact on fruit growing was magnified by his contributions to landscape design. His *Treatise on the Theory and Practice of Landscape Gardening*, first published in 1841, defined the popular landscape aesthetic of the nineteenth century; his influence spread to architecture, even to vernacular tastes in furniture. Landscape historians, who often begin their studies of the history of American landscape architecture with Downing, are, I suspect, surprised by his unrelenting passion for such a utilitarian field as fruit growing. For Downing, "fine fruit is the most perfect union of the useful and the beautiful that the earth knows," and scientific pomology was an essential complement to his theories of landscape gardening.[1]

Thomas Jefferson was also an indefatigable fruit grower, who like Downing possessed a diversity of talents and interests, including the design of ornamental pleasure grounds (fig. 3). One of Jefferson's central visions for the landscape at Monticello was to create a *ferme ornée*, an ornamental farm, by "interspersing the articles of husbandry with the attributes of a garden." The theme of the delightful and useful is an accessible way of defining both his architectural and horticultural world. Elaborately designed spiral labyrinths of Scotch broom were juxtaposed with experimental field crops, farm roads were lined with ornamental trees, and fishponds not only provided fresh food for the table but also introduced the cooling element of water into the dry mountaintop landscape. These features were the landscape equivalents of the numerous household gadgets—the seven-day clock, the writing machine, and the dumbwaiter—that enthrall today's visitors and distinguish, for some, the genius of Monticello.

Fig. 1. Andrew Jackson Downing, from *Theory and Practice of Landscape Gardening*

1

THE

FRUITS AND FRUIT TREES

OF

AMERICA;

OR,

THE CULTURE, PROPAGATION, AND MANAGEMENT, IN THE GARDEN AND
ORCHARD, OF FRUIT TREES GENERALLY;

WITH

DESCRIPTIONS OF ALL THE FINEST VARIETIES OF FRUIT,
NATIVE AND FOREIGN, CULTIVATED IN THIS COUNTRY.

BY A. J. DOWNING.

CORRESPONDING MEMBER OF THE ROYAL BOTANIC SOCIETY OF LONDON; AND OF THE
HORTICULTURAL SOCIETIES OF BERLIN; THE LOW COUNTRIES; MASSACHU-
SETTS PENNSYLVANIA; INDIANA; CINCINNATI, ETC.

What wondrous life is this I lead?
Ripe apples drop about my head;
The luscious clusters of the vine
Upon my mouth do crush their wine;
The nectarine and curious peach
Into my hands themselves do reach.
                                   MARVELL.

NINTH EDITION, REVISED.

NEW YORK:

JOHN WILEY, | G. P. PUTNAM,
161 BROADWAY. | 155 BROADWAY.

1849.

Fig. 2. Title page of Downing's
Fruits and Fruit Trees of America

Fig. 3. Thomas Jefferson, by Thomas Sully, 1856 copy of 1821 life portrait

Even a Jefferson plan for the north, or farm, orchard at Monticello was stamped with his novel imagination in an effort to exploit a functional part of the plantation for ornamental purposes (fig. 4). The longitudinal rows, up and down the slope of the hill, were aligned like the spokes of a wheel emanating from a wide hub, the first roundabout road.[2]

Both A. J. Downing and Thomas Jefferson would agree that fruit growing is the crowning glory of the ornamental farm, providing fresh food and spirited liquors for the table as well as a visual bouquet of flower and fruit—the ideal blend of the "articles of husbandry" with the "attributes of a garden." Jefferson cultivated over 170 varieties of the finest temperate fruits known at the time. He set an example as an enthusiastic and pioneering experimenter, a model steward of the land. The gardens at Monticello were his laboratory; the fruits and fruit trees of Monticello the most intriguing of his experiments.

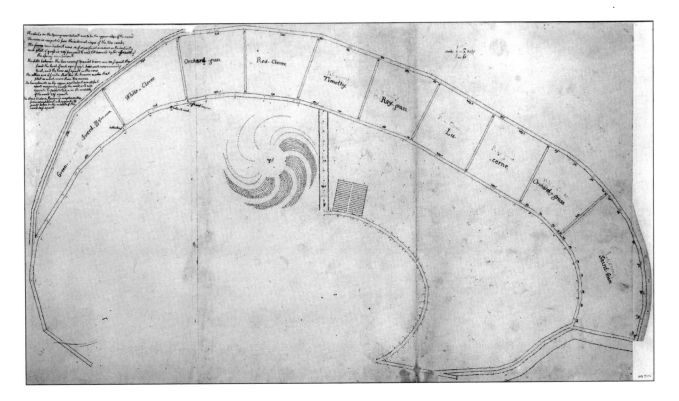

Fig. 4. Jefferson's undated plan for an ornamental farm on the hillside of Monticello, probably from the 1790s. As designed, the north orchard's latitudinal rows emanated down from the allée of honey locust trees along the first roundabout. The pinwheel was to be planted with broom. The house would be near the bottom of the drawing.

TO BE SOLD,

By WILLIAM PRINCE,

At *Flushing Landing*, on LONG-ISLAND, near *New-York*,

A large Collection, as follow, of

Fruit Trees and Shrubs.

English Cherries.

MAY Dukes,
Black hearts,
White hearts,
Carnations,
Bleeding hearts,
Ox hearts,
Amber,
Red hearts,
Duke cherry,
Cluster cherry,
Double blossom cherry,
Spanish hearts,
Honey cherry,
Kentish cherry,
Mazarine cherry,
Morello cherry.

Plumbs.

Green gage plumbs,
Yellow egg plumb, as big as a hen's egg,
White sweet plumb, bigger than a hen's egg,
Orleans plumb, very large and fine,
Red Imperial plumb,
The wild Allegany plumb, and red and yellow, two sorts,
Catharine plumb,
Cherry plumb,
Matchless plumb,
Large pear plumb,
White imperial plumb,
Drab d'or plumb,
Apricot plumb,
White bonum magnum plumb,
Whitton plumb,
Jeanhative plumb,
Precous detour plumb,
Fotheringham plumb,
Red perdigron,
Brignole plumb,
White damson plumb,
Large red sweet plumb,
Large Holland plumb,
Early sweet damson plumb,
Red bonum magnum plumb,
Winter damson frost plumb.

Apricots.

Large early apricot,
Large French Brussels apricot,
Orange apricot,
Masculine apricot,
Blanche apricot,
Algier apricot,
Roman apricot,
Turky apricot,
Small sweet apricot,
Large moor park or peach apricot.

Nectarine.

Fairchild's early nectarines,
Large green clingstone nectarine,
Yellow nectarine,
Red Roman nectarine,
Yellow Roman nectarine,
Elruge nectarine,
Temple's nectarine,
Italian or Brugnon nectarine,
Newington nectarine,
Genoa nectarine,
Brinyon nectarine.

Peaches.

The scarlet nutmeg peach,
White nutmeg peach,
Green nutmeg or early ann, ripe in July,
The rare ripe peach,
Old newington peach,
New newington peach,
Large early clingstone peach,

Large red peach,
Large red clingstone, weighs from 11 to 12 ounces,
Yellow clingstone, called the Carolina Canada, weighs a pound,
The white blossom peach,
Fine large French peach call'd murketong,
Fine red clingstone, equal to a pine apple for goodness,
English swalch peach,
Large red stone peach, weighs from 10 to 15 ounces,
Large Yellow clingstone, weighs 10 or 12 ounces, ripe October 15th,
Large white clingstone, weighs 14 ounces,
Large lemon clingstone,
Lemon peach,
English double blossom peach,
Large winter clingstone peach,
Large yellow malagatune peach,
Large yellow clingstone peach,
Large white stone peach,
White winter clingstone peach,
Blond peach,
Carolina clingstone peach,
Western newington peach,
Barcelona yellow clingstone,
Elizabeth peach,
Yellow Catharine peach,
Red cheek malagatune peach,
Large blood clingstone peach,
Large heath peach,
Green Catharine peach.

Pears.

Bergamot pear,
Catharine pear,
Vergal'eu pear,
Joly pear,
Monsieur jean pear,
Amber pear,
French primitive pear,
Winter bonne cretienne pear,
Easter bergamot pear,
Choumontelle pear,
Russellet pear,
Early sugar pear,
Beure vert pear,
Burre de roy pear,
Colmer pear,
Swan's egg pear,
Cressan pear,
Spanish bonne cretienne pear,
Large bell pear,
Citron de camis pear,
Summer bergamot pear,
Autumn bergamot pear,
Lent St. Germaine pear,
Brocaus bergamot pear,
Winter bergamot pear,
Jargonelle pear,
Roussilon pear,
Cuisse madam pear,
Green Catharine pear,
Dr. Avedale's St. German pear,
Large winter pear, weighs near 2 pounds,
Pear wardens,
Large summer baking pear,
The black pear of Worcester, or Parkinson's warden,
The skinless pear.

Apples.

Newtown pippins,
Æiopus spitzenberg,
Peermains,
Vandevils,
Large pippins, weigh a pound or more,
Large red and green sweet apple, ripe at Midsummer, weighs a pound or more

Large early apple, two or three weeks earlier than either junating or bow apple,
English codlin,
Red streaks,
Early bow apple,
Early junating,
Newtown spitzenbergs,
Jersey greening,
Golden pippins,
Russettings,
Golden rennets,
Lady-apple,
Nonpareil,
Yellow bell flower,
Swaar apple,
Rhode-Island greenings,
Large white sweeting,
Bell flowers,
White pippins,
Late bow apple,
Seek no farther apple,
Virginia crab apple,
Holland pippin apple,
Quince apple,
Everlasting apple,
Newark pippin apple.

Mulberries.

Large black English, 2s.
Black American mulberry, 1s. 6d.
White mulberry, 1s. 6d.

Fig Trees, 2s. each.

Currants, 6d. each.

Large red currants,
Large black currants,
Large white currants.

Quince Trees.

Madeira and Lisbon grapes, 1s. each vine,
Large Syrian grape, 2s.
American wild grapes, many sorts, 1s. each.

Goosberries.

Great amber,
Large yellow oval,
Green goosberry, 9d. each.

Rasberries.

White rasberries,
English red rasberries,
American rasberries, 3d. each.
Large Canada rasberries, 6d.

Strawberries.

Large hautboy strawberries, 1s. per doz.
Chili strawberries, 1s. do. do.
Red wood strawberries, 4d. do.
Hudson strawberry, very large, fine flavoured, and great bearers, 2s. per doz.

Roses.

Moss Provence rose, 3s.
Yellow rose, 1s. 6d.
Rosa Mundi, 2s.
Large Provence rose, 1s. 6d.
The monthly rose, 2s.
The red damask rose, 1s.
The white damask rose, 1s.
Primrose, 1s.
Musk rose, 2s.
Cinnamon rose, 1s.
Thornless rose, 1s.
American wild rose, many sorts, 6d.

Evergreen Trees and Shrubs.

Red-Virginia cedar, 1s. 6d.
Weymouth's pine, 1s. 6d.
Black spruce fir, 1s. 6d.

Hemlock spruce fir, 1s. 6d.
The Kingsbridge laurel, 2s.
Large silver fir, 1s. 6d.
The balm of Gilead fir, 2s.
Pitch pine, 1s. 6d.
Jersey pine, 1s. 6d.
Virginia pine, 1s. 6d. each.

Timber Trees and flowering Shrubs.

American white oak, 1s.
American black oak, 1s.
Large New-England white oak, 1s.
Pin oak, 1s.
Scarlet oak, 1s.
English passion flower, 2s.
American passion flower, 1s. 6d.
Oleander, with red flowers, 2s.
American white thorn, 6d.
Scarlet maple, 1s.
Sugar maple, 1s. 6d.
Fringe tree, or Venetian sumach, 2s.
Snow-drop tree, 2s. 6d.
Pride of China, 2s.
Benjamin tree, 1s. 6d.
Scarlet flowering horse chesnut tree, 2s.
Andromeda, 1s. 6d.
Dwarf cypress, 2s.
Lombardy or Italian poplar,
Bladder Sena,
Monthly honey-suckle, 6d.
Late white American honey-suckle, 1s. 6d.
Dwarf acacia, with red flowers, 2s.
Carolina kidney bean tree, with purple flowers, 2s.
Threethorn'd acacia, with white flowers, 1s.
Leburnum, with yellow flowers, 1s. 6d.
The slender bome, or lime tree, 1s. 6d.
Liquid amber tree, 1s. 6d.
American medler, 1s. 6d.
Weeping willow, 1s. 6d.
The sweet-scented shrub from Carolina, 2s. 6d.
The aspe tree, 1s. 6d.
Catalpa flower tree, 1s. 6d.
Broad leav'd dog-wood, 1s. 6d.
White dog-wood, 1s. 6d.
Hard shell almonds, 1s. 6d.
Sweet almonds, 1s. 6d. each.
Magnolia, 4s.
Tulip tree, 2s.
Snow-ball tree, 1s.
Bastard tamarind tree, 1s.
Locust tree, 9d.
Button tree of Virginia, 1s.
Blue lilac, 1s.
The balsam Peru, 1s. 6d.
White lilac, 1s. 6d.
Syringas, 1s. 6d.
Standing American honey-suckle, 1s. 6d.
Candle-berry myrtle, 9d.
Sugar birch, 1s.
Saffafrass, 1s.
Poplar, 1s.
Carolina bird cherry, 1s.
Yellow willow, 1s.
Double flowering almond, 2s.
Carolina allspice, 1s. 6d.
Rhododendrun, 2s.
The balsam willow, 2s.
Madeira nut, 2s.
Long black walnuts, 1s.
Round black walnuts, 1s.
White walnuts, many sorts, 1s. 6d.
American hazle-nut trees, 1s.
Barcelona nuts, 1s. 6d.
Filberds, 1s. 6d.
White althea frutex, 1s.
Purple althea frutex, 1s.
Double tube rose roots, 1s.

ALL the above are inoculated and grafted fruit trees and will bear well upon the mountains or highlands in the West-Indies; They are put up with such safety that scarce one in an hundred dies. I have sent them to the West-Indies these twenty years, and they thrive and bear well; the apples grow very large and fine; the peaches, apricots and nectarines, grow as large and fine as they do in any part of America; the pears, and many sorts, bear well. Should any person incline to purchase, there are now many thousands of a proper size; and if wanted to send over sea, will be safely put up in either mats, casks or boxes. Persons in New-York having a mind for any of the above trees, can have them sent every day in the week, as boats constantly go from Flushing landing to that city, and may commonly be found at Burling's-Slip near the Fly-market ferry-stairs.

The Price of the Fruit Trees is One Shilling and Six Pence each.

NEW-YORK, October, 1790.———Printed by Hugh Gaine, at the Bible, in Hanover-Square.

Fig. 5. William Prince nursery broadside, 1790

THE ORIGINS OF AMERICAN HORTICULTURE

Public interest in fruit growing has diminished significantly in the United States over the last hundred, fifty, even twenty years. This decline reflects the increasing homogeneity of our culture and our peculiarly suburban alienation from the land. Although limited in its variety and shipped unripened across continents, fresh fruit is readily available in the supermarket. Fruit trees take up an inordinate amount of space in the suburban yard, and they are difficult to maintain without active pest control, pruning, and fertilization. As the low-maintenance yard or garden becomes more desirable, fruit trees become less so. Although specialty fruit nurseries are common, relatively few gardening books are published about pomology. While trends in garden interest come and go—perennial borders, rock gardens, roses, native plants, vegetable gardening—the diminishing interest in fruit growing seems more permanent.

Until 1820, and to a lesser extent until 1860, horticulture meant fruit growing for most Americans. Perhaps 90 percent of the plants sold by commercial nurseries before 1820 were fruit trees (fig. 5). Most of the garden literature before 1860 dealt with apples, peaches, and grapes; eighty-nine pomological books were published before 1860, and about three hundred between then and 1920. The first horticultural cultivars developed by Europeans in North America were fruit varieties: the Rhode Island Greening and Roxbury Russet apples were discovered in seventeenth-century New England, while the Virginia White apple emerged around 1700. The Hewes Crab, a cider apple, was the most commonly grown horticultural cultivar in eighteenth-century Virginia. The horticultural cultivar grown commercially for the longest period in United States history is the Newtown Pippin apple, first planted for the export trade to Europe north of New York before 1800 and still grown today on the West Coast. Indigenous North American species, especially plums, strawberries, grapes, and raspberries, were among the first plants domesticated by European immigrants. For the earliest natural historians of the eastern North American landscape, no plant—fruit, vegetable, flower, or grain—promised as much

as the native vine. Experimental grape culture before 1830, when the first successful commercial vineyards were finally established, dominated the interests of the country's most active horticulturists. Cherry trees were among the first plants used ornamentally, to decorate a farmer's yard or the entrance road to a gentleman's estate. Most deliberate scientific plant breeding done in this country before 1850, beginning before 1800 with the work on plums by Joseph Cooper in Philadelphia and William Prince, Jr., in New York, concentrated on the improvement of European species of fruit.[3]

Although thousands of peach, apple, cherry, and other fruit cultivars were developed in North America, their parents were Old World species, many originating in Asia Minor. But the pomological potential of the numerous native American fruits has led botanists and scientists to wonder about the effect on our cultivated fruit if North America had been the original cradle of civilization: if the native plums, cherries, crabs, grapes, and mulberries had been cultivated for thousands of years in the New World rather than in Europe. Sweeter, more delicately flavored, and larger fruits—qualities developed in the Old World species—would have been more diligently selected from naturally occurring hybridization, and at the same time the vigor and adaptability of the native species would have been preserved. Eastern North American grapes, blueberries, cranberries, raspberries, strawberries, and to a lesser extent plums and gooseberries eventually played major roles in the development of our cultivated pomology. The fruit species that generally flourished at Monticello were native fruits such as the Chickasaw plum or indigenous grape and strawberry species, New World apple and peach cultivars derived from European species, or else species like the peach tree, which originated in a similar continental climate. On the other hand, European plums, pears, almonds, apricots, raspberries, currants, and gooseberries generally suffered at Monticello.[4]

A study of the evolution of American fruit growing reveals this continuing tension between the influence of a European heritage—Old World varieties and species, traditional English cultural practices such as espaliered trees and sophisticated propagation methods, even European weeds, insects, and diseases introduced with the first settlers—and the development of North American cultivars and horticultural methods. A review of agricultural publications before 1825, from the *Memoirs* of the Philadelphia Society for Promoting Agriculture to Baltimore's *American Farmer*, shows how American fruit growers developed new plants and distinct traditions. As James Fitz, author of the *Southern Apple and Peach Culturist*, said in 1872, "The Englishman prepares his borders while the American will dig his holes." Large-scale peach orchards were planted with seedling trees (trees raised from seeds rather than by budding or grafting) as producers of animal fodder. Hogs, the principal beneficiaries of the ripe fruit, were considered the best cultivators of an orchard as well, manuring the trees, keeping down weeds, and devouring destructive insects like the plum curculio. In 1817 William Coxe, author of *A View of the Cultivation of Fruit Trees*, the first American horticultural work to make a clean break from European traditions, urged his readers to banish the Old World fruit garden and all its affectations—dwarf and espaliered trees, walls, and even European varieties—and to replace it with a sprawling field of American cider apples. Cider production, though a demanding art, should be the essential role of the orchardist. The cultivation of native and European grapes in the eastern United States required new ways of spacing, trellising, and protecting the vines. Native pests— disease, insects, and weeds—and an extreme continental climate demanded the adaptation of traditional practices to uniquely new conditions.[5]

Vernacular techniques for propagation, fencing, pest control, and fertilization emerged to further define the American pomological experience. Chestnut snake and cedar rail fences and even ditches protected apple and peach orchards and ordered the larger rural landscape. Budding and grafting, complicated and expensive, were irrelevant when the function of the harvest was to feed the hogs or to make alcoholic beverages. And since asexual propagation, the only certain means of duplicating the qualities of a parent, was generally distrusted before 1800, and to a lesser extent before 1850, fruit orchards were commonly planted with trees propagated from seeds, rather than with budded or grafted plants. The unique genetics of each seedling fruit tree essentially creates a new variety. Many of these seedling trees, however, in all

their accidental variations, produced qualities worthy of preserving—whether a juicier peach or a particularly flavorful apple—and subsequently perpetuated by budding or grafting. Ultimately, the common planting of seedling orchards resulted in the development of unique North American cultivars better suited to the climate, soil, and needs of the new land and its people. Effective techniques for pest control emerged in the young United States, including theories of biological control, the use of tobacco as a pesticide, and the creative use of whatever repellents were available: soapsuds, pickle brine, and tanbark mulch. Strawberry beds were burned in the spring to stimulate earlier and more robust fruiting. Even the European attitude toward bearing orchards changed radically in North America when fruit became part of the common domain and was considered freely accessible to wayside travelers. Thomas Jefferson gardened in the dawn of this developing American horticulture—during the emergence of regional fruit cultivars, homespun cultivation techniques, and a distinctly American character for orchards, vineyards, and fruit gardens.

THOMAS JEFFERSON, PLANTER

> If you should have any plants to spare of what you deem excellent pears, peaches, or grapes, they will then be most acceptable indeed, and I shall be able to carry & plant them myself at Monticello where I shall then begin to occupy myself according to my own natural inclinations, which have been so long kept down by the history of our times.
>
> —*Jefferson to Timothy Matlack, October 19, 1807*

Thomas Jefferson's first documented mention of the name Monticello occurs in a terse notation for August 3, 1767, in his lifelong horticultural diary, the Garden Book: "inoculated common cherry buds into stocks of large kind at Monticello." This was Jefferson's first mark on the land, and perhaps represents his ultimate identification with it. Grafting fruit is a choice symbol for the civilization of nature, the union of cultivation and the wild, and in this case, the marriage of the Old World and the New. Jefferson was attempt-

Fig. 6. Jefferson's fruit garden ranges below the 1,000-foot-long kitchen garden

ing to improve the native wild cherry ("common cherry") by budding it on the roots of the "large kind," the European bird cherry, *Prunus avium*. Jefferson budded his cherries nine months before he contracted with John Moore to begin leveling the top of the mountain and two years before the red clay cellar was excavated for his south pavilion, the first structure on top of his "little mountain." While the numerous impracticalities of frontier existence on a mountain—the inconveniences of obtaining well and spring water, the distance from the riparian avenues of transportation and commerce (in this case, the Rivanna River, one mile downhill)—might weigh heavily against the romantic possibilities of such a site—the grand prospects, the symbolic eminence—one must acknowledge the preeminent practicality of Monticello as a place for fruit growing. Jefferson was not alone in his priorities: it was not an uncommon practice for eighteenth-century American homesteaders to plant their orchards before beginning construction of their dwellings.[6]

Monticello's six-acre fruit garden, or "fruitery" as Jefferson called it in 1814, eventually included the 400-tree south orchard; two small vineyards (northeast and southwest); "berry squares" of currants, gooseberries, and raspberries; two nurs-

eries where Jefferson propagated fruit trees and special garden plants; and "submural beds," where figs and strawberries were grown to take advantage of the warming microclimate created by the kitchen garden retaining wall (fig. 6). The fruitery's broad, sunny southeastern exposure and an elevation that warded off the late spring frosts so devastating to Jefferson's neighbors were savvy horticultural arguments favoring his mountain homestead. On the other side of his "little mountain," Jefferson's north orchard was reserved for three varieties of cider apples and seedling peaches.[7]

The Monticello fruitery (including the south orchard) and the north orchard reflected the two distinct forms of fruit growing that emerged in eighteenth-century Virgina. The north orchard was typical of the "field" or "farm" orchards found on most middle-class farms: it was large, with 200 trees on average, and consisted of only peach or apple trees. The fruit was harvested for the production of what John Smith called "most comfortable and excellent drinks," usually cider or brandy, or as livestock feed. The universality of fruit liquors in the eighteenth century lends credence to numerous historians' tongue-in-cheek remark that it was a significant event when Americans began eating their fruit rather

Fig. 7. Artist's rendering of Monticello fruit garden with vineyard, vegetable garden wall, and garden pavilion

than drinking it. The trees in these utilitarian orchards were often propagated from seed, resulting in unpredictable variations and few named varieties, and the orchard received little horticultural attention such as pruning or pest control. Because of its large, sprawling scale and its function, the north orchard was more an agricultural feature of the plantation than part of an ornamented or experimental landscape.[8]

The Monticello fruitery, on the other hand, was reserved for over 170 varieties of thirty-one of the finest temperate species of fruit, cultivated in Jefferson's words, for the "precious refreshment" of its fancy fruit (fig. 7).[9] In some ways it resembled a gentleman's fruit garden in the Old World horticultural tradition and was similar to the diverse recreational plantings of other wealthy Virginians such as John Hartwell

Cocke, St. George Tucker, and George Washington. These Virginia fruit connoisseurs purchased the most esteemed European fruit varieties from urban nurseries, such as the William Prince nursery on Long Island. They used progressive propagation methods, including dwarfing rootstocks. Their fruit gardens, also characterized by a wide spectrum of varieties that included unusual species like apricots, almonds, and nectarines, were often planted within tidy kitchen gardens, mixed with small fruits and berries, sometimes vegetables and even ornamental plants, and were tended by trained gardeners guided by the directions of European pomological writers.

Jefferson's fruitery, however, was unique because it was both an Old World fruit garden and a colonial Virginia farm orchard. Seedling peaches and Virginia cider apples were planted alongside French apricots, Spanish almonds, and English plums. Its sprawling American scale was defined by manageable, specialized compartments: intensively cultivated nurseries, two terraced vineyards, berry "squares" of small fruit, fig gardens, blocks of cherry trees, and plots of experimental field crops planted between the orchard rows. Like Jefferson himself, it represented the best of the European heritage combined with a distinctive New World vitality and personality. Along with the "hanging" kitchen garden that hovered over it, Jefferson's fruitery was an essential feature of Monticello's experimental laboratory of new and unusual plant introductions from around the world.

Jefferson's journey into fruit cultivation is important because he wrote so much about it. Few American fruit growers kept such extensive and detailed notes on pomology: mapping the plantings, noting the grafting of trees in his nursery, and writing to friends to assemble the most esteemed fruit-tree varieties. However, like many of his horticultural and agricultural ventures, Jefferson's vision extended beyond what he was able to accomplish; his "natural inclinations" were stymied by the diversions of political life, long absences from home, and a lack of skilled labor. The need to make the Monticello farms self-sufficient—to plant wheat as a cash crop and to build a nailery for nail production—also diverted his pomological attentions. Jefferson's interest in fruit growing was formed, in part, from the agrarian ideal of the classical Enlightenment, yet, if we are to accept his own image, the orchards succumbed to "entire decay" from the realities of plantation life on the Virginia frontier: rotting fences, peach tree borers, hares, fire blight, chaotic labor management, plum curculio, searing droughts, aphids, downy mildew, shot-hole fungus, briers, adolescent vandals, peach tree yellows, fruit-hungry sheep, bricklike soil, killing frost, brown rot, simple neglect.[10] Jefferson's tireless persistence should be saluted, his dedication to experimenting with a wide spectrum of varieties applauded, for fruit growing on a little mountain in central Virginia is hard work.

Nevertheless, there is some question about Thomas Jefferson's skill as a fruit grower. He was undoubtedly successful with certain species: peaches, figs, cherries, strawberries,

specific apple cultivars, sometimes grapes. Edmund Bacon, Monticello overseer from 1806 to 1822, recalled, "I have never seen such a place for fruit." Yet Jefferson's repeated plantings of the same site, his failure to record cultural techniques like pruning or fertilization, and his retirement from fruit growing after 1814 demonstrate a perennial struggle with, and ultimate abandonment of, his fruit garden.[11] Jefferson's influence on American pomology and horticulture in general is also difficult to gauge. Jefferson's pioneering advocacy of American viticulture—his association with the leading grape growers in the United States, his perennial experimentation with a rainbow of *Vitis* cultivars—is perhaps his most enduring horticultural legacy despite a losing battle with vine cultivation at Monticello. As president he served as a model in his promotion of scientific agriculture, botany, and horticulture, yet his orchards, like his vineyards, probably were not an example of cultural expertise. His favorable account of the Taliaferro apple was published in the *Memoirs* of the Philadelphia Society for Promoting Agriculture, a journal of progressive farming, but the Taliaferro has disappeared from cultivation and remains Monticello's mystery apple today. Many of the Italian grapes, peaches, and apricots he received from Philip Mazzei were unique introductions into American gardens, yet most of them died before he was able to distribute them to friends and other growers. Some nineteenth-century authors credited Jefferson with introducing and naming Ralls Genet, an eighteenth-century Virginia apple and parent of Fuji, a Japanese apple developed in 1962 that some forecast as the commercial fruit of the future, but the claim is difficult to verify. Jefferson was also a pioneer in the culture of the Newtown Pippin apple in Albemarle County. Later known as the Albemarle Pippin, this fine keeping apple generated a large and profitable commercial industry in the county from the mid-nineteenth century until World War I. However, Jefferson was not close to being the introducer.

Simply because he planted so many species and wrote so much about the subject, fruit growing influenced Thomas Jefferson and our image of him. He kept remarkably detailed records, as reflected in the 1778 and 1811 plans for the orchard or in his consistent recording of nursery plantings in his Garden Book—documents of unparalleled detail in the early history of American gardening. Jefferson was an experimenter in a casually scientific manner; drought, frost, weeds, insects —commonplace threats to the health of his fruitery—were studied curiosities rather than horticultural plagues and reflected a healthy, holistic approach to garden and farm management. Fruit growing, like so many of his other Monticello activities, provided a retreat from the slings and arrows of political life. On March 25, 1807, during one of the most traumatic periods of his presidency, while in the throes of a searing headache during the contentious Aaron Burr treason trial, Jefferson was busy planning the replanting of his vineyards in his Weather Memorandum Book. This document, detailing the planting of twenty-five European grape cultivars, is the most comprehensive American vineyard plan that survives from the first half of the nineteenth century. Jefferson's identification with the spirit and natural bounty of the New World—his vocal advocacy of North American plants and their cultivation—was also reflected in his efforts at fruit growing. At the same time he was influenced by the style and wisdom of the Old, shown in his preference for Mediterranean foods and methods of agriculture. With its elevated southern exposure, man-made terraces, and abundance of vines and figs, the Monticello fruitery resembled the estate of an Italian villa. Finally, Jefferson was a planter: 1,031 fruit trees, 130 varieties in the south orchard alone; 33 grape cultivars in his two vineyards; hundreds of strawberries, figs, and other berries. The history of fruit growing at Monticello is not so much a testament to his pomological wizardry as it is a reflection of the Jefferson spirit—expansive, optimistic, epicurean, innocent; altogether, very American. Thomas Jefferson was a planter rather than a cultivator. Planting was his rite of spring, his sermon of faith, his prayer for the future.[12]

Part
I

The Farm Orchard and the Fruit Garden

Jefferson's forty-seven-year sojourn in pomology (1767–1814) was influenced by both the Virginia regional tradition, the farm orchard, and the English example, the fruit garden. The European tradition was expressed by the literature in the Monticello library and reflected in the orchards and plantings of other gentlemen fruit growers. Few travelers' descriptions of the seventeenth- and eighteenth-century Virginia and mid-Atlantic landscapes ignored the presence of abundant orchards. The initial reports on fruit growing abounded in images of the fertile soil, gentle climate, and luxurious fruitfulness. A common theme before 1800 was the ease with which fine fruit was grown. One seventeenth-century recorder said, "All sorts of excellent Fruits will grow there in full perfection; you may sleepe while they are growing; after their setting [planting] or engrafting, their needs no more labor but your prayers that they prosper." The 1701 diary of Frenchman Francis Louis Michel included references to the "great abundance" of fruit trees: apples so common that they fell to the ground unharvested, peaches so plentiful they were "fed to the pigs," and cultivation so easy that "everything grows that is put into the ground." John Banister in his often-copied *Natural History*, written around 1690, commented on the plentiful and excellent fruit that, remarkably, often bore twice in a season.[1]

The theme of effortless abundance continued through the 1700s. Robert Beverley, in *The History and Present State of Virginia*, first published in 1705, said: "The Fruit-Trees are wonderfully quick of growth, so that in six or seven years time from the Planting, a Man may bring an Orchard to bear in great plenty, from which he may make store of good Cyder, or distill great quantities of Brandy. . . . Yet they have very few, that take any care at all for an Orchard; nay many that have good Orchards, are so negligent of them, as to let them go to ruine." John Lawson, whose *History of Carolina* was published in London in 1714, described numerous cultivated fruits (including seventeen English apple varieties) known in the Carolinas and Virginia. He marveled over peach trees that grew like weeds and said, "They generally bear so full that they break great part of their Limbs down." William Eddis in 1772 declared: "Throughout the whole of this province [Maryland], fruit is not only plentiful but excellent in various kinds. There are very few plantations unprovided with an apple and a peach orchard; the peach trees are all standards [rather than espaliers], and without the assistance of art frequently produce fruit of an exquisite flavor." By the end of the century Richard Parkinson, an English gentleman transplanted to a rural Maryland farm in 1798, reported that "it would astonish a stranger to see the quantity of fruit in these parts [eastern Maryland], which makes the country to look beautiful twice a-year when the trees are in blossom, and when the fruit is on the trees ripe. But the fruit is chiefly for the use of hogs, and can be applied to no better purpose."[2]

Many commentators who observed this casual approach to American pomology disapproved of what they saw. A German observer, Johann David Schoepf, reported in 1784, "The American cares little for what does not grow of itself, and is satisfied with the great yields of his cherry, apple and peach trees, without the thought to possible and often necessary betterments." The celebrated French botanist François André

Michaux concluded from his journeys across the continent that "the Americans are by no means so industrious or interested in this kind of culture [fruit growing] as the European states." Jasper Danckaerts, a leader of a Labadist colony in Maryland, wrote that "tobacco is the only production in which planters employ themselves. . . . Some have begun to plant orchards, which all bear well, but are not properly cultivated." The "American Farmer," probably William Cobbett, who edited William Forsyth's popular *Treatise on the Culture and Management of Fruit Trees* in 1803 for a United States audience, chastised his contemporaries for their inattention to the literature of fruit, their haphazard pruning techniques, their planting of "stunted" nursery-grown trees, and their careless cultivation efforts. He concluded his lament over their slovenly pomological efforts by saying: "In a word, very generally *fruit* is shamefully neglected by the *American farmers.* They *plant* and they *neglect!*" Such criticism seems to argue that the Americans' abundant harvests were unearned, as nothing of the gardener's art was needed to produce them.[3]

When eighteenth-century Virginians tried to sell their farms, they often mentioned their orchards in advertisements in Williamsburg's *Virginia Gazette.* Of the 370 farm advertisements listed between 1736 and 1780 that described the types of fruit trees, nearly all had an apple orchard while 244 had a peach orchard. Few noted plantings of cherries, pears, and plums. More than 150 farms had more than one orchard, and these were segregated plantings of apples or peaches. Among the 59 advertisements that referred to the size of the orchard, the typical apple orchard consisted of 250 to 300 trees; the norm for a peach orchard was about 1,000 trees. Richard Parkinson, whose six-acre orchard was equally planted with apples and peaches, bluntly explained what species most mid-Atlantic growers preferred: "Americans have two kinds of fruit worth mentioning, apples and peaches; all the others are but trash." The large average size of the typical orchard also suggests the agricultural function of the fruit itself: the harvest from a thousand peach trees was intended for the distillery or the bellies of hogs, not the dinner table. The function of the orchard also determined how trees were propagated; the use of seedling trees was another feature that defined the typical Virginia farm orchard.[4]

THE FRUIT GARDEN

In contrast to the traditional Virginia farm orchard, the fruit gardens of wealthy planters were considerably smaller and cultivated more intensively; they often were associated with vegetable or flower gardens and included grafted fruit varieties, often nursery grown and usually of European origin. Professional gardeners occasionally were employed to care for the trees, which were sometimes espaliered against walls. Large and diverse varietal collections were assembled, and home nurseries were reserved for the asexual propagation of those varieties sent by friends and neighbors. Fruit gardens included types of trees other than peaches and apples: apricots, nectarines, pears, and plums. The pomological directions given by English horticultural authorities Batty Langley, Philip Miller, and William Forsyth were consulted and followed as diligently as Virginia's severe continental climate and its unruly plantation structure would allow.

The traditional fruit gardens of horticultural writers such as Philip Miller and Bernard McMahon, two writers commonly consulted by Jefferson, were a part of the kitchen garden. Such a garden, enclosed by walls (ideally twelve feet tall and constructed of brick) and divided into geometric squares and borders, was decidedly hidden yet conveniently accessible to the kitchen itself and often included espaliered fruit trained on its defining walls. Miller even questioned the need for a family orchard "since a kitchen-garden well planted with espaliers will afford more fruit than can be eaten while good." Squares of berries and figs were included, and McMahon thought "you may have the Kitchen, fruit, and pleasure-garden all in one. . . . The back part of them planted with a range of espalier fruit-trees, surrounding the quarters [or squares]."[5]

The fruit gardens of three of Jefferson's contemporaries —St. George Tucker, George Washington, and John Hartwell Cocke—demonstrate how the English horticultural tradition was blended with an occasional New World flourish, the planting of seedling peaches and distinct Virginia cider apple varieties, for example, and the use of regional fence styles: ditches, palings, or split-rail fences. A brief account of these Virginia fruit gardens, all of which were complemented by field orchards similar to Jefferson's north orchard, provides a

Fig. 8. St. George Tucker, by Saint Mémin

view of the state of the art of eighteenth- and early nineteenth-century fruit growing and a context for the pomology practiced at Monticello.

ST. GEORGE TUCKER

Like Jefferson, St. George Tucker (1752–1827) was a student of Williamsburg's George Wythe, whom he later succeeded at William and Mary as professor of law (fig. 8). Tucker became a prominent Virginia judge and political figure after serving as a lieutenant colonel in the Revolutionary War. Like many Virginians, he jotted notes in his copies of the yearly editions of the *Virginia Almanac*, published in Williamsburg. There Tucker recorded the births of his children, wrote impromptu poems, made architectural sketches, and documented numerous fruit-tree plantings between 1784 and 1792. Like Jefferson, Tucker had at least two orchards: the "little orchard," planted with Virginia apples purchased from a Surry County nursery owned by Thomas Sorsby, and a "fruit garden" along the entrance and crosswalks of the vegetable garden and in

the two "yards" closer to the house at Matoax, an estate near Petersburg which Tucker acquired through his marriage to Frances Bland Randolph in 1778.[6]

Tucker organized his vegetable garden into traditional "squares," or planting beds: a geometric pattern of rectangles bordered by pathways of turf, gravel, or some other dry, firm surface. The 122 fruit trees he purchased in 1787 from the William Prince nursery on Long Island were planted to form allées and borders for these squares. For example, 12 apple trees, probably spaced equally, were planted "on the left side of the Walk at the Entrance of the Garden," and 12 more apples were set on the right side. The crosswalks had similar rows of cherries, pears, and peaches. A small, three-row, 18-tree plum orchard was planted in the "North yard," and a similarly designed peach, nectarine, and apricot orchard of 23 trees was set out in the "South yard," somewhere between the garden and the house. Many of these trees died, probably because their roots dried out while being transported the 350 miles from New York, but Tucker persevered nonetheless, transplanting the surviving yard trees into the garden in order to preserve the planting symmetry of his ornamental crosswalks.[7]

Altogether, Tucker documented planting as many as eighty-five varieties of nine different species of fruit trees, including twenty-five peach cultivars, thirteen plum, fourteen pear, fifteen apple, ten cherry, and a few each of apricot, quince, almond, and nectarine. He often propagated his own trees and experimented by budding two different cherry varieties, the May Duke and Oxheart, on one rootstock and by grafting apples on quinces, a technique he also used to dwarf his pear trees. Like Jefferson, he freely exchanged seeds, scion wood, and young trees with his neighbors and friends, such as John Hartwell Cocke and Peyton Skipwith, the husband of Lady Jean Skipwith of Prestwould, a most ambitious eighteenth-century Virginia flower gardener. Tucker's comments on fruit growing were sometimes playful: he noted on April 1, 1784, that "in honor of this day I made B:M's experiment on the slips of apple trees." Tucker probably was budding every apple limb with a different cultivar, creating a surprising and no doubt perplexing apple collection. While his fruit garden was well dressed with the latest European varieties, he also had a typical Virginia farm orchard where he cultivated the

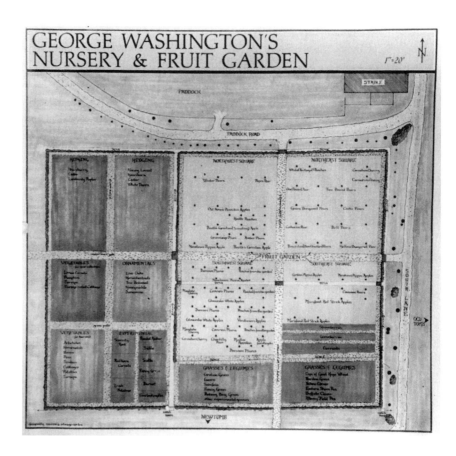

Fig. 9. Conjectural drawing of George
Washington's Mount Vernon fruit garden

Northern Yellow flint corn between the rows of trees. Tucker used the borders of his vegetable garden as a nursery, where he and his slave Lyphax planted the stones of plums and peaches, later set out in the "little orchard" as seedling trees.[8]

GEORGE WASHINGTON

George Washington was the most traditional of all Virginia fruit growers in the way he adhered to the pomological directions of eighteenth-century English garden writers like Philip Miller, whose *Dictionary* resided in the Mount Vernon library. One visitor remarked, "After seeing his house and his gardens one would say that he had seen the most beautiful examples in England of this style." Washington referred to his "Fruit Garden," a four-acre area which was the site of a failed

vineyard below the lower, or south, garden (fig. 9). In 1786 a large portion of the fruit garden was divided into four symmetrical squares or quadrants, each with nine rows and space for five trees in a row—180 trees in all. It was planted with approximately twenty-five varieties of apple, plum, pear, peach, and cherry, most of which came from Washington's nephew William Washington. Earlier fruit gardens had been planted within the one-acre, brick-walled upper and lower gardens that directly reflect the structure and layout of Philip Miller's kitchen garden: the division of the garden into formal squares, or "quarters," of vegetables and the use of borders and walls for espaliered fruit. The diaries of Washington's gardeners provide the only documented account of the use of walled, espaliered fruit trees in eighteenth-century Virginia. Mount Vernon's "Cherry Walk" was either an allée of standard cherries along the "curved" or "straight" walkways or perhaps a border of espaliers. Another early Mount Vernon orchard planted in 1760 included 177 trees—58 cherries, 12 plums, 54 pears, and 53 apples—planted in six mixed rows. Washington cultivated as many as eight varieties of apple, nineteen pear, five plum, eleven cherry, three apricot, and three nectarine. The large number of pear and cherry varieties again reflects the European influence on the pomological style at Mount Vernon. References abound in Washington's diaries to both the grafting of fruit and the employment of English or Scottish gardeners, whose first responsibility was often the propagation of young fruit trees. Like St. George Tucker and his April Fool's Day grafting joke, Washington became playful when discussing unnatural unions in his fruit garden: "And my Gardener to shew his cunning, grafted ten Pairs . . . on Plumb scions."[9]

Washington also had numerous farm orchards. Some were exclusively of unnamed seedling peaches surrounded by Virginia split-rail fences. Others, like the cider orchard at River Farm, were reserved by Washington in 1785 for 215 Maryland Red Streaks, a popular cider variety. Through the autumn months 120 gallons of cider or mobby (apple or peach brandy) were produced daily at Mount Vernon, a staggering amount resulting from the vast amounts of land planted in farm orchards. The importance of these functional plantings was suggested by the stipulations Washington laid down for his leased land: "Within three years there shall be planted an orchard of 100 apple trees, at forty feet distance either way from each other, and 100 peach trees, the same to be kept always during the continuance of said lease well pruned, fenced in and secured from horses, cattle and other creatures that might hurt them."[10]

JOHN HARTWELL COCKE

John Hartwell Cocke (1780–1862) was a friend of Jefferson's who developed his 3,184-acre estate, Bremo, into a model agricultural and architectural village along the James River forty miles southeast of Monticello. Cocke was a talented pioneer, a visionary pragmatist like few early Americans: he was variously a general in the War of 1812, an abolitionist, a progressive agriculturist, the first president of the American Temperance Society, and one of the founders and designers of the Univer-

Fig. 10. Upper Bremo, the home of John Hartwell Cocke

sity of Virginia. He possessed both a suberb command of the practical arts and an inspired creative genius. The Palladian-style Upper Bremo, one of the three architectural masterpieces he designed and built at Bremo, was described by Samuel Eliot Morison and Henry Steele Commager as "perhaps the most beautiful country house in America today" (fig. 10). His farms were a model of skilled management and included grandiose stone barns, pisé stone walls constructed from a compacted mixture of mud and straw, unusually productive fields of wheat, corn, and tobacco, and two handsome neo-Jacobean houses at the Recess and Lower Bremo. Still today, Bremo is the most magical of settings, a testament to the creative imagination and the practical skill of a diversely talented genius.[11]

In many ways Upper Bremo challenges and even surpasses Monticello in the beauty of its design. The Bremo collection of fruits, including thirty cultivars of pear and thirty-five varieties of the finest native Virginia apples, was just as diverse and extensive as Jefferson's. Cocke was also a horticultural activist: his essay on a clever technique for the eradication of peach tree borers was published in the *American Farmer*, a Baltimore-based journal of progressive agriculture. Cocke organized the local Fruit Tree Association, a society of twenty-two residents formed "to promote the introduction and diffusion of the finest kinds of fruit trees." They purchased over $1,000 worth of fifty-eight varieties of cherries, pears, nectarines, apricots, peaches, and almonds from the Benjamin Prince nursery in 1815. Cocke owned the best American and most recent European works on pomology, including William Forsyth's *Treatise on the Culture and Management of Fruit Trees*, 2d ed., 1803, and William Coxe's *View of the Cultivation of Fruit Trees*, 1817. According to his first wife, Ann Barraud Cocke, he was "so deeply engaged in planting our orchard, by a mathematical rule, that he is off directly after breakfast and sometimes does not return until midnight." In 1815 Cocke planted an "elegant orchard of the finest fruits" to celebrate and commemorate the peace treaty ending the War of 1812, and he employed a skilled Scottish gardener, Archibald Blair, who, with the help of two slaves, Peter and Dick, planted at least three orchards in 1817.[12]

Fig. 11. Recess cottage at Bremo. Cocke's fruit garden was behind the stone wall to the left of the house.

Cocke's "fruit garden" or "fruitery" included a mix of vegetables, figs, berries, grapes, and fruit trees, which were often planted along border beds, in "compartments," or on the edge of the garden "squares." Initially defined by a paling fence, this garden, which was located near the Recess cottage (fig. 11), was later surrounded by handsome stone walls that sheltered tender fruits and flowering ornamentals cultivated by Cocke's sons and daughters. Jane Nicholas Randolph, the wife of Jefferson's grandson Thomas Jefferson Randolph, described a fruit fight that erupted in this pleasure garden in 1827 after a Bremo wedding: "After [tea] we went into the gardens [of the Recess] where the girls & young men, John Cocke [son of John Hartwell] at the head of them, pelted each other with green fruit until they were tired, while I stood in all the dignity of a new acquaintance who could not be taken liberties with, in safety, while the fruit flew round my head never missing its aim & never touching me, while the girls screamed & the young men shouted & there was a real right down romp; so much for Norfolk manners." Grapes from this garden still survive, and figs growing nearby may be original as well.[13]

There were at least three other orchards at Bremo before 1820: two fenced farm orchards of peaches and cider apples and an orchard at "U.B. [Upper Bremo] in Low Grounds," reserved for fancy varieties purchased from commercial nurseries. Cocke also had his own nursery, probably a part of the Recess garden, where he planted seeds and grafted and budded scion wood from neighbors and friends, including St. George Tucker, a mentor in architecture as well as gardening. Cocke personally budded or grafted his peaches and apples, and his apple collection seems especially noteworthy because he assembled the finest Virginia varieties—Pryor's Red, Limbertwig, Golden Wilding, Father Abraham, Carthouse, Virginia Greening, Hewes Crab, Red June, Cherry Cheeks, Shacklehills, Virginia Spice, Cherokee Wilding, Taliaferro, and Winter Cheese—and apparently recognized the advantages to Virginia fruit growers of cultivating regional apples.[14]

Fruit gardeners like Cocke, Washington, and Tucker were not alone in their inclusion of fruit trees within the confines of the vegetable garden. Luigi Castiglioni, a traveling Italian botanist who visited Monticello in 1786, noted that on the typical Virginia farm, "a large garden is not lacking, in which the most delicate vegetables are varied, and also plum trees, cherries, European apples, and other fruit trees brought over from Europe." Farm advertisements in the *Virginia Gazette* in the eighteenth century occasionally mentioned household gardens of mixed vegetables, herbs, flowers, and fruit trees. Philip Fithian, a Princeton-educated tutor for the Carter family at Nomini Hall in 1773 and 1774, often strolled in the pleasure garden of plum trees, figs, and young grafted apricots as well as honeysuckle vines, primroses, and asparagus. John James Spooner, a visitor to Prince George County in 1793, described the "most beautiful and enchanting" orchard of David Meade of Maycox along the James River; it was noteworthy for an arrangement probably inspired by Batty Langley's recommendation that fruit trees be integrated into the landscape at large. "Forest and fruit trees are here arranged, as if nature and art had conspired together to strike the eye most agreeable. Beautiful vistas, which open as many pleasing views of the river; the land thrown into many artificial hollows or gentle swellings, with the pleasing verdure of the turf; and the complete order in which the whole is preserved; altogether tend to form it one of the most delightful rural seats that is to be met with in the United States, and do honor to the taste and skill of the proprietor, who was also the architect." Fruit gardens were more common in the yards of middle-class merchants and artisans in urban centers like Baltimore and Philadelphia. The absence of large cities in Virginia determined, to some extent, the relative scarcity of artfully arranged mixed plantings of flowers, vegetables, and fruit. Such refinements reflected the tastes of prosperous and horticulturally sophisticated Virginians for whom fine fruit was a handsome and useful companion to the ornamental flourishes provided by honeysuckle vines and flowering lilacs. A ripe pear or juicy peach was a prized culinary achievement to be brought to the table, discussed with pride, and consumed along with precious imported food. Fruit gardening in Virginia around 1800 was not only a recreation but a reflection and affirmation of one's place in the world.[15]

Fruit-Tree Culture at Monticello

Jefferson's south orchard and fruitery formed a complex area of specialized compartments similar, at least in a whimsical way, to the human body. The Monticello fruit library provided the cultural advice: directions on varietal selection, pruning, planting, fertilizing; it was the mind of fruit. The various enclosures—paling fences, ditches, hawthorn hedges—defined the body of cultivation and formed a protective skin. The nurseries that constantly revived Jefferson's plantings, providing young grafted or seedling trees, were the heart of his pomological world. The trees and soft fruit required nourishment and a beneficent environment: food and water, sunshine and air, manure and summer rain, an open prospect and drying winds. Weeds, disease, and insects were health-threatening plagues, especially to poorly nursed trees or species and varieties unacclimated to Monticello's heavy clay soil and central Virginia's harsh continental climate.

JEFFERSON'S FRUIT LIBRARY

Jefferson's extensive library included hundreds of books and pamphlets on agriculture, botany, horticulture, and pomology. For a gentleman gardener unpracticed in the art of planting, pruning, and grafting, his reference books were as indispensable as his nursery was in providing young trees or his paling fence was in protecting them. Jefferson admitted his reliance on literary sources in 1809 when he wrote, "In agriculture I am only an amateur, having only that knolege which may be got from books, in the field I am entirely ignorant, & am now too old to learn." Four books stand out in his diverse

collection because of their relevance to contemporary conditions; their specificity regarding the choice, planting, and care of trees; their popularity among early American gardeners; and the way they stimulated technical advances in fruit growing.[1]

Batty Langley's *Pomona: or, The Fruit-Garden Illustrated*, 1729, was the most complete, accurate, and handsome work on English fruit growing in the eighteenth century (fig. 12). Langley, like A. J. Downing or Jefferson himself, was also a surveyor, architect, and landscape designer. His *New Principles of Gardening* was owned by George Washington and influenced the design of the grounds at Mount Vernon. Langley's fruit garden was composed of espaliered trees trained on walls. This method of cultivation was popular not only for the trees' ornamental value but also because the cool, cloudy English climate required the supplemental heat radiated from brick walls. *Pomona*, with its seventy-nine folio plates of fruit varieties, documented progressive pomology and the latest English fruit of the early eighteenth century.[2]

Jefferson owned two editions, including the eighth edition of 1768, of Philip Miller's *Gardener's Dictionary*, acknowledged as one of the finest horticultural works ever published and certainly the definitive garden book of the eighteenth century in both America and Europe (fig. 13). Miller was the head gardener for forty-three years at the Chelsea Physic Garden, where he introduced plants from around the world. Peter Kalm, a Swedish botanist who recorded his impressions of the natural history of the mid-Atlantic states in the middle of the eighteenth century, noted the influence of Miller on American gardeners: "I have asked several of the greatest and best

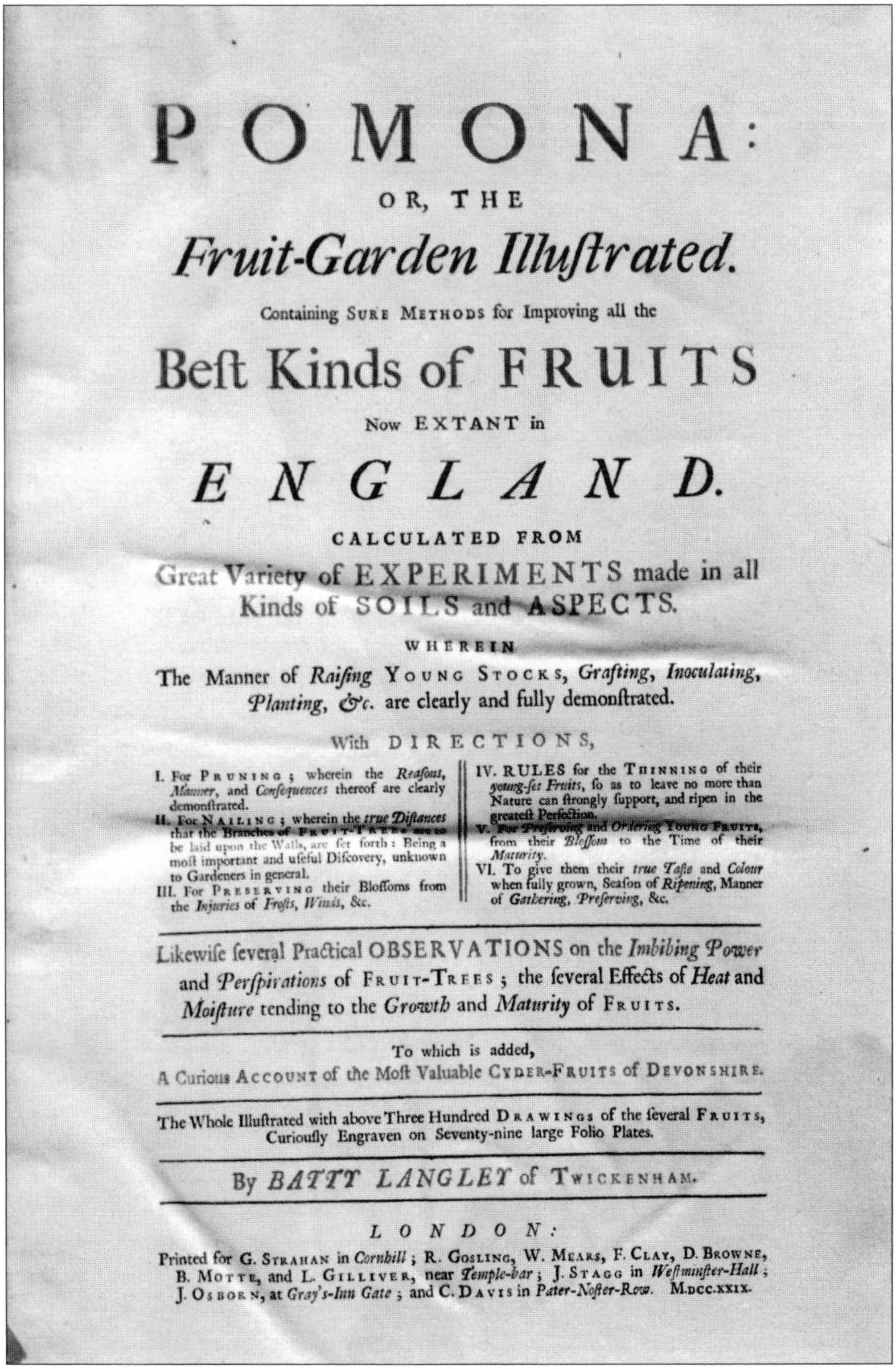

POMONA:

OR, THE

Fruit-Garden Illustrated.

Containing SURE METHODS for Improving all the

Best Kinds of FRUITS

Now EXTANT in

ENGLAND.

CALCULATED FROM

Great Variety of EXPERIMENTS made in all
Kinds of SOILS and ASPECTS.

WHEREIN

The Manner of *Raising* YOUNG STOCKS, *Grafting, Inoculating,
Planting, &c.* are clearly and fully demonstrated.

With DIRECTIONS,

I. For PRUNING; wherein the *Reasons, Manner,* and *Consequences* thereof are clearly demonstrated.
II. For NAILING; wherein the *true Distances* that the Branches of FRUIT-TREES are to be laid upon the Walls, are set forth: Being a most important and useful Discovery, unknown to Gardeners in general.
III. For PRESERVING their Blossoms from the *Injuries* of *Frosts, Winds,* &c.

IV. RULES for the THINNING of their *young-set Fruits,* so as to leave no more than Nature can strongly support, and ripen in the greatest Perfection.
V. For *Preserving* and *Ordering* YOUNG FRUITS, from their *Blossom* to the Time of their *Maturity.*
VI. To give them their *true Taste* and *Colour* when fully grown, Season of *Ripening,* Manner of *Gathering, Preserving,* &c.

Likewise several Practical OBSERVATIONS on the *Imbibing Power*
and *Perspirations* of FRUIT-TREES; the several Effects of *Heat* and
Moisture tending to the *Growth* and *Maturity* of FRUITS.

To which is added,
A Curious ACCOUNT of the Most Valuable CYDER-FRUITS of DEVONSHIRE.

The Whole Illustrated with above Three Hundred DRAWINGS of the several FRUITS,
Curiously Engraven on Seventy-nine large Folio Plates.

By *BATTY LANGLEY* of TWICKENHAM.

LONDON:

Printed for G. STRAHAN in *Cornhill*; R. GOSLING, W. MEARS, F. CLAY, D. BROWNE,
B. MOTTE, and L. GILLIVER, near *Temple-bar*; J. STAGG in *Westminster-Hall*;
J. OSBORN, at *Gray's-Inn Gate*; and C. DAVIS in *Pater-Noster-Row.* MDCCXXIX.

Fig. 12. Title page of Batty Langley's *Pomona,* the only work in Jefferson's library devoted solely to fruit growing

Fig. 13. Frontispiece of Philip Miller's *Gardener's Dictionary*,
8th ed., 1768

Fig. 14. William Cobbett, c. 1831 by an unknown artist

horticulturists both in England and in America, what author and what book they had found and believed to be the best in horticulture. . . . They all answered with one mouth, Miller's *Gardener's Dictionary* was the best of all, and that when one has it, no other book is afterwards required." George Washington, Lady Jean Skipwith, and numerous other eighteenth-century Virginia gardeners made liberal use of Miller's work. It was offered for sale in the *Virginia Gazette*, Williamsburg's newspaper, and Jefferson often used the *Dictionary* as a botanical and horticultural reference. Miller devoted more space to

peach culture—ten pages with nearly eleven thousand words —than to any other garden species, suggesting the importance of pomological skills to the eighteenth-century gardener.[3]

Jefferson also owned a copy of the American edition of William Forsyth's *Treatise on the Culture and Management of Fruit Trees*, 1802, with an introduction by William Cobbett (fig. 14). *A Treatise* was inspired by Forsyth's evangelical devotion to a radical pruning technique called "heading down" and to the use of his personal wound-healing compound, "Forsyth's Composition"(fig. 15). Both controversial, these practices set

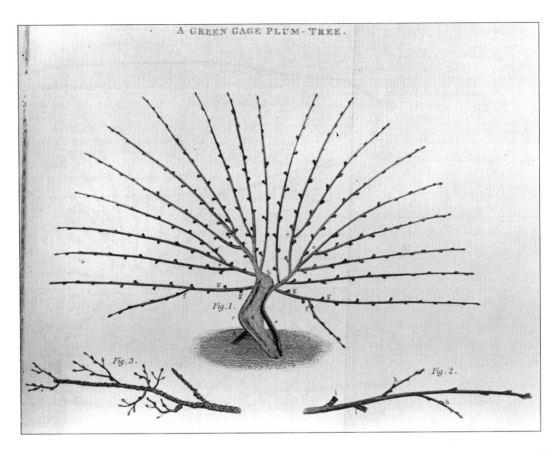

A GREEN GAGE PLUM-TREE.

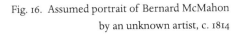

Fig. 15. A Green Gage plum "headed down" according to William Forsyth's *Treatise on the Culture and Management of Fruit Trees*, 2d ed., 1803

a horticultural standard to which future writers and gardeners reacted, postively or negatively. Cobbett, a staunch Forsyth convert and author of *The American Gardener*, 1821, "one of the spiciest books in the whole history of American horticulture," was moved to edit and publish *A Treatise* by the "swift decay" of peach and apple orchards in the mid-Atlantic states. An abridged American edition, *An Epitome of Mr. Forsyth's Treatise on the Culture and Management of Fruit Trees* by "an American Farmer," was published in Philadelphia in 1803 and, according to one writer, "was the most widely read book on fruit during the first decades of the nineteenth century." *An Epitome* pro-

Fig. 16. Assumed portrait of Bernard McMahon by an unknown artist, c. 1814

vided a valuable critical commentary on the unfulfilled potential of American fruit growing.[4]

Bernard McMahon's *American Gardener's Calendar* (Philadelphia, 1806) was the most comprehensive American horticultural work of the first half of the nineteenth century and was
published in eleven editions until 1857 (fig. 16). McMahon forwarded the newest vegetable and flower varieties to Jefferson,
who would often follow the *Calendar* step by step, whether
planting tulips in his flower beds or sea kale in his vegetable
garden. McMahon borrowed extensively from English works,
especially those of Miller and John Abercrombie, despite his
claim that "however excellent and useful these works are in
the regions to which they are adapted, they tend to mislead
and disappoint the young *American* Horticulturist." Still,
McMahon made a concerted effort to break away from English traditions in the way he celebrated the use of native
American ornamentals, acknowledged the desirability of
large-scale cider and seedling peach orchards that could be
grazed with livestock, and frankly admitted the harsh realities of North America's climate. McMahon was concerned
about "the universal inattention paid to the greater number
of our orchards," and the *Calendar* was the first American
book to provide at least a rudimentary guide to the care of
fruit trees.[5]

NURSERIES

A nursery is the sheltered yet often bustling workshop where
a gardener distinguishes his skill as a propagating horticulturist; where cherished seeds carefully sown in rows spring from
the earth; where treasured scions, often gifts from friends, are
married to ordered rows of rootstocks. Home nurseries were
essential around 1800 because of the scarcity of commercial
sources and the difficulties of shipping perishable plants over
great distances. Perhaps most importantly, propagating one's
own tree helped to ensure that the fruit variety was true to
name, a vexing problem since the beginning of commercial
horticulture. As early as the seventeenth century, the English
herbalist John Parkinson had said, "It is an inherent quality almost heriditative with most of them [commercial nurseries]
to sell any mean and ordinary fruit for whatsoever rare fruit

he [the consumer] shall ask for: so little they are to be trusted."
Jefferson occasionally purchased fruit trees from commercial
sources, such as the William Prince nursery on Long Island or
the Thomas Main and Alexander Hepburn nurseries in Washington, yet his home nurseries played a central role in supply-
ing the Monticello orchards.[6]

Jefferson had at least two nurseries: the "old nursery" rested
below the kitchen garden wall below squares IV–VI of the
garden (fig. 17), while the "new nursery," mentioned as early
as 1783, was an extension of the northeast end of the garden.
In 1810 Jefferson began leveling it into nineteen terraces, each
devoted to a particular fruit-tree species. Although the propagation of fine fruit—sowing seed for rootstock, budding, and
grafting—was the most important function of the Monticello
nurseries, the list of plants he grew in them included the favorite species of his gardening experience. Jefferson's nurseries were home to plants discovered by the Lewis and Clark
expedition and first grown at Monticello, like the Arikara bean
and Quarantine corn; a sampling of his pet ornamental trees,
like the chinaberry and Kentucky coffee tree; and potentially
important economic species he hoped would be the salvation
of southern agriculture, such as the sugar maple, sesame, and
Gloucester hickory. Jefferson documented the propagation of
fifteen kinds of shrubs, twenty-nine species of ornamental
trees, twenty-one vegetable varieties, six kinds of grasses, and
sixty-four fruit and nut varieties in the Monticello nurseries.
They were the heart of his horticultural world, continually
pumping new plants into his gardens.[7]

The Monticello nurseries were also ornamental gardens
in themselves. Cherry and other fruit trees occasionally were
left to grow to maturity, and when blended with Jefferson's
choice vegetables, flowering shrubs, and experimental plots
of forage grasses, they provided a happy composition of flowers and foliage texture. The nurseries were protected with a
variety of fences, usually palings or narrow boards; however,
in 1812 Jefferson recorded planting a castor bean hedge "in a
row round the Nursery," perhaps because of its tropical, ornamental effect or the castor bean's reputation as an animal
repellent. The "new nursery" was organized into four-foot-
wide terraces, which contained rows of seedlings. Sticks
marked where rows began and often were numbered to cor-

Fig. 17. Re-created "old nursery" in the fruit garden

respond to Garden Book notations. The names of the sources for his seed and scion wood were as important as the variety name itself. If the seeds failed to germinate, replacements could be obtained; if, after bearing, seeds or scions were supplied to other gardening friends, the source could be accurately identified. For Jefferson, plants were intimately associated with people — friends, neighbors, children — and nowhere is this more evident than in his nursery record. Other Virginia gentlemen fruit growers had nurseries, including George Washington, who puttered in his "botanic garden," his nursery of rare and tender plants, but none seems to have been as intensively cultivated as Jefferson's.[8]

Bernard McMahon provided detailed instructions — more than sixty pages divided into monthly responsibilities — on the cultivation of the home nursery. According to his *Calendar*, plantings should be recorded in a separate "Nursery book," seed rows labeled with old wooden wagon-wheel spokes, and a special "quarter," or square, set aside as a "seminary," where seeds were sown in rows. The quality of the soil in the nursery was a subject much debated by early writers. Philip Miller, for example, felt the nursery soil should be no better than that of the orchard. Richard Peters, a prominent Pennsylvanian fruit grower and frequent correspondent with Jefferson, agreed: "Trees or plants brought from a worse to a better soil, always improve." McMahon, however, insisted that young plants, like children, should never be neglected or malnourished in their infancy. The controversy continued well into the nineteenth century as correspondents in the *American Farmer*, published in Baltimore by John Skinner, argued the merits of high-quality nursery soil. One writer, after citing past arguments, including those of Philip Miller, "the father of horticulture in England," said, "Surely at a time when our public papers are in a dispute on such a topic, agriculture must be in its infancy." In 1824 Skinner concluded, "Young fruit trees, as well as young animals, should neither be stuffed nor starved, but fed with food convenient for them."[9]

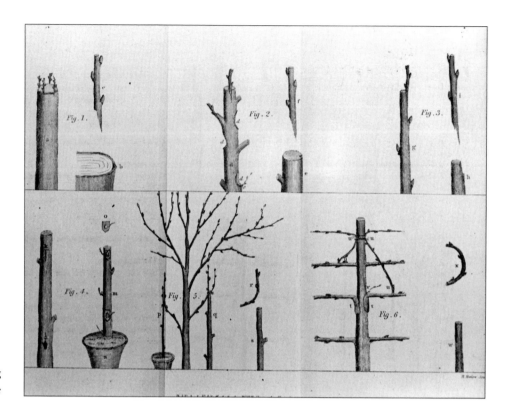

Fig. 18. Budding and grafting
techniques from Forsyth's *Treatise*

PROPAGATION

In theory, every time one plants a seed of an apple or peach, the ensuing seedling is a new variety. The only means of duplicating the parent is by asexual means: budding or grafting (fig. 18). Most eighteenth-century Virginia farm orchards were planted with seedling trees because this was simpler and any fruit would suffice when apples were harvested for cider or peaches were picked for brandy. Seedling orchards were crucial to the development of unique New World cultivars: if a seedling tree produced some exceptional character—an apple particularly suited for cider or a notably late-season peach, for example—it would be budded or grafted, then given a name, often in reference to the fruit's discoverer (Hewes Crab), season of bearing (Red June), appearance (Lemon Cling peach), or place of origin (Gloucester White). Distinctive Virginia apple varieties appeared late in the eighteenth

century, replacing, at least for many growers, the seedling orchards of the colonial era. This might be regarded a progressive, populist movement, carried on not by the grand names of early American gardening, who generally purchased European varieties from urban nurseries in Baltimore, Philadelphia, and New York, but by middle-class farmers. The fruit from the gardens of Virginia squires was intended for the dinner table; preserving the dessert qualities of a Newtown Pippin apple or Carnation cherry was essential, so the trees were grafted.[10]

Although Jefferson commonly planted seedling peaches, he usually grafted or budded his other fruit species in the Monticello nurseries. In a letter from Paris late in 1786, Jefferson commented on the different propagation practices used on the two continents: "Of fruits, the pear, & apricots alone [in Europe] are better than ours, and we have not the Apricot peche at all. But the stones of good apricots & of the peach-apricot would answer well. The fruits of the peach-class do not degenerate from the stone so much as is imagined here. We have so much experience of this in America that tho' we graft all other kinds of fruits, we rarely graft the peach, the nectarine, the apricot or the almond. The tree proceeding from the stone yields a faithful copy of its fruit, & the tree is always healthier." Grafting and budding are genuine tests of the gardener's art, and usually Jefferson contracted the task to outside specialists—Patrick Morgan in the 1770s, Antonio Giannini in the 1780s, Robert Bailey in the 1790s, and Isaac Coles, a friend and neighbor, in 1811. Urging Coles to come to Monticello, Jefferson wrote: "I am the more interested in it as you were so kind as to say you would come over in the inoculating season and give us a lesson in that art. I wish to have Maydukes & Carnations inoculated as mine are on the decline, and your example and instruction may enable my grandson to perform that operation hereafter."[11]

FENCES

A fence is an indispensable feature of an orchard in the way it both defines the body of cultivation and protects the fruit from domestic animals, deer, rabbits, and other pestilential invaders. Like everything else, the character of the enclosures at Monticello evolved as fences fell down and as the perpetual mending and repair work required making do with the materials at hand. Jefferson's 1778 orchard plan shows a fence, probably constructed of posts, rails, and vertical, hand-riven chestnut pales, enclosing three sides of the orchard and garden. Jefferson's numerous directions that it be mended and repaired, especially in the early 1790s when he returned from France, suggest a perennial maintenance headache: "I beg that Mr. [Thomas Mann] Randolph will employ the whole force, he has been so kind as to direct, in repairing the inclosure in preference to every other work I had proposed. Nothing can be placed in competition with the loss of the produce of the garden during the season."[12]

A fashionable solution to the problem of expensive repairs to rotting fence posts and fallen palings was the installation of a Washington hawthorn hedge, *Crataegus phaenopyrum*, a Virginia native. Jefferson wrote to William Hamilton, "As a

thorn for hedges nothing has ever been seen comparable to it certainly no thorn in England which I have ever seen makes a hedge any more to be compared to this than a log nut to a wall of freestone." William Cobbett agreed: "And why should Americans not possess this most beautiful and useful plant? She has English gew-gaws, English play-actors, English Cards and English Dice and Billiards . . . why not English *Hedges*, instead of post and rail and board fences which are sterile-looking and cheerless?" Jefferson purchased 4,000 plants from the Thomas Main nursery of Georgetown in March 1805 and 16,000 seedlings in 1806 and 1807. The thorns were planted six inches apart around part of the south orchard and the entire north orchard (see fig. 32); however, later documents from 1809 and 1811 indicate that most of the thorn hedge was abandoned. Many of the six-inch-high seedlings undoubtedly died in transit, and others were surely strangled and smothered by weeds or, particularly on the south side where the hedge was never established, parched and killed by the hot summer sun. Chastened in his efforts to establish an English-style hedge, Jefferson wrote in August 1807 to J. P. Reibelt, who also hoped to establish a model ornamental farm in the harsh New World: "The luxuriance of the soil by its constant reproduction of weeds of powerful growth & stature will bid defiance to the keeping your grounds in that clean state which the English gardens require." Perhaps learning a lesson, Jefferson purchased the drought-resistant, fast-growing privet, *Ligustrum vulgare*, in 1808 for a hedge in his newly terraced vegetable garden. Privet would be much simpler to establish for it could more easily dominate weedy competitors.[13]

Unfazed by failure, Jefferson planned another fence in 1808, "a large inclosure of garden & orchard." This monumental barrier, ten feet high and nearly three-quarters of a mile long, was recalled by Jefferson's slave Isaac: "My Old Master's garden was monstrous large: two rows of palings, all 'round ten feet high." The extreme height of the fence probably was necessary in order to secure the orchard from both human invaders and browsing deer, who could jump ten feet if under duress. Locust posts, spaced ten feet apart, supported a double row of riven chestnut palings, thin boards or wide pickets (fig. 19). The paling may have been only a temporary enclosure. In 1814 Jefferson alluded to the construction of a ha-ha

Fig. 19. A sample of the re-created paling fence that surrounds the fruit and vegetable garden

BARRIER

In 1814 a ditch 500 yards long was dug to keep grazing animals off the west lawn. The rails that were laid across the banks reminded a visitor in 1823 of "a common post and rail straight fence, blown down across a ditch."

The present re-excavation, still in progress, is by staff archaeologists.

Fig. 20. Re-created ha-ha ditch

by the slaves Wormley and Ned, and in 1823 a Monticello visitor, William Hooper, described an earthen enclosure above the fruitery, along Mulberry Row, that resembled a cattle guard more than the traditional European ha-ha (fig. 20).[14]

Palings, hedges, and ditches had long been ways of enclosing an orchard. In 1639 the Virginia assembly enacted a law requiring large landowners, those holding over one hundred acres, to "establish a garden and orchard carefully protected by a fence, ditch, or hedge." In 1686 William Fitzhugh's 2,500-tree apple orchard in the Northern Neck was "well fenced with a locust fence, which is as durable as most brick walls." Most eighteenth-century fruit growers used the Virginia worm-style, split-rail chestnut fence, which historian Philip Bruce described as "one of the most familiar features of the Virginian plantation, a monument, like the fence law itself, of the perpetuation of agricultural conditions beginning with the very foundation of the Colony." George Washington, for example, "laid in part the Worm of a fence round my Peach orchard and had it made." Richard Parkinson, an English gentleman transplanted to a rural Maryland farm in 1798, described the enclosures in northern Virginia: "There were none but snake-fences; which rails laid with the ends of one upon another; from eighteen to sixteen in number, in one length." Although worthless against most native animal pests and human intruders, the split-rail fence was easily constructed from readily available materials that would last for decades. In many cases the snake fence functioned to keep domestic animals within the orchard, especially hogs that were nourished by fallen peaches.[15]

Although Jefferson's "monstrous large" orchard fence required a lock and key, it was not enough to ward off a band of mischievous intruders sometime between 1806 and 1808. Overseer Edmund Bacon recalled the incident:

Almost every Friday evening Jeff Randolph [Jefferson's grandson Thomas Jefferson Randolph] would bring a lot of his mates to Monticello to play and eat fruit. If they did not come on Friday, they were pretty certain to come on Saturday. I gave them the keys to the house and garden, and very often they all stayed there overnight. One Saturday a lot of the schoolboys that were not invited concluded that they would come also and help themselves to fruit. They went around the back side of the garden, broke off the palings, and got in. They then climbed the trees and broke off a good many limbs, and did a great deal of damage. The other party attacked them, and they had a tremendous fight. The party that had broken in was much the largest, and they could not drive them off. They threw stones at the old gardener and hurt him very badly.[16]

The exaggerated security provided by the paling fence was unusual according to some eighteenth-century landscape descriptions, which suggested that cultivated fruit was part of the common domain. Thomas Anburey, who, like many travelers in the late eighteenth century, was surprised by the large number of peach orchards near Richmond, Virginia, also observed, "It is deemed no trespass to stop and refresh yourself and your horse with them." Peter Kalm noted that the tradition was just as pervasive farther north in Pennsylvania: "All travelers are allowed to pluck ripe fruit in any garden which they pass by, provided they do not break any branches; and not even the most covetous farmer hindered them from so doing. It was a common custom, and any countryman knew that if the farmer tried to prevent it, he would be abused in return." For Richard Parkinson, who owned a six-acre peach and apple orchard near Baltimore around 1800, such a custom was the symbol for American republicanism escaping the bounds of civilized behavior: "The idea of liberty and equality destroys all the rights of the master, and every man does as he likes. Even taking fruit out of your garden, or orchard, is not looked upon as theft." Parkinson defied the tradition by vigilantly guarding his fruit to ward off the plague of local fruit snatchers. "But what was the consequence? I received such abuse from the lower sort of people; they called me a mean English rascal . . . and it was frequently hinted that I must take care, or I should be shot." William Cobbett of Long Island, another transplanted Englishman, was perhaps more forgiving: "Gardeners may scold as long as they please, and lawmakers may enact as long as they please, mankind never will look upon taking fruit in an orchard as *felony* nor even as *trespass*."[17]

THE SITE

Although not elevated enough for general climatic changes, Monticello, at 867 feet, is high enough that during the spring and fall months, as cold air settles in the bottomlands, warm air rises over the mountain—effectively preventing frost damage to blooming fruit trees. Jefferson was especially attentive to the dates of the last spring frost, and one senses him gloating when describing how his lowland neighbors had lost their fruit while his mountainside trees remained unscathed. Thomas Mann Randolph perhaps shared Jefferson's smugness when he wrote his father-in-law in 1792 that "another unproductive year in the orchards of the low country increases the value of the mountains by giving reason to think that their summits in a short time will be the only region of Virginia habitable by fruit trees." Overseer Edmund Bacon recalled:

"I have never seen such a place for fruit. It was so high that it never failed" (fig. 21). The southeastern exposure was also a critical factor in determining which species could be successfully grown at Monticello. Tender trees—almonds, pomegranates, apricots—and fruits, such as peaches and grapes, suited to warm, sunny environments were ideal for such a setting. On the other hand, apples, pears, plums, gooseberries, and currants suffered from the climate that resembled an environment hundreds of miles to the south. This partly explains why the peach was Jefferson's favorite fruit tree and why the north orchard was developed for cider apples, perhaps in response to the hot, dry microclimate of Monticello's south orchard and fruitery.[18]

Siting an orchard on a mountainside certainly was not unique in Virginia. Rich bottomland was reserved for more profitable crops like tobacco, and the utilitarian farm orchards

Fig. 21. Monticello and its southeastern slope

of middle-class farmers were often planted on exhausted and abandoned agricultural fields or on uncultivatable hillsides. In 1785 Robert Dickson reported that Maryland orchards were planted on "the very Meanest and hilly lands," and in 1732 William Hugh Grove, an English traveler through the Virginia countryside, observed apple and peach orchards cultivated "in the worst of their ground in order to Improve it." Peach trees, in particular, were thought capable of ameliorating soil worn out by tobacco, especially when the orchards were grazed by manure-producing hogs and other livestock. William Coxe said that the soil for the standard orchard should be good wheat-growing land, characterized as well drained, of mild but not excessive fertility, and often associated with the uplands. There was no typical site for gentlemen's fruit gardens, except that they were often close to the main house and associated with a kitchen garden. They could be along the bluffs overlooking a river, as at Bremo, the home of John Hartwell Cocke on the James River, or even on an island in the Roanoke River, where Sir Peyton Skipwith of Prestwould cultivated the finest French pears in his "Island Orchard."[19]

PLANTING

Jefferson usually planted bare-root fruit trees in March or April, probably from three to five feet in height, one or two years after they were grafted or budded. As long as the tree is dormant, the time of planting in central Virginia is not a critical factor. Interestingly, in 1799 William Prince, Jr., the son of the founder of what is considered the first commercial nursery in the United States, observed that it was a common practice for peach trees to be planted when in full bloom, a procedure discouraged by modern horticulturists. Prince also refused to sell his nursery-grown fruit trees unless they were taller than six feet, which would be the largest size one could obtain today from most commercial fruit-tree nurseries. Perhaps the practice of selling and shipping such large trees explains why so many of Prince's trees died in transit to Virginia growers like St. George Tucker and John Hartwell Cocke. William Coxe's reliance on an "intermediate" home nursery that was planted with four-year-old trees seven to eight feet

Fig. 22. Williamsburg's John Custis, oil painting by Charles Bridges, c. 1725

tall, which were then grown for still two or three more years before setting in the orchard, also suggests that fruit trees were planted in larger sizes than is customary today. In 1785 George Washington, incredibly, directed the transplanting of a thirty-three-inch-caliper Carnation cherry and a twenty-one-inch apricot, "little expecting that either will live." One eighteenth-century planting technique was described in 1738 by Williamsburg's John Custis, who commonly nursed his fruit trees in soil-filled baskets: "The basket and tree [were] buried together. The basket soon rotted so that the tree was never stunted in the least; and 'tis great odds if another method will ever do" (fig. 22).[20]

Jefferson sent directions home from Washington in 1798 for the planting of ornamental trees recently shipped to Monticello: "He [John, a gardening slave] would do well perhaps to dig his holes before hand, to mellow the earth. All the trees to be well staked, & the numbers preserved." Preparing a planting hole by heaping the excavated soil into piles exposes the soil to the effects of freezing and thawing and also effectively drains Monticello's heavy red clay, assuring that the tree's roots, once planted, are covered with friable "mellow" dirt. Garden writers were unanimous in recommending large planting holes, especially if the land was uncultivated. For instance, Dr. Nicholas Collin, a Pennsylvania apple grower, said, "The too common fault of squeezing them into small holes, has ruined many trees; they must be wide enough to extend at least one foot beyond the limits of the longest roots, and the mould be made quite mellow." Archaeological investigations in the Monticello south orchard in 1980 discerned square-cut holes, a more convenient method than round ones because of the square-shaped spades used in the eighteenth century. Most authors also agreed on the desirability of staking fruit trees to prevent their roots from being disturbed by strong winds. For larger transplants, McMahon suggested a teepee system of three large stakes. At Poplar Forest, his summer retreat, Jefferson supported young trees with "strong stakes 12. f. long stuck by such of the young trees as grow crooked, [tied] to the stake in as many places as possible," and in 1774 he documented the use of yucca leaves to tie up his grapevines, a practice he may have used with young planted trees as well. George Washington recorded how he often had to "right my Trees and ram round them," probably because he neglected to stake them.[21]

There is no documentation to suggest Jefferson watered any garden plant at Monticello. Surprisingly few early fruit writers stressed the importance of watering planted trees, now considered essential to establish intimate contact between the roots and the soil, and there was more opposition to this now-common practice than there was support. Although he preconditioned his trees by soaking in water for eight to ten hours before planting, Philip Miller warned against overwatering. One early Pennsylvania fruit expert with whom Jefferson exchanged scion wood, Timothy Matlack, believed that watering fruit trees during hot weather rotted their roots, while William Cobbett felt that irrigation encouraged "mould and canker." Few early American orchardists

possessed the resources to irrigate their established orchards. An exception was John Bartram, who developed a sophisticated liquid fertilization system at his Philadelphia home. Bartram channeled water, mixed with horse dung, ashes, and lime, to his fruit trees from a small spring a mile and a half away. A more typical example was John Custis, who lost nearly all his young trees during a drought in 1738, "notwithstanding I kept 3 strong Nigros continually filling large tubs of water and put them in the sun and water'd plentifully every night, made the shades and arbors over all the garden almost; but abundance of things perished notwithstanding all the care and trouble."[22]

CULTIVATION

Jefferson cultivated the south orchard with a variety of field crops, a practice consistent with his agricultural theories: "From an opinion entertained by Mr. Jefferson that the heat of the sun destroys or at least dries up in great measure, the nutritious juices of the earth, he judges it necessary that it should always be covered . . . therefore . . . [his fields] never lie fallow." It was not until the 1790s, however, when Jefferson had returned from Europe with experimental plans to revive his exhausted fields, that there is documentation for planting among the trees. In 1791 he wrote his overseer Nicholas Lewis: "You know how much I have at heart the preservation of my lands in general, & particularly the hill side where my orchard is, below the garden, & round the North side of the hill. I will therefore repeat my request to have as much white clover seed gathered & bought as can be, and sowed first in the orchard." In succeeding years the orchards were planted with a diversity of agricultural crops, mostly with the purpose of improving the soil. "Mazzei's corn" was planted in the southwest angle of the south orchard in 1794, the same year corn, sainfoin, and succory were cultivated among trees in the north orchard. The following year Jefferson noted in his Farm Book that the south orchard had been "grubbed" free of weedy native vegetation, probably a preliminary step to planting. Again in 1806 Jefferson directed his overseers to first "clean up," then plant peas, potatoes, oats, and clover in the fruitery and Irish potatoes in the north orchard.[23]

Jefferson's choice of cover crops was particularly progressive, especially the use of field peas, sainfoin, and burnet — soil ameliorators not usually chosen by early fruit growers. Tilling the soil and growing crops between the fruit trees was a common practice only among the most sophisticated early Virginia orchardists. George Washington grew turnips and wheat in his orchards in 1763 and 1765, Landon Carter planted tobacco, and both he and St. George Tucker cultivated corn. John Hartwell Cocke cultivated sweet potatoes in his orchard, while Colonel James Gordon grew oats. Some crops were controversial. Jefferson's endorsement of white clover, "the best improver of lands," was typical of many Virginian growers, yet writers such as Coxe described its effect as "pernicious," and Henry Wynkoop, a progressive Pennsylvania pomologist, thought clover was a haven for field mice. The failure to cultivate orchards was seen by authorities as the symbol of pomological laziness. In 1829 a writer in the *American Farmer* lamented the condition of mid-Atlantic orchards: "It is said that 75 or 100 years ago, apple trees grew almost spontaneously, being properly set out, nothing more was necessary, the work was finished. Now we might as well think of raising a field of corn without the use of a plough or hoe, and the application of manure, as to rear an orchard without labour and cultivation." In 1842 the editor of Richmond's *Southern Planter* observed that "ninety nine young orchards in a hundred have been rendered worthless" by allowing grass to grow around the trees. The pervasive complaints about this issue suggest that orchard cultivation did not become a standard practice until later in the century. A writer in the *American Farmer* concluded: "It is surprising to notice the inattention of our farmers to their Orchards. Some think it unnecessary to cultivate any fruit at all. . . . A farmer with an orchard of 80 or 100 trees, is too often contented if 4 or 5 of them bear a palatable apple. 'The rest,' he says, 'will do to make cider.'"[24]

Stable manure, river muck, leaf mold, oyster shells, lime, and ashes were among the fertilizers favored by progressive fruit growers in the mid-Atlantic states around 1800. Many orchardists discovered beneficial effects, as well as increased land efficiency, from using the orchards as feed lots. McMahon observed, "As to manure, it is well known that where hogs and poultry are constantly running over the ground, the trees seldom fail of a crop, which is the best proof that manure is necessary." An editorial in the *Southern Planter* in 1842 endorsed the traditional Virginia practice of using hogs as insect destroyers and manurers by fencing them within orchards and letting them graze. As late as 1872 a central Virginia pomologist, James Fitz, wrote, "The hogs are the MOST SERVICEABLE IN THE ORCHARD, BUT THEY MUST BE WATCHED." Mulching, especially with mixtures of rotted manure and litter, was also generally endorsed. In 1821 Charlottesville residents were urged to use tanbark (the residue from tannin manufacturing) mulch by Massachusetts's John Gates in an essay reprinted in the local newspaper, the *Central Gazette*. Gates spread one-half to two bushels of bark around his fruit trees every two years and marveled at his healthy trees "wholly free from the ravages of caterpillars, canker-worms, grubs, and every kind of insect."[25]

PRUNING

Jefferson included the task "lop cherry trees" in a list of garden responsibilities for 1770 and referred to trimming orchard trees in an 1812 garden calendar—documentation so sparse one wonders if trees were pruned at all at Monticello. Nineteenth-century American garden writers generally reacted to the controversial principles popularized by William Forsyth, who promoted the severe practice of "heading down" young as well as older decayed trees; the ensuing wounds were to be covered immediately with the healing paste of his celebrated "composition" (fig. 23). Young trees, particularly those recently planted from the nursery, were cut down to three or four buds to prevent "long naked branches." Mature, declining specimens were virtually cut off at the base. In both cases the resultant vigor, according to Forsyth, would rejuvenate the failing trees and increase fruitfulness in the younger ones. Of course, Forsyth maintained, such radical surgery would only be successful if followed by the application of his composition, which consisted of "one bushel of fresh *cow-dung,* half a bushel of *lime rubbish* of old buildings (that from the ceilings of rooms is preferable), half a bushel of *wood-ashes,* and a sixteenth part of a bushel of pit or river *sand,*" mixed into a smooth plaster and applied to the wound.[26]

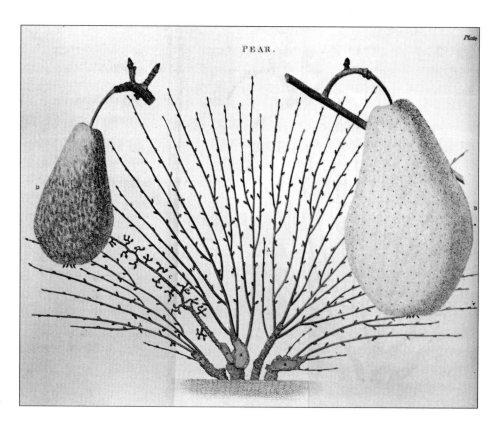

PEAR.

Fig. 23. "Heading down" a
pear tree as illustrated in
Forsyth's *Treatise*

William Coxe was especially wary of Forsyth's techniques: "Excessive pruning is very apt to generate an infinite number of suckers . . . our great heat and dry atmosphere, render close pruning less necessary here than in England, whence we derive most of our instruction on this point." Coxe also passed judgment on the composition: "It was a common practice, some years since, to apply Mr. Forsyth's celebrated composition to large wounds produced by pruning: that novelty . . . has finally lost its popularity." Instead, said Coxe, large wounds should be sealed with tar or thick paint and smaller scars with cow dung. Despite Coxe's dismissal of Forsyth's techniques, writers were still advocating their use throughout the nineteenth century. Nevertheless, pruning in early orchards was casual at best. The "American Farmer" who edited an American edition of Forsyth's *Treatise* in 1803 acknowledged, "Heading-down, training and pruning are practised by many people in their own *some-how way*," and both McMa-

hon and William Coxe admitted it was among the least understood, and worst executed, of the horticultural arts. Peter Yates of Albany, writing in the American edition of Forsyth's *Treatise*, said: "To the neglect of pruning fruit trees . . . may be ascribed the bad and unfruitful state of some of the orchards in America. This inattention and mismanagement . . . subjects them to disease, mortification and death."[27]

PESTS

Jefferson best summarized his philosophy of pest control in a letter to his daughter Martha after she complained of insect-riddled plants in the Monticello vegetable garden: "We will try this winter to cover our garden with a heavy coating of manure. When earth is rich it bids defiance to droughts, yields in abundance, and of the best quality. I suspect that the insects which have harassed you have been encouraged by the feebleness of your plants; and that has been produced by the lean state of the soil. We will attack them another year with joint efforts." Responding to reports of the damage inflicted by the Hessian fly on his wheat crop in 1791 while he was in Philadelphia serving in the president's cabinet, Jefferson wrote: "I do not think that [the natural history] of the weavil of Virginia has been yet sufficiently detailed. . . . Bartram here tells me it is one & the same insect which by depositing its egg in the young plumbs, apricots, nectarines & peaches renders them gummy & good for nothing. He promises to shew me the insect this summer. I long to be free for pursuits of this kind instead of the detestable ones in which I am now labouring without pleasure to myself, or profit to others." Jefferson's expression of entomological interest in the curculio, which he incorrectly associated with the Hessian fly, rather than complaining about his lost harvest, demonstrated his detached, coolly scientific, what would today be called "holistic," approach to pomology.[28]

Many modern authorities believe that because numerous harmful diseases and insects have since been imported, fruit trees grown in American orchards around 1800 enjoyed a virtually pest-free environment. An early twentieth-century pomologist, S. W. Fletcher, said, "There were no serious insect or fungus pests [in eighteenth-century Virginia orchards]; the trees bore lavishly, even under neglect." U. P. Hedrick remarked, "There were far fewer orchard pests at that time than now [1950]," and L. H. Bailey in 1900 stated, "For generations insect pests were not common." William Cobbett wrote in 1821 that in America "there are no blights of fruit trees worth speaking of," and "fine trees and fine fruit and large crops may be had in a country where blights are almost unknown." The list of fruit pests introduced from abroad since 1820 is extensive and includes the Japanese beetle and San Jose scale. Because there were no natural predators, these pests became plaguelike soon after being introduced. Other common maladies—from spider mites and aphids to apple scab and powdery mildew—are native to the New World yet were rarely mentioned by early ninteenth-century fruit writers. Many of these indigenous pests only became problems when their populations exploded as a result of intensive, man-made agricultural activity, when large-scale, monocultural commercial

orchards developed around urban settlements and provided a fertile breeding ground for their spread. For example, the peach tree, an Oriental native, thrived before 1800 because of the lack of introduced pests; European grapes, on the other hand, suffered because they had no immunity to New World diseases and insects like black rot and phylloxera. In many cases, however, before 1800, perhaps even 1820, American orchards enjoyed a virgin age of innocence in regard to fruit pests.[29]

Were pests uniformly less serious in 1800 than they are today? In some cases, no. Jefferson's failure to successfully cultivate European varieties of plum and pear was likely the result of an inability to combat plum curculio and fire blight. John Bartram, perhaps colonial America's most committed gardener, failed perennially in growing nectarines and apricots, to the surprise and consternation of his London patron, Peter Collinson, who recommended various remedies "to prevent the depradations of the Beetle." One eighteenth-century New York fruit grower, Hector St. John de Crèvecoeur, said, "Our country teems with more destructive insects and animals than Europe." Another New Yorker, Governor DeWitt Clinton, observed that "unfortunately our country, as much perhaps as any on this globe, abounds with such insects." Jefferson's daughter Martha reported from Monticello, "I am going on with such spirit in the garden that I think I shall conquer my *oponent* the *insect* yet, tho hither to they have been as indifatigable in cutting up as I have been in planting."[30]

The most serious fruit-tree pests before 1820 were peach borers and plum curculio, but others were becoming especially virulent. The yellows, a bacterial infection that infests the peach, killed millions of trees in the mid-Atlantic states in the first half of the nineteenth century. In 1824 a writer in the *American Farmer* noted, "You could not have found a [live] peach in a day's drive" across central Pennsylvania; "the dry dead skeletons presented a most dismal aspect." Fire blight, according to some authors, prohibited the culture of the pear entirely. Peach tree borers, perhaps because they are both lethal and visually obvious, rivaled the curculio, which devastated fancy fruits such as apricots, nectarines, and plums, as the most commonly discussed destructive insect. Many growers probably felt that spotted, fungus-infested fruit was part of the innate character of a particular species or variety. William Coxe's daughters, who illustrated American fruit varieties for an intended second edition of their father's *View toward the Cultivation of Fruit Trees*, made no effort to hide the various smuts, mildews, and rusts inevitably found on untreated peaches, apples, and pears (pl. 1). This enabled a twentieth-century pathologist, P. L. Richter, to identify early American diseases in 1924. Richter found such modern maladies as codling moth, apple scab, flyspeck, leaf blight, and peach scab. Some of these may have been ignored, particularly by growers who tolerated superficial damage such as a rotten spot (brown rot) in an apple or a discoloration of the fruit's skin (mildew or flyspeck). Although the populations of many diseases and insects had not yet become epidemic, and while many pests could be overlooked, there were serious problems in orchards by 1820.[31]

One of the best-known and most commonly cited essays on pest control was written by Benjamin Barton, a Philadelphia botanist who named the *Jeffersonia diphylla*, or twinleaf, in Jefferson's honor. Barton insisted on the need to study the life cycle of destructive insects and also celebrated the effect of insect-devouring birds—bluebirds, woodpeckers, house wrens, even vultures. He suggested gardeners and farmers procure "10 or 15 pair of these small birds," who would perform the service of "a whole plantation of negroes, men, women and children" in the tedious chore of removing destructive insects from garden plants. "Moreover," Barton continued, "they are a very agreeable companion to man, for their notes are pleasing." Barton's arguments for biological control were reaffirmed by later writers; for example, New York governor DeWitt Clinton hailed Barton's pioneering scientific approach in 1819: "Dr. Barton has very justly remarked, that it is an object of the first importance to investigate the natural history of those insects which are peculiarly injurious to us in any way." James Worth, a correspondent in the *American Farmer* in 1823, observed that "many species of insects have increased to an alarming extent, and unless timely checked, they will be the means of causing a famine in our land." Worth noted the scarcity of wrens, blackbirds, and woodpeckers and blamed the increase in destructive insects on nature "being out of balance." He recommended rather benign control measures—knocking rose bugs

Fig. 24. Tent caterpillars at Monticello

into water jars and letting hogs into the peach orchard to control the plum curculio—and was curiously optimistic that a grower's garden would return to "the pristine state when he has dominion over all the natural world." Obviously, biological control was the first weapon in defense against fruit insects. John Bartram's success with plum growing was attributed to the trees' proximity to his home: by frequently shaking the tree he "tumbled off" the curculios. In a letter to John Custis, Peter Collinson described how he rid his orchard of moles by attacking them with a shovel. William Coxe suggested that the best means of controlling tent caterpillars, "one of the worst enemies to an orchard," was simply to crush them in their nests; Worth claimed that "by a little attention one person can rid a farm of them in a single day" (fig. 24).[32]

While some early American orchardists expressed innocence and others scientific detachment, still others found military analogies to describe their war on destructive pests. In 1808 Pennsylvania judge Richard Peters, whom Jefferson called "an excellent farmer," presented a dirge on the fate of his orchards in the *Memoirs* of the Philadelphia Society for Promoting Agriculture. His article "On Peach Trees" suggested how problems boomed with the increased horticultural intensity during his lifetime: "In my youth, excellent *plumbs* grew here; now we can obtain none, but those of inferior species. In *grapes* we were never successful; though much more so than at present. . . . Our *apple orchards* do not produce, as they did in early times. There must therefore be some change in our climate; and new races of vermin, not known to our ancestors." Peters's lament continued with further explanations for a resurgence of fruit disorders. The conclusion of his essay, however, was punctuated with pugilistic ardor.

Trees, like animals, have inherent diseases peculiar to their species. The peach seems most subject to this tendency; pears are liable to blights from the electric fluid. Iron hoops, old horse shoes etc. hung on these trees, attract and conduct for a time, this floating fluid. But when the air is surcharged, destruction partial or total is certain. Cherries are fatally operated upon, by what is called the four o'clock sun. Plumbs too are exposed to peculiar disasters. . . . Particular insects and vermin have their respectively favorite tree, or plant to prey on. They pursue the dictates of nature, for their own propagation and support; while, by destroying our sustenance and comforts, they become hostile to us. They compel us to wage against them a perpetual warfare.[33]

Another typical lament, as expressed by "Veritas" in the *American Farmer* in 1821, repeated Peters's nostalgic grief over the depletion of the native soil: "In the early years of our country the earth needed only the seed to be sown to produce a rich harvest, for its bosom was softened and enriched by natural manure. The case is now different—it has been skimmed by grandfather, father and son, twice or thrice re-

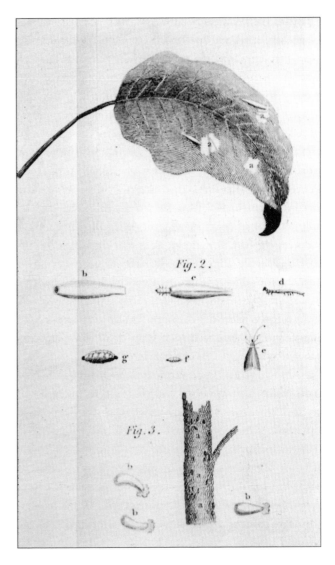

Fig. 25. Insect pests of the pear, from Forsyth's *Treatise*

peated until its face is sadly wasted." Grim reports of entire landscapes riddled with the skeletons of dead peach trees, apple trees whose trunks were "drilled with holes; its branches covered with moss; many of the trees bent or crooked; much old naked, barren, and even dead wood upon them, and scarcely one that bears every year" made it clear that the age of innocence for American fruit growing had come to an end (fig. 25).[34]

By 1820 American agricultural journals included a variety of general tonics and homemade recipes for sick fruit trees. "Ringing" limbs by peeling off a thin (one-quarter to one inch wide) strip of bark was a common practice popularized in part by André Thöuin, the head gardener of the Jardin des Plantes in Paris and a frequent horticultural correspondent of Jefferson's. Ringing small branches, when done sparingly, is a scientifically legitimate way of promoting fruit production. American fruit growers were astonished at the resurgence of fruit after doing this. "Barking" trees was a more unconventional and controversial practice that usually will result in the tree's death. After printing the pros and cons of stripping the bark from the trunk of a sickly fruit tree in the *American Farmer*, editor John Skinner concluded that such a "mischievous" and "hazardous" practice was applicable only as a last resort. Prophylactic liquid tonics, usually involving lime, tobacco juice, and soapsuds, similar to Forsyth's composition, often were endorsed. Many of these general tonics were obviously experimental, some suspiciously so, and one senses a growing pessimism as farmers experienced the dark side of fruit growing. William Cobbett, for example, wrote: "When orchards are seized with diseases that pervade the whole of the trees . . . the best way is to cut them down. They are more plague than profit. . . . However, as there are persons who have a delight in quackery, who are never so happy as when they have some specific to apply, and to whom rosy cheeks and ruby lips are almost an eye sore, it is perhaps fortunate that the vegetable world present them with patients."[35]

The Monticello orchards were admirably adapted to resist some of the most destructive eighteenth-century enemies to fruit: their elevation warded off late spring frost, the enclosures protected the trees and soft fruit from human and animal invaders, and Jefferson's selection of varieties was oriented toward Virginia cultivars well adapted to Monticello's climatic and soil situation. U. P. Hedrick argued that because of the protection provided by nearby virgin forests, most early orchards received minimal frost damage due to a climate that was "probably more equable." However, the frequent reference to frost damage in eighteenth-century Virginia orchards suggests otherwise. Some growers concocted frost protection

remedies, the equivalent of modern smudge pots and circulating fans. Samuel Preston observed that plaster of Paris applied at the base of his apple trees prevented the frost damage that had blasted the fruit on untreated trees. Richard Peters commented that such a technique "has been observed by others; moisture will [also] keep off frost, common salt has had this effect, when scattered around trees. A straw rope, with one end twisted round the fruit trees, and the other immersed in water, conveys moisture and repels frost." An anonymous contributor to the *American Farmer* in 1824 recommended a mulch of snow or ice.[36]

WEEDS

A weed is often defined subjectively, "a plant out of place." For Jefferson, weeds, "spontaneous herbage," the native and introduced plants that populated his garden, orchard, and nonforested abandoned or cultivated land, were a satisfactory soil ameliorator in an agricultural system of crop rotation: "It is well known here that a space of rest greater or less in spontaneous herbage, will restore the exhaustion of a single crop." Jefferson's naive yet positive perception of the place of the weed, like his ideas on pest control, reflected a kind of horticultural innocence. The most troublesome weed in Virginia orchards today, poison ivy, was considered an ornamental by Jefferson, probably because of its striking autumn color. Crabgrass, presently the second most common weed in Virginia orchards and the third most economically damaging species in American cropland, was listed as a legitimate pasture and lawn grass in his *Notes on the State of Virginia* and was commonly sowed by early agriculturists. Still, Jefferson recognized that certain plants were "out of place" and realized the necessity of controlling them. In a letter to Charles Willson Peale in 1813 he discussed his theories on weed control, cultivation, and agriculture. "The spontaneous energies of the earth are a great gift of nature, but they require the labor of man to direct their operation. And the question is so to husband his labor as to turn the greatest quantity of this useful action of the earth to his benefit. Ploughing deep, your recipe for killing weeds, is also the recipe for almost every good thing in farming. The plough is to the farmer what the wand is to the sorcerer. Its effect is really like sorcery." Thomas Mann Randolph, who often managed the farmland at Monticello, read a paper in 1824 before the Agricultural Society of Albemarle in which he discussed his method of ridding wheatlands of horse nettle. Sheep were introduced into the fields in late spring as the nettles were blooming. Although they abhorred the foliage of this prickly weed, they would graze on the flowers, eliminating the species' ability to reproduce itself. This was efficient biological control: man, domestic beast, cultivated plant, and escaped weed in environmental harmony.[37]

Old World plants became naturalized soon after the European settlement of America, and many turned into pests that are with us today. For example, the two most common weeds in modern Virginia orchards, foxtail and crabgrass, were European introductions observed by Richard Parkinson in Maryland before 1800. John Smith noted the appearance of "all manner of herbs and roots we have in England" in the fields about Jamestown in 1629. John Josslyn, an English explorer and naturalist who visited New England in 1638 and 1663, compiled a list "Of Such Plants as have sprung up since the English Planted and kept Cattle in New-England" in his *New England Rarities*. These are plants still common wherever the ground is disturbed, virtually everywhere the forest has been removed. John Bartram, a hundred years later, compiled a similar list of the most troublesome weeds in eastern Pennsylvania, and like later writers, he found plant pests both native and alien. The two worst weeds observed by Peter Kalm in 1748 were the indigenous pokeweed and the naturalized jimsonweed (*Datura stramonium*), named "Jamestown weed" for its association with the Virginia settlement where it reputedly was grown as an ornamental. For William Cobbett, dandelions and dock were "the gardener's two *vegetable devils.* . . . Nothing but absolute *burning*, or a sun that will reduce them to *powder*, will kill their roots." Archaeological excavations in 1985 in the orchard of Charles Carroll, an eighteenth-century fruit grower at Mount Clare in Baltimore, also uncovered seeds of jimsonweed as well as other Old World herbs.[38]

Whatever their source, early American orchard weeds had to be eliminated by fruit growers eager to bring their trees to full productivity. Most growers relied on cultivation (Peale's "recipe for killing weeds"), grazing the orchard, or simply hoeing up or mowing down the offending plants. John Bartram eliminated most of his weeds with "the hoe and plough," but the two "most mischievous," wild snapdragon, or butter-and-eggs (*Linaria vulgaris*), introduced as an ornamental, and the European Saint-John's-wort (*Hypericum perforatum*), required more drastic measures. Bartram described the futile efforts of his neighbors to rid their fields of the *Linaria*: "Some people have rolled great heaps of logs upon it, and burnt them to ashes, whereby the earth was burnt half a foot deep, yet it put up again, as fresh as ever." John Boulster, a correspondent of Baltimore's *American Farmer*, wrote of wild garlic, "If you can't get rid of it, learn to live with it." Another writer in the *American Farmer*, John Armstrong, described how he rid his farms of the Canada thistle by dumping the salty brine from his pickled fish, pork, and beef on the offending plants.[39]

FRUIT VARIETIES

Perhaps the most important pomological achievement of Thomas Jefferson was the varietal collection he assembled at Monticello. He planted over 170 varieties (of which 125 were tree fruits), and although grown over a period of nearly fifty years, they represent the state of the art of fruit cultivars available to an early nineteenth-century gardener. Jefferson's favorite choices usually were reaffirmed by the pomological authorities later in the nineteenth century, such as A. J. Downing or William Kenrick. At a time when most Virginians were planting seedling peaches, which could not be identified with a cultivar name, Jefferson was growing the premier American types: Heath Cling, Oldmixon Free and Cling, Lemon Cling, and Morris's White and Red Rareripe. He also grew the finest European, especially Italian, varieties like the Breast of Venus (Poppa di Venere), Vaga Loggia, and Green Nutmeg, an old English cultivar. He cultivated and cherished America's two greatest nineteenth-century apples, the Newtown Pippin and Esopus Spitzenburg, and the most popular fruit-tree cultivar in eighteenth-century Virginia, Hewes Crab (fig. 26). He repeatedly exchanged the regional Taliaferro apple, not widely known, with friends and lauded it in agricultural journals after his tests proved it "the best cyder apple exist-

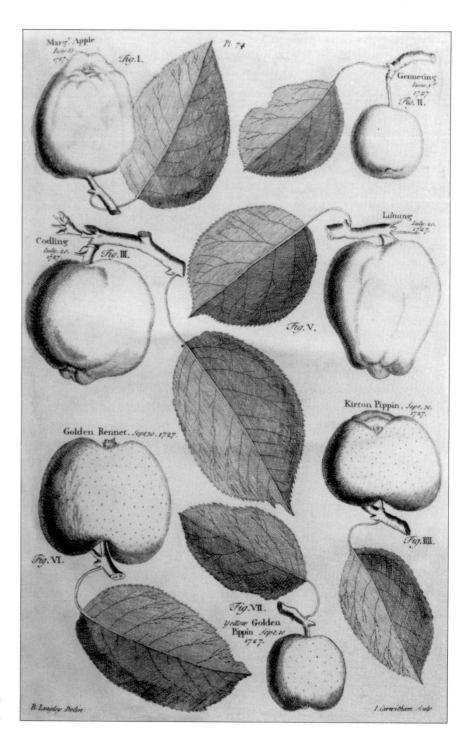

Fig. 26. Apple varieties
from Langley's *Pomona*

ing." Jefferson cultivated the most highly acclaimed New World pear, the Seckel, after failing with the finest available eighteenth-century French varieties, Beurré Gris, Crassane, Royal, and Virgouleuse. Most of the 27 European plum varieties died at Monticello, yet the Green Gage, the one variety at the top of the pomological chart, and the native Chickasaw plum, a fascinating experiment as a cultivated orchard tree, survived attacks of pestilence and drought. Jefferson's trials with European cherries were also a successful venture, including the two most vaunted cultivars, the May Duke and Carnation, his personal favorite. Jefferson's collection of small and soft fruit was also extraordinary. The Hudson strawberry, Marseilles fig, and Antwerp raspberries became legendary cultivars while Jefferson's documented grape collection was unparalleled among American viticulturists before 1850. In his varietal selection Jefferson had the best of both fruit worlds, the Old and the New. Although there were notable exceptions, it was the American varieties that thrived at Monticello —the Seckel pear; Taliaferro, Pippin, Spitzenburg, and Hewes Crab apples; and seedling peaches. In the same way, New World varieties, particularly of apples and peaches, had superseded the European cultivars in the nursery catalogs of American growers and the recommended lists of fruit authorities by the middle of the nineteenth century. But it was also the blend of varieties that makes Jefferson's collection so striking; he grew not only the finest dessert varieties but also functional, utilitarian fruits like cider apples and seedling peaches designed for the cider press, the drying lot, or the brandy keg—the best varieties for the farm orchard as well as the fruit garden.

The South Orchard

The south orchard, like most of Jefferson's landscape and architectural ventures, evolved by fits and starts from the first plantings in 1767 until 1815, when in Jefferson's seventy-third year planting seemed to cease. Jefferson grew apples, peaches, cherries, pears, plums, apricots, nectarines, quinces, almonds and even some nut trees, mulberries, olives, and tender pomegranates in the orchard, which extended below the vegetable garden wall and formed a horseshoe-shaped grid of about five and one-half acres around two vineyards, the northeast and southwest, and the berry terraces.

The detailed early references to fruit growing at Monticello—in 1767, 1769, 1774, and 1778—make it seem likely that the pomological potential of his "little mountain" was a chief motivation for Jefferson's settling there. Monticello may have been the site of an earlier orchard before Jefferson's first planting there in 1767. He wrote in his *Notes on the State of Virginia* in 1780 that "I have known frost so severe as to kill the hiccory trees round about Monticello, and yet not injure the tender fruit blossoms then in bloom on the top and higher parts of the mountain; and in the course of 40 years, during which it has been settled, there have been but two instances of a general loss of fruit on it; while, in the circumjacent country, the fruit has escaped but twice in the last seven years." Although this suggests fruit was being grown on the mountain as early as 1740, perhaps planted by Jefferson's father, Peter, or even by Native Americans, one might also interpret "fruit" as a botanical term, referring to indigenous cherries, plums, even oaks and hickories, rather than cultivated species such as apples or peaches.[1]

In 1769 Jefferson recorded the first intensive planting at Monticello (fig. 27). His plan reflects his immediate awareness of the warm microclimate created by a south-facing slope as well as his knowledge of European cultural practices: his curiosity about sophisticated grafting combinations (almonds and apricots on peaches) and tender Mediterranean plants (pomegranates, figs, and almonds) suggests an Old World influence. On the one hand it is the experimental orchard of a young man (Jefferson was twenty-five) eager to import Mediterranean culture to the Virginia frontier, yet this plan also included grafted trees of the Newtown Pippin ("New York apples"), the most widely distributed of all American varieties and often acknowledged as the finest. The first record of harvest, an indication that his initial plantings were at least marginally successful, occurred on October 8, 1772, when Jefferson noted that he "gathered 2. plumb-peaches at Monticello." "Plumb-peaches," a distinctly eighteenth-century American expression, were clingstone types in which the flesh adheres tightly to the peach stone, or pit. From the beginning Jefferson's fruit garden revealed the studied influence of both Old and New World species and cultural techniques.[2]

Another major European influence on the early plantings in the south orchard was Philip Mazzei, a Tuscan farmer, wine merchant, and later a Revolutionary War patriot, who in 1773 settled with Jefferson's blessings at a farm adjacent to Monticello that he named Colle. Mazzei imported oranges, lemons, olives, and European grapes in an effort to establish Italian agriculture on the Virginia frontier. Although his attempts at growing such tender fruits failed, Mazzei's influence on Jefferson was revealed by the Italian fruit names he used in the 1774 Garden Book: apricots were "Meliache e Albiocche," and the cornelian cherry (actually a dogwood, *Cornus mas*) was "Ciriege corniole." Jefferson also planted olive roots, some of which survived the winter of 1774, sour orange trees, eighty-six almond seeds, and "198 Cherries of different kinds from Italy" that came from Colle. Mazzei's incongruous commu-

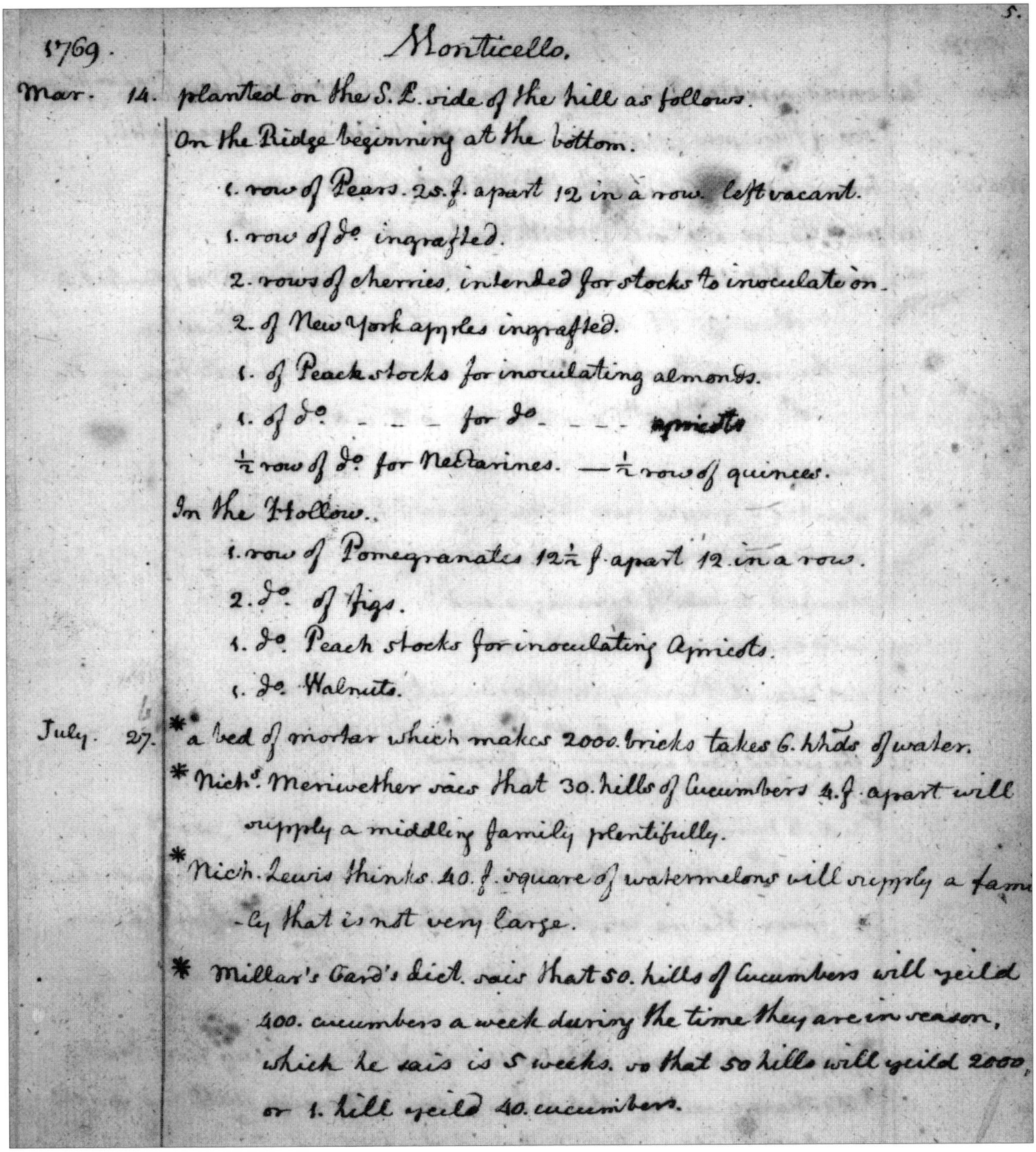

5.

1769.

Monticello.

Mar. 14. planted on the S. E. side of the hill as follows.

On the Ridge beginning at the bottom.

1. row of Pears. 25. f. apart 12 in a row. left vacant.

1. row of do. ingrafted.

2. rows of cherries. intended for stocks to inoculate on.

2. of New York apples ingrafted.

1. of Peach stocks for inoculating almonds.

1. of do. ___ ___ for do. ___ ___ ~~apricots~~

½ row of do. for Nectarines. —½ row of quinces.

In the Hollow.

1. row of Pomegranates 12½ f. apart 12 in a row.

2. do. of Figs.

1. do. Peach stocks for inoculating Apricots.

1. do. Walnuts.

July. 27. * a bed of mortar which makes 2000. bricks takes 6. whds of water.

* Nichs. Meriwether saies that 30. hills of Cucumbers 4. f. apart will supply a middling family plentifully.

* Nich. Lewis thinks. 40. f. square of watermelons will supply a family that is not very large.

* Millar's Gard's dict. saies that 50. hills of Cucumbers will yeild 400. cucumbers a week during the time they are in season, which he saies is 5 weeks. so that 50 hills will yeild 2000, or 1. hill yeild 40. cucumbers.

Fig. 27. Garden Book page from 1769 with early fruit-planting plans for Monticello

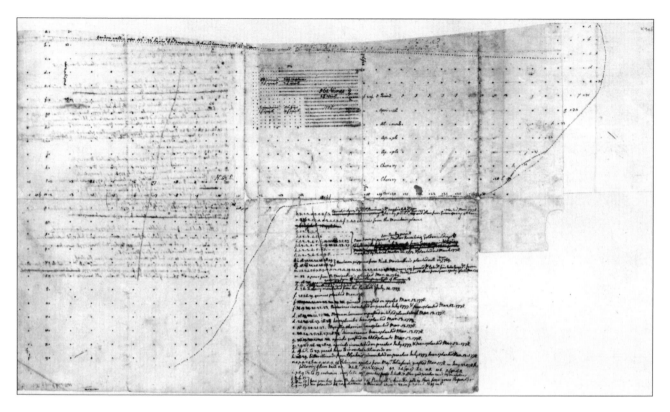

Fig. 28. Jefferson's 1778 orchard plan

nity of Italian workmen dissolved with the outbreak of the Revolutionary War, yet two gardeners, Antonio Giannini and Giovannini da Prato, remained employed by Jefferson at Monticello. Giannini worked in the orchard sporadically from 1778 to 1791, occasionally grafting trees and working in the vineyards, while Giovannini, described by Jefferson as "sober, industrious, & honest," worked as a gardener at Monticello in 1782. Mazzei's pomological influence was perhaps most profoundly felt after he retired to Pisa in 1792 and, ten years later, shipped to Jefferson various peach and apricot varieties previously unknown in the United States.[3]

The 1778 orchard plan, composed during a year in which Jefferson was often in Williamsburg serving in the Virginia assembly, included his first map of an enlarged orchard and was his most detailed and ambitious scheme in its evolution (fig. 28). In fact, there is no other surviving document on an American eighteenth-century orchard with such meticulously organized notes on tree locations, propagation techniques, and planting failures and successes. Jefferson's notes reflect the uncommon perseverance and patience of a dedicated horticulturist. The depth and detail of these early plans suggest at least his presence on site, perhaps directing the grafting or planting, perhaps participating in the process himself. Two memorandums, the first jotted down in the spring, the other entitled "State of fruit trees. Nov. 1778," record plantings between 1769 and 1778 (fig. 29). The fruit trees were organized into a grid system defined by latitudinal rows across the hillside, designated by letters (a–y), and longitudinal rows up and down the mountain, referred to by numbers (1–43). Although the map segregates species into specific rows—the apple row, the apricot row, etc.—Jefferson's notes indicate that he regularly deviated from such a plan. For example, he planted apples in seventeen different rows and cherries in six, isolating the Taliaferro apple in the southern corner and cherry trees

Fig. 29. Jefferson's notes for his 1778 orchard plan

on the northeastern edge of the orchard. Jefferson wisely allotted the large growing apples, cherries, and pears to the southwestern side of the orchard, where trees were spaced at 25 by 40 foot intervals. He also planted many of the smaller peach trees at a 25 by 20 foot spacing in the central sections. Otherwise, species were casually integrated at intervals of 25 by 25 feet. By 1811, however, many of the apples were growing in cramped quarters in the heart of the orchard, while peaches wastefully occupied the generously spaced eastern side.[4]

The 1778 planting memorandums delineated the introduction of 312 trees, including more than twenty-eight varieties of ten species: 147 apple trees, 41 peaches, 25 pears, 31 cherries, 19 plums, 23 apricots, 11 almonds, 6 nectarines, more than 6 quinces, and 3 walnuts. Jefferson continued to experiment with unusual grafting combinations, testing the compatibility of quinces grafted upon apples and apricots on wild plum and peach seedlings. The trials were performed by either Giannini or Patrick Morgan, a local horticulturist. Al-

though the plan has a pleasing balance in the number of species, the planting exhibited an unusual variety, which again attests to the experimental character of the orchard. As well, Jefferson dutifully recorded a diversity of sources. Trees, cuttings, and seeds came from nearby estates such as Blenheim and Mountain Plains as well as plantations in eastern Virginia near Williamsburg like Sandy Point and Green Spring. Neighborhood friends such as Nicholas Meriwether, Isaac Coles, and James Walker; Jefferson's own workmen such as Abraham Balyal; and Williamsburg's Major Richard Taliaferro also contributed grafting material. The exchange of scions, seeds, and trees was a token of friendship, a living manifestation of the "humanized horticulture" that enlivened the letters, and surely the conversations, between Jefferson and his friends, neighbors, and even political allies. The south orchard did not exist in a horticultural vacuum but rather was nourished generously by a society of Virginia gardeners. The following autumn, on the reverse side of his map, Jefferson recorded the

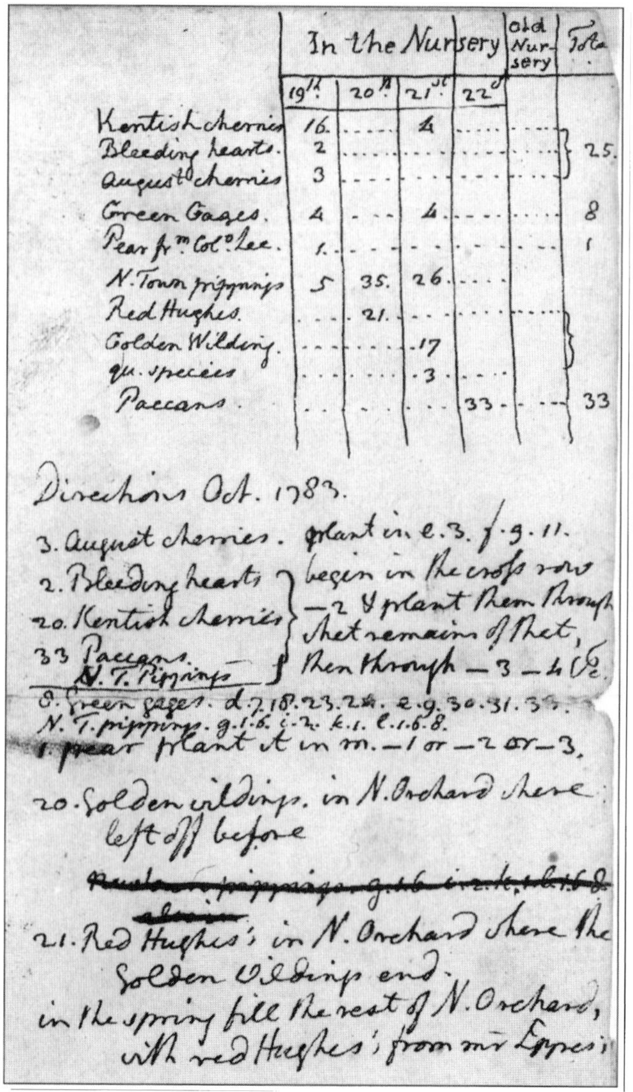

	In the Nursery 19th.	20th.	21st.	22d.	Old Nursery	Total.
Kentish cherries	16.		4			} 25.
Bleeding hearts.	2					
August cherries	3					
Green Gages.	4		4.			8
Pear fr. Col. Lee.	1.					1
N. Town pippings	5	35.	26.			
Red Hughes.		21.				
Golden Wilding.			17			
qu. species			3			
Paccans.				33		33

Directions Oct. 1783.

3. August cherries. plant in e.3. f.9.11.
2. Bleeding hearts } begin in the cross row
20. Kentish cherries } —2 & plant them through
33 Paccans. } that remains of that,
N. T. Pippings } then through —3 —4 &c.
8. Green gages. d.7.18.23.24. e.9.30.31.33.
N. T. pippings. g.1.6. i.2. k.1. l.1.6.8.
1. pear plant it in m.—1 or—2 or—3.
20. Golden wildings. in N. Orchard where left off before
21. Red Hughes's in N. Orchard where the Golden Wildings end.
in the spring fill the rest of N. Orchard, with red Hughes's from mr Eppes's

Fig. 30. Jefferson's notes on the contents of the Monticello nurseries and "Directions Oct. 1783," planting plans for the south and north orchards

fate of many of the 1778 plantings, detailing expanded plantings and propagating activities during the summer. Many trees survived the long Virginia summer, but when any failed, Jefferson was diligent enough to replant the empty spaces.[5]

The history of the orchard parallels the extent of Jefferson's residency at Monticello; when he was away as governor of Virginia, member of Congress, minister to France, vice-president, and president, attention to fruit growing inevitably suffered. On the other hand, he always returned from public service with plants, plans, and renewed energy to direct toward the improvement of his estate. During two interludes in 1783 Jefferson left planting memorandums. "Revisal of my Fruit, 1783" specified locations for ninety-seven new trees, twenty-two of which were replacements. He remarked on the dates they were budded or grafted (either "inoc'd" or "graf'd") and transplanted ("transp.," "trp'd," etc.) into the orchard. Jefferson also commented on the fate of thirty-three of the trees noted in the 1778 memorandum, particularly the years in which they began to bear fruit. A notable success were the cherry trees, most of which still survived and were producing. "Revisal, 1783" also documents the expansion of the southwest and northeast sides of the orchard as Jefferson added cherry trees in the former and "Balyal's peaches" in the latter. (See chart on page 47.)

Another plan later the same year, "Directions Oct. 1783," provides a further definition of the way Jefferson was beginning to isolate species and varieties not so much by the original 1778 map—in latitudinal rows—but by planting them in blocks along "cross rows," which ran up and down the hill (fig. 30). It gave directions for replacing the dead trees and the completion of the north orchard with cider apples from Francis Eppes, a friend as well as Jefferson's brother-in-law. The nursery, admirably self-sufficient, held 154 trees, including 33 pecans and 66 Newtown Pippins, and was the sole source for the October plantings. Antonio Giannini was employed by Jefferson as a custom grafter and probably concentrated his efforts there. This memorandum is the first documented reference to the north, or farm, orchard at Monticello.[6]

Jefferson left for Paris the following year to serve as minister to France, and in his absence there was little record of specific activity in the orchard. While abroad he wrote the Reverend James Madison about the comparative quality of American- and European-grown fruit trees. "They have no apples [in France] to compare with our Newtown pippin. They have nothing which deserves the name of a peach; there being not sun enough to ripen the plum-peach [clingstone] and the best of their soft [freestone] peaches being like our

REVISAL OF MY FRUIT, 1783

a 1. −1.−2. Kentish cherries transpl. Ap. 1782
     2.   Cherry from Mount. Plains. transpl. Mar. 1778. bore 83
     3.   Cherry
   33.34.35.36. Balyal's peaches trp'd Oct. 177[?].
b. 1   cherry from the nursery transpl'd spring 83
     2.   ([same as a.2])
     3.   Carnation from Greenspring or Sandy point tr'd. Mar. 78 bore 83
   33.34.35.36. (a.33)
 −1   Kentish cherry tr'd. Apr. 82.
 −2   Carnation from Allen's tr'd. Apr. 82.
c. 2.4. (a.2)   3. (b.3)   33.34.35.36. (a.33)
    1.2.   large Morellas tr'd. Apr. 82.
d. 1.4.   cherries from nursery transpltd. spr. 83
   2 (a.2)   3. (b.3)   5.6. Mag. bon. tr'd 80
   8   Green gage inoculated June 83.
   9.10.11. Green Gages grafted on Wild plumb stocks.
   19.   green gage [?] June. 83.
   21.22.   Magnum bonums on Wild plumb stocks. Mar. 78 bore 82.
   20.25.   (do.) grafted 1781.
   26.   Horse plumbs tr'd. Mar. 78. bore 82.
   27.28.30.31.32.33. Prunes tr'd Apr. 82.
   29.   Damascenes tr'd 81.   34.35.36. Balyal's peach
 −1.   May Duke tr'd Ap 82.   −2. Large Morella tr'd Ap: 82.
e. 1   [?] the nursery trd. spr. 83.   2.4. (a.2)
   5.10.   plumbs of a parcel of yellow eggs, large white sweet, Orleans, Imperatrice. Red Imperial, White Imperial,
          Drap d'or, Royal & Apricot plumbs from N. York grafted on Wild plumb stock Mar. 80.
   6.8.   Green Gages ind. June 83   7.11. Orleans plumbs tr'd. Apr 82.
   18.19.20.21.22. Morellas tr'd. Mar. 78. bore 82.
   23.24. & many others of about 1780. 1781 are believed to be Carnation, Kentish or Morellas substituted in vacancies
          and not noted.
   25.   Magnum bonum grafted 81.
   26.27.   Damascenes tr'd Mar. 78. bore 82.
   28.   apricot plumbs tr'd. Ap. 82.
   29.   Green gage grafted 80. qu.
   30.35.36. Balyal's peaches
   32.   cherry from nursery tr'd. spr. 83.
 −1.−2.   May Dukes tr'd. Ap. 82.   Dead. [?]30.31.33.
f. 1.   Carnation tr'd Apr. 8 Allen's   2.4.5. (a.2)   3. (b.3)
   6.7.8.   Allen's Carnation from Brandon graft'd 80.
   10.   Green gage inoc'd 83.
   20.   Plumb Nectarine from E. Carter inoc'd [?] tr.d 78. bore 82.
   18.19.21.22.23. Peach stocks for inoculation
   25.26.29. (do.) planted Mar. 69.   28. (do.) pl'd. Nov. 78.
   30.31.32.33.34.35. Balyal's peaches
 −1.−2.   Carnation from Allen's tr'd Apr. 82   Dead. 9.11.24.27.
g. 2.3.4.5. of a parcel of New T. pippins from Sandy Point. Medlar Russetins, Gold Wildings fr'm Gr. Spr. graft'd. 73.
          tr'd Mar. 78. begin to bear 82.
   7.8.10.11. Green gages in'd. 83.   9. Apricot from the stone pl't. 81.
   25.   an apricot inoc'd. July 1772. bore 82.
   20.23.   ditto grafted 81.   ditto tr'd' Apr. 82.
   18.19.21.22.24.26.27.28.29.30.32.33.34. ditto gr'd & in'd. 83.   Dead. 1.6.[7]

autumn peaches. Their cherries and strawberries are fair, but
I think lack flavor. Their plums I think are better; so are their
gooseberries, and the pears infinitely beyond anything we possess." The story of fruit growing in America, particularly in
the South, is that of the adaptation of alien species and varieties to a unique continental climate. Jefferson thus succinctly
reported that apples and peaches, in particular, reached an exalted level of flavor and fruitfulness when brought to eastern
America, but plums, pears, and gooseberries remained species
best cultivated in the Old World.[8]

While in Paris, Jefferson was eager to learn of the state of
his orchard and sent home directions to Antonio Giannini:
"Graft me a good number of the fine white, red, & yellow
plumb peaches from Balyal's, taking the grafts from the old
trees remaining at Balyal's, to plant these in the room of all
those which die in my orchard, and in the room of such as
are found to bear indifferent peaches. I hope this has been
done & if not, that you will do it the first season. I depend
also that you will fill up my apple orchard on the North side
of the mountain with the kinds of trees I directed, and wind-
ing the rows on a level round the hill as was begun before I
came away: and always as soon as any fruit tree dies, replant
another of the same kind in it's place." Giannini responded
to Jefferson later in the year: "The apples in the orchard below
the garden are producing abundantly. All of the varieties of
cherry trees are growing well. The 'Magnum bonum' plumbs
are turning out marvelously, and so are the green gages. The
apricots are growing. Some died but have been replanted. The
almonds are still alive but are not improving. The peaches are
doing well."[9]

Giannini was aided in his curatorship by a Monticello slave,
Great George, who handled more of the day-by-day responsibilities—grubbing weeds from around the trunks, pulling
out dead trees, and harvesting. Nevertheless, when Jefferson
returned from Europe late in December 1789 he found his
farm and orchard deteriorating, and he soon planted directly
in the orchard the Royal, Crassanne, St. Germaine, and Virgouleuse pears, "melon" apricot grafts, seeds of "French
peaches," and the Marseilles and Angelica figs. By March he
was off again, departing for New York to become secretary
of state. The following spring, returning to Philadelphia, the

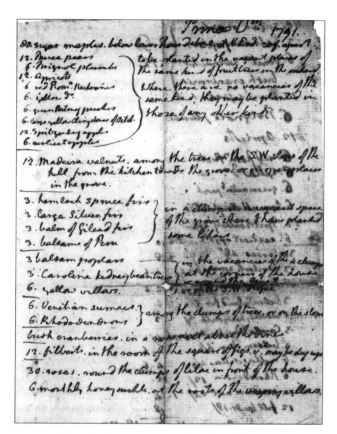

Fig. 31. Jefferson's planting memorandum for William
Prince order in 1791

government's new seat, from a botanical excursion with
James Madison through New England and upstate New York,
Jefferson stopped at the William Prince nursery on Long Island and placed a large order that included sixty fruit trees of
nine varieties. These young trees were "to be planted in the
vacant places of the same kind of fruit trees in the orchard."
Where there are no vacancies of the same kind, they may be
planted in those of any other kind" (fig. 31). Such directions
suggest that Jefferson hoped to maintain his 1778 planting pattern, but in reality vacancies were planted with whatever
species was convenient. The Prince order marked the introduction of the Esopus Spitzenburg apple, a variety which Jefferson first encountered on his northern journey and which
he planted as many as seven different times in later years.

Other fruit trees obtained from Prince included the Beurré Gris pear, Red Roman and Yellow Roman nectarines, Brignole plum, Early Harvest apple, Green Nutmeg peach, and the "large yellow clingstone peach of October." Thomas Mann Randolph, who often managed Monticello's garden and farm affairs while Jefferson was away, wrote to his father-in-law: "I am happy to inform you that a great part of your young trees from Longisland is alive notwithstanding the hardships they underwent during the Winter. The apple, peach, Nectarine & plumb trees . . . are evidently reviving."[10]

From 1793, when Jefferson returned from service in Philadelphia as secretary of state, until his departure for the office of vice-president in 1797, his focus at Monticello was the institution of a systematic and scientific agricultural scheme for his farms. The few references to fruit centered on their agricultural function: the improvement to the farm, or north orchard, the planting of ornamental peach hedges between his fields, and the possibilities of using peach trees as a firewood source. Appropriately, the era's largest fruit-tree planting scheme was recorded in the Farm Book:

Peach trees planted Dec. 1794.	trees
Monticello. in the North orchard	
between the apple trees	263
dividing lines between the fields	537
do. between the Quarry field & Long field	70
Lego. dividing lines between the fields	287

It seems doubtful Jefferson's nurseries were large enough to supply 1,157 peach trees; perhaps the trees were dug from wild, naturalized colonies on the property. Two years later, in 1796, Francis Eppes, a supplier of many of the north orchard apple trees, observed that this orchard contained only three cider varieties—Hewes Crab, Golden Wilding, and Clarke's Pearmain—but did not mention its 263 peaches. Scotsman Robert Bailey had been hired in 1794 to serve as gardener, and it seems likely the south orchard responded so well to his horticultural attentions that Jefferson's immediate supervision and detailed record keeping became unnecessary. A road between rows *h* and *i* through the heart of the orchard was named "Bailey's alley" in 1805, perhaps as a tribute to his pomological success.[11]

Plantings continued at Monticello while Jefferson served as president between 1801 and 1809. Upon the request of Meriwether Lewis, in 1804 John Armstrong of Cincinnati sent Jefferson scion wood of six fruit varieties that had originated in Detroit, an early center of fruit growing. They were planted in the orchard the following March along with other trees assembled from a variety of sources: neighbors George Divers of Farmington and William D. Meriwether, who lived only a mile away; the private orchard of Robert Bailey; the Thomas Main nursery of Washington; General James Jackson of Georgia; and also Philip Mazzei, who in 1802 and 1804 had shipped both peach stones and young trees from Italy. This 1805 planting was recorded in the Garden Book (though it has never been included in a published version).[12]

While Jefferson was president much of the activity in the orchard revolved around the shipments of stones and trees from Philip Mazzei. Jefferson's interest in fruit was beginning to focus on peaches, and in 1801 he wrote to Mazzei for "plants of good fruit, and especially of peaches and *eating grapes.*" Mazzei responded with a series of shipments of cuttings and seeds of grapes, plums, peaches, and apricots, many of which were unknown in the United States, such as the Peach apricot and the Breast of Venus, Alberges, and Vaga Loggia peach varieties. As with all his shipments, Mazzei sent detailed instructions on the proper propagation techniques—whether the stones should be cracked before planting, the time expected before they would germinate—and also brief varietal descriptions. In 1801 Mazzei wrote, "The stones are tested and all good and so I advise planting them in place so as not to submit them to transplantation, and consequently to the loss of a year." Despite Mazzei's advice, Jefferson planted the stones in his nursery where at least ten of the peach seeds apparently germinated, yet these young trees languished for eight years until transplanted into the orchard in 1810. Jefferson seemed intent on doing the opposite of what Mazzei suggested. Mazzei also noted that he had never seen the Vaga Loggia or Apple peach ("Pesca mela," mistranslated by Jefferson as the Melon peach) grown outside of Italy, and they may have been among the fruit varieties Jefferson helped introduce into the United States.[13]

Jefferson's Italian fruit connection continued in 1804, when

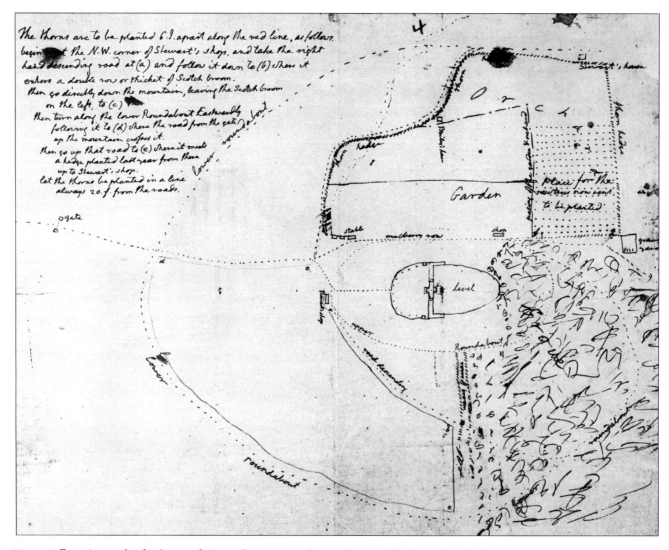

Fig. 32. Jefferson's 1806 plan for the top of Monticello mountain, showing locations for the south orchard, vegetable garden, and hawthorn hedge

Mazzei forwarded a larger shipment of grafted and seedling trees, including five Angelica apricots, which Mazzei had himself "baptised" or discovered; two grafted trees of the often-praised Peach apricot; two grafted Alberges peaches; and three seedling Breast of Venus peaches. Mazzei also shipped "a case of stones" that included three apricot, five plum, and seven peach varieties. Jefferson set out six of the plants in the orchard the following year, although the Peach apricot, "the finest fruit which grows in Europe," was reportedly stolen in transit from Washington to Monticello. Jefferson also gave Alexander Hepburn, a Washington nurseryman, the case of stones to propagate. Hepburn produced 150 trees, and they were forwarded to Monticello along with 4,000 hawthorn seedlings in the spring of 1806. The hawthorns were planted as a living fence for an expanded southwestern section of the orchard and as an enclosure for the north orchard (fig. 32).[14]

Jefferson provided his overseer John Freeman with explicit planting instructions and encouraged him to plant "with all your force the moment" the trees arrived: "Jerry with the light car & 2. mules had better set off [for Washington] as speedily as you can get him ready. . . . The purpose of his coming is to carry home a number of trees to be planted. For these the ground lying Westward from the garden pales to the young hedge must be entirely cleaned up. Where peach or other fruit trees already exist there in the regular rows, they may be left; but all out of the rows must be taken up. The trees he will carry will fill the whole space between the pales & hedge from East to West, & up & down the hill from North to South from hedge to hedge." The "light car" contained 122 peach trees (1 Apple, 5 Alberges, 37 Vaga Loggia, 12 freestone Vaga Loggia, 29 Breast of Venus, 18 St. James, and 20 Magdalen), 9 apricots (8 Peach apricot and 1 Angelic), and 19 plum trees (14 Mirabelle, 4 Regina). There is no record of their planting or fate in later documents, particularly the 1811 orchard plan; however, the shipment apparently had arrived at Monticello because of Jefferson's discouraging message to Freeman, concerning the condition of the "very foul" hawthorns later that season. Freeman was dismissed in 1806. The hedges later were replanted by his successor, Edmund Bacon, but the Italian peach varieties were irreplaceable. The Peach apricot had been forwarded again by Mazzei and fortuitously landed in the possession of Jefferson's friends John Threlkeld and William Meriwether. By 1809 Threlkeld's trees had produced sufficiently to repay Jefferson.[15]

Other disasters befell the orchards during Jefferson's absence, partly due to having to communicate long distances and to transport live plants in open wagons along bog-riddled roads. Timothy Matlack, a progressive Pennsylvania farmer and fruit grower, sent ten notable fruit-tree varieties, including the Moor Park apricot, Seckel pear, and five highly esteemed American peaches, to Monticello in February 1807. They were planted in orchard vacancies on April 21 but evidently had dried out during the arduous journey: "The bundle of trees you so kindly sent me, were longer coming than they should have been, but going hence to Monticello in a cart, they were out in the remarkable severe weather we had in the middle & latter part of March, and by the impassable-

ness of the roads & breaking down of the cart were so long out that not a single one survived." Undaunted, Jefferson asked Matlack for more trees of "excellent pears, peaches, or grapes" that might be forwarded to Monticello after his retirement. When Jefferson wrote Charles Willson Peale in 1811 that the joy of gardening was demonstrated by "the failure of one thing repaired by the success of another," he was expressing two of the great virtues of horticulture, persistence and patience. Obviously, he needed such traits during the orchard trials of 1806 and 1807.[16]

Jefferson's major horticultural concerns upon his retirement to Monticello in 1809 were the completion of the terracing of the vegetable garden and the establishment of flower beds and borders around the house. By 1810, activity in the orchard began again as he recorded in the Garden Book a planting of eighty-one trees and reorganized his nursery into ten terraces, where intensive grafting and seed planting was also taking place (fig. 33). Jefferson planted mostly peaches in 1810, a trend that would distinguish the plantings after 1800 from earlier ones. He expressed his choice for a favorite fruit tree in 1807 when he wrote John Threlkeld that "I am endeavoring to make a collection of the choicest kinds of peaches for Monticello." Jefferson also added three longitudinal rows, numbered minus one to minus three, to the southwestern section where the Hepburn-propagated Italian varieties evidently failed. Although the nursery was newly organized so that species were relegated to specific terraces, the orchard was mixed; apples were planted next to pears and peaches alongside cherries. Jefferson introduced peaches into eleven different rows, planting them in the area once reserved for the cherry collection. Many of the trees originated from earlier introductions into the Monticello nursery, including the Italian varieties and an 1807 planting of 500 peach stones. Jefferson finally retrieved the much-vaunted Peach apricot, which had been saved, propagated, and returned to him by Threlkeld. The trees produced fruit in 1809.[17]

In March 1811 Jefferson made a systematic chart of the location of the orchard's 384 trees and a map of the area (figs. 34, 35). There were 160 peaches, 84 apples, 48 cherries, 7 apricots, 5 nectarines, 5 quinces, 2 pears, 2 plums, and 71 vacancies, which were intended to be filled the following autumn, mostly

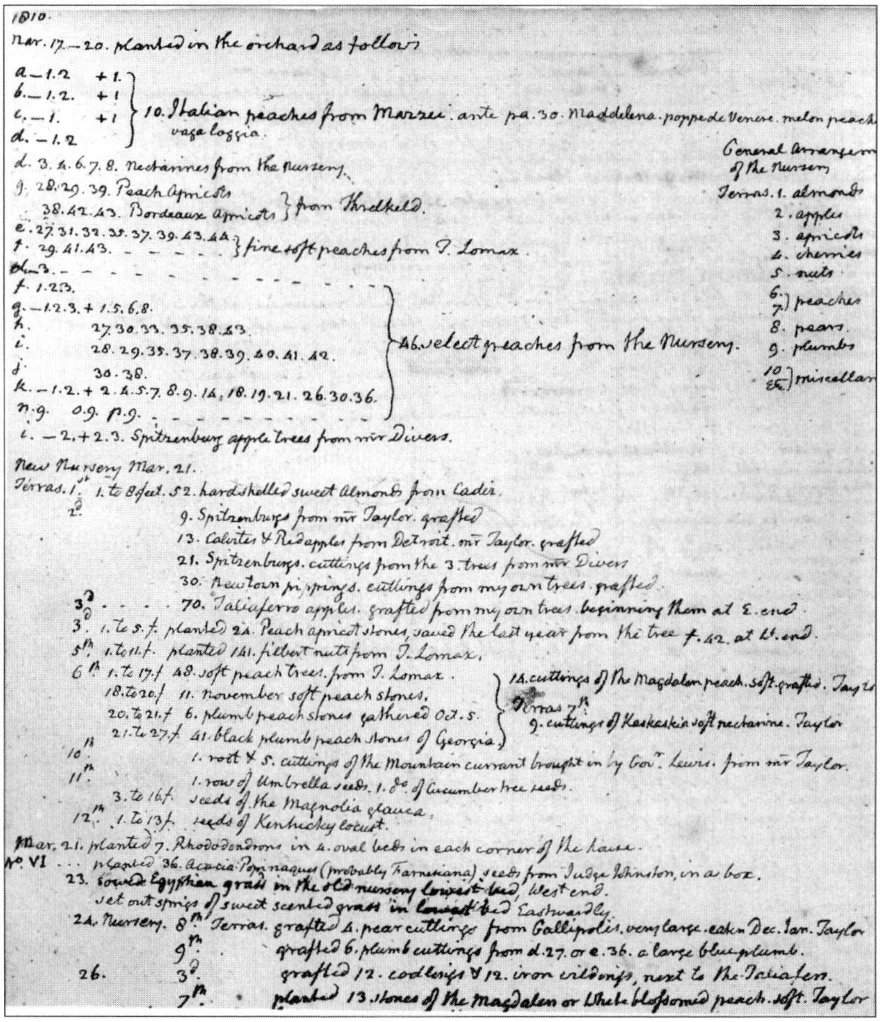

1810.
Mar. 17–20. planted in the orchard as follows
a–1.2 +1. }
b.–1.2. +1 } 10. Italian peaches from Mazzei. ante pa. 30. Maddelena. poppe de Venere. melon peach
c.–1. +1 } vaga loggia.
d.–1.2 }
d. 3.4.6.7.8. nectarines from the nursery.
g. 28.29.39. Peach apricots } from Threlkeld.
38.42.43. Bordeaux apricots }
e. 27.31.32.35.37.39.43.44 } fine soft peaches from T. Lomax.
f. 29.41.43. }
f. 1.23.
g.–1.2.3.+1.5.6.8.
h. 27.30.33.35.38.43.
i. 28.29.35.37.38.39.40.41.42. } 46. select peaches from the Nursery.
j. 30.38.
k.–1.2.+2.4.5.7.8.9.14, 18.19.21.26.30.36.
n.9. o.9. p.9.
l.–2.+2.3. Spitzenburg apple trees from mr Divers.

General Arrangement of the Nursery
Terras. 1. almonds
2. apples
3. apricots
4. cherries
5. nuts
6. 7.} peaches
8. pears.
9. plumbs
10. Etc.} miscellan.

New Nursery Mar. 21.
Terras. 1st. 1. to 8 feet. 52. hard shelled sweet almonds from Cadiz.
2d. 9. Spitzenburgs from mr Taylor. grafted
13. Calvites & Redapples from Detroit. mr Taylor. grafted
21. Spitzenburgs. cuttings from the 3. trees from mr Divers
30. Newtown pippings. cuttings from my own trees. grafted.
3d. 70. Taliaferro apples. grafted from my own trees. beginning them at E. end.
3. 1. to 5. f. planted 24. Peach apricot stones, saved the last year from the tree f. 42. at W. end.
5th. 1. to 11. f. planted 141. filbert nuts from T. Lomax.
6th. 1. to 17. f. 48. soft peach trees. from T. Lomax.
18. to 20. f. 11. november soft peach stones.
20. to 21. f. 6. plumb peach stones gathered Oct. 5.
21. to 27. f. 41. black plumb peach stones of Georgia.
14. cuttings of the Magdalen peach. soft. grafted. Taylor
Terras 7th. 9. cuttings of Kaskaskia soft nectarine. Taylor
10th. 1. root & 5. cuttings of the Mountain currant brought in by Gov. Lewis. from mr Taylor.
11th. 1. row of Umbrella seeds. 1. do. of Cucumber tree seeds.
3. to 16. f. seeds of the Magnolia glauca.
12th. 1. to 13. f. seeds of Kentucky locust.
Mar. 21. planted 7. Rhododendrons in 4. oval beds in each corner of the house.
No. VI ... planted 36. Acacia Popinaques (probably Farnesiana) seeds from Judge Johnston, in a box.
23. sowed Egyptian grass in the old nursery lowest bed, West end.
set out sprigs of sweet scented grass in lowest bed Eastwardly.
24. Nursery. 8th. Terras. grafted 4. pear cuttings from Gallipolis. very large. eaten Dec. Jan. Taylor
9th. grafted 6. plumb cuttings from d.27. or e.36. a large blue plumb.
26. 3d. grafted 12. codlings & 12. iron rildings, next to the Taliafers.
7th. planted 13. stones of the Magdalen or White blossomed peach. soft. Taylor

Fig. 33. Garden Book from 1810, listing the "General Arrangement of the Nursery" and planting plans for south orchard and "New Nursery"

with his favorite apple varieties. The 1811 profile of the mature orchard does not suggest the myriad collection of fruit trees that Jefferson had assembled over thirty years of planting and replanting but rather reveals the success of peaches, apples, and cherries, mostly because they are easier to grow. The chart also suggests Jefferson's inability to successfully cultivate pears or plums, of which he planted twenty-three varieties during his fruit-growing career at Monticello. Nearly all the varieties of plum and pear grown in American orchards around 1800 were of European origin, and they were especially susceptible to pests, from fire blight to plum knot, encouraged by the heat and humidity of Virginia summers. On the other hand, American peach and apple varieties that were particularly adapted to regional growing conditions emerged in the eighteenth century. Jefferson cleverly pinpointed each site's species with a compass-inspired code. The eight types of trees were identified or coded by the different alignments of a dot to either a vertical or horizontal line. For example, apples were "• |," while peaches were "| •."[18]

On March 17 and 18 of the following year, 107 fruit trees

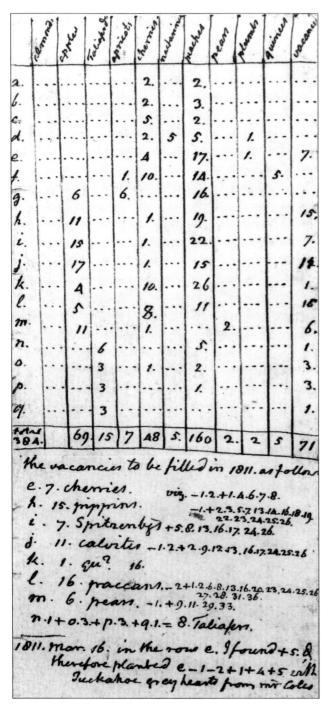

Fig. 34. Jefferson chart reflecting the state of the south orchard in 1811

were planted, including numerous late-season, undescribed peaches; the Esopus Spitzenburg, Taliaferro, and Newtown Pippin apples; and Carnation cherries (fig. 36). Jefferson was now planting his favorite fruits, particularly the types that he could successfully cultivate, rather than experimenting with new and unusual ones. In 1813 he filled his nursery with 273 peach stones, and in 1814, now referring to the south orchard as part of the "fruitery," he transplanted 66 successfully grown young apples and peaches from his nursery to the orchard on March 19. This is the last mention of an orchard planting in Jefferson's records. After forty-seven years in which he documented the introduction of 1,031 trees into his south orchard, 814 peach trees along Monticello field boundaries, 526 apples and peaches in the north orchard, and over 2,000 seeds sown in the nursery, he wrote in 1816 to a friend and neighbor, James Barbour, that "my collection of fruits went to entire decay in my absence and has not been renewed."[19]

Perhaps this statement was only the nervous apology expressed by a performer about to assume the stage, or in this case, fulfill Barbour's request for trees and plants from the Monticello gardens and orchards. Jefferson's 1811 profile of the orchard documented 384 existing trees, hardly "entire decay," and he planted over 300 additional trees from 1810 to 1814. He also sent Barbour cuttings of the Carnation cherry, "so superior to all others that no other deserves the name of cherry," and Taliaferro apple, "the best cyder apple existing," reflecting at least a continued enthusiasm for his experimental trials and the "precious refreshment" of the finest fancy fruit known at the time.[20]

Yet Jefferson's silence concerning his orchard activities after 1814 suggests a pomological malaise resulting from tree failures, physical inactivity, and the more pressing need to develop financial stability on the Monticello farms. He had recorded the fate of earlier plantings in 1778, 1783, and 1794, or at least their immediate demise or survival, but upon his return from the presidency, he ceased to make such notations. With the exception of yearly vegetable garden activity, there was quiet in regard to other gardening activities as well. Although many Monticello visitors reported on the majestic native forest and the ornamental plantings around the house, few mentioned the orchards in their descriptions of the Mon-

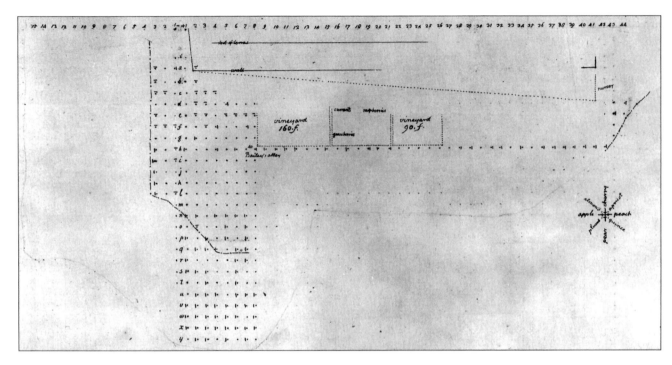

Fig. 35. The 1811 orchard plan. Note the compass-inspired code for identifying the species of each fruit tree: •| = apple, |• = peach.

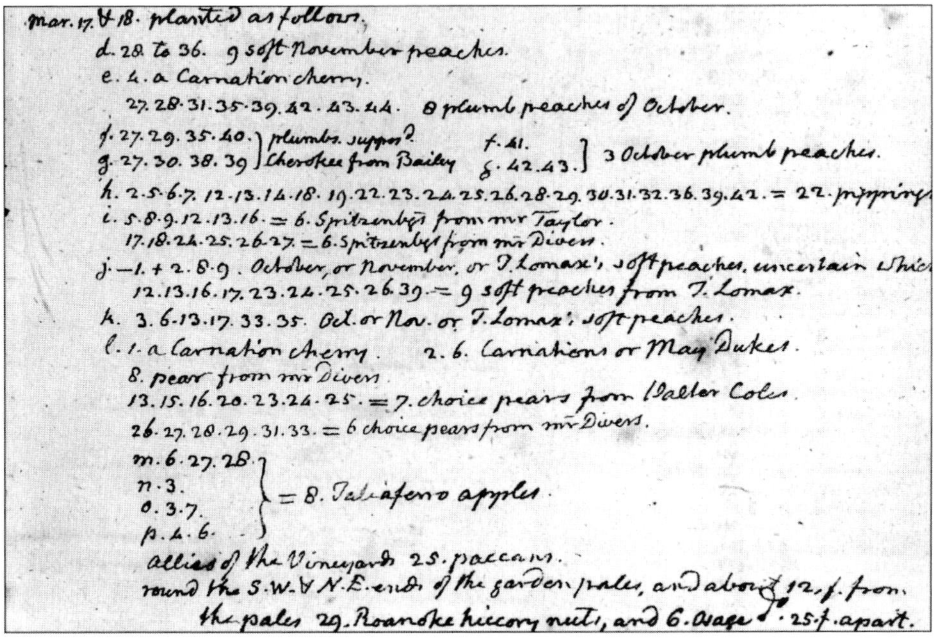

Fig. 36. Planting record from 1812 Garden Book

ticello landscape. Luigi Castiglioni, an Italian botanist who visited in 1786, alluded to Jefferson's "abundant orchard of the best European varieties," and Lieutenant Francis Hall, an English traveler whose reports on American horticulture in 1817 were later published in J. C. Loudon's *Encyclopædia of Gardening*, said the eastern (actually, southeastern) and western (northern) sides of Monticello were "covered" with orchards. Numerous reports documented the widespread vandalism of Monticello's landscape upon Jefferson's death. In 1827, only a year after Jefferson died, Frank Stockton observed that all the orchards, in fact most of the cultivated landscape features, had "all disappeared." Advertisements were placed in the Charlottesville *Central Gazette* begging souvenir hunters to desist from "digging up plants and flower roots" from Monticello. Jefferson's granddaughter Virginia Trist recalled how "Mama's choicest flower roots were carried off, one of her yellow jesmins, fig bushes . . . grape vines and everything and anything that they fancied." Much blame has been accorded James Barclay, a Staunton druggist who purchased the property in 1831 and has been vilified for cutting down Jefferson trees to plant mulberries for silk production and for reputedly plowing up the west lawn and planting corn up to the portico. With the possible exception of a fig bush growing below the vegetable garden wall, nothing of Jefferson's fruit garden survived until Monticello's restoration efforts began in the early 1980s.[21]

Part
II

Apples

"OUR DEMOCRATIC FRUIT"

The apple was a standard, everyday fruit at Monticello. Cider was an integral part of the Jefferson dining tradition. He drank it with the main course of his meals and, from some reports, relished apple and mince pies, "as he eschewed ice cream or any form of rich or elaborate dessert." Jefferson's cultivation of the apple was exceptionally discriminating as he concentrated on only four varieties that were either unrivaled for cidermaking—Hewes Crab and Taliaferro—or as a dessert fruit for the table—Newtown, or Albemarle, Pippin and Esopus Spitzenburg. His cultivation of only eighteen apple cultivars was surprisingly limited. Native apples were the finest expression of eighteenth- and early nineteenth-century Virginia pomology, yet Jefferson, the experimental plant collector and pioneering proponent of the indigenous products of his native land, expressed little interest in assembling a varietal collection. Nevertheless, with the exception of the peach, apples were the most commonly cultivated fruit tree in the south orchard, beginning in 1769 with the planting of two entire rows of grafted Newtown Pippins. In his orchard plan of 1778 Jefferson noted that he had 164 apples compared to only 41 peaches; however, by 1811 there were twice as many peaches as apples. Such a reversal of species dominance was probably due to the unfavorable microclimate of the south orchard, which is simply too hot for apples, and the development of the cooler north orchard as a repository for cider varieties.[1]

Although it seems likely Jefferson preferred the peach as a dessert fruit, apples were more common on eighteenth-century Virginia farms. When plantations were advertised for sale or lease in Williamsburg's *Virginia Gazette* between 1736 and 1780, nearly every advertisement that named the types of fruit trees included apples among them. There were 369 plantations with apple orchards of some size compared to 244 that possessed peaches. Of the 123 estate advertisements listed in the *Maryland Gazette* between 1728 and 1774, 61 specifically mention apple orchards on the property, and 5 describe estates containing two apple orchards. "Every American farm has some sort of an apple orchard," said the "American Farmer" in 1803. In the eighteenth and early years of the nineteenth century, "horticulture" meant fruit growing, which in turn usually meant apple growing. A relatively casual breeding process, initiated not by grand gentlemen gardeners like Jefferson and Washington but by middle-class farmers, resulted in the first improvements of American and Virginian garden plants, the first horticultural cultivars of eastern North America. Eighteenth-century Virginia nurseries offered a broad range of native cider and dessert apples, and when the word *orchard* was used without qualification, it generally was in reference to an apple orchard. L. H. Bailey noted around 1900 that "there was practically only one general horticultural commodity a hundred years ago, and that was the apple." The American apple was the star of the pomological show, eliciting praise from such distinguished British authorities as William J. Hooker, who wrote from Glasgow in 1825, "Our most highly flavoured dessert apples are imported from America."[2]

The apple is an apt symbol for the diversity and complexity of America's melting-pot culture. No cultivated fruit has so many delightful variations as the apple; there are almost as many apples as there are people, each with its own unique history and personality. A 1905 publication of the U.S. Department of Agriculture, *Nomenclature of the Apple*, lists the names of ap-

PACKING HIS ALBEMARLE PIPPINS.
ORCHARD OF J. T. O'NEILL, CROZET, ALBEMARLE CO., VA.

Fig. 37. Harvest time at an Albemarle, or Newtown, Pippin orchard in Albemarle County, Virginia,
from Virginia State Horticultural Society, *Report,* 1910

proximately seventeen thousand apple varieties that appeared in nineteenth-century American publications. During that era there was an apple for every community, for every function, whether for cider, storage, baking, drying, or eating out of hand; there was an apple for every taste, crunchy, soft, sweet, and tart, and an apple for every season, especially in the winter when few fruits or vegetables were available. The apple is to America as the potato is to Ireland or the olive to Italy. The cultural diversity and natural wealth of the New World were reflected in its apples, which, with the peach, became a distinctly American fruit that evolved relatively untinged by the European past. "The apple," as James Fitz proudly proclaimed in 1872, "is our democratic fruit."[3]

Apples were popular in Virginia because of the fruit's culinary usefulness, its storage capability, and its English heritage. The apple grows well in Virginia, and an important industry evolved in the more mountainous western sections of the state by the turn of the twentieth century. Geared mostly for the export trade, Virginia's ten million apple trees that produced over six million bushels of apples ranked it among the top five states in the country by 1910, and Jefferson's native Albemarle County was the most productive apple-growing county in the state (fig. 37). But, at least in the eighteenth century, the importance of the apple was due to the universality of cider production: "From the founding of Jamestown to the time of George Washington . . . every plantation owner made cider, drank cider, and bragged about his cider." The marquis de Chastellux, who visited Monticello in 1782 and recorded many vivid images of its landscape and proprietor, also commented that cider was a staple beverage of most piedmont Virginia farmers: "As for drink, they are obliged to content themselves with milk and water, until their apple trees are large enough to bear fruit." John Taylor of Caroline, whose *Arator* was in the Monticello library, succinctly defined the apple's diversity in 1813: "The apple will furnish some food for the planters' hogs, a luxury for his family in winter and a healthy liquor for himself and his labourers all the year. . . . Good cyder would be a national saving of wealth." Peter Kalm was "frequently surprised at the prudence of the inhabitants" of Pennsylvania, whose "first concern," like Thomas Jefferson's, was the planting of an apple orchard, even before the construction of a dwelling. Sweet cider has been described as the "Coca Cola (as hard cider was the beer) of colonial America"; the two ciders evolved into the country's "national beverage" by the 1820s.[4]

Apple seeds, scions, and even young trees were brought to Virginia by the earliest settlers, and most were described in the traditional nomenclature of the Old World, such as "pearmains," with fruit shaped like a pear; "pippins," from trees originally raised from a pip or seed; or "russetings," apples with a tough, reddish-brown, spotted skin (figs. 38, 39). There is mention of apple trees at George Menefie's estate, Littleton, in 1623, and by 1629 John Smith noted that apples were bearing in Jamestown. By 1642 Governor Berkeley's Green Spring estate, from which Jefferson purchased trees in 1778, had an orchard of 1,500 apple trees. Thomas Glover in 1676 noted "fair and large orchards some whereof 1200 trees and upward, bearing all sorts of English apples . . . of which they make great store of cider." Apple orchards were commonly mentioned in Virginia land leases and wills, and cider had become an important economic commodity, regularly used as barter in the seventeenth century. In 1686 William Fitzhugh's Westmoreland County orchard included 2,500 grafted trees, consisting of "mains" (pearmains), "pippins," "russentens," "costards" (large, heavily ribbed, greenish-skinned cooking apples), "marigolds" (apples with skin striped like a marigold flower), "kings" (a large red apple), "magitens," and "bachelors." Fitzhugh declared that the cider produced from his apple trees possessed an economic value equal to 15,000 pounds of tobacco. The earliest apple varieties grown in Vir-

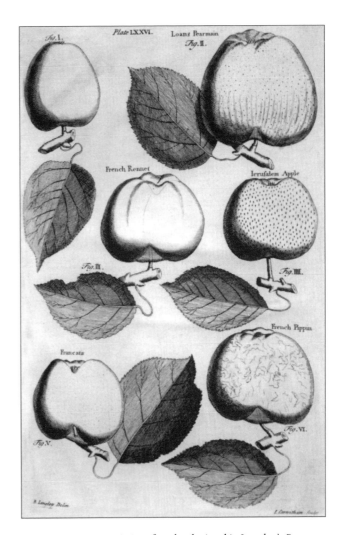

Fig. 38. European varieties of apples depicted in Langley's *Pomona*

ginia were English in origin. John Lawson, in describing the fruits of North Carolina in 1714, mentioned twelve English varieties: Golden Russet, Winter and Summer Pearmain, Harvey (a tough cooking and cider apple), Leathercoat, Juniting (Geneting, Juneating, or June-eating: an early season variety), and Codling. William Byrd's annotated list of 1737, from his *Natural History,* also included thirteen European varieties, nearly half of which were used for cider. He also mentioned varieties noted by Lawson such as the Golden Russet, Red Streak, Golden Pippin, and the Winter as well as Summer Pearmain. By 1701 Francis Michel remarked that in Virginia "the apple trees are exceedingly fruitful. I was at many places

Fig. 39. Old World apples, including the Calville grown
by Jefferson, from Langley's *Pomona*

where I could not estimate the large quantities which were
rotting on the ground. They are the nicest apples I have ever
seen."[5]

As apple growing evolved in Virginia in the eighteenth
century — as the grafted English varieties suffered from the
colony's heat and humidity, and as planters chose the easiest
method of propagation, by seed — new apples that both
thrived in the extreme summer climate and were best suited
for the production of cider were selected. The evolution was
slow because many planters thought a seedling apple pro-

duced a decent enough copy of the parent. Robert Beverley
wrote in 1705 that "apples from the Seed, never degenerate
into Crabs or Wildings, but produce the same, or better Fruit
than the Mother tree, (which is not so in England) and are
wonderfully improved by Grafting and Managing; yet there
are very few Planters that graft at all, and much fewer that
take care to get choice Fruits." Although seedling orchards
were the rule rather than the exception, distinct Virginia cultivars, these accidental miracles, were eventually named and
propagated asexually, from the Virginia White apple to the
Hewes Crab, Taliaferro, Gloucester White, Carthouse, Ralls
Genet, Pryor's Red, Limbertwig, Father Abraham, Lowrey,
Winesap, Milam, Pilot, and Royal Pearmain.[6]

The apples sold by the William Smith nursery of Surry
County in 1755 reflect the transitional stage of Virginia apple
growing that was emerging in the mid-eighteenth century
(fig. 40). Of Smith's twenty-two apple varieties, seven were
Virginia cider cultivars, including Hewes, White, Clarke Pear-
main, and Father Abraham. Seven others were of European
origin, such as Golden Pippin, Nonpareil, Golden Russet, and
English Codling. Another Williamsburg nurseryman, Thomas
Sorsby, on November 4, 1763, published a varietal list nearly
identical to Smith's. It is interesting to compare the lists of
Smith and Sorsby with the varieties planted by a northerner,
Cadwallader Colden of Newburgh, New York, in 1735.
Colden, lieutenant governor of New York and an avid
botanist, planted the Pippin and Spitzenburg, but the rest of
his orchard was composed of old English varieties such as the
Golden Pippin, Golden Russet, Nonpareil, and Red Streak.
The golden age of the American dessert apple had not yet arrived in Virginia by the mid-1700s; aside from the Newtown
Pippin, none of the famous New England and mid-Atlantic
table varieties—Roxbury Russet, Rhode Island Greening, Yellow Bellflower, or Esopus Spitzenburg—were included. By the
end of the century, however, indigenous varieties dominated
the lists of Virginia nurserymen. For example, the Spotsylvania County nursery of Stratchan and Maury offered twenty-
two apples in 1798, and only the Vandevere, Newtown Pippin,
and the European Hereford Red Streak are recognizable as
non-Virginia natives. Samuel Bailey's New Kent County nursery sold twenty-four American varieties in 1804, but only

Pl. 1. Newtown, or Albe-
marle, Pippin from William
Coxe's unpublished second
edition of "A View"

Pl. 2. Newtown Pippins from the south orchard

Pl. 4. Esopus Spitzenburg
from Coxe's "View"

Pl. 3. Esopus Spitzenburgs from the south orchard

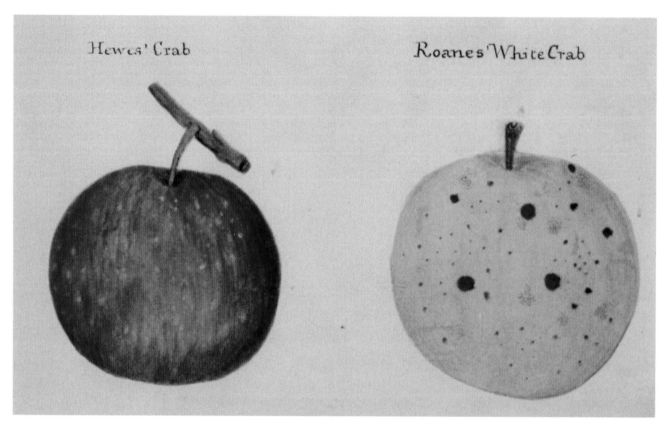

Pl. 5. Hewes Crab and Roan's White Crab from Coxe's "View"

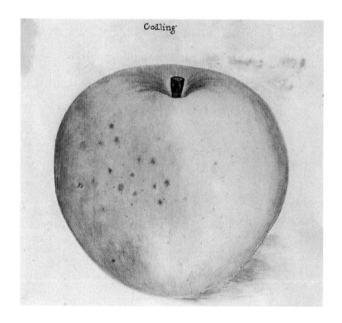

Pl. 6. English Codling from Coxe's "View"

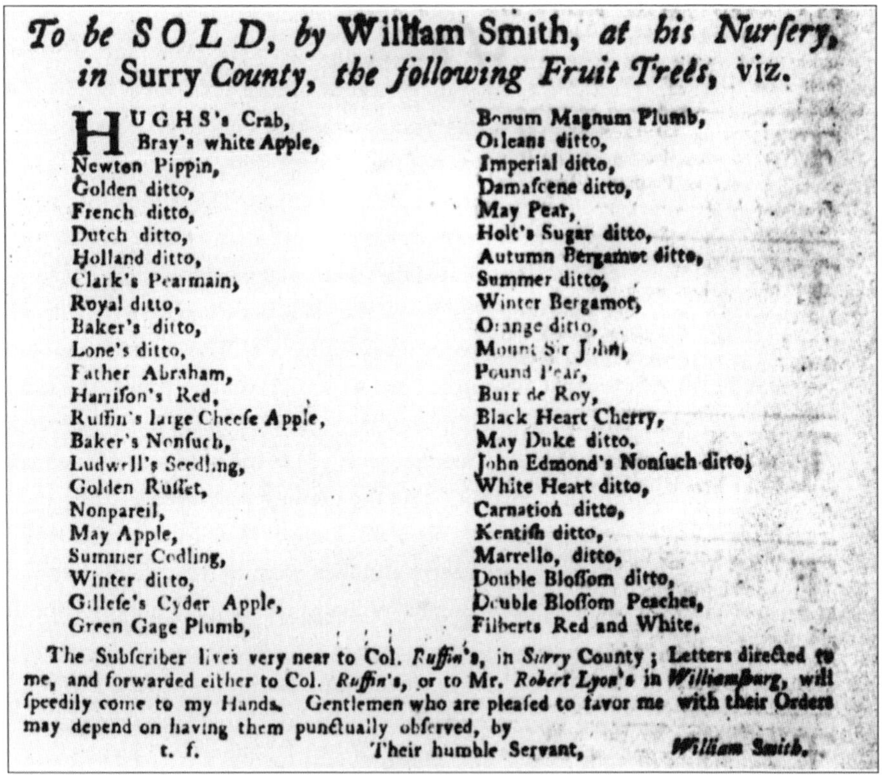

To be SOLD, by William Smith, at his Nursery, in Surry County, the following Fruit Trees, viz.

HUGHS's Crab,
Bray's white Apple,
Newton Pippin,
Golden ditto,
French ditto,
Dutch ditto,
Holland ditto,
Clark's Pearmain,
Royal ditto,
Baker's ditto,
Lone's ditto,
Father Abraham,
Harrison's Red,
Ruffin's large Cheese Apple,
Baker's Nonsuch,
Ludwell's Seedling,
Golden Russet,
Nonpareil,
May Apple,
Summer Codling,
Winter ditto,
Gillese's Cyder Apple,
Green Gage Plumb,

Bonum Magnum Plumb,
Orleans ditto,
Imperial ditto,
Damascene ditto,
May Pear,
Holt's Sugar ditto,
Autumn Bergamot ditto,
Summer ditto,
Winter Bergamot,
Orange ditto,
Mount Sir John,
Pound Pear,
Burr de Roy,
Black Heart Cherry,
May Duke ditto,
John Edmond's Nonsuch ditto,
White Heart ditto,
Carnation ditto,
Kentish ditto,
Marrello, ditto,
Double Blossom ditto,
Double Blossom Peaches,
Filberts Red and White.

The Subscriber lives very near to Col. Ruffin's, in Surry County; Letters directed to me, and forwarded either to Col. Ruffin's, or to Mr. Robert Lyon's in Williamsburg, will speedily come to my Hands. Gentlemen who are pleased to favor me with their Orders may depend on having them punctually observed, by

t. f.   Their humble Servant,   William Smith.

Fig. 40. Advertisement for William Smith nursery of Surry County, Virginia, from Williamsburg's *Virginia Gazette,* September 26, 1755

three—Bellflower, Sheepnose, and Early Harvest—originated outside the state. Bailey was the first nurseryman to offer the Winesap, an apple with muddled origins yet so well adapted to the state's soil and climate that it remains today one of the chief contributions to the apple industry (pl. 8).[7]

The progressive movement in Virginia toward the development and culture of regional cultivars preceded and at the same time was more pronounced than that in the North. L. H. Bailey observed in 1900 that in the United States "there has been a noticeable tendency toward the origination of varieties of apples and the subsequent exclusion of varieties of European origin." However, the domination of American apple varieties on the nursery lists of large northern urban nurseries was not so emphatic as in Virginia. In 1788 a Baltimore nursery operated by Philip Walten advertised thirteen apples in the *Maryland Gazette and Baltimore General Advertiser,* yet the Newtown Pippin was the only American variety offered. About half of the varieties were European on the apple lists of the Prince nursery on Long Island, considered the best and most common source of nursery stock in the country until 1830, the Landreth nursery in Philadelphia in 1811, and the Booth nursery of Baltimore in 1810.[8]

By the middle of the nineteenth century the Virginia apples, nearly all of them cider apples or keeping varieties that were eaten in the late winter and spring, flourished in the burgeoning apple country of the Ohio River valley, where the frontier need for self-sufficiency made apples that could be stored all winter especially valuable. Southern Ohio, Indiana, Missouri, and Kentucky also have a severe summer climate similar to Virginia's. Many of these notable eighteenth-century Virginia varieties—Ralls Genet, Father Abraham (fig. 41), Limbertwig, Pryor's Red, Carthouse, Spice, Milam, Winesap, and Virginia Greenings—were extensively cultivated by the fruit growers and praised and recommended by the pomological writers of the American heartland but received sparse notice from sophisticated eastern authorities like A. J.

No. 98. Father Abraham.

Fig. 41. Father Abraham, popular eighteenth-century Virginia apple, from William Coxe's *View of the Cultivation of Fruit Trees*

Downing (New York), John Jay Thomas (New York), and William Kenrick (Boston) or from urban nurseries along the Atlantic seaboard. When the central Virginia Fruit Tree Association, composed of around twelve gentlemen farmers from three piedmont counties, ordered $1,043 worth of trees in 1815 from the Benjamin Prince nursery, apples were not included because the best cultivars could be purchased locally. The development of regional apple varieties, like those in Virginia, was essentially a rural, populist movement.[9]

CIDER

L. H. Bailey's tongue-in-cheek remark about the role of cider in early American culture rings true: "The gradual change in customs, whereby the eating of the apple (rather than the drinking of it) has come to be paramount, is a significant development." Merely by examining the character of the emerging Virginia apple cultivars, one sees the importance of cider to the colonists. As well, many contemporary reporters fo-

cused on the quality and alcoholic effect of Virginia cider. They include a Frenchman, Durand of Dauphiné, who described a rather dizzy visit to Gloucester County in 1686: "It was cidermaking time. Everywhere we were required to drink so freely that even if there were twenty, all would drink to a stranger & he must pledge them all. They drank also some bottles of a rhum much stronger than brandy. When they were not intoxicated they usually let me drink in my own way, & generally I just kissed the glass: but when they were drunk they would have me drink at their will. This so much annoyed me that as soon as I had a room, I went no more. The cider made me ill; I think it was too new." William Byrd's report of cider-induced merriment suggests the potency of Virginia's "liquid dynamite": "In the evening we played at cards and I won 5 [pounds]. We drank some of Will Robinson's cider till we were very merry and then went to the coffeehouse and pulled poor Colonel [William] Churchill [a burgess] out of bed."[10]

Cider was consumed by all classes, from planter to common man; its universality extended to its use as a form of currency. Teachers, ministers, and doctors were paid by bartering cider. Historian Philip Bruce has claimed that cider was found on the table of every planter in the colony: "There was hardly a residence of any pretension which did not keep a supply of this liquor on hand; and some planters had as much as one hundred and fifty gallons stored away in their cellars." By 1800 Richard Parkinson, whose jaded views of American culture arose from the frustrations of an English gentleman farmer transferred to the rude New World, nevertheless felt "the making of cyder is a better business" than any other form of American agriculture. Benjamin Rush, an acquaintance of Jefferson's, George Washington's friend and personal physician, and signer of the Declaration of Independence, recommended "in the room of spirits, in the first place, Cyder. This excellent liquor is perfectly inoffensive and wholesome." In the 1820s patriotic cider proponents writing in the *American Farmer* attempted to lead crusades for cider as the "national beverage," pointing out the apple tree's ease of culture and the beverage's superiority to "ardent spirits."[11]

In 1819 Jefferson wrote, "Malt liquors & cyder are my table drinks"; and Francis Calley Gray, a visitor to Monticello in 1815,

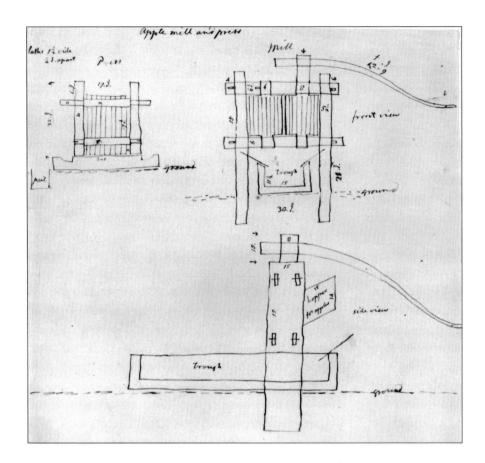

Fig. 42. Jefferson's drawing of
an apple mill and press

described a dinner that included "table liquors [of] beer and cider and after dinner wine." Cider was certainly important at Monticello; the north orchard was devoted to the cultivation of about 265 cider apples, and Jefferson sang high praises of the cider-making qualities of the Taliaferro and Hewes Crab. He sketched plans for a cider mill and a cider press (fig. 42), and overseer Edmund Bacon recalled how the March bottling of cider was part of the yearly work routine. In 1799, 120 gallons were produced from seventy bushels of the Taliaferro and the Hewes Crab. Although these seem like adequate quantities for home consumption, Jefferson's production was meager in comparison to a comparably sized cider orchard of Hewes Crabs owned by Henry Wynkoop of Bucks County, Pennsylvania. Wynkoop reported that 200 trees on five acres, about the size of the north orchard at Monticello, produced annually forty hogsheads, or 4,480 gallons of cider.[12]

Jefferson occasionally noted difficulties both in harvesting the fruit at its proper maturity and in bottling the liquor from casks or hogsheads. In 1793 Martha Randolph reported fireworks in the Monticello cellar: "Of 140 bottles that were put away you will hardly find 12. It flew in such a manner as to render it dangerous going near them. Those [bottles] that were carelessly corked forced their corks, the rest burst the bottles amongst which the havoc is incredible." Jefferson later wrote from Washington to his son-in-law Thomas Mann Randolph lamenting the death of Jupiter, a trusted slave responsible for cider making: "I must get Martha or yourself to give orders for bottling the cyder in the proper season in March. There is nobody there but Ursula who unites trust & skill to do it. She may take anybody she pleases to aid her." Two years later Jefferson wrote from Washington about his French staff at the President's House and again suggested that there were specific technical skills required of a cider bottler: "My people (who are foreigners) know nothing of it [cider making and bottling], nor is there any body in this place who does. Hence a great inequality in the bottles, from some being better or worse corked, and an inequality in the casks from their not understanding the true state of the liquor for bottling."[13]

A delicate distinction exists between cider apples that are mature yet well mellowed and those that are rotten. John Spurrier of Delaware, author of the *Practical Farmer,* which he dedicated to Jefferson, said, "It should be the first care of every one concerned in making cider, to let his apples ripen on the trees, till they arrive at their full maturity." Jefferson's plea to Edmund Bacon in 1817 was perhaps the result of years of careless harvesting: "We have saved red Hughes enough from the North Orchard to make a smart cask of cyder. They are now mellow & beginning to rot. I will pray you therefore to have them made into cyder immediately. Let them be made clean one by one, and all the rotten ones thrown away & the rot cut out. nothing else can ensure good cider." In 1796, when copying down the advice of Francis Eppes in regard to the north orchard, Jefferson noted that "the Golden Wilding must not be mellowed before pressed; it will yield nothing. It must be pressed as soon as gathered. mixed with the red Hughes they make the best cyder & yield best." These admonitions were an effort to avoid the problems expressed by a Pennsylvanian, Lewis Evans, in 1753: "Every Body has an Orchard and makes commonly Cyder enough, but so much worm eaten and rotten Apples are used that it is often nauseous."[14]

THE CULTURE OF THE APPLE

Despite the admonitions of garden writers about proper soils, fertilizer, and pruning, apple growing for most Virginians was a rather casual pastime. In 1811 John Tayloe, whose Virginia farm was described as "among the best in the state," wrote that "orchards succeed tolerably well here, though I think the peach preferable to the apple for produce. I have no defence for either, except to have the trees looked over, and pruned once a year." In 1825 a self-styled "Rusticus" found "almost every orchard in the United States with the body of the trees drilled with holes; its branches covered with moss; many of the trees bent or crooked; much old naked, barren, and even dead wood upon them, and scarcely one that bears every year." Even as late as 1902 a Virginia pomologist asked, "Is there one farmer in ten in Virginia who actually cultivates his apple orchard as though it were a valuable crop? No."[15]

Varietal selection is perhaps the most important element in determining the health and vigor of an apple. The many native Virginia varieties that originated in the eighteenth century were well adapted to the state's soil and especially its warm, humid summers, a condition generally inimical to the production of the fine-flavored, crisp-textured eating apples that became famous in the northern states. James Fitz, in the *Southern Apple and Peach Culturist,* cited the opinion of a respected University of Virginia professor: "Experience teaches us that almost all northern apples of high reputation are comparatively worthless when cultivated as far south as Virginia." Virginia's apple advocate, John Taylor, wrote as early as 1813 that southern apples underwent "premature decay and death" because of "sunstroke," while William White lamented in Athens, Georgia, in 1859 that "a tree full grown, and entirely free from disease, is a rarity." Fortunately, many of the indigenous varieties grown by Jefferson flourished in Monticello's severe summer weather, particularly the Virginia cider apples: Taliaferro, Hewes Crab, White, Golden Wilding, and Clarke Pearmain. The Newtown Pippin, although originating on Long Island, adapted famously to Albemarle County, especially the rich and damp coves of its more mountainous, western terrain. The Roxbury Russet, originally from Massachusetts yet recommended as a home fruit by Virginia authorities; Calville Blanc, from France; and Early Harvest, from New York, also seem suited to the suffocating humidity and red clay soils of central Virginia.[16]

PESTS

Pest control has become the most difficult and expensive factor in today's apple industry, yet many apple diseases and insects were ignored by fruit writers until the 1820s. One early twentieth-century Virginia fruit scientist described the apple's fall from innocence: "In the early days, when the country was new and the soil in its virgin condition, it was full of available

Fig. 43. Fire blight on apple at Monticello. Notice the characteristic crook on the tip of branch.

Fig. 44. Cedar-apple rust can lead to the defoliation of entire trees

less cosmetic fruit spotting; bitter rot (*Glomerella cingulata*), a serious problem on many varieties; and fruit spot (*Cylindrosporium pomi*). Richter also observed apple scab (*Venturia inaequalis*), which results in brown lesions on the leaves and fruit. Apple scab was not named until 1819 in Sweden and not reported in America until 1834. Coxe's daughters surely regarded these spots as part of the fruit when they made the drawings, as none of the diseases except bitter rot were discussed by their father. Cedar-apple rust (*Gymnosporangium juniperi-virginianae*) and the less obvious but more harmful quince rust (*G. clavipes*) are the most insidious diseases today in the restored south orchard at Monticello (fig. 44). Although the former is a New World native, it is dependent upon a symbiotic relationship with an alternate host, the red cedar tree (*Juniperus virginiana*), which apparently was introduced into Albemarle County, even though it is now at home in the fields, woodland edges, and forests of the county. According to Jefferson, his brother-in-law James Bolling planted Albemarle's first cedar tree, to which the present population owes its parentage, at Shadwell, Jefferson's birthplace, in 1755. It seems doubtful that the rust, which incited controversial state laws allowing twentieth-century apple growers to destroy any plantations of red cedars within ten miles of their orchards, was so alarmingly prevalent by 1810.[17]

Insects injurious to apples, unlike those of peaches, received relatively little attention from early garden writers. Visually obvious insects, however, were the exception. They included the tent caterpillar (*Malacosoma* sp.), which Coxe declared the greatest threat to the orchard, and the seventeen-year locust, which Richard Parkinson noted "causes great injury to the fruit" after it girdles the tree's stems and twigs. Coxe suggested merely crushing the tent caterpillars individually as they emerged from their nests in the spring, and Peter Kalm observed Pennsylvanians setting the nests on fire. Many pests became problems only because of horticultural progress or the inevitable advances of urban civilization. The damage inflicted by the European red mite, today's most serious mite in Virginia apple orchards, did not become noticeable until after World War II when organic phosphate insecticides like Carbaryl eliminated its various predators. Populations of deer and pine voles or mice, which John Taylor had noted were

plant food and there were almost no insects, nor fungus and bacterial diseases to affect the apple tree or its fruit. Now it is a hand to hand fight with impoverished soil, insects by the billion, and sporadic diseases that attack all parts of the tree." William Coxe mentioned only one apple disease in the first, 1817, edition of his work—fire blight (*Erwinia amylovora*), which is more common in the pear yet potentially a lethal problem with the apple (fig. 43). When twentieth-century pathologist P. L. Richter analyzed the various fruit spots revealed in the illustrations for the unpublished second edition of Coxe's book, particularly on the apples, he identified leaf blight (*Fabraea maculata*); flyspeck (*Microthyriella rubi*), a harm-

Fig. 45. Carolina parrot, from Mark Catesby, *The Natural History of Carolina, Florida, and the Bahama Islands*, 1731

harmful to apples as early as 1813, expanded dramatically once the virgin forest was removed. Increased amounts of sunlight reaching the woodland floor of second- and third-growth forests stimulated dense undergrowth, native and introduced shrubs and vines like Japanese honeysuckle, which are desirable forage crops. The woolly aphid, according to at least one English expert, was a problem in the United States around 1800; its introduction from America (or France, depending on the writer) to London alarmed numerous early fruit scientists, who recommended soapsuds, sulfur, manual removal, and linseed oil as preventive measures. The American technique, touted as effective, involved excavating and burning one to two feet of soil around the tree's roots; the hole was then filled with charcoal soot and rich mold. As late as 1872 James Fitz believed that "the apple trees of Virginia, and the South generally, are not infested with insects to any serious extent. . . . Our losses are but small when compared with those of the North. There they have vast armies of insect enemies to contend with." Thirty years later another twentieth-century Virginia pomologist used a military image to describe the battlefield of man and insect when he observed "the great

army of insects and fungous diseases increasing in the same ratio as our fruit plantations." Coxe mentioned only one major apple insect in 1817, and Downing listed seven in 1848. L. H. Bailey's catalog of thirty-four insects specific to the apple in 1914 is both a tribute to the evolution of horticultural science and a statement about the spread of native and the invasion of foreign pests from around the world. A notable exception, however, was the Carolina parrot, which devastated North Carolina apple orchards early in the eighteenth century (fig. 45). It is now extinct.[18]

RALLS GENET

The well-known cider and dessert apple Ralls Genet was reputedly introduced and named by Jefferson (fig. 46). The *Report* of the American Pomological Society, 1871, noted that Jefferson obtained scions of the variety from the controversial French minister to the United States, Edmund Charles Genet, in 1791. Jefferson relayed them to an Amherst County nurseryman, Caleb Ralls, who, according to Howley, propagated the cuttings and disseminated the tree throughout Virginia

Fig. 46. Ralls Genet apple, parent of today's Fuji, from S. A. Beach, *The Apples of New York*

and the western territories. S. A. Beach, author of the comprehensive *Apples of New York,* 1900, doubted the veracity of the Jefferson link: "This claim does not seem to have been made in print till about one hundred years after the time of its alleged occurrence and as there are no records to verify it, its truth seems problematical." Nevertheless, the incongruous connection that inspired the variety's name—Ralls, a frontier fruit grower and neighbor to Jefferson's summer retreat, Poplar Forest, and Genet, a cosmopolitan diplomat—could easily have been nurtured by a worldly central Virginian plantsman like Jefferson. Ralls Genet was listed by the Stratchan and Maury nursery in 1799 in Fredericksburg and the Samuel Bailey nursery in New Kent County in 1804, was sold in Charlottesville markets by 1819, and by the middle of the nineteenth century was especially cherished by western fruit growers in Ohio, where it was described as "a prime favorite" by the Cincinnati Horticultural Society. Ralls Genet, which acquired numerous synonyms like Neverfail or Rock Rimmon, is distinguished by its retarded flowering period, which enables the nascent fruit to avoid fruit-killing frost. William Kenrick's praise could not have been more favorable. He said the Ralls possessed a "flesh more fragrant, more juicy and of superior flavor to the Newtown Pippin, and keeps equally well." Ralls has been used extensively in breeding, particularly by the Japanese, who developed the promising Fuji in 1962 from a cross of the Ralls and Red Delicious.[19]

NEWTOWN PIPPIN

In comparing the fruits of Europe to those of America, Jefferson wrote from Paris, "They have no apples here to compare with our Newtown pippin" (pls. 1, 2, 7). The Pippin, with the possible exception of the Taliaferro, was the most commonly planted fruit variety in the south orchard. Two rows were planted in 1769, and over 170 trees added over the next thirty-five years. After 1783 Jefferson either did not note a source for his Pippins or else, as in 1810, said budwood was taken from his own trees. This suggests some horticultural success, and with good reason: the appellation Albemarle was given to the Pippin because of its adaptability to Jefferson's home county.[20]

The Pippin originated at Newtown, New York, on Long Island across the East River from Manhattan in what is now Queens, early in the eighteenth century as a seedling discovered in a swamp on the estate of Gershom Moore. The original tree reputedly died in 1805 after being maimed by decades

No. 72. Yellow Newton Pippin.

No. 73. Green Newton Pippin.

Fig. 47. Many question the difference between the Green and Yellow forms of Newtown Pippin, illustrated here from Coxe's *View*

of graft hunters who repeatedly exhausted it by excessive cutting. Its appearance in the Virginia nurseries of Sorsby and Smith in 1755 and 1763 and the orchards of numerous eighteenth-century Virginians suggests the widespread distribution and reputation the Pippin achieved at an early date. Aside from the Hewes Crab, it was the most commonly noted of

all Virginia apple varieties before 1780. George Washington, St. George Tucker, Lady Jean Skipwith, and John Hartwell Cocke cultivated the Newtown Pippin, and Richard Parkinson declared it the New World's "best apple" in 1799.[21]

The Newtown Pippin was almost universally acknowledged as the aristocrat of the species in the nineteenth century. New York nurseryman Benjamin Prince in 1815 said, "The Newtown Pippin is valued generally as the best Winter Apple in America or in fact in the World." William Coxe, who was the first writer to distinguish two distinct cultivars, the Yellow and Green Newton (fig. 47), agreed that "this is in most of its varieties the finest apple of our country, and probably of the world," while Downing declared that "the Newtown Pippin stands at the head of all apples, and is, when in perfection, acknowledged to be unrivaled in all the qualities which constitute a high flavoured desert apple."[22]

The name Albemarle Pippin first appeared in print on the editorial page of the *Southern Planter* in 1843 when a disgruntled Richmond writer complained about the importation of northern apples to Virginia when "the very best pippin we know, is grown in the county of Albemarle." New Yorker U. P. Hedrick boldly asserted in 1950 that "there is no doubt that, as grown in the mountains of Virginia, this variety is better than when grown in its home in New York," and Virginia pomologists attempted to identify the qualities of good Pippin land — soil, climate, elevation, aspect, and moisture — that proved so amenable to "the greatest apple of the Piedmont." By 1849 John J. Thomas in New York described the Albemarle Pippin as a distinct variety, and later pomological writers debated the synonymity of the names Albemarle and Newtown. The consensus was summarized by a Virginia university pomologist in 1900: "We have Albemarle Pippin from two sources in Virginia and the Newtown Pippin from New York all growing side by side and they prove to be identical."[23]

A local story attributed the Pippin's introduction to Albemarle County to a seedling tree that in 1765 was noted for its fine fruit in North Garden, ten miles from Monticello across the Southwest Mountains and very close to the property of Nicholas Meriwether, who provided Jefferson with "Newtown Pippins" in 1769. Perhaps a more plausible account relates how Dr. Thomas Walker, a Jefferson acquaintance, of-

GATHERING AND PACKING ALBEMARLE PIPPINS.   ONE DAY'S WORK, 151 BARRELS.
DR. PARSONS' ORCHARD, MASSIE'S MILLS, NELSON CO., VA.

Fig. 48. Central Virginia Pippin orchard, from the Virginia State Horticultural Society, *Report*, 1910

ficer in the Virginia militia at Braddock's defeat in Pennsylvania, and owner of Albemarle's Castle Hill, returned home via Philadelphia with scion wood of the Newtown Pippin in 1755 and distributed the tree throughout the county.[24]

The Newtown Pippin was the only American fruit to achieve lasting fame and fortune in England. Benjamin Franklin is credited with importing barrels of the fruit in 1759 when he was in London, while John Bartram supplied scion wood to the English plantsman Peter Collinson a few years later once word of the quality of this apple had spread. Collinson thanked Bartram for the scions and added that "what comes from you is excellent. I wish our sun may bring it to the like perfection." Trade undoubtedly began very soon; Collinson's son Michael wrote to Bartram in 1773 that "your American apples have been an admira[b]l[e] substitute this season [for a failed English crop], many of our merchants having imported great quantities of them." By 1807 the Newtown Pippin appeared on the Horticultural Society of London's "Select List" of apples. In 1838 Andrew Stevenson of Albemarle County, the American minister to the Court of St. James, imported two barrels of locally grown Pippins "in as good a state of preservation as we have them in Richmond, and never did a barrel of apples obtain such a reputation for the fruits of this country!" Stevenson presented them to the new queen, Victoria, who responded to his graciousness as well as the fine flavor of the variety ("a great sensation at the palace") by lifting an English export tax on imported apples. "They were eaten and praised by royal lips, and swallowed by many aristocratic throats." The fame of the Pippin soon spread throughout England. By 1848 exported fruits "commanded the highest price in the Covent Garden Market, London," and by 1898, when it was grown commercially primarily for export, the Pippin sold at prices three times those of other American varieties in the markets of Liverpool. No other American apple reaped such a profit for the grower. The Albemarle County Pippin industry, profitably based on foreign exportation, thrived in fertile elevated mountain coves on the spurs of the Blue Ridge until the end of World War I, when the British government reinstated import taxes on American apples in order to promote the apple industries of its Commonwealth countries (fig. 48). The Pippin continued to be grown for applesauce in California until the 1970s, enjoying the exalted status of being America's oldest agricultural or horticultural commercial crop.[25]

One local story attributes the Pippin's loss of popularity and its inability to find a market in the United States after World War I to a tendency of impatient growers to harvest the fruit too early in the season. Blame has also been accorded the tree's biennial bearing habit and the extended period, as long as eighteen years on seedling rootstock, that exists between planting and first harvest—unfortunate traits in an age of efficiency. The Pippin is not a handsome apple, and its winter-long keeping qualities were irrelevant once refrigeration became common at the turn of the twentieth century. The variably green-skinned, yellow-fleshed Pippin is both sweet and tart; crisp and tender at the same time. The citruslike aroma (some describe it as "piney") lingers in the mouth like

a dear memory. Reason enough for the Pippin to continue to enjoy its status as "the prince of apples."

ESOPUS SPITZENBURG

Although Jefferson never planted the Spitzenburg in large quantities, there are more documentary entries concerning its planting than for any other fruit variety—seven (fig. 49, pls. 3, 4). Jefferson purchased young trees from the William Prince nursery in 1791 and the Thomas Main nursery in 1805 and 1807, received grafts from his friends George Divers of Charlottesville and James Taylor of Norfolk, and reserved the heart of his south orchard, row i, for at least three separate plantings—in 1810, 1811, and 1812. It is difficult to successfully grow the Spitzenburg in a warm climate, and Jefferson's repeated plantings suggest he may have had trouble establishing this variety, perhaps the finest of all American dessert apples. As well, in his Garden Book in 1810, Jefferson noted that he was obtaining grafts of the Newtown Pippin from his own or-

No. 44. Esopus Spitzemberg.

Fig. 49. Esopus Spitzenburg from Coxe's *View*

No. 86. Hewes's Crab.

Fig. 50. Hewes Crab, also known as Virginia Crab or Hughes's Crab, from Coxe's *View*

chard, while at the same time he was relying on George Divers, an outside source, for his Spitzenburg budwood.[26]

Esopus Spitzenburg was discovered early in the eighteenth century at Esopus (pronounced today as E-soap´-us) along the Hudson River sixty miles north of New York, presumably by a horticulturally astute Dutch settler named Spitzenburg. Lady Jean Skipwith, an avid and proficient eighteenth-century Virginia gardener, declared it "the finest Am. table apple next to the Newtown Pippin." In the nineteenth century the Spitzenburg was the most widely acclaimed of all apple varieties. William Coxe said it "possesses great beauty, and exquisite flavor"; Downing described it as "a handsome, truly delicious apple . . . unsurpassed as a dessert fruit"; and even S. A. Beach, often frugal in his praise, said the Spitzenburg was "unexcelled in flavor and quality." Although the Spitzen-

burg never achieved the international reputation of the Pippin, it received a blue ribbon when displayed with other American apples at a Parisian exhibition in 1900.[27]

The Spitzenburg tree forms a distinctive slender, open shape with its long, hanging, willowlike limbs that create an upright, almost vase-shaped habit. The fruit is easily identified by its bright, vivid orangish-red skin. Biting into a Spitzenburg produces an explosion of flavor; the yellow flesh is crisp, firm, tender, juicy with an extremely rich, aromatic flavor: the ultimate gourmet apple.

HEWES CRAB
("Hughes's," "red Hughes," Virginia Crab)

The Hewes Crab—a cider apple, the most common fruit variety of eighteenth-century Virginia—was grown by Jefferson only in the north orchard (fig. 50, pls. 5, 12). In an 1814 letter to James Mease published in the *Memoirs* of the Philadelphia Society for Promoting Agriculture, Jefferson attempted to recall the history of the Hewes: "I remember it well upwards of 60. years ago, & that it was then a common apple on the James river." Another recollection, by Colonel John Roan of Virginia, suggests that orchards of only Hewes Crabs were planted in the tidewater very early in the eighteenth century. In property advertisements in the *Virginia Gazette* between 1755 and 1777, the Hewes Crab appeared more times, thirteen, than all other described fruit varieties combined. It was the first fruit variety listed by William Smith in 1755, and Thomas Sorsby's nursery in 1763 included three types of the Hewes, the names deriving presumably from the person who propagated them: Lightfoot's, Sorsby's, and Ellis's. Roan's White Crab, another seedling of the Hewes, was celebrated by Thomas Pickering in the *Memoirs* in 1814. Jefferson wrote home from Chestertown, Maryland, in 1797 and suggested the superior reputation of Hewes cider: "It will be worth his [Thomas Mann Randolph's] while to have the making of his crab cyder well attended to hereafter, as I learn here that good cyder of the qualities commonly at market sell for a quarter of a dollar the bottle, wholesale. Crab cyder would probably command more." John Hartwell Cocke proclaimed that the Hewes produced "the best cider I have ever seen," and its reputation had spread throughout the country by the nineteenth century. The Hewes was described by writers as far away as Boston (Kenrick, 1845) and Cincinnati (Hooper, "surpassingly fine," 1856), and it was widely distributed among urban nurseries in the North in the early 1800s. Although described in 1872 by James Fitz as "the old and popular cider apple of the South," its popularity declined with the flagging interest in southern cider making in the nineteenth century, and it was omitted from Beach's *Apples of New York* in 1900. Today the Hewes is only a historical curiosity.[28]

The Hewes is a maverick apple. Its vigorous, thrifty growth habit suggests that it may be a cross between a native American crabapple, *Malus angustifolia,* and the domesticated apple of horticulture. Landon Carter's "crabs" were the only apple unhurt by a late spring frost in 1772, and in 1814 Henry Wynkoop of Pennsylvania lamented the unexplained decline in the health of his dessert apples yet rejoiced in the "smooth and fair" progress of his Hewes Crabs: two testaments to the Hewes's native heritage. The fruit is very small, one to two inches round, with a bright to dull red, sometimes pinkish-red, skin. When pressing the Hewes for cider, the juice "runs through the finest flannel like spring water," or, according to another writer, "the liquor flows from the pumice as water from a sponge." The juice, described as "ambrosia" by a gardener at Colonial Williamsburg today, is both sugary and pungently tart; cinnamon-flavored and delicious.[29]

TALIAFERRO
(Robinson, "Robertson")

The Taliaferro (pronounced "Toliver") is Monticello's mystery apple. While Jefferson praised it as "the best cyder apple existing," producing cider "more like wine than any other liquor I have tasted which was not wine," the Taliaferro was ignored by national pomological writers. The lack of a detailed description of its qualities makes retrieval of the Taliaferro virtually impossible. Yet the enigma of the extinct Taliaferro has enhanced its stature as a lost treasure. Unprecedented quantities of this apple were planted in a select location in the southwest quadrant of the south orchard (rows *n* through *y*) beginning in 1778, when "96 Robinson apples from Major Tali-

aferro. grafted" were set out. This was one of the few early plantings at Monticello that endured into the next century.[30]

In a letter to James Mease in 1814, Jefferson described this apple's history. The process by which the Taliaferro was discovered, named, and propagated was typical of the evolution of many of the apples that originated in North America:

It is not a crab, but a seedling which grew alone in a large old field near Williamsburg where the seed had probably been dropped by some bird. Majr. Taliaferro of that neighborhood remarking it once to be very full of apples got permission of the owner of the ground to gather them. From these he made a cask of cyder which, in the estimation of every one who tasted it was the finest they had ever seen. He grafted an orchard from it, as did his son in law our late Chancelor Wythe. The cyder they constantly made from this was preferred by every person to the [Hewes] Crab or any other cyder ever known in this state, and it still retains its character in the different places to which it has been transferred. I am familiar with it, and have no hesitation in pronouncing it much superior to the Hughes's crab. It has more body, is less acid, and comes nearer to the silky Champaigne than any other. Majr. Taliaferro called it the Robertson apple from the name of the person owning the parent tree, but subsequently it has more justly and generally been distinguished by the name of the Taliaferro apple, after him to whom we are indebted for the discovery of its valuable properties. It is the most juicy apple I have ever known, & is very refreshing as an eating apple.[31]

William Kenrick described the Taliaferro in 1835: "The fruit is the size of a grape shot, or from one to two inches in diameter; of a white color, streaked with red; with a sprightly acid, not good for the table, but apparently a very valuable cider fruit. This is understood to be a Virginia fruit, and the apple from which Mr. Jefferson's favorite cider was made." Taliaferro was sold by the Stratchan and Maury nursery in 1799. Robinson became an accepted synonym that was listed by William Booth of Baltimore in 1810 and by the McMahon

No. 61. White Calville.

Fig. 51. White Calville (Calville Blanc d'Hiver) from Coxe's *View*

Fig. 52. Calville Blanc d'Hiver from Henri Louis Duhamel Du Monceau, *Traité des arbres fruitiers*, 1768

nursery of Philadelphia in 1819. In 1872 James Fitz provided the last, though unfortunately imprecise, statement on the Taliaferro: "Robinson's White: Medium, crisp, juicy and delicate flavor, a good bearer, highly esteemed; Nov. to Jan. in the Valley of Virginia."[32]

OTHER JEFFERSON APPLES

Calville Blanc d'Hiver. John Armstrong of Cincinnati sent Jefferson cuttings of the "Calvit apple which is without comparison the best apple that ever was Eaten" in 1804. Jefferson then transcribed it as "Calvite," an anglicization of the famous French variety Calville Blanc d'Hiver, introduced very early by the French into the Michigan frontier (figs. 51, 52, pl. 9). Although the nineteenth-century reviews of this sixteenth-century French apple were mixed, Calville is admired today by fruit connoisseurs for its high vitamin C content and spicy, bananalike aroma.[33]

Clarke Pearmain ("Clark's pear-main," synonymous with Golden Pearmain?) was a North Carolina cider apple grown in the north orchard (pl. 10). This firm, rough-skinned, green-

ish-yellow variety was widely distributed among eighteenth-century Virginia growers.[34]

"Detroit large white" was sent with the Calville by John Armstrong. White Bellflower or Ortley, possible synonyms popular in the Midwest in the nineteenth century, was a white-fleshed, yellow-skinned variety described in 1857 as "one of the best apples known."[35]

Detroit Red ("Detroit large red") was also sent to Jefferson from Ohio in 1805. At first a regional variety, its choice dessert qualities — an unusually smooth, dark red skin and snow-white, crisp flesh — stimulated its popularity in Virginia late in the nineteenth century.[36]

Early Harvest ("Large early harvest") was purchased by Jefferson in 1791 from the William Prince nursery, which pop-

No. 2 Prince's Harvest.

Fig. 53. Early, or Prince's, Harvest from Coxe's *View*

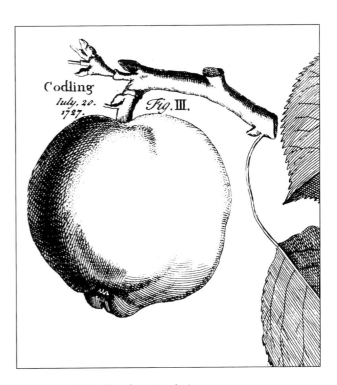

Fig. 54. English Codling from Langley's *Pomona*

ularized this well-known and widely distributed early-season apple (known by some as "Prince's Harvest") with its bright, smooth, straw-colored skin and white, juicy flesh (fig. 53). Benjamin Prince said Early Harvest was "the earliest of all apples, fit for tarts in June, and when ripe is an excellent table fruit," while Downing referred to it as "the finest early apple yet known."[37]

English Codling ("codlin") was planted in 1778, 1794, and 1810 (fig. 54, pl. 6). An ancient cooking cultivar, the "codlin" was mentioned by John Lawson in 1709 ("no better and fairer fruit in the world") and was one of the few European varieties described by early American writers as either vigorous or fruitful. William Coxe was enthusiastic in his praise of the Codling, which he said was "a very fine fruit for pies and stewing, and is also a pleasant table apple: it grows very large and fair . . . is uncommonly handsome, vigorous, and fruitful . . . [and] is one of the most profitable apples for the market." Best suited for stewing or baking, when the rich, buttery taste was most evident, English Codling's early popularity diminished later in the nineteenth century, and it seems to be extinct today.[38]

Golden Wilding was the only apple variety grown in both

Monticello orchards. John Hartwell Cocke wrote that it was "said to be superior to any in Virginia for cyder." This golden yellow, yellow-fleshed apple was grown on only a limited scale in Virginia and apparently has disappeared from cultivation.[39]

"Iron wilding" was planted in the Monticello nursery in 1810.[40]

"Mammoth" (synonymous with Gloria Mundi?) was among the plants Dr. James Wallace of Washington intended to send Jefferson in 1809.[41]

Medlar Russetin, occasionally sold and grown in Virginia around 1800, was planted in 1771 and 1778. Although never described in the literature, it was probably a russet apple with similarities to a medlar, *Mespilus germanica,* a cultivated fruit with a dark brown skin and an astringent flesh that mellows with age or cooking.[42]

"Ox-eye striped" (synonymous with Vandevere or Newtown Spitzenburg?) also was sent by John Armstrong, who said it was "ripe in the fall, highly flavored, weighs from 16 to

20 oz." Jefferson planted eleven trees in 1804, sixteen more in the nursery in 1805.[43]

Pomme Gris ("pumgray"), also sent from Cincinnati in 1804, migrated east from French North America and was first sold along the Atlantic seaboard by the Benjamin Prince nursery in 1815 (pl. 11). Praised by Downing as "one of the finest dessert fruits for a northern climate," this russet-skinned, small, greenish-gray to cinnamon brown apple was popular for its storage capabilities, but it is also an excellent dessert apple.[44]

"Russetins" (Golden Russet or Roxbury Russet) were planted by Jefferson in 1778 and sent to Poplar Forest in 1782. A russet is a generic term for an apple with a rough, pimpled, brownish skin. Jefferson possibly was alluding to either Roxbury Russet, which originated near Boston early in the seventeenth century and, according to U. P. Hedrick, was among the three most common American apples in the eighteenth century, or Golden Russet, an old English variety widely distributed in eighteenth-century Virginia.[45]

Virginia White ("White") is the oldest documented Virginia apple cultivar, mentioned as early as 1716 in the York County records and sold by Sorsby in 1755 and Smith in 1763. William Byrd drank "exceeding good" cider from the White apple in 1732. Jefferson planted grafted "White" apples in 1778.[46]

Pl. 7. Newtown Pippin from George Brookshaw's Horticultural Repository (London, 1823)

Pl. 8. Winesap from Coxe's "View"

White Calville

Pl. 9. White Calville, or Calville Blanc d'Hiver, from Coxe's "View"

Pl. 10. Golden Pearmain, possibly synonymous with the Clarke Pearmain Wilding that Jefferson planted in the north orchard

Pl. 11. Pomme Gris in the south orchard

Pl. 12. Hewes Crab in the
south orchard

Pl. 13. Breast of Venus, or Poppa di Venere, peach from Giorgio Gallesio's *Pomona italiana*

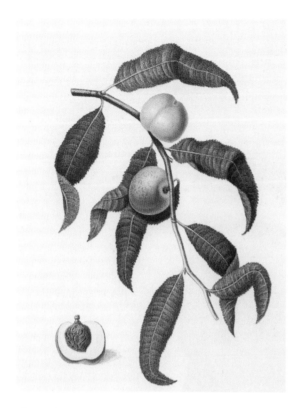

Pl. 14. Alberges from Gallesio's *Pomona italiana*

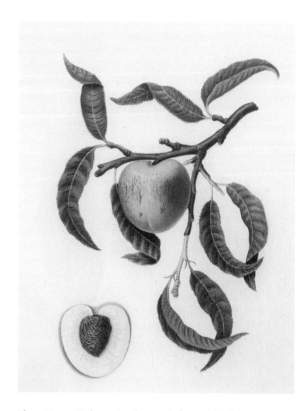

Pl. 15. Pesca Mela, or Apple, peach from Gallesio's *Pomona italiana*

Pl. 16. Vaga Loggia from Gallesio's *Pomona italiana*

The Luxury of the Peach

We abound in the luxury of the peach.

—Jefferson to Martha Randolph, August 13, 1815

The peach tree was an early image for the bounty of the New World's natural productions. By the beginning of the eighteenth century peach trees had naturalized so abundantly throughout the southeastern and mid-Atlantic colonies that John Lawson said they grew as luxuriantly as weeds: "We are forced to take a great deal of Care to weed them out, otherwise they make our Land a Wilderness of Peach-Trees." As well, the vast quantities of peaches planted in Virginia defined a distinctive form of New World pomology based on casually cultivated seedling orchards geared toward utilitarian uses—as an animal fodder or a source for peach brandy—rather than as a dessert fruit. Jefferson also regarded the peach as a fancy delicacy for the table, and if one measures his appreciation of a fruit by the frequency with which he had it planted or by the number of varieties in his collection, the peach would easily be considered his favorite fruit tree. Peach cultivars were seldom documented in eighteenth-century Virginia literature. George Washington, for example, mentioned only two specific varieties for his Mount Vernon orchard. Jefferson, however, cultivated over thirty-eight in his south orchard alone. By 1811 he had twice as many peach trees as apples. The peach was the queen bee, the workhorse of tree fruits at Monticello because of its abundance and its many uses, but also because, simply, Thomas Jefferson liked peaches.[1]

Jefferson planted peach trees not only for the "precious refreshment" of their fruit but, like most Virginia farmers before 1820, to exploit them as an agricultural commodity as well. For example, in one year, 1794, Jefferson planted 1,157 peach trees in his north orchard and as a boundary fence to his fields. Peaches were planted as a timber product, as a source of firewood, and as a living fence defining boundary lines. The harvested fruits were manufactured into peach liquors—mobby and brandy—and although Jefferson leaves no record that suggests he used the peach as livestock fodder, it was a common practice among his contemporaries. But perhaps more importantly, at least for Jefferson, peaches are easy to grow, and they bear relatively soon after planting. They provide a kind of instant gratification unique among tree fruits by bearing after two or three years, particularly in the sunny microclimate of the south orchard. Their quick growth suggests a perennial vegetable rather than, for example, a venerable, centuries-old apple. Peaches are also easy to propagate; they sprout readily from the stone, and Jefferson himself distinguished the peach as one of the few fruits whose seedling would produce a faithful copy of the original. Finally, the peach is the most sensuous of fruits: juicy, sweet, delicately perfumed, and desirable only at its peak of ripeness. This partly explains the vivid imagery used to describe its place in the early American landscape.[2]

One of the reasons the peach is so amenable to the New World climate and soil is that it is native to continental China. China and North America have similar climates, and there are intimate botanical links between the two continents: most North American genera have comparable copies in the flora of China. At the same time the absence of a North American peach species eliminated the danger of indigenous pests that would find cultivated trees a suitable host. The "luxury of the peach" was a theme found not only in the earliest descriptions of botanically oriented European explorers but in travelers' accounts of the eighteenth- and nineteenth-century southern landscape. The peach was one of our first naturalized weeds, so precocious and abundant, so curiously yet delightfully out of place to European observers.[3]

THE PEACH IN VIRGINIA

From Pennsylvania south, peach trees merged into the surrounding vegetation so completely that the earliest natural historians, even John Bartram, America's first great botanist, assumed the peach was a native tree. In fact, the peach was introduced either by the Spanish settlers in St. Augustine, Florida, in 1565 or by the French to an isolated Gulf of Mexico settlement in 1562. It was probably grown in Mexico at an even earlier date. Whatever its first date and place of introduction, Indian peach culture migrated north with the travels of Jesuit and Franciscan missionaries and with the Indians themselves. Cultivated trees escaped into the landscape and were among the first alien species to naturalize around settlements. William Penn observed wild "Indian peaches" as far north as Philadelphia in 1683, and a few years later John Banister wrote that in Virginia, "Peaches and Nectarines I believe to be Spontaneous . . . for the Indians have, and ever had greater variety, and finer sorts of them than we. . . . I have seen those they call the yellow plum-peach that have been 12 or 13 inches in girt." Luigi Castiglioni noted a hundred years later that "peach trees are so abundant in Virginia that often, upon cutting away a pine wood, these fruit trees, which previously could not multiply because of the shade, quickly grow in such quantity that in a short time they cover the whole terrain." It seems odd that today there is no place where peach trees dominate "the whole terrain" in Virginia; instead, they are reported as relatively uncommon in about half of its counties.[4]

Aside from the trees cultivated by the Indians and the naturalized Indian peaches, the European settlers in Virginia planted the fruit in enormous quantities. Robert Beverley, echoing John Banister, described the "luxury of the peach" in early Virginia orchards: "Some of these [peaches] are 12 or 13

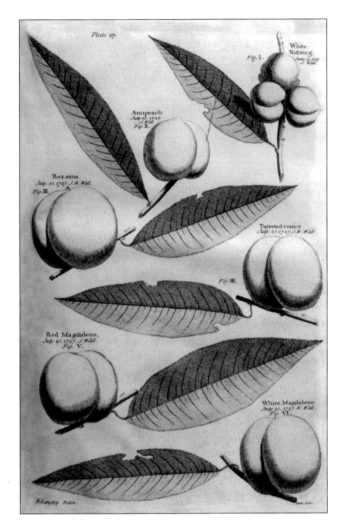

Fig. 55. English peaches from Langley's *Pomona*

Inches in the girthe, These sorts of fruits are raised so easily . . . that some good Husbands plant great Orchards of them, purposely for their Hogs; and others make a Drink of them, which they call Mobby, and either drink it as Cider, or Distill it off for Brandy." He also noted that "the flavor of Virginian fruit was superior to the flavor of that of England, this being true in the most marked degree of the peach" (fig. 55). Peter Collinson wrote that Virginia "is reported to have the finest peaches in the world." Evidently, the quality varied, for William Grove observed in 1732 that the insipid flavor of Virginia peaches was the result of lazy cultivation and an inordinate attention to tobacco growing. Travelers such as Josiah Quincy of Boston observed peach orchards as large as thirty acres in 1773: "Through Virginia you find agriculture carried to great perfection, and large fields are planted with peach trees, which all in bloom made my journey vastly agreeable." When farms were advertised for sale between 1736 and 1780 in Williamsburg's *Virginia Gazette*, the size and character of the orchard were important in evaluating the plantation's value. Of approximately 369 notices that mentioned an orchard as part of the farm to be sold, 244 mentioned a peach orchard. Their median size was 1,000 trees, significantly more than in the apple orchards. U. P. Hedrick described an orchard in Accomack County, planted in 1814, which included 63,000 trees that yielded nearly ten thousand gallons of peach brandy. The peach continued to be the standard southern commodity as late as 1859, when William White of Athens, Georgia, said, it was "the favorite, and in many instances, the only fruit tree cultivated by our planters."[5]

THE USES OF THE PEACH

Philip Vickers Fithian, a Princeton-educated tutor living at Nomini Hall on the Northern Neck of Virginia, commented on a killing May frost in a 1774 journal entry and then remarked, "The peaches here . . . are wholly destoy'd, & these were the choisest expectation of some, who think Brandy their most valuable commodity!" Later the same year Fithian visited a plantation where, despite the frost, "people were shaking the trees to prepare the Peaches for brandy." Luigi Castiglioni a few years later explained the reasons for the popularity of brandy and the techniques Virginians used to make it: "The difficulty and expense of obtaining rum and other liquors in regions far from the sea induced the Virginians to make their own brandy from peaches. Peach trees, which grow spontaneously everywhere in Virginia, produce annually a great deal of fruit, which, crushed by a wheel driven by a horse as is done with apples, produce a large quantity of juice, which, passed through a still, comes out as a clear, limpid liquor of excellent flavor and odor. This liquor is very strong, has a pleasing and delicate fragrance, and is drunk

mixed with sugar or syrup like maraschino, or simply mixed with water like rum and brandy." Jefferson recorded the production of mobby in 1782: "20 bushels of peaches will make 75 galls. of mobby, i.e. $\frac{5}{12}$ of its bulk." Mobby was peach juice, sometimes distilled; William Byrd found it "much more agreeable than apple juice or pear juice."[6]

Although Jefferson never alluded to the use of the peach as an animal fodder, that also was a common practice in eighteenth-century Virginia. The biological symmetry of grazing livestock caretaking the peach orchard—fertilizing the trees, devouring destructive insects, fattening themselves on unwanted fruit—presents an enduring lesson in the wholesome stewardship of the land. Goochland County's William Mayo in 1731 said, "I have had this year such a plenty [of peaches] and have found such a benefit by letting my Hogs come into the Orchard that I prepare to plant 6 acres more." In 1741 John Oldmixon observed that "there's such plenty of them [peaches and other fruits] that they are given to the hogs." In 1774 Landon Carter planted nearly three thousand peach trees, primarily for this purpose. William Byrd said peaches "bear so very fruitfully, that many of their branches break, and one gives them to the swine as fattener because of their great quantity, although they are also employed for other useful things. Unbelievable amounts of them are dried." Peach chips—sliced, boiled, sugared, and sun-dried—were also popular, and Jefferson noted in a letter to his daughter Martha in 1815 that one of the Monticello slaves, Cate, "is busy drying peaches for you."[7]

When Jefferson wrote his practical-minded son-in-law Thomas Mann Randolph in 1792, he described a unique use for the peach tree:

> I thank you for your experiment of the Peach tree. It proves my speculation practicable, as it shews that 5. acres of peach trees at 21. feet apart will furnish dead wood enough to supply a fireplace through the winter, & may be kept up at the trouble of only planting about 70. peach stones a year. Suppose this extended to 10. fireplaces, it comes to 50. acres of ground, 5000 trees, and the replacing about 700 of them annually by planting so many stones. If it be disposed at some little distance,

Fig. 56. William Cobbett's directions for peach pruning, before (fig. 2) and after (fig. 3), in *The American Gardener*

say in a circular annulus from 100. to 300. yards from the house, it would render a cart almost useless. —When I indulge myself in these speculations, I feel with redoubled ardor my desire to return home to the pursuit of them, & in that of my neighbors.—But I must yet a little while bear up against my weariness of public office.

U. P. Hedrick, writing in 1950, felt that Jefferson must have been a poor horticulturist if five acres of peaches provided enough deadwood for ten winter fireplaces. In Jefferson's defense, however, it seems he regarded the species as a forestry product: the deadwood was the result of the vigorous pruning of live branches (fig. 56). Jefferson also speculated on the possibilities of using pollarded willow trees as a firewood source, a traditional European practice.[8]

The peach is also a handsome ornamental tree with its rich foliage and striking display of pink, or rarely white, flowers.

Jefferson noted their flowering at Monticello at least twelve times as a barometer of the season. He also planted the double flowering peach, a pure ornamental, in 1805. In 1829, three years after Jefferson's death, Nicholas Trist sent "good peach stones" to Edgehill's Jane Randolph, wife of Jefferson's grandson Thomas Jefferson Randolph, and said, "Let them be distributed among the negroes and thus in a few years there will be two or three trees about every cabin." The species' aggressive growth habit and its ornamental qualities also make the peach suitable for a living fence. In 1794 Jefferson noted the planting of nearly nine hundred peach trees as "dividing lines" between his agricultural fields at both Monticello and Lego, an adjacent plantation across the Rivanna River. The duc de La Rochefoucauld-Liancourt observed these trees, a "single row" around the fields, in 1796. There seems to have been a Virginia tradition for using the peach as a hedge. As early as 1732 William Hugh Grove observed that Virginians made "strong hedges of Peach plants in their gardens."[9]

PEACH CULTURE

In 1754 John Bartram described the Indian peaches he found growing wild as "large, healthy, and fruitful." The reports of colonial peach growing suggest this overwhelming abundance: orchards so productive the ground was slippery with fallen peaches, a fruit so common it was used as animal fodder, a tree so precocious as to be considered a common weed. One would assume that serious cultivation would only improve the "luxury of the peach," if trees were manured, kept free of weeds and pests, and pruned. The champion seedling peaches described by Beverley and Banister around 1700 were the size of grapefruits, thirteen inches in circumference, but by 1819, one avid peach observer thought an eleven-inch, ten-ounce peach was a world record of museum quality "for the inspiration of the curious." By 1845 William Kenrick believed intensively cultivated eight-ounce (eight or nine inches) peaches most remarkable. In 1815 Jefferson remarked that the peach harvest was "as fine here now as used to have in Albemarle 30 years ago, and indeed as fine as I ever saw anywhere." This comment perhaps suggests that for thirty years the "luxury of the peach" had not existed. There were other disturbing suggestions of a general peach malaise. Benjamin Barton, in his journal of a botanical visit to Virginia in 1802, expressed surprise that "the diseases which affect the peach-trees in so many parts of the N. States, have even reached this secluded spot" along the Blue Ridge Mountains north of Monticello. Barton reported evidence of both the plum curculio and the peach borer: "They [peaches] are gummy, and also subject to the worm." The chief inspiration for William Cobbett's preparation of an American edition of William Forsyth's *Treatise* in 1803 was the "swift decay" of peach trees in the mid-Atlantic states. In 1811 Richard Peters said, "There are so many misfortunes attending this species of tree, and so much has been in vain attempted to establish some general rules for its culture, that we hesitate to pronounce any decided opinions." The success of American peaches degenerated with cultivation, the depletion of virgin soils, and the ravages of three virulent plagues: peach yellows, plum curculio, and peach tree borers.[10]

Richard Peters noticed the appearance of the yellows at his Pennsylvania farm in 1790 when his entire 150-tree orchard suddenly died after the leaves turned yellow and the "bodies blackened in spots." This description is considered the first allusion to any fruit virus in the United States. Peters attributed the source of the epidemic to "some morbid affection in the air." By 1849 Downing said the yellows was "the greatest enemy of the peach planter for the last thirty years." He laid the blame for the spread of the disease to poor cultivation techniques, exhausted soil, and overbearing trees, then compared the casual cultural methods used by American growers to the more meticulous care exercised by Europeans. One wonders how prevalent the disease was at Monticello. While Maryland was considered near the center of the epidemic, William White observed from Georgia that "we entirely escape the yellows, except in the case of northern importations." Today the yellows is an insignificant problem, its control aided by the use of virus-free rootstock.[11]

In 1791 Jefferson described a "weavil" to Thomas Mann Randolph which "by depositing its egg in the young plumbs, apricots, nectarines & peaches renders them gummy & good for nothing." The most popular contemporary way to combat the plum curculio (Jefferson's "weavil") was to allow grazing hogs in the orchards. McMahon's *Calendar* included a dissertation on the curculio by James Tilton. Tilton's remedy was to allow hogs in the orchard: "The fact is, hogs render fruits of all kinds fair and unblemished, by destroying the curculio." He recommended that "little bits of board" dipped in tar be suspended from the tree branches as a deterrent. In an address to the Agricultural Society of Annapolis in 1819, Joseph Muse looked scientifically at the life cycle of the curculio, then suggested a control measure: paving of the ground around the tree with brick, stone, or shells to prevent the larvae from penetrating the soil. Nevertheless, many growers despaired of ever finding an effective, permanent solution.[12]

In 1798 Jefferson recorded William and Moses Bartram's observations on peach insects:

The insect which lays it's egg in the plumb, apricot, nectarine, peach, etc. is a Curculio. William Bartram. Probably the Curculio Cerasi. (Note the Curculio segatum is the weevil.) wm.

That which destroys the Peach tree is an Ichneumon. Wm. Bartram. It lays it's egg in the peach tree a little within the surface of the earth soon after harvest. It hatches. The worm eats downward, and becomes winged and escapes in May following. Moses Bartram. Boxing round the root, with 4. shingles or boards staked down and filled with dung, prevents the insect. Idem.

Jefferson undoubtedly was referring to the borer, the "Ichneumon," in 1824 when he wrote that "Gen. Cocke says the Peach tree worm is hatching all July, Aug. Sep. and lays it's egg immediately on being hatched. It may be seen & taken out from Mar. to June. It should always be done before harvest." The peach tree borer was the most commonly discussed southern fruit pest before 1840. Among the most effective controls was General John Hartwell Cocke's use of cured tobacco leaves, which were wrapped around the base of the tree's trunk: "I have now several hundred young peach trees, in perfect health and full bearing, which I attribute entirely to the use of this remedy." Richard Peters, writing in the *Memoirs* of the Philadelphia Society for Promoting Agriculture, 1808, recommended pouring boiling hot soapsuds around the base of the tree; Walter Coles of Charlottesville also endorsed this practice in the *American Farmer* in 1821. John Ellis of New Jersey described an elaborate banded-straw barrier that encircled the trunk. The *Southern Planter* in 1841 suggested interplanting cedar trees among the peaches. The solutions to borer control were as numerous as the growers who seriously cultivated the tree.[13]

Many growers were giving up. In 1825 a North Carolina correspondent to the *American Farmer* reported that the peach was the "most uncertain of any fruit in its produce. . . . Hence, esteemed as this fruit is, it is not much cultivated; and I think is becoming still more and more neglected." Thomas Say, who in 1824 reviewed the literature on borer eradication by Tilton, Coxe, and Cocke, concluded, "We still found that our orchards are decaying . . . [and are] little better than a barren waste of dead and decaying limbs." Another correspondent, after detailing numerous experiments to ward off both the borer and curculio—sand and tobacco mulches, recycled sand-filled waterspout sleeves for the trunks, repeated cultivation

—was forced simply to replace his dead trees. Solutions became more unconventional, even desperate. One writer in the *American Farmer* applied a thick mulch of charcoal, and the "trees flourished to an unparalleled degree ever since; not one of them evincing any symptoms of decay or disease."[14]

Richard Peters concluded that the solution to peach culture was to treat the trees as perennials that would only produce three or four crops, then die. The grower should "keep up a constant succession, by setting out a few [trees] every year." Peters described a successful planting by a respected Delaware grower. Peach kernels were set twenty-five feet apart among the spring corn planting. The pits sprouted and grew three to four feet a year. "The knife is never applied to the standard trees, it being found injurious. . . . The crops are certain, abundant, and well flavored. In size, they are little inferior to those on pruned trees. . . . They often fruit in three years in plenty: and the trees have been known to endure fifty years. No worms or disease assail them. They are so easily propagated, and renewed, that cutting down a peach orchard for a course of tillage . . . is not uncommon." Thomas Coulter of Bedford, Pennsylvania, discussed his relatively effortless peach growing in the *Domestic Encyclopedia*. Coulter planted seedling trees sixteen feet apart. They were left unmolested for two years except "you may plough and harrow amongst [them], paying no regard to wounding them or tearing them." Apparently following the dictates of William Forsyth, he then had the trees cut off at the ground so that five or six suckers would immediately arise from the stump. Coulter believed the bushy sucker growth shaded out weeds, made cultivation unnecessary and manure useless, and ensured that his trees would live a hundred years. His adage, "The poorer the soil the better the fruit," seemed generally accepted by early peach growers.[15]

In 1808 Richard Peters discussed his unrelenting failures in peach cultivation and the various unsuccessful techniques he used to ward off the plague of diseases and insects that were destroying his orchards:

I have failed in many things, in which others are said to have succeeded. Straw . . . surrounding the trees, from the root, at all distances, from 5 inches, to 3 or 4 feet—

white washing, painting, urinous applications, brine, soot, lime, frames filled with sand, oil, tar, turpentine, sulphuric acid or oil of vitriol, nitrous mixtures, and almost every kind of coating. I ruined several trees, by cutting them down, and permitting the stump to throw up new shoots, and branch at pleasure. All teguments kept the exsudation from evaporating with freedom. The pores being closed, or too open, were alike injurious. Teguments of straw or bass made the bark tender; and threw out under the covering, sickly shoots. The more dense coating stopped the perspiration. The oil invited mice and other vermin, who ate the bark thus prepared for their repast and killed the tree. I planted in hedge rows and near woods, I paved, raised hillocks of stone—I have suffered them to grow from the stone only, grafted on various stocks and budded, hilled up the earth in the spring and exposed the butt in the fall, sometimes I have used the knife freely—frequently have left the tree to shoot in every direction—I have scrubbed the stocks or trunks . . . I had temporary success, but final disappointment.

Peters, perhaps like Jefferson, concluded that the solution to peach culture was to treat the trees as perennials that would only produce three or four crops, then die.[16]

Jefferson recorded little information on specific techniques he used in cultivating this fruit. The south orchard is an ideal site for peaches. Thomas Mann Randolph reported to Benjamin Barton that "the best peaches, in this country [central Virginia], grow neither upon the low nor upon the highest grounds, but upon hills about 300, or 400, feet high." Although not precisely fulfilling such a requirement, the south orchard's range of elevation—from 650 to 750 feet—provides air circulation, protection from cold winds, and frost protection. In a letter to Jefferson in 1780, George Mason of Gunston Hall suggested that at least one variety of peach required some degree of attention: "Almost all my Portugal peaches were stolen this year, before they were ripe; but I have saved the few stones I send you myself, & know they are the true sort. I have observed this kind of peach requires more care than most others, & if the trees are not tended, & the Ground cul-

tivated, the fruit is apt to be coarse & harsh; with due culture the peaches are the finest I ever tasted." While Jefferson may or may not have given his peaches their "due culture," it seems more likely that peach trees were simply planted and harvested, then replaced when they died.[17]

PROPAGATION

Because the culture of peach trees for hog feed or peach brandy did not require a specific type of peach, there was little need to preserve or propagate particular varieties. Before 1820 varieties were seldom mentioned. While eighteenth-century Virginia nurserymen sold the Hewes Crab and Newtown Pippin apple, neither William Smith nor Thomas Sorsby, Surry County nurserymen, sold specific peach types, only "peach" trees. At Mount Vernon, George Washington did basically the same thing when planting large quantities of peaches between 1775 and 1786, although he did mention the Heath and the Portugal varieties. Lady Jean Skipwith planted the stones of about ten different peach types in 1791 and fifteen in 1792, all described by their basic physical characteristics or else the source of the seed. William Cobbett was critical of this varietal imprecision: "It is curious enough, that people in general think little of the *sort* in the case of *peaches*, though they are so choice in the case of *apples*. A peach is a *peach* it seems, though I know no apples between which there is more difference than there is between different sorts of peaches." There were exceptions: Peter Collinson sent John Custis the Catherine and Nutmeg varieties; St. George Tucker received at least eight named varieties, and John Hartwell Cocke as many as sixteen, from the Prince nurseries, which offered budded trees by 1791. In 1817 William Coxe wrote about the techniques for budding trees in August, although he assumed that most of his readers would purchase budded trees from competent nurseries. As horticultural sophistication increased, nurseries developed, and pomological works were published, gardeners began to realize the need to bud or graft peaches in order to preserve the varietal purity of distinct cultivars. Yet the practices advocated by writers and the most sophisticated gardeners were not followed out in the field. One wary writer in Richmond's *Southern Planter* attributed the decline in peach quality in 1841 to the newly awak-ened interest in grafting. There were millions of peach trees in America before 1825, but until that time there were only a few named varieties.[18]

Most gardeners, including Jefferson, were convinced that a seedling peach not only produced a true copy of the parent but also was superior in its robust and hardy growth. He wrote that "we rarely graft the peach . . . the tree proceeding from the stone yields a faithful copy of its fruit, and the tree is always healthier." Although it was a standard practice with most other tree fruits, Jefferson rarely budded or grafted a peach. He wrote to William Short in 1791 that "I cannot as yet gratify the Duke's [the duc de La Rochefoucauld-Liancourt] desire as to engrafted peach trees. The Peach of Pennsylvania is not that which is to be offered as of first quality, and in Virginia you know we have attended chiefly to the clingstone peach; and moreover have never engrafted either kind. I must therefore desire a friend to choose the ensuing season a tree of the best soft peaches at Monticello, and engraft from it the ensuing spring." Goochland County's William Mayo expressed the nearly universal smug satisfaction with seedling peaches: "I have had Peaches from the Stones you gave me when you was at my House. It is a good Peach and large but I think I have better & much larger & some has measured 14 inches about & I think of as rich a juice as a Pine[apple]."[19]

JEFFERSON'S PEACHES

I am endeavoring to make a collection of the
choicest kinds of peaches for Monticello.

—*Jefferson to John Threlkeld, March 26, 1807*

Jefferson's collection of peaches was a thorough blend of Old and New World varieties, early and late producers, freestones and clingstones, yellow-fleshed and white-fleshed peaches. He received young budded trees from the William Prince nursery in New York and the Thomas Main and Alexander Hepburn nurseries in Washington; he obtained peach stones from friends like George Mason, Timothy Matlack, Isaac Coles, James Taylor, and William Meriwether. He was sent a shipment of choice Italian varieties by Philip Mazzei, many

of which could be considered Jefferson introductions into the United States, including the Vaga Loggia, Maddelena, and the Apple peach. He received local types from his own Monti-cello workmen, such as Abraham Balyal, who worked in the vegetable garden. The Monticello collection had many fa-mous American varieties as well, among them the Heath Cling, America's first named peach, the Oldmixon Cling, Mor-ris's Red Rareripe, and the Indian Blood Cling. Although U. P. Hedrick stated that "there were millions of peach trees in America before 1825, but until that time there were but a few named varieties," nearly half the thirty-eight varieties grown by Jefferson at Monticello were described in the pomological literature—a tribute to the depth of his collection and the sin-cerity of his interest in fine fruit. Monticello peaches could be harvested from late June, when the Green Nutmeg first bears fruit, until the end of November, when the many un-described large yellow freestones finally ripen. Jefferson's col-lection of peaches was large enough to fulfill any need.[20]

Peach varieties are naturally divided into clingstones, also known as pavies or, as Jefferson referred to them, "plumb peaches"; and freestones: clear stones, melocotons, or "soft peaches." The flesh of the former adheres closely to the stone or pit, like a plum, while the flesh of the latter separates eas-ily, or clearly. Eighteenth-century Virginians seemed to pre-fer the clingstone types, and the "American Farmer" included a definition of how each kind was cherished: "Within the states of America, *clear-stone* peaches are preferred for food to hogs, and for making brandy; perhaps also to be eaten in country families, with milk; but the cling-stone sorts are pre-ferred when of a good sort, well ripened, to be eaten as fruit undressed." Because of the surging popularity of freestone peaches by 1849, A. J. Downing thought this historical pref-erence for clingstones as dessert fruit and freestones as hog food rather amusing. Jefferson grew as many freestone vari-eties as he grew clingstones, including the Poppa di Venere, Oldmixon Free, Vaga Loggia, Morris's Red Rareripe, and Green Nutmeg. Most of his late-season "soft peaches" pos-sessed only generic descriptions and probably were used for brandy production or preserves. These late-season, yellow-fleshed peaches often were described as "melocotons": "as big as a lemon and resemble it a little." White-fleshed peaches were considered significantly more flavorful by nineteenth-century American fruit connoisseurs.[21]

Many difficulties arise in attempting to pinpoint Jefferson's peach varieties. Most were grown from pits, and although Jefferson was sincere in his insistence that a seedling peach was as true to variety as a budded one, this was probably not the case. Jefferson regularly used personal descriptions to refer to specific types—for example, "the fine, soft peaches of August." Some of the named varieties of peaches Jefferson received, such as those from Timothy Matlack, were sent as cuttings or small branches and probably did not live once they were planted in the nursery. Although Jefferson was attempting to assemble a collection of peach varietals, the more successful plantings seem to have been of undescribed types. Furthermore, he planted so many peaches from seeds, which proliferated into countless types, and differentiating the qualities of one peach from another is so difficult sometimes, that relying on Jefferson's nomenclature for peaches is perhaps riskier than with any other Monticello fruit. Just as American apples gradually supplanted European cultivars on nursery lists, so American peaches began to dominate the collections of nineteenth-century nurseries. McMahon's 1806 *Calendar* listed thirty-four peaches, mostly European imports. Of the forty-five varieties listed in 1810 by William Booth, a Baltimore nurseryman, only ten were American peaches. The balance was reversed by 1849 when the ninth edition of Downing's *Fruits and Fruit Trees of America* described seventy-six peaches; twenty-eight were of European origin, and the rest were American. By 1850 American nurseries were offering over four hundred peach varieties, and by the turn of the century, over a thousand.[22]

HEATH CLING

In 1813 Jefferson recorded planting "4. fine Heath peach stones. Carysbrook," in the nursery (fig. 57, pls. 18, 19). He received them from Wilson Cary of Fluvanna County. Heath Cling is not only considered the first named American cultivar but was also the most highly acclaimed. In 1803 the usually skeptical "American Farmer" labeled it the "noble Heath peach. . . . Best of all peaches, perhaps of all fruits." There are two theories

No. 13. Late Heath.

Fig. 57. Late Heath, or Heath Cling, from Coxe's *View*

on its origin. The first was espoused by William Coxe, who said the Heath was "the finest in our country" and credited Daniel Heath of Maryland with introducing the seed from the Mediterranean before the American Revolution. The second attributed its introduction to the Prince nursery of Flushing, New York, where, after finding a naturalized seedling growing on a barren Long Island heath, William Prince, Sr., cultivated it for "many years before the revolution."[23]

The fruit of Heath Cling is very large, sometimes weighing a half pound, and it terminates in a point at the head. It ripens in September yet is frequently stored and eaten during October and November, a unique feature among peaches. The skin is creamy white, sometimes with a red blush, and "the juice is so abundant, as to make it difficult to eat this peach without injury to the clothes." The Heath was especially admired when preserved in sugar or brandy, "imparting a pleasant flavor of peach-pit bitterness." It was universally sold by nineteenth-century American nurseries and praised throughout the literature. John Hartwell Cocke, St.

George Tucker, and George Washington grew the Heath, which is still in cultivation.[24]

OLDMIXON CLING AND OLDMIXON FREE

In 1807 Timothy Matlack sent Jefferson cuttings of both the "much boasted" Oldmixon Cling peach and Oldmixon Free, "a fine peach" (pls. 20, 21). They differ in the way that the flesh adheres to the stone. The Oldmixon Cling ranked second only to the Heath in the praise it received from pomologists. Coxe declared it "an uncommonly fine fruit." The tree's origin is attributed to John Oldmixon, author of *The British Empire in America*, 1741, and it rivals the Heath as the oldest named American peach. Oldmixon Free originated very early in the nineteenth century from a seedling of the Cling, and by 1811 it was listed by the Landreth nursery of Philadelphia. Coxe described it as a "beautiful large peach" in 1817. The juice of the Oldmixon peaches is uncommonly candy-sweet.[25]

LEMON CLING
("Carolina Canada," Kennedy Carolina, "Lemon," Large Yellow Pineapple)

Jefferson also was sent cuttings of the "Carolina Canada" peach by Timothy Matlack, who said "when fully ripe, [it is] the most juicy and highest flavoured of all the Clingstone peaches. For preserving it is the best of all peaches. It retains more of the peach flavour in *brandy* than any other." Matlack undoubtedly was referring to Kennedy's Carolina, so named because a New Yorker, Robert Kennedy, brought the peach north from Charleston, South Carolina, before the Revolution to the Prince nursery, where William Prince, Sr., popularized it. Kennedy's Carolina was later known as Lemon Cling and Large Yellow Pineapple and likely was the "Lemon peach" Jefferson received from Walter Coles in 1816 (fig. 58, pl. 17). Coles's brother Isaac wrote that the seeds of the Lemon peach "will prove a great treasure if they can be defended against the attacks of the worms." Downing praised Lemon Cling as "one of the largest, and most beautiful of all the yellow fleshed clings." Named for its very large and lemon-shaped fruit, Lemon Cling was commonly sold in American nurseries be-

No. 8. Large Yellow Pine Apple.

Fig. 58. Large Yellow Pineapple, probably synonymous with Lemon Cling, from Coxe's *View*

ginning in 1790. It was still popular in California as a canning peach in the first half of the twentieth century.[26]

INDIAN BLOOD CLING
("black Georgia plumb peach," "Blood," Cherokee)
INDIAN BLOOD FREE
("black soft peach of Georgia")

One "Blood" peach tree was sent Jefferson in 1807 by the Washington nurseryman Thomas Main (fig. 59, pl. 17). In 1810 Jefferson planted forty-one stones of the "black plumb peach of Georgia" in the "New Nursery." These likely came from William Meriwether, who had passed on "black soft peaches of Georgia" in 1804 and "Georgia black" peaches in 1809. When pomological writers such as Miller, Coxe, Downing, and Hedrick discussed the Blood Cling peach, they attributed its origin to a French variety known as Sanguinole, a curiosity suitable mostly for preserving. Today the peach is known as the Indian Blood Cling, a name which unites the "Blood" peach of the French Sanguinole with the "Indian" peach that grows wild in the southeastern states of Georgia and Florida and was obtained by Jefferson as the "black plumb peach of Georgia." The fruit, entirely splashed and mottled with scarlet, tigerlike stripes, is sometimes twelve inches round. The skin resembles a beet: scarlet, tough, stringy, and meaty, although pleasantly flavored and brisk. Blood Cling is a fine peach to eat out of hand but is mostly used for pickling and preserving. It was commonly listed by early nineteenth-century nurseries and is still offered in the trade.[27]

POPPA DI VENERE
("Teat," Breast of Venus, Teton de Venere)

Philip Mazzei shipped stones and cuttings of Poppa di Venere to Jefferson at Monticello and in Washington, where nurseryman Alexander Hepburn custom propagated trees for the president (figs. 60–62, pl. 13). The Breast of Venus originated

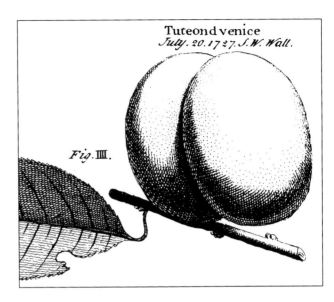

Fig. 60. Teton de Venere from Langley's *Pomona*

Fig. 59. Bloody peach, possibly synonymous with Jefferson's "Blood" or "black plumb peach of Georgia," from Langley's *Pomona*

Fig. 61. Teton de Venus from Duhamel's *Traité*

No. 12. Teton de Venus.

Fig. 62. Teton de Venus from Coxe's *View*

Alberge Jaune.

Fig. 63. Alberges peach from Duhamel's *Traité*

in France before 1667; according to Mazzei, his Italian version, the Poppa di Venere, was "much larger than those of France, I have had them in my garden up to eleven ounces." Most early pomologists concurred in describing the taste of the Breast of Venus as "melting" and "rich." The fruit is large, roundish, and straw-colored with a bright red marbled blush on the exposed side. Coxe mentioned a long furrow "running from the stem to the point at the head of the fruit, which is so large as to characterize it." Hedrick described the nipple as "prominent" and "obtuse," while Miller labeled it a "dug" or "bubby." Jefferson was among the first Americans to grow the Breast of Venus, which was regularly offered by nurseries beginning in the early 1800s.[28]

OTHER JEFFERSON PEACH VARIETIES

Alberges, another variety in the Mazzei shipment, was carried to Monticello in 1806 from Washington (fig. 63, pl. 14).

It originated in France in the seventeenth century and was the parent of a race of yellow-fleshed peaches known in America as melocotons. Giorgio Gallesio, an Italian pomologist, noted in 1817 that while Alberges "was quite valuable for its beauty I have seen it only in the garden of the late Signor Filippo Mazzei."[29]

Algiers Yellow ("large yellow clingstone") was ordered by Jefferson in 1791 from the Prince nursery, the exclusive distributors of this "handsome round fruit, weighs 12 ounces, ripe October 15th."[30]

Apple ("Pesca Mela," "melon"), according to Mazzei, "is a freestone with a greenish-white skin. It melts in the mouth like the Poppa di Venere; it also keeps until the last stages of maturity a little bit of acidity, which makes it particularly tasty" (pl. 15). Gallesio said it was "not without value, having a delicateness and perfume, but so singular for its exterior aspect that . . . one could not exclude it from a collection." Gallesio described the apple-shaped fruit as flattened, irregular, with greenish-white skin tinged with red. This variety was likely among the unique Jefferson introductions into the United States.[31]

"General Jackson's" was obtained from General James Jackson of Georgia and was mentioned casually by Jefferson in 1807.[32]

Green Nutmeg was also purchased from the William Prince nursery in 1791. More commonly known as Early Ann, this small-fruited, white-skinned English variety with white flowers was the earliest of all peaches. Despite criticisms of its slow growth and uneven productivity, the freestone Green Nutmeg was readily available commercially.[33]

"Lady's favorite" was sent to Monticello by Timothy Matlack, who described it as "a small yellow peach of exquisite flavor—a late importation from France—ripens full of juice."[34]

Maddelena was still another Italian peach from Mazzei, who said it "matures so quickly that its last fruit precedes the first of all other kinds." Gallesio said it was "one of the most valuable of Italian peaches": medium-sized, white fleshed, irregular-shaped, with skin a fresh red on a foundation of yellowish-white. Its name arose because it is harvested around the time of the feast of Magdalene, July 22.[35]

"Magdalene" (Red or White Magdalene) cuttings were sent to Monticello by James Taylor in 1806. Trees were then planted in the orchard four years later. Taylor said he had "never seen any of the kind in Virginia." Taylor's "Magdalene" is likely the French Red Magdalen or White Magdalen, both of which were described by Coxe and Downing and, according to Mazzei and Gallesio, were distinct from the Italian Maddelena.[36]

Malta stones were planted in the nursery in 1813. An old European cultivar that received mixed reviews in the United States, the large fruit of Malta has a pale-green skin blotched with purple and a greenish flesh.[37]

"Mammoth" cuttings were sent by Matlack, who described the variety as "large, perfectly beautiful and ripens tender—a clingstone."[38]

Morris's Red Rareripe ("Italian red-freestone") and Morris's White Rareripe ("Italian White-freestone") were also sent by Matlack, who said they had been imported into the United States by Robert Hunter Morris, governor of Pennsylvania. According to Downing, the Red "is everywhere justly esteemed for its acknowledged good flavour, beauty, and productiveness," while the White "is everywhere cultivated." Both late-season freestones, the Red has a handsome red and white skin and a rich, sugary taste; the White has creamy, slightly downy skin and white flesh. Some still refer to particularly juicy peaches as "rareripes."[39]

"October" peach stones were sent to Monticello by Washington nurseryman Thomas Main in 1807 (fig. 64). The Monticello nursery was enlarged to accommodate them. Late-season varieties generally were esteemed for preserving purposes.[40]

"Plumb" peaches were clingstones, which were especially treasured by gardeners around 1800 as dessert fruits. Jefferson cultivated numerous "plumb" peaches, usually described by the color of their flesh; for example, in 1786 he directed the planting of "fine white, red, & yellow plumb peaches from Balyal's [a Monticello workman]." They seemed a particular source of pride to Jefferson when he wrote that France did not have "sun enough to ripen our plumb peach."[41]

Portugal was a European clingstone also grown by Washington at Mount Vernon. Jefferson received stones from George Mason of Gunston Hall in 1780 ("they should be secured from moles with slabs, or some such thing, let into the ground") and trees from Thomas Main in 1807. The Portugal is a mid-to-late-season, very large clingstone with spotted dark red fruit and white flesh that turns red at the stone.[42]

San Jacopo was among the Italian varieties sent by Mazzei. Also known as St. James, it was described by seventeenth-century herbalist John Parkinson as a "faire great yellowish browne peach, ripe at Bartholmew tide, of a very pleasant taste."[43]

"Soft" peaches were freestones, usually late-season preserving types, also called melocotons. Jefferson grew at least ten kinds of "soft" peaches: "very late soft peaches from J. Scott," 1778; "soft peaches from T[imothy] Lomax," "October soft peaches," and "November soft peaches," 1810; "early soft peaches from Mr. Clay," "large yellow soft peaches," "fine white soft," "large white soft," and "fine soft peaches of August," 1812. The late-season, yellow-fleshed freestones were popular for preserving purposes, and Downing felt they derived from the French Alberges.[44]

Vaga Loggia peaches, both freestone and clingstone, were among the shipments from Mazzei, who said that this variety "matures with a red and yellow skin. The taste is different and distinct but excellent. To make it more pleasing it is necessary to remove the skin because the part closest to the skin is best" (pl. 16). Mazzei also noted that he had never seen the Vaga Loggia outside of Italy. Gallesio said they were named for the ducal garden, Vaga Loggia, outside of Florence during the reign of the Medici.[45]

Fig. 64. October peaches ripening in the south orchard

Cherries

FOR USE OR DELIGHT

When he [Jefferson] walked in the garden and would call the children to go with him, we raced after and before him,
and we were made perfectly happy by this permission to accompany him. Not one of us in our wildest moods
ever placed a foot on one of the garden beds, for that would violate one of his rules. . . . He would gather fruit for us,
seek out the ripest figs, or bring down the cherries from on high above our heads with a long stick,
at the end of which there was a hook and a little net bag.

—Virginia J. Trist, 1839

Unlike the two major fruits, the cherry was hardly a farm necessity; neither a cider fruit nor a livestock feed, it was a culinary luxury that supplied "precious refreshment" early in the season when few fruits were ripe. Cherries were the third most common fruit tree at Monticello, as they were in colonial Virginia, and in 1811 the south orchard contained 48 cherry trees along with the 84 apples and 160 peaches. Many Virginia farms had cherry trees, but orchards including only cherries, or even with cherries, were unusual. The choice English cultivars like Carnation or May Duke were mostly reserved for the fruit garden as connoisseur dessert fruits, while seedling sour cherries, Morellos, and sweet Black Hearts were planted casually in the yard for pies and preserves or decoratively along roads. There was a type of cherry for everyone. They did not necessarily function as orchard trees but could be a dooryard ornament, a border around the kitchen garden, or an allée for a decorative lane or avenue.[1]

Two Old World species, *Prunus cerasus*, the sour or pie cherry, and *Prunus avium*, the sweet cherry, are the chief cultivated types. Both species, particularly the sour, are adaptable to a range of soils and climates, and of all fruit trees, the cherry probably requires the least amount of care and provides the greatest return under a gardener's neglect—unusual

for an Old World fruit tree. But the cherry is also a spectacular ornamental tree. Its snow-white storm of flowers appears early in the spring, followed in May or June by shiny red berries crowning the tree. Jefferson recognized the cherry as a barometer of the spring season, and his thirteen notations regarding its blooming date at Monticello reflect his regard for its ornamental qualities. The sweet cherry grows to forty feet in height, and its cone-shaped, regular habit and form distinguish the species as an elegant shade tree. The sour cherry is smaller, for a horticulturist more manageable, and its crown is rounded, spreading, symmetrical, and regular.[2]

In a Garden Book entry of 1810 Jefferson noted "the cherry trees along the brow of the garden wall." These seven trees—May Dukes, Carnations, and Black Hearts—formed an irregularly spaced decorative and shady border along Monticello's 1,000-foot-long kitchen garden (fig. 65). Jefferson's acknowledgment of the cherry's ornamental value continued a long-standing custom of planting trees along walkways, roads, and within the garden enclosure. In 1768 Philip Miller noted that the French lined their avenues with the Black Heart cherry. In eighteenth-century Virginia, George Washington had a "cherry walk" at Mount Vernon, and William Byrd observed "an avenue of cherry trees" in 1732 at Governor Spotswood's Enchanted Castle west of Fredericksburg.

Fig. 65. Cherry tree
on the border of the
kitchen garden

George Mason planted an intriguing double avenue of Black Heart cherries at Gunston Hall, 1,200 feet long. The four rows of trees radiated from the house like the spokes of a wheel to create clever optical illusions. Outside Baltimore in 1777 John Adams observed "two fine rows of large cherry trees" leading from the elegant house at Chatsworth (later Gray's Gardens) to the public road. While in Pennsylvania about the same time, Swedish botanist Peter Kalm observed cherries "planted in great quantities before the farmhouses and along the highroads," and in New York he "found them very common again, near the gardens." William Robert Prince, the fourth proprietor of the Prince nursery, reported that Long Island roads were lined with *Prunus avium*, "and hundreds of children regale themselves with the fruit at the period of its maturity." Today, fruiting cherries have been replaced by sterile-fruited crabapples or flowering cherries, or by other purely ornamental flowering trees such as the flowering dogwood; but as late as 1914 U. P. Hedrick remarked, "The cherry is probably the most popular of temperate climate fruits for the home yard, being planted more commonly than any other tree-fruit . . . in the dooryard, garden, and along the roadside."[3]

In 1981 archaeological excavations at Monticello uncovered four wine bottles filled with preserved cherries in a kitchen yard dry well, which was a storage pit that had been covered over with soil (fig. 66). The cherries, of which there were between 175 and 232 in each bottle, were in a remarkable state of preservation. A similar discovery occurred at Wetherburn's Tavern in Williamsburg in 1965 when forty-seven bottles, filled with murky liquid, cherry pits, stalks, and between 72 and 249 intact cherries, were unearthed. The large quantities in each bottle suggest that the cherries were not being brandied, a common practice in colonial Virginia, but that they were being stored and preserved for later use. William Byrd in 1709 discussed such a technique: "Then we had some cherries which had been scalded in hot water which did not boil and

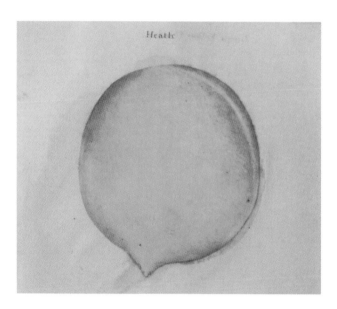

Pl. 18. Heath Cling from Coxe's 'View"

Pl. 17. Large Yellow Pineapple (*top*), considered synonymous with Lemon Cling, and the Cherokee, or Indian Blood Cling, from Coxe's "View"

Pl. 19. Heath Cling peach ripening in the south orchard

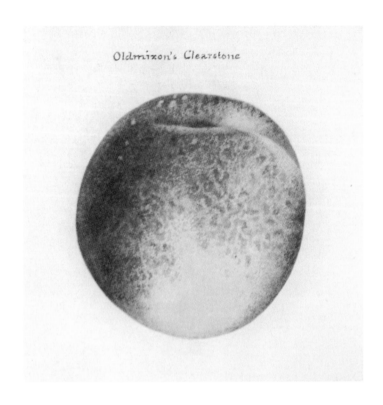

Pl. 20. Oldmixon Cling from Coxe's "View"

Pl. 21. Oldmixon
Free peaches

Pl. 22. May Duke cherry from William Hooker's *Pomona Londinensis*, 1817

Pl. 23. Carnation (*top*) and White Heart (*bottom*) from Coxe's "View"

Pl. 24. Red Heart, White Heart, and Black Heart from Brookshaw's *Horticultural Repository*

Pl. 25. Kentish, English Bearer, and Carnation from Brookshaw's *Horticultural Repository*

Pl. 26. Seckel pear in the
south orchard

Pl. 27. Seckel pear from Coxe's "View"

Pl. 28. Beurré Gris, or Brown Beurré, pear from Hooker's
Pomona Londinensis

Pl. 29. Crassane pear from Hooker's *Pomona Londinensis*

Fig. 66. Cherries discovered by archaeologists in a dry well, an earthen storage pit, at Monticello in 1981

tionaries made with both sweet and sour cherries. But cherries are also a common wayside fruit; one eats them out of hand while walking through the orchard or as a refreshing interlude while weeding the garden. Jefferson implied that American cherries were superior to their European counterparts when he wrote that French "cherries and strawberries are fair, but I think lack flavor." The "American Farmer," on the other hand, said, "The sorts preferred in the country places seem to be the thick, tough, indigestible sorts, which are now and then the cause of sudden death in people who make too free in eating them." William Byrd, however, perceived the cherry as a therapeutic remedy for his ailing stomach: "In the afternoon I played billiards with my wife and was exceedingly griped in my belly. I ate as many cherries as I could get for it, but they did no good."[5]

Unlike apples and peaches, which were altered dramatically when cultivated by New World gardeners, the cherry is a distinctive European fruit that has retained a genetic stability since cultivated by the Romans. The cherry varieties listed and described by John Parkinson, Philip Miller, Batty Langley, and William Forsyth were familiar sorts and included the Carnation, Jefferson's favorite; Kentish, formerly called the "English" or Common Red cherry; May Duke, a cross between the sweet and sour species; Morello, the popular choice for preserves or brandy; and the various sweet "heart" cherries: Black Heart, Ox Heart, White Heart, and Bleeding Heart (fig. 67). Because of their traditional status in English horticulture, cherry scions were imported by the Virginia Company as early as 1622, and George Menefie, a merchant who arrived in 1623 and settled at Littleton on the James River near Jamestown, had a notable orchard that included cherries. In 1676 Thomas Glover said, "The meanest Planter hath store of Cherries, and they are all over Virginia as plentiful as they are in Kent. The Cherry-Trees grow more large generally than they do in England, and bear more plen[ti]fully without any painstaking of digging about them, or pruning them." Francis Michel and Hugh Jones observed that cultivated cherries were abundantly planted and reached "great perfection" in the early eighteenth century, and William Byrd procured fifty trees for Governor Berkeley at Green Spring in 1711. By the middle of the 1700s, when established peach varieties were virtually unknown, the

then [put] in bottles without water in them. They were exceedingly good." Cherries, as many as thirty pounds a year, also were dried at Monticello.[4]

Like apples and peaches, cherries were commonly made into refreshing liquors. Francis Michel admired Virginian cherry wine in 1702, and Mary Randolph's *Virginia House-wife* in 1826 included recipes for cherry brandy and cherry shrub, liquified cherries doctored with a small quantity of brandy. Cherry tarts, which Landon Carter ate "heartily of" in 1771, dried cherries, pies, and puddings were also common confec-

Fig. 67. Cherries from Langley's *Pomona*. Jefferson grew Carnation and Morello.

names of cherry cultivars began to appear in the listings of Virginia growers. William Smith's Surry County nursery listed the familiar cultivars — Black Heart, Carnation, Kentish, Morello, and May Duke — making it likely that some fine Old World dessert cherries were available to rural, middle-class growers.[6]

At Monticello, Jefferson made more references to the budding of cherries, fifteen, than to the asexual propagation of

any other fruit, and he noted a surprisingly large number of sources for both cherry trees and scion wood, ten, which suggests the widespread culture of cherry cultivars among Virginians. His forty-five notations regarding the planting of cherry trees at Monticello exceeded those for any other fruit-tree species. Most of the cherry plantings occurred in 1778 and 1783, and Jefferson's few allusions after the initial establishment of cherry trees suggest that he was reasonably successful as a cherry gardener. He wrote to Isaac Coles in 1811 to announce the need to revive his collection; for this reason he looked forward to having Coles come over and teach his grandson Thomas Jefferson Randolph how to inoculate his grandfather's cherries. According to one visitor, George Ellicott, cherry trees were still bearing at Monticello fifteen years after Jefferson's death.[7]

Although Hugh Jones admired the "great perfection" of Virginia's cherry crop early in the 1700s, he acknowledged that the trees themselves suffered a certain malaise, probably because of fungus infestations. Both sour and sweet cherries suffer in the heat and humidity of Virginia, and they are sometimes stripped of their foliage by the first of August by attacks of various diseases such as powdery mildew, black knot, and cherry leaf spot, or shot-hole fungus (*Coccomyces hiemalis*), still a serious problem at Monticello. William White admitted that southern growers faced grave defoliation problems: "In cooler climates, some of the varieties are quite ornamental on account of their fine foliage and early white blossoms, but it stops growing and drops its leaves too early in this climate to be esteemed for this purpose." James Worth, a frequent correspondent to the *American Farmer*, complained in 1822 of "the premature decay of our [Morello] trees" due to a trunk excrescence caused by the plum curculio. He urged his readers to scrape away the decayed bark and apply a soap-based tonic to the wound. He also recommended that cherry trees be pruned to shade the trunk from the sun. Still, the cherry was not important enough as an economic crop for the earliest Virginians to counter with experimental control measures, and the cosmetic blights associated with this species usually do not weaken the tree enough to reduce its production of cherries substantially. The "American Farmer"'s assertion, "as it is with so little done to them, they are a common, and rather a mean fruit," is a fair statement about the horticultural management, although not necessarily the quality, of American cherries around 1800.[8]

CARNATION

The Carnation was Jefferson's favorite variety of cherry, "so superior to all others that no other deserves the name of cherry" (pls. 23, 25). He obtained budwood from Mordecai Debnam of Sandy Point in 1773 and from the Brandon estate along the James River east of Richmond a few years later. By 1783 when some of the Carnations began to bear, more than thirty-three trees were prospering in the south orchard. Trees were renewed in 1807 and 1811. Carnation was first mentioned by British botanist John Rea in 1676 and is generally identified with English pomology despite having originated on the Continent. It was widely distributed among Virginia growers— Tucker, Skipwith, George Mason, Washington, William Smith, and John Hartwell Cocke—and praised by William Coxe as "one of our most excellent cherries." Downing considered it "very handsome . . . highly esteemed here for brandying and preserving," and Hedrick said that "for a home plantation, it would be hard to name a better cherry of its kind." The name Carnation is derived from its variegated, immature fruit; however, being a sour cherry, the fruit was often dismissed from the table except when preserved or sugared in some way. The low-growing, spreading, almost drooping habit of the tree is a unique feature among cherry cultivars. The fruit is large and round, the skin at first yellowish-white but becoming a lively marbled red when ripe, and the flesh, which separates easily and freely from the stone, is unusually light and delicate. According to Coxe, the fruit's thin pulp kept the Carnation free from assaults by birds or insects.[9]

OTHER CHERRY VARIETIES GROWN BY JEFFERSON

August cherries were planted in 1783. William Prince said this late-ripening, acidic variety was best for preserving or brandy.[10]

Black Heart. In 1778 Jefferson recorded planting in row *i*

six "latter black heart" and one "forward black heart," both kinds budded from James Walker of nearby Castle Hill (pl. 24). Two Black Hearts were sent to Poplar Forest four years later, and in 1810 Jefferson said that "perhaps a black heart" was growing along the "long walk" of the vegetable garden. The Black Heart, a variety of *Prunus avium*, was praised by William Prince ("a fine cherry"), William Coxe ("a very fine, large, rich, cherry"), and Downing, who said "its great fruitfulness and good flavour, together with the hardiness and the large size to which the tree grows, render it every where esteemed." Black Heart was very popular and widely disseminated among eighteenth-century Virginia growers like William Smith, Tucker, Skipwith, Washington, and, later, John Hartwell Cocke. Downing noted that it was the most popular cherry variety in America in the middle of the nineteenth century. The Black Heart originated in Europe in the sixteenth century. It is a tall, handsome tree with a distinctively large and glossy sweet cherry leaf. The fruit is heart-shaped, somewhat irregular, medium-sized with shiny purple skin that turns a deep black when fully ripe.[11]

Bleeding Heart was transplanted from the nursery in 1783. Jefferson was one of the first American growers of this late-season sweet variety. William Coxe said it was a "very fine rich cherry . . . of very superior quality," and William Robert Prince heralded Bleeding Heart as "one of the largest and most beautiful cherries." The curious dark red fruit is heart-shaped and remarkable for the teardrop at its base.[12]

"Broadnax" was planted in 1773. This undescribed variety may have had its American origins with Colonel John Broadnax of York County whose family owned a notable Kentish cherry orchard, Harbleden Hill, in England.[13]

Cornelian (*Cornus mas*). Jefferson planted four seeds of "Ciriege corniole. (a particular kind of cherry)" in 1774. This is not a true cherry but a European dogwood, *Cornus mas*, once cultivated for its preservable fruit but now grown mostly as an ornamental.[14]

English Morello. Five "Myrilla" cherries were planted at Monticello in 1778 and four "large Morella" cherries in 1782. The English Morello, listed by Parkinson as early as 1629, is a late-season sour cherry reserved for culinary or preserving purposes. Coxe said, "It is the finest cherry we have, for pies,

Fig. 68. Kentish cherry from Langley's *Pomona*

cerasus—was, according to Downing, Late Kentish: "It is emphatically the Pie Cherry of this country, being more generally grown than any other sort, the poorest and most neglected affording so hardy a fruit in abundance." Early Richmond grows taller (15 to 18 feet) with a roundish, spreading head. The large, sour fruits ripen three weeks earlier. Hedrick described it as "the leading Sour Cherry of its season . . . possibly the most cosmopolitan of all cherries" because of its adaptability. Virginians such as St. George Tucker and John Hartwell Cocke, who ordered their Kentish cherries from the Prince nurseries, were surely growing the Late Kentish, the "pie cherry"; however, when William Smith listed the Kentish in 1755, he was likely referring to the Early Richmond, the Kentish cherry of England. Both were widely distributed among cherry fanciers.[16]

"May," "Large May" (Early Richmond?). In 1767 Jefferson inoculated the "May" cherry on four unidentified rootstocks and in 1790 recorded the location of two "large May" cherries obtained from Dr. George Gilmer. Miller's "May" was the May Duke; Virginia May and May were common nineteenth-century American synonyms for Early Richmond; and Parkinson's and Langley's "May" was *Prunus fruticosa*, a dwarf and very ornamental European species.[17]

May Duke ("May," "Duke"), a hybrid of *P. avium* and *P. cerasus*, is distinguished by rounded fruit, thin skin, and juicy, rather sweet flesh (fig. 69, pl. 22). Its English name, first mentioned by Rea in the seventeenth century, originated either from the French region where it flourished, the Medoc, or simply because it bears in May. Downing said the "invaluable" May Duke "is one of the most popular sorts in all countries," and it rivaled Black Heart in popularity around 1800. May Duke is remarkable for its tall-growing (30 feet), vase-shaped habit that is unique among cherry cultivars. It is one of the first cherries to ripen, in May. Jefferson planted trees in 1778 and 1782.[18]

"Tuckahoe grey heart" was planted in 1811. The trees, apparently named for the ancestral home of the Randolphs along the James River in Goochland County, were sent to Jefferson by Isaac Coles, who supplied many of the Monticello cherries.[19]

White Heart, first mentioned by Philip Miller in 1734, was

for brandy, for preserves, and for drying: it will keep in high perfection, when bottled, without sugar or spirits." The beverage bottles unearthed archaeologically at Colonial Williamsburg in 1965 contained Morello cherries. The most commonly mentioned cherry variety in eighteenth-century Virginia, English Morello is a small tree with a spreading, roundish crown and drooping branches. The tart fruit, at first a dark purple, becomes black when ripe, and the juice is a dark purple color similar to the fruit of the mulberry (the name Morello is derived from the genus name of the mulberry, *Morus*). The cherries are large, round, and somewhat heart-shaped.[15]

"Kentish" (synonymous with Early Richmond or Late Kentish) was planted by Jefferson in 1778 and 1783 (fig. 68, pl. 25). The Kentish cherry of England, of the county Kent, was first named Early Richmond in 1803 by William Prince, Jr., because the source for his nursery trees was the Virginia capital. Another "Kentish" cherry—very similar to the wild *P.*

Fig. 69. May Duke cherry
from Duhamel's *Traité*

widely distributed among early Virginia growers (pl. 24). The earliest of the Heart cherries, White Heart forms a large, somewhat erect tree, and its sweet, juicy fruits are medium-sized, heart-shaped, and colored a dull whitish-yellow that is tinged and speckled with red on the cherry's sunny side. Jefferson planted budded trees in 1778.[20]

Pears

LEISURE-CLASS FRUIT

Jefferson probably felt that pear cultivation in Virginia was hardly worth the effort as he wrote from Paris that European pears were not simply "better than ours" but "infinitely beyond anything we possess." He had only two trees growing in the south orchard in 1811, and despite writing the following year to his neighbor George Divers that he was "engaged in planting a collection of pears," Jefferson never provided specific varietal names for the few plantings that ensued. Jefferson's lack of enthusiasm for the pear reflected the species' relative unimportance on eighteenth-century Virginia farms. Until the 1820s orchards of only pear trees were unknown in Virginia; when pears were grown, they were planted as part of the apple orchard, in the garden, or isolated along a fence line, at the edge of a field, or along a roadway. The pear had no essential economic, culinary, or even ornamental functions; the best varieties were either difficult to locate or yet undiscovered; and most importantly, the pear is the most complex of all fruit trees to grow successfully, especially in Virginia's warm and humid climate, particularly in the microclimate of the south orchard.[1]

Unlike the cherry, apple, or peach—all democratic fruits widely disseminated throughout the social spectrum—a good pear was a distinctly connoisseur's treat, a gentleman's specialty, the fruit of the leisure class. William Byrd, as early as the 1720s, described twenty-nine varieties in his *Natural History*, more than any other species of fruit. George Washington fancied eighteen of the finest European varieties, all obtained from friends and neighbors and usually planted at the edge of the garden rather than among the more common orchard fruits. John Hartwell Cocke cultivated twenty-five va-

rieties, again often planting them as a garden border. The pear was associated with the Old World fruit garden, and nearly all the varieties grown in America until the middle of the nineteenth century were European in origin (fig. 70). Although Jefferson languished in his cultivation of the pear, a notable exception was his esteem for the Seckel, which originated near Philadelphia and was universally praised throughout the pomological world.[2]

Except for the Oriental pears, such as the easily grown yet poor-flavored Kieffer, that were introduced in the middle of the nineteenth century, most Old World cultivars suffer immeasurably in the hot, humid, drought-ridden Virginia summer. Perhaps most importantly, the prevalence of the dreaded fire blight, a bacterial disease first observed along the Hudson River in 1780 and documented in 1794, eliminated most commercial pear culture in the eastern United States and sooner or later destroyed or severely maimed any plantings of the species. The pear also compares unfavorably with other fruits that bear at the same time. Juicy, fragile plums, cherries, and peaches, unless preserved, require immediate consumption because they store so poorly, while the pear, to be at its best, requires a storage period of at least two weeks. Thomas Knight, the most respected of early nineteenth-century European fruit authorities, acknowledged that pears were "little subject to be stolen in situations where fruit does not abound." Although not nearly so common as cider, the fermented juice of the pear, perry, was a popular by-product whose production was begun in Britain by the Romans and peaked in England during the seventeenth and early eighteenth century. Orchards of perry pears were well known in cider districts such as Herefordshire, and perry varieties were

Fig. 70. Pear varieties from Langley's *Pomona*

distinguished by a curious transformation of the juice—from being harsh, rough, and astringent when eaten out of hand to a pleasing rich, sweet, sugary flavor when crushed. William Byrd referred to the "excellent" pear juice and apple juice that "in the Summer are much more pleasant, much sweeter and more healthful than wine. For [this] reason everyone drinks it." Despite Byrd's praise, there were few allusions to perry production in Virginia before 1820.[3]

Most travelers' descriptions assigned the pear only a supporting role in the evolving pageant of New World fruit. Thomas Glover in 1676 said, "There are some sorts of Pears,

but at very few Plantations; I have seen the Bergamy [Bergamot], Warden, and two or three other sorts, and these are as fair, large and pleasant as they are in England." Francis Michel in 1701 added that "there are also pears of all kinds, but they are not as common as the apples." John Lawson's listing of North Carolina pear varieties in 1709 matched those of the English herbalist John Parkinson eighty years earlier. By the middle of the eighteenth century, regional pear cultivars began to appear on the lists of Virginia nurseries. William Smith's Surry County nursery offered nine pear varieties in 1755, including May pear and Holt's Sugar, which were probably local seedlings of some quality that were named and consequently grafted. The trend toward the culture of native cultivars was also noticed in the varieties sold by Thomas Stratchan, a Richmond nurseryman, in 1795: Moore's Winter, Taylor's September, Lewis's Fine, and Maury's Fine were named for their local discoverers.[4]

Charles Carroll of Baltimore, George Washington, St. George Tucker, and John Hartwell Cocke almost exclusively cultivated European varieties purchased from northern nurseries or even Europe. None of them were planted in large quantities; most were the same cultivars—Bergamots, St. Germaine, Pound, Jargonelle, the Bon Chretiens, Warden, and the French types grown by Jefferson. It might be safe to assume, however, that gardeners lower on the social pyramid, without European contacts, the financial resources to send for fruit trees 500 miles away, or even the access to major urban nurseries, were growing native varieties selected by local horticulturists like Thomas Stratchan or William Smith, especially since the regional selections would be easier grown, possibly more resistant to fire blight, and surely better adapted to the Virginia climate. The pears offered by the Prince nurseries in 1771, 1790, and 1815, those sold by nurseries in Baltimore and Philadelphia before 1822, and the varieties described by William Coxe in 1817 were, with one or two exceptions, entirely of European origin. Another reason for the pear's limited popularity before 1820 was the failure of fruit growers to develop and popularize distinct American varieties.[5]

"An American Farmer"'s assessment of the extent to which the species was grown in 1803 was probably a fair generalization: "Pears in America are only from some one or two trees in the farmer's apple orchard or garden; merely for the fruit eaten, or for preserves or present culinary purposes." Peter Kalm blamed the failure of North American pears on a lack of care in their culture. Richard Parkinson, as blunt and scornful as usual, said pears "will not produce fruit at all in many parts of America, nor are they worthy of bearing the name here, and are only fit for hogs, as they have no flavour of the fruit in England." In 1950 U. P. Hedrick wrote, "The pear did not reach so high estate as the apple in colonial America, and one somehow feels that a great opportunity was missed." In *The Pears of New York* Hedrick dramatized the living monuments to early American pear culture near Boston, along the Detroit River, and in a few other isolated, French-settled midwestern towns—giant, to 100 feet, seedling pear trees that were still alive and standing near the turn of the twentieth century. Hedrick's marveling observations of the enormous seedling trees along the Detroit River, monarchs remarkable for their size, vigor, fruitfulness, disease resistance, and longevity, surely inspired his comment "that a great opportunity was missed," and in Virginia, one wonders if Thomas Stratchan's Maury's Fine pear might not have been one of those "opportunities."[6]

Fire blight (*Erwinia amylovora*) is the most virulent of orchard pests. Its vernacular name describes the effect of this malignant bacterial infection; leaves, flowers, twigs, branches, and entire trees suddenly wilt and take on a scorched, withered appearance as if blasted by a fiery torch. "No other disease causes such comfortless despair to the grower," remarked U. P. Hedrick in 1921. Fire blight is a peculiarly American disease, of little consequence to European-grown trees, and it was first described in 1794 in New York by William Denning. Judge Richard Peters attributed the disease in 1808 to atmospheric electricity: hanging iron objects like old horseshoes on stricken trees would only control "this floating fluid," until it built up in the air; at that point, "destruction partial or total is certain." Although William Coxe described sixty-five selected varieties, he remarked that successful pear culture was "doubtful" because of fire blight, which "arises from the rays of the sun operating on the vapour, or clouds, floating in the atmosphere, either by concentration or reflection." William Forsyth of London said blight was induced by "certain trans-

parent flying vapours" or the "reflection of the sun's rays from hollow clouds." By 1837 the Pennsylvania Horticultural Society was offering a $500 bounty for a fire blight cure. Deterrents included rags wrapped in sulfur, nails driven into the trunk, and a liquid drenching of soapsuds. A few years later A. J. Downing, while on the one hand acclaiming the pear "the favourite fruit of modern times," acknowledged that the blight was "the terror and despair of pear growers."[7]

SECKEL

Fruits and cuttings of the Seckel were sent to Jefferson in 1807 by Timothy Matlack, who described it as "a small pear to be gathered about the 10th of October—They are red upon the tree & ripen in about two weeks to a beautiful lemon colour —They are juicy and tender as the best of the Burser [Beurré] pears, and much sweeter" (fig. 71, pls. 26, 27). Jefferson subsequently planted the cuttings but later wrote to Matlack apologetically that they had not survived exposure to a spell of in-

No. 25. Seckle Pear.

Fig. 71. Seckel pear from Coxe's *View*

clement weather. However, after tasting the fruits sent by Matlack, Jefferson said, "They exceeded anything I have tasted since I left France, & equalled any pear I had seen there."[8]

The Seckel was not widely distributed among American fruit growers until William Coxe popularized it through his praise in *A View of the Cultivation of Fruit Trees* in 1817. He said, "It is in the general estimation of amateurs of fine fruit . . . the finest pear of this or any other country." Like the Newtown Pippin apple, the Seckel pear soon achieved an international reputation in 1819 when the prominent New York physician and horticulturist David Hosack sent the Seckel to England, where the London Horticultural Society pronounced it superior to their own autumn varieties. A. J. Downing extended the praise in 1849 when he wrote: "We do not hesitate to pronounce this American pear the richest and most exquisitely flavoured variety known. In its highly concentrated, spicy, and honied flavour, it is not surpassed, nor indeed equalled, by any European variety . . . [and] we consider no garden complete without it." Virginia fruit growers awarded the Seckel a "10" for its quality and adaptability to the state's soil and climate in 1903. Finally, U. P. Hedrick in 1914

remarked that the Seckel was "the standard of excellence," that it "stands alone in vigor of tree, productiveness, and immunity to blight, and is equalled by no other variety in high quality of fruit."[9]

The Seckel originated before the Revolution south of Philadelphia along the Delaware River on property originally owned by a German immigrant known familiarly as "Dutch Jacob," a popular cattle trader and noted hunter. Dutch Jacob would secretively distribute the pears to his friends late in the fall yet never divulged the location of the original tree, which may have been a seedling of an old German variety, Rousselet. It was not until the land was purchased by a Mr. Seckel that the pear was named and generally disseminated, at first around Philadelphia (Jefferson's source, Timothy Matlack, was from Lancaster), where it was sold by Landreth's nursery in 1811, then throughout the country.[10]

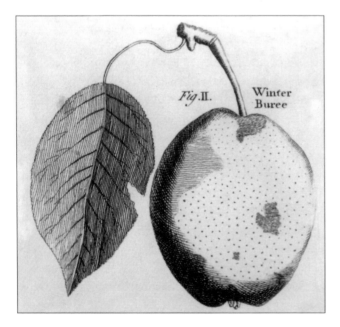

Fig. 72. Brown, or Winter, Beurré, or Beurré Gris, from Langley's *Pomona*

Fig. 73. Beurré Gris from Duhamel's *Traité*

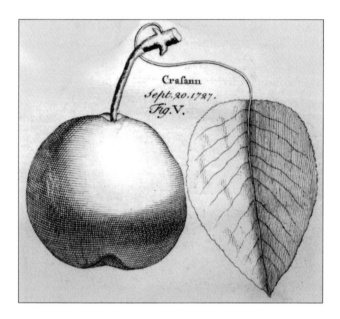

Fig. 74. Crassane pear from Langley's *Pomona*

Fig. 75. Crassane pear from Duhamel's *Traité*

Because of its American heritage, the Seckel is a vigorously growing tree with a regular form and dark, rich foliage. The small, trim, uniquely shaped fruit is formed in distinctive clusters. The skin, which imparts its characteristic flavor as much as the flesh, is usually colored a light brown, with a red blush toward the sun. The white flesh is melting, buttery, juicy, perfumed, and delicately flavored. Seckel is still an important commercial pear.[11]

OTHER PEAR VARIETIES GROWN BY JEFFERSON

In addition to the varieties described below, Jefferson commonly referred to pears by their season of bearing or the source of his trees. In 1778 he planted twenty trees from either Sandy Point or Green Spring and from Isaac Coles: "forward," "late," "fine late large," and "3 kinds of English"; in 1783, "a pear from Col. Lee"; in 1810 he "grafted 4 pear cuttings from Gallipolis. very large. eaten Dec. Jan. Taylor"; and in 1812 he planted "8 pears from Divers, 7 from Walter Coles," and "6 choice pears from Divers."[12]

Beurré Gris ("Bursé," Brown Beurré) was ordered from the William Prince nursery in 1791 (figs. 72, 73, pl. 28). This French cultivar, acclaimed "the finest pear in the world" by Sir Peyton Skipwith of Prestwould around 1800, was widely distributed among Virginia gentlemen growers and sold by northern nurseries in the early nineteenth century. Downing described it as the "prince of pears," yet William Kenrick in 1845 relegated Brown Beurré to his list of "outcast" varieties. The fruit is large, plump, nearly elliptical with a thick russeted yellowish-green skin.[13]

Crassane. In 1789 Jefferson returned home from France with nineteen pear trees, including four varieties: Royal, "Crassane," St. Germaine, and Virgouleuse. Crassane, named for the thickness (*crassus*) of the skin, was discovered by Jean de La Quintinye, gardener to Louis XIV, in the middle of the seventeenth century (figs. 74, 75, pl. 29). Like all the old French varieties, the popularity of Crassane diminished with the introduction of the famous Von Mons Belgium pears early in the

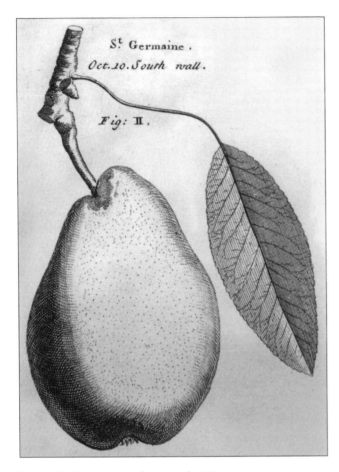

Fig. 76. St. Germaine pear from Langley's *Pomona*

Fig. 77. St. Germaine pear from Duhamel's *Traité*

1800s. The bright greenish-yellow fruit, flattened at either end, was "liable to canker and blight," according to Kenrick.[14]

Meriwether was noted by Jefferson in his 1778 orchard plan. John Hartwell Cocke detailed Jefferson's experience with this variety:

> On a visit he once made to Mr. Nick Meriwether, he informed [Meriwether] that he had once put up a parcel of these pears packed in tow in a trunk. Twelve months after supposing the pears were all used in getting some tow to wash his gun he found one of the fruit and that it was in a candied state like a preserve. The following year Mr. Jefferson put up some of this fruit in the like manner packed it in tow and in the course of the following winter went on to Congress then sitting at An-

napolis, from whence he was sent on a mission to France where he remained seven years. Upon his return to Monticello to his great astonishment he found his pears in the state of candied preserve.

Charles Downing, brother of Andrew, said the Taylor, or Meriwether, originated with Nicholas Meriwether, Jefferson's good friend and neighbor. The medium-sized fruit with a light green skin was mottled with a darker green russet.[15]

Royal, or Winter Royal, was less commonly distributed than the other French pears. Its name comes from an association with Louis XIV, who reputedly imported it from Constantinople. Royal has a large, somewhat triangular-shaped lemon-green fruit. Kenrick described Royal as "blighted and worthless."[16]

St. Germaine, or Richmond. Cuttings of the "Richmond" pear were sent in 1807 to Jefferson by Timothy Matlack, who

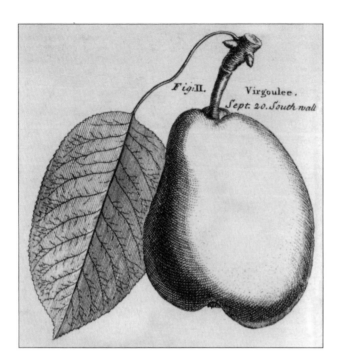

Fig. 78. Virgouleuse pear from Langley's *Pomona*

Fig. 79. Virgouleuse pear from Duhamel's *Traité*

said they were "worth particular attention." Richmond was a synonym of St. Germaine, one of the most widely distributed pear varieties, grown by Washington and Cocke and sold by every major early nineteenth-century nursery (figs. 76, 77). William Coxe said the St. Germaine was "a fine winter pear . . . sprightly beyond any other pear when the season is favorable," and Downing noted that it "is scarcely surpassed by any other juicy pear." Nevertheless, by 1848 Kenrick would state that it "has long since become an outcast and abandoned variety." This seventeenth-century pear, named for the French village where it originated, has a large, irregularly shaped greenish-yellow fruit.[17]

"Sugar" (Sucre Vert or Early Sugar?), planted in 1778, is a convenient term easily applied to any seedling pear that had a favorable taste.[18]

Virgouleuse originated in 1659 in the village of Virgouleé in the Limousin (figs. 78, 79). It was sold by major nurseries from 1771 to 1822, and Coxe said it was "highly deserving of extensive cultivation." The lemon-yellow, smooth-skinned fruit has a rich, perfumed flavor.[19]

Plums of the Old World and New

Three species of wild plum were the only native fruit-tree species planted in the south orchard: these included the "Horse Plum," likely *Prunus americana*, a small tree with variable yellow fruit found along streams; the Chickasaw, or "Cherokee," plum *Prunus angustifolia*, a large-growing shrub with small glossy leaves, red-barked branches, and smaller yellow or red fruit; and the "Florida" plum, probably *Prunus umbellata*, the hog or sloe plum. Most of our cultivated tree fruits originated in their wild form in the landmass somewhere between Asia and Europe. Although thousands of peach, apple, cherry, and other fruit cultivars were developed in America, their parents were these Old World species. But because of the pomological potential of the numerous native American fruits such as the indigenous plums, botanists and scientists have wondered about the effect on our cultivated fruit if America had been

Fig. 80. Flowering Chickasaw plum in the south orchard

the original cradle of civilization; if the native plums, cherries, crabs, grapes, mulberries, and walnuts had been cultivated for thousands of years in the New World rather than in Europe. Sweeter, more delicately flavored, and larger fruits —qualities developed in the Old World species—would have been more diligently selected from naturally occurring hybridization, and at the same time the vigor and adaptability of the native species would have persevered. Asa Gray, an early nineteenth-century American botanist, said, "It would be curious to speculate as to what our pomology would have been if the civilization from which it, and we ourselves, have sprung, had had its birthplace [in continental America] instead of the Levant, Mesopotamia, and Nile, and our old world had been open to us as a new world less than four hundred years ago." Although none of the cultivars which emerged from these native plums have found favor in European orchards, and they are scarce in commercial American production today, the potential of our American plums is probably greater than that of any other New World tree fruit. Of all the tree fruits grown at Monticello today, the Chickasaw plum is the healthiest and most vigorous with its clean, shiny, pest-free foliage and abundant fruit production (fig. 80). Unfortunately, while numerous cultivars did emerge from these wild plums, their place as a dessert fruit has been insignificant compared to the European and Japanese plum, *Prunus triloba*, which was introduced in 1876 and whose shiny, brightly colored fruits are now standard on supermarket shelves. As with the cultivated pear, it seems a great opportunity has been missed in the development of North American plums.[1]

Although Jefferson grew a surprising number of plum varieties, twenty-three, by 1811 there were only two plum trees in the entire south orchard. The cultivated plum, at least in the eighteenth century, was a distinctly European fruit which Jefferson himself acknowledged was better than those grown in the New World. European plums are difficult to grow in Virginia because of destructive fungi encouraged by the summer heat and humidity and the species' susceptibility to the plum curculio. Although a ripe plum is indeed a connoisseur's treat, the domestic uses of the fruit—for confectionary desserts, prunes, or plum liquors—never achieved popularity as they did in Europe. When the various plum species were

planted in Virginia around 1800, they were usually placed in a small corner of the orchard or in the gentleman's fruit garden. Still, Jefferson's trials with the plum were laudable. He planted nineteen plum trees in 1778, of which thirteen survived the first season and five began bearing in 1783, when he set out twenty-eight more trees that included fourteen varieties. He not only planted the three species of native plum but experimented with the choicest European varieties known at the time.[2]

The garden plums grown at Monticello emerged from the bloodlines of a diverse collection of European, American, and Asian botanical species. *Prunus domestica*, probably a naturally occurring hybrid of *P. cerasifera* and *P. spinosa*, was the parent of four of the most celebrated and historically significant cultivars. These include the standard of excellence in plums, Reine Claude, or Green Gage, with its handsome, round, bluish-green fruit; Prune plums, the source of an important commercial industry in Hungary as early as the sixteenth century; Yellow Egg, or Magnum Bonum, plums, distinguished by their large, oval fruits; and the dark blue Imperatrice types. Many of the earliest references to European plums in American gardens before the Revolution mentioned the Damson, *Prunus insititia*, legendary for its preserving and cooking qualities. The spicy Damson is also more adaptable to the climatic extremes of the continental United States. The mirabelle plums such as Drap d'Or (pl. 30) with their very sweet, freestone, round yellow fruit form another division of *P. insititia*. They were cherished by the French for the making of pastries, preserves, jellies, and prunes (fig. 81). A third European species, *P. cerasifera*, or Myrobolan plum, was also grown in eighteenth-century American gardens as a rootstock for *domestica* cultivars and as a distinct variety, Cherry plum (see pl. 30).[3]

Native plums, particularly *P. americana* and *P. angustifolia*, were among the first wild fruits to be domesticated in the New World. Although the European species adapted adequately to cultivation in northern gardens, their inability to thrive in other parts of North America left an opening for the development and breeding of native plums. Despite their difficulty in identifying the exact species — persimmons and cherries were often labeled "plumbs," and the native *Prunus* or plum flora that so readily hybridizes is remarkably com-

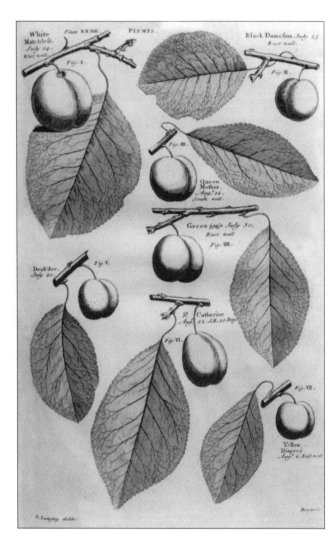

Fig. 81. Plums from Langley's *Pomona*, including Green Gage,
Queen Mother, and Drap d'Or, grown by Jefferson

with the Damasene [Damson]." John Lawson in 1714 described five American "plums," including two sorts of "Indian plums." Although the potential of the native plums was recognized by the earliest commentators on the natural history of the South and New England, it was not until after 1814 that the first indigenous cultivar, Miner, emerged from seedlings of *Prunus angustifolia* in Knox County, Tennessee.[4]

The cultivated plum's relative inability to thrive in Virginia gardens and orchards and its resultant secondary role were noted in the earliest landscape narratives. In 1676 Thomas Glover mentioned "some sorts of English plums but these do not ripen so kindly as they do in England," Francis Michel said they were "not common," and both John Lawson in 1714 and John Custis in 1736 concurred that plums "do not do well in this hot country." Like John Bartram in Pennsylvania and John Custis in Williamsburg, Byrd had complained to his English correspondent Peter Collinson about the "gumming of his plumbs, apricots, & nectarines." Prefacing his various solutions to this malady, probably caused by the curculio, Collinson wrote Byrd, "It is a great misfortune that you are deprived of tasting those fruits in their highest perfection & is very surprising it should happen so with you for I always imagin'd your climate much happier than ours, in perfecting delicate fruit." Richard Parkinson, from his farm outside of Baltimore in 1799, said that plums "have no flavour of the fruit in England," while the "American Farmer" in Forsyth's *Epitome* related how "very little attention [is] observed towards the *plum*." Bernard McMahon also referred to the "utterly destroyed" curculio-ridden plums and omitted them from his list of fruits suitable for an orchard. William Cobbett was puzzled by the plum's lowly status in the New World: "How is it that we see so few plums in America, when the markets are supplied with cartloads in such a chilly, shady and blighty country as England. . . . I have never tasted a better Green Gage than I have at New York." Except for the vigorous and adaptable Damson, plums were generally reserved for the fruit garden. Luigi Castiglioni noted plums in Virginia home gardens, and William Coxe suggested they were more suitable for the "private garden" than the orchard.[5]

As with apples, most plums grown in Virginia were identified by their cultivar name, particularly the queen of plums,

plex and botanically variable—the New World's first natural historians favorably reviewed wild plums. John Smith compared the red and white plums in Virginia to "our [European] hedge plums," William Strachey identified the Chickasaw plum (*Prunus angustifolia*) as a cherry, and William Fitzhugh mentioned the "Indian cherry," again probably the Chickasaw. Robert Beverley observed "the Black and the Murrey Plum, both of which are small, and much the same Relish

Fig. 82. Green Gage plum from Coxe's *View*   Fig. 83. Green Gage plum from Langley's *Pomona*

Green Gage (figs. 82, 83). Elizabeth Cocke of Williamsburg, wife of the colonial secretary, raved about Green Gage as early as 1751. Plum varieties grown before 1790, and by Jefferson, were familiar sorts, the favorites of such English gardeners and writers as Parkinson, Langley, and Miller. For example, William Smith's Surry County nursery offered Green Gage, Yellow Magnum Bonum, Orleans, Imperial, and Damascene, or Damson, in 1755, and a Baltimore nursery operated by Philip Walten sold Green Gage, Magnum Bonum, and Prune plums in 1788. The most obvious commercial source, at least for prosperous Virginians, was the William Prince nursery on Long Island, which sold thirty-one European plums in 1771. St. George Tucker ordered ten *domestica* varieties from the Prince nursery in 1784, and John Hartwell Cocke ordered ten cultivars from the Benjamin Prince nursery in 1816. Deliberate breeding of the European plum began in 1790 when William Prince, Jr., planted twenty-five quarts of Green Gage plum pits, which produced some remarkably desirable varieties: White Gage, Red Gage, and Prince's Gage. By 1811 the Landreth nursery in Philadelphia was listing not only these Green Gage seedlings but also three varieties developed by Joseph Cooper of Philadelphia, including Cooper's Large plum that was grown by Jefferson at Monticello and sold in

Philadelphia as early as 1800 (see pl. 30). The appearance of these American cultivars as seedlings of *Prunus domestica* proved to A. J. Downing that the European plum was "admirably suited" to the soil and climate of the mid-Atlantic states.[6]

There are few references to how plums were used in Virginia around 1800, explaining in part why the species were scarce in orchards. The choicest European cultivars obviously were treasured as a dessert fruit when they ripened in late July and August. In 1720 William Byrd wrote that he had "eaten so many plums that I could not sleep," and plum-induced flatulence, as it does today, perhaps restricted the fruit's popularity. During his journey through Provence, Jefferson encountered the French prune industry, which in the nineteenth century shipped dried plums around the world. Specific sugary varieties are considered necessary for the dried fruit to achieve its high-flavored expression, and Jefferson soon forwarded to William Drayton of South Carolina the Brignole plum, named for the town famous for its prunes. Dried Damson plums were probably more common than prunes. In 1629 London's John Parkinson mentioned that they were imported from France after being dried and stored in hogsheads. Landon Carter, who purchased dried plums in

Natural Drap d'or.

Yellow Gage.
or
Drap d'Or

Cherry Plum.
or
Mirobalan

Gualdi Plum.

Cooper's Plum.

Pl. 30. Plums from Coxe's "View"

The Green Gage!

Pl. 31. Green Gage plum from Hooker's *Pomona Londinensis*

Pl. 32. Green Gage plum in the south orchard

Pl. 33. Moor Park apricot from William Hooker's *Pomona Londinensis*

Albicocca di Germania

Pl. 34. German, or Peach, apricot from Gallesio's *Pomona italiana*

Pl. 35. Violet Hative nectarine, the oldest nectarine variety still in cultivation, from Hooker's *Pomona Londinensis*

bulk, complained in 1777 that "yesterday damson Pudding tormented me all the evening and places in the night I was really tormented awhile with wind." Mary Randolph's *Virginia House-wife* included a recipe for damson pudding, and the "American Farmer" also alluded to Damson-based tarts. Other European plums could be boiled, bottled, and preserved in sugared brandy just as cherries were.[7]

Jefferson planted both seedling and grafted ("inoculated") plums in the orchard, and his propagation techniques were similar to the efforts of other progressive fruit growers. Like John Hartwell Cocke and St. George Tucker, he experimented with the use of "wild plum" rootstock for the budding of his choicer European varieties. The "American Farmer" described how he grafted his weak-growing Green Gages on one native Chickasaw plum and a number of Damson stocks. The single tree on the Chickasaw stock produced ten times the fruit of the five Damson-based roots. "It was wonderful and curious to observe how like ropes of onions the gages grew along the twigs and small limbs of the Chickasaw grafted tree." The European tradition as espoused by Miller and Langley involved the use of seedling rootstock from vigorous-growing variants of the three Old World species: the Myrobolan from *Prunus cerasifera*, the Muscle from *Prunus domestica*, or the St. Julien from *Prunus insititia*. Peter Collinson, who often sought to bridge the gap between European and American horticulture, recommended that John Custis use wild plum rootstocks for his almonds, and he urged William Byrd and John Bartram to use seedling peach understock for their sickly plums or else avoid grafting altogether. Many growers, including the Virginia fruit gardeners, agreed with Peter Collinson and Robert Beverley that seedling-grown plum trees were healthier.[8]

The care of the plum received little specific attention from garden writers until later in the nineteenth century. An exception was Peter Collinson, who composed a detailed five-point plum cultivation program for William Byrd in 1730. In addition to the use of trees grown from seeds or on peach rootstock, he recommended planting the plums on the sides of streams for a constant supply of moisture, binding the trunk and mulching the roots with fresh green moss to prevent dessication from the sun, and radical pruning. The dis-

cussion by later American writers revolved around the most effective techniques for ridding the trees of the curculio. Correspondents in the *American Farmer* during the early 1820s recommended soil drenches of soapsuds, tar and fish oil, or mercury and mulches of clam and oyster shells. Downing, for whom the insect was an "uncompromising foe," as well as William White and John J. Thomas, recommended that plums be grown in heavy clay soils to partially seal the insect from its winter home. Downing's techniques for the eradication of the curculio mirrored the writings of most nineteenth-century pomologists: he recommended shaking the tree, paving the ground around the plum's roots, thinning the fruit, and turning livestock into the orchard. He was unique in advocating salt-based fertilizers specifically for the plum, and it was perhaps his cultural success that inspired his enthusiasm for the species. Nevertheless, one can gauge the vigor and health of European versus southern American–grown plums by the spacing recommended by the fruit authorities of the respective regions: London's Philip Miller urged gardeners to plant the trees twenty-four to thirty feet apart while William White of Athens, Georgia, suggested a twelve-foot spacing.[9]

CHICKASAW (*Prunus angustifolia*) ("Cherokee")

In 1812 Jefferson planted "plumbs, supposed Cherokee from Bailey" in eight south orchard locations. Once a Monticello gardener, Robert Bailey had become a Washington nurseryman by this date. Jefferson also included the "Cherokee" in a list of esculent plants in his *Notes on the State of Virginia*. The Chickasaw plum was often associated with Indian settlements by the earliest recorders of the region's natural history, and John Bartram assumed it had been brought east from the Mississippi by Indian tribes; however, modern botanists consider it indigenous to the piedmont and coastal plain of the Southeast.[10]

George Washington planted "Cherokee" plums in his fruit garden, St. George Tucker and the "American Farmer" used the "Indian plumb" as rootstock for European varieties, and Bernard McMahon included the Chickasaw in his list of "select" fruit varieties. Like most native plants the Chickasaw was not considered a marketable item by early nurseries, but it probably was cultivated to some extent by frontier gardeners without access to commercial sources. William White, providing his uniquely southern perspective, was among the first writers to urge its introduction into the garden; he said "the fruit is much enlarged by garden culture." Many later nineteenth-century fruit writers called for horticultural improvements, and by 1900 promising cultivars named Newman, Pottawattamie, Wild Goose, Miner, Wayland, Ogeechee, and Transparent were considered offspring of *Prunus angustifolia*.[11]

The Chickasaw plum grows twelve to fourteen feet with a cinnamon-colored cherrylike trunk, a suckering, thorny habit, and a thick bushy head. The leaves resemble those of the peach but are half the size and shinier. The fruit, three-quarters of an inch in diameter in the wild, are round, thin-skinned, and either yellow or red. The trees are prolific and universally healthy and vigorous.

GREEN GAGE

The Green Gage is the most celebrated plum variety of the last four centuries (pls. 31, 32). Jefferson planted twenty-one budded trees, some grafted on wild plum rootstock, in the south orchard in 1783. At the beginning of the sixteenth century, Francis I, king of France, named it Reine Claude after his wife, Claudia. Although described by Parkinson in 1629 as Verdoch, it did not receive its English name until John Gage, a Roman Catholic priest in Paris, sent young trees before 1724 to his brother, Sir Thomas Gage, near London, where the gardener lost the label. The fame of Green Gage soon spread throughout the English-speaking world. Elizabeth Cocke of Williamsburg wrote to a friend around 1751: "I met with the Green Gage plumb so much celebrated of late years. I've sent you some of the stones." Its appearance on the nursery list of William Smith in 1755 and in the fruit gardens of many nineteenth-century gentlemen — St. George Tucker, John Hartwell Cocke, the Skipwiths, and George Washington — suggests the popularity this variety had achieved in Virginia at an early date. Green Gage was the most intensively documented of Jefferson's 170 fruit varieties (see appendix).[12]

The popularity of the Green Gage only increased through the nineteenth and into the twentieth century. William Forsyth praised its "exquisite taste" that "eats like a sweetmeat," William Coxe proclaimed it "universally acknowledged to be the finest plumb of this or any other country," and Downing said, "The Green Gage is universally admitted to hold the first rank in flavour among all plums, and is everywhere highly esteemed." The Green Gage's handsome greenish-blue fruit, sometimes with a faint reddish russet on the sun side at maturity, is the variety's most striking feature. The flesh is pale green with a melting, juicy, rich, and candy-sweet flavor.[13]

MAGNUM BONUM
(Yellow Egg, Mogul, White Imperial)

Jefferson planted three Magnum Bonum plums in 1778, grafted on wild plum rootstock, and he set out three more grafted trees in 1781 that were thriving by 1783. This *domestica* plum had numerous synonyms; the "Mogul" plum Jefferson planted in the nursery in 1778 and the Yellow Egg scions he grafted in 1780 from the Prince nursery were Magnum Bonum. In February 1804 John Armstrong sent scions of the Egg plum, "as large as a hens egg light coloured rich & sweet with a small stone. will succeed by Engrafting on a Damson, Wild Plum or Peach Stock, I generally cut my cions at this Season of the year, and place one end of the cuttings about two inches in the ground in a perpendicular position and there let them remain until the proper season for placing them into the stock—I practice Tongue Grafting, and seldom lose five trees out of one thousand, have had trees to bear the second year after ingrafting them."[14]

The Magnum Bonum was first mentioned in 1676 by John Rea, and it became a standard English cultivar described by Langley and Miller. Not a choice dessert fruit, this plum was reserved for baking, preserving, or sweetmeats and was especially esteemed for its large, handsome golden yellow appearance. Magnum Bonum was sold by William Smith in 1755, was grown by Tucker and Washington, and was common in nursery offerings in the early 1800s. The synonym Yellow Egg, a distinctly American name which accurately describes the fruit's appearance, first appeared in William Prince's 1771 catalog. Coxe said this "most beautiful bright yellow fruit" was the "most superior plum for preserving," Downing described it as "very popular." Many nineteenth-century pomologists were disappointed that the promise of such a large, handsome fruit was not fulfilled when eating out of hand. The yellow flesh, especially acidic before ripe, achieves a mild sweetness when finally mellow late in the season (mid-August in Charlottesville), and the flavor is "very pleasant and much superior to most preserving plums," according to Coxe. The Magnum Bonum was still a commercial plum early in this century and today is available for the home orchard.[15]

OTHER JEFFERSON PLUMS

Nine *domestica* plum varieties were grafted by Jefferson in 1780: "yellow eggs, large white sweet, Orleans, Imperatrice, Red Imperial, White Imperial, Drap d'or, Royal & Apricot plumbs from N. York grafted on Wild plumb stock Mar. 80" (fig. 84). He designated orchard locations for two trees of the Orleans and one of the Apricot in 1782, but the remaining seven varieties were illogically intended for only two sites in row *e*, perhaps because only two trees survived his propagation efforts. The source for the scions was undoubtedly the Prince nursery, the only large commercial nursery in New York at the time and the only American source for such a collection.[16]

Apricot was also purchased from the Prince nursery by St. George Tucker and John Hartwell Cocke. It was described as early as 1629 by John Parkinson: "a good plum when in perfection, but that is seldom because of a tendency to crack." Apricot has a middle-sized, roundish, freestone fruit with yellow skin covered by a white bloom.[17]

Brignole. After sampling the celebrated Brignole prunes when touring through Provence and shipping sixteen "prunieres" to William Drayton in 1789, Jefferson purchased four trees of this prune variety from the William Prince nursery in 1791. Philip Miller proclaimed Brignole "the best Plum for sweetmeats yet known." American growers soon found such a variety, suited to the sunny Mediterranean skies of Provence, would not thrive in the eastern United States. The dry, yellow, sugary flesh was ideal for drying.[18]

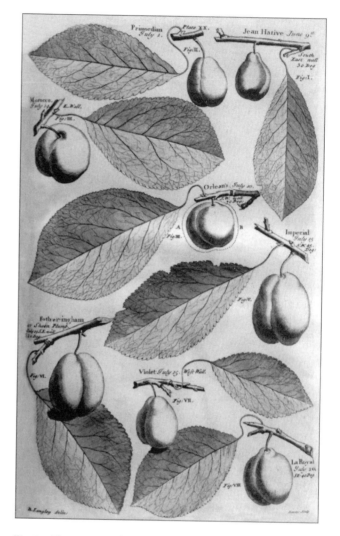

Fig. 84. Plum varieties from Langley's *Pomona*, including Royal, Imperial, and Orleans, grown by Jefferson

Cooper's Large. In 1807 Timothy Matlack sent Jefferson "Coopers plum, a seedling from the Green Gage grafted on the Wild Plum." Joseph Cooper of Gloucester County, New Jersey, was, according to U. P. Hedrick, "the first man in America to undertake as his life work the breeding of plants." Coxe said Cooper's Large was the largest plum he had ever seen (see pl. 30). The oval-shaped, dark purple fruit has a rare blend of sweetness and acidity.[19]

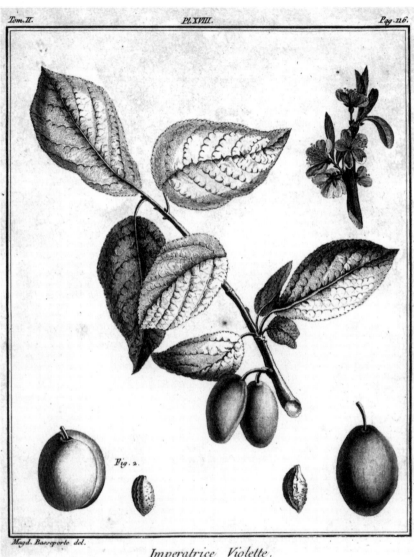

Fig. 85. Blue Imperatrice plum
from Duhamel's *Traité*

Damsons ("Damascene") were planted at Monticello in 1778, and two trees were bearing by 1783. The ambiguous name Damson may refer to the botanical species, the horticultural group of preserving plums, or the particular cultivar Jefferson was probably growing, the Common Damson. As early as 1629 Parkinson described four different varieties of Damson—Black, Large, Blue, and White—reflecting its pop-

ularity in England. Hedrick believed that most of the allusions to plum growing before the Revolution referred to the Common Damson, and this preserving plum was well known in Virginia, cultivated by Washington and Cocke and the source of Landon Carter's indigestion in 1777. Named for the city of Damascus and little changed in two thousand years, this ancient fruit comes true from seed and escapes easily from cul-

Fig. 86. Mirabelle plum from Duhamel's *Traité*

tivation. In 1849 Downing said the "common, oval, blue Damson is almost too well known to need description." The distinctive and beautiful dark Damson skin, purple with a thick blue bloom, provides the astringency and tartness necessary for good preserves.[20]

Drap d'Or, an *insititia* cultivar from the seventeenth century, was endorsed by Miller ("full of excellent juice") and Langley ("a most valuable plum") (see pl. 30). Although uncommon in early nineteenth-century nurseries, William Coxe said the Drap d'Or was "a most valuable fruit." The yellow fruit, streaked with red when exposed to the sun, has a rich, yellow, sugary flesh.[21]

"Florida" (*P. umbellata*?). In 1814 Jefferson "planted stones of the native Florida plumb, said to yield fruit in 2. years from the stone." There are at least three native Florida plum

species, including hog plum, *Prunus umbellata*, which produces a small orangish-red to purple fruit suitable for culinary purposes but barely edible otherwise.[22]

Six Horse plums (*P. americana* or *P. insititia*) were planted in 1778. The European "Horse" plum was often regarded as a Damson seedling in the American pomological literature, yet the native *P. americana* was also called "horse." Downing said *P. americana* was "a very common and inferior fruit, which reproduces itself from seed, and is sometimes naturalized in the gardens of the middle states."[23]

Imperatrice was another ancient European plum with numerous synonyms: Imperial, Imperial Violet, and Blue Imperatrice (fig. 85). "One of the finest of the late plums," according to Downing, the intensely violet-black clingstone fruit has a rich, sugary flavor best enjoyed when shriveled on the tree.[24]

"Large white sweet." In his 1771 catalog William Prince, Sr., said the White sweet plumb was "bigger than a hen's egg." It was probably a promising seedling of the Yellow Egg, or Magnum Bonum.[25]

Mirabelle. Philip Mazzei included plum stones of the Mirabelle in his shipment to Jefferson in 1804 (fig. 86). Seedlings were carried to Monticello in 1806. Mirabelle is a very old French variety of the Damson group, *Prunus insititia*, little known in America until the middle of the nineteenth century. Downing said Mirabelle was "a very pretty little fruit, exceedingly ornamental on the tree." Its yellow-skinned, red-speckled fruit has a sweet orange pulp valued for preserving because of its perfume.[26]

Muscle (*P. domestica*), a primitive form of the species European plum, was planted by Jefferson in 1767, probably at Shadwell. Although Parkinson described three types of "Mussel plumme's" ("of very good taste"), by the mid-eighteenth century it was regarded as suitable only as a rootstock. The teardrop-shaped dark red or black fruit has thin skin and a dry, insipid pulp.[27]

Orleans, except for Magnum Bonum, was the most widely distributed of the Prince plum varieties sent to Jefferson. It was sold by Smith and many early nineteenth-century nurseries; grown by Tucker, Washington, and Cocke; and described by Langley ("very valuable"), Miller, and Coxe ("fine and delicate"). Cultivated chiefly for its productiveness, the Orleans has a dark red to purple fruit and yellow flesh.[28]

Red Imperial (Red Magnum Bonum) was celebrated early in the seventeenth century by the English plant explorer and renowned gardener John Tradescant, Sr. Downing felt the flavor "harsh," yet it was "seen in abundance in our markets" by 1848, mostly because of its culinary possibilities. The shape of the large, dark red, egg-shaped fruit is similar to its yellow-skinned cousin, but the flesh is coarser, dry, and of only fair quality.[29]

"Regina" (Queen Mother, or Damas Violet?). Along with Regina Claudia (Reine Claude, or Green Gage), Mirabelle, White Imperial, and Boccon del Re, this was another plum sent by Mazzei in 1804. The Queen Mother plum was briefly described and illustrated by Parkinson and Langley, named the Damas Violet by Miller, and called "a neat little reddish plum, long known in European gardens" by Downing. The Queen Mother has a small, roundish-ovate, reddish-violet fruit. Like Mirabelle and Boccon del Re, this might have been a Jefferson introduction into North America.[30]

Royal was a unique Prince offering until well into the nine-

teenth century. Miller praised its "fine sugary juice," Forsyth found it "equal to the Green Gage," and Downing said it was "undoubtably one of the richest plums." The fruit is distinguished by the remarkable thick bloom on its reddish-purple skin.[31]

OTHER PLUMS

Boccon del Re, translated as the "King's morsel," or colloquially, "bull's balls," was one of the five varieties of plum stones sent by Philip Mazzei to Jefferson in 1804, but apparently Alexander Hepburn, the Washington nurseryman and propagator of this Italian shipment, failed to successfully germinate this variety. In 1810 Jefferson noted that he grafted six "large blue" plums in the nursery from south orchard trees located at either *d.27* or *e.36*, both sites of an earlier planting of the "Horse" plum, *Prunus americana,* or Damson, *P. insititia*. The "small green plums" he planted in the nursery in 1778 were possibly Green Gage, while the "purple prune" he received from Timothy Matlack is nearly impossible to identify precisely.[32]

Apricots

PRECIOUS BUT PRECARIOUS

Apricots are variously eaten, some delighting to eat when crisp, others when mellow, or a little soft, but not mealy—
which last, in my humble opinion, is the best because then all the Juices are in their utmost Perfection. Some delight
to eat them from the Tree; others not until the next Day after gathering, which of the two forms seems to
be the best, being gathered in the Cool of the Evening, and laid singly on dry Vine leaves.

—Batty Langley, *Pomona,* 1729

Although he admitted that the flavor of European-grown apricots (*Prunus armeniaca*) was superior, Jefferson planted as many as fifty-four trees in the south orchard, including eight varieties, more than any other Virginian before 1820. He set out sixteen grafted trees in the south orchard in 1778 and diligently replaced them with fourteen more in 1783. In 1790 he ambitiously sowed seventy-two apricot stones directly into the orchard and in 1809 planted sixty-eight seeds in the nursery. Jefferson received apricot trees, scions, and seeds from George Wythe, William Prince, Philip Mazzei, John Threlkeld, George Jefferson, and Timothy Matlack. Jefferson documented his admiration for the Melon apricot, "the best fruit in this country [France]," and Peach apricot, "the finest fruit which grows in Europe," and he also grew the standard of apricot excellence for the last two hundred years, Moor Park. Jefferson experimented with a variety of propagation techniques, using both peach and plum rootstock as well as apricot seedlings. Despite his relentless efforts, by 1811 there were only seven apricot trees in the south orchard, the fruit and trees themselves likely succumbing to the twin devils of apricot culture: spring frost and curculio.[1]

Although the apricot was not common in Virginia orchards around 1800—in fact, only three farm-sale advertisements in the *Virginia Gazette* between 1736 and 1780 mention the species—trees were cherished by wealthy and sophisticated growers. The apricot is the ultimate fruit garden tree: a handsome ornamental with its white flowers late in winter, cherrylike bark, and large, healthy, glossy leaves. When St. George Tucker considered the role of the nine species of 122 trees he purchased from the Prince nursery in 1787, it was an apricot that he planted out as a landscape specimen. The species' need for a warm sheltered place also makes it ideal for training on walls, and George Washington planted espaliered trees on both sides of his greenhouse at Mount Vernon. As Batty Langley attested, the apricot is among the most delicious temperate-climate fruits: to harvest the richly colored sunset-orange fruit, delicately spiced with a citruslike aroma, the skin soft and supple in ripeness, the silky flesh sweet and tender, surely endeared the tree to aristocratic fruit epicures (fig. 87). The tree is difficult to grow in non-Mediterranean climates. The early flowering period of the apricot, usually near the middle of March at Monticello and before every other fruit tree except the almond, repeatedly dooms the possibility of a legitimate harvest. If the nascent fruit survives a blast of March or April cold air, it still provides an easy target for the curculio, more devastating to the smooth and thin-skinned apricot than even plums or peaches. The minor

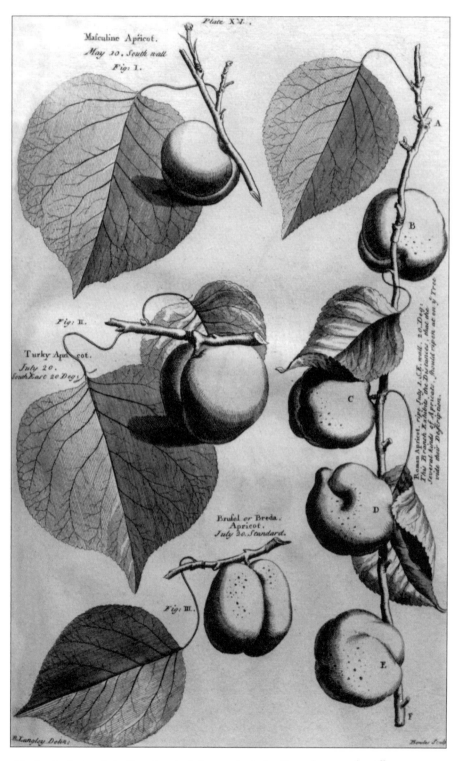

Fig. 87. Apricot varieties from Langley's *Pomona*, including Brussels, grown by Jefferson

miracle of actually harvesting a fresh apricot in central Virginia forbade its use in a more functional culinary role—drying or cooking in large quantities. The apricot, at least in the eastern states of North America, is too precious for its own good. Nevertheless, it seems to be among those fruits whose popularity has significantly diminished over the last two hundred years.[2]

The name apricot derives from *praecox*, or "early ripening," seemingly an allusion to its early flowering and bearing season. Apricots were usually mentioned by the earliest narrators of the New World, sometimes included with the tropical fruits like oranges and lemons that prospered in the grower's sleep. In 1709 John Lawson saw "the biggest Apricock tree I ever saw" in eastern North Carolina. Two decades later William Hugh Grove said: "Apricots were plenty at York[town] but not high flavor[ed.] I have seen none since." William Byrd in his *Natural History* noted that "apricot trees grow very tall and thick here." Mrs. Robert Carter proudly pointed out her grafted apricot trees, planted decoratively alongside the asparagus beds, to Philip Fithian in the garden at Nomini Hall. She also provided St. George Tucker with stones of the Early and Late apricots. Tucker himself ordered two varieties, Large Early and Brussels, from William Prince, while George Washington sent to England for three cultivars. Washington planted trees in his fruitery as formal espaliers on each side of his greenhouse and also scattered a few apricots among his apple and peach orchards. Eighteenth-century Virginians rarely mentioned named varieties. Richard Warren, a Philadelphia nurseryman, advertised the Green, Newington, and Roman apricots in the *Virginia Gazette* of 1792; Charles Carroll of Baltimore cultivated Orange, Turkey, Breda, and Roman; and John Hartwell Cocke grew five varieties, including Moor Park, Large Early, Peach, Black, and Davis's Clingstone. The latter was an esteemed apricot named for a Williamsburg fruit grower, challenging U. P. Hedrick's claim that there were "no new apricots named in America before 1860."[3]

After a lifetime of planting hundreds of young apricot trees and stones, it was surely disappointing for Jefferson to record only seven trees in his mature 1811 orchard. Seventeenth- and eighteenth-century gardeners often grumbled about the difficulties of apricot growing. In 1676 Thomas Glover noted that Virginia apricots "do not ripen so kindly as they do in England." While William Byrd's New World Eden, as described in his *Natural History*, included "very tall" apricots with "beautiful" fruit, privately he (as well as John Bartram) complained to Peter Collinson that "our apricots are worm eaten before they are ripe, which surely you virtuoso's know how to prevent." William Cobbett described American apricots as "hard, and not above one third as large as the same fruit in England," due to inattention to proper cultivation. Richard Parkinson lamented that apricot fruits "dwindle away before they grow ripe," probably because of curculio damage, and a writer in the *Domestic Encyclopedia* concluded that apricots were only successful "in confined paved yards in our cities," probably because the pavement restricted the insect's life cycle and the urban fruit garden provided a sheltered warm environment.[4]

The site of the south orchard is ideal for the survival of established apricot trees, which respond favorably to warmth and shelter, yet its exaggerated balmy microclimate would have induced premature flowering, increasing the chances for frost damage to the flower buds or young fruit. Fruit writers, from Batty Langley to A. J. Downing, recommended a sheltered site but urged their readers to avoid a southern exposure in favor of a northern slope or even the shade of buildings. After numerous unsuccessful trials with various frost deterrents, William Forsyth enthusiastically endorsed the use of fishnets, folded three times and carefully draped around the crown of the tree. Peter Collinson provided sage advice in a letter to John Bartram in 1746: "If your Apricots are too forward, plant them under all disadvantages possible; that is, in the most exposed places, and in all the coldest, shadiest aspects that can be found. Perhaps, when mountains come to be settled, the north sides may succeed with this fruit and others, and may not be so much frequented by the Beetles." While the elevation of the south orchard was ideal, its aspect negated effective frost protection.[5]

Curculio damage to the apricot is as threatening as frost, and Monticello apparently was not sufficiently isolated to avoid "the depredations of the Beetle." The "American Farmer" inaccurately attributed dropping and withered fruit to cultivation: "*Apricots* come when there is a scarcity of other fruits; which makes them more desirable. In the green stage, they make an agreeable tart. In ground dug or stirred about the trees . . . are apt to drop their fruit and wither." Remedies were numerous; for example, Collinson recommended that the roots be soaked with manure water or that the afflicted trees be mercilessly shaken to jar the curculios from their leaves. This was a technique still used in New York orchards in the early 1900s because lead arsenate insecticides burned the apricot's foliage: one man would shake the tree while another would catch the fallen insects in wheelbarrow-driven cloth hampers.[6]

MOOR PARK

Jefferson ordered Moor Park, the most popular apricot variety of the last two centuries, from William Prince in 1791, and he also received scions from Timothy Matlack in 1807 (pl. 33). Moor Park, introduced into England in 1760 by Admiral Lord Anson, was named for the estate where this apricot first fruited, the home of Sir William Temple near Watford in Hertfordshire. British nurserymen began listing it in 1777. Moor Park's status was reflected in the dialogue of Mrs. Norris and Dr. Grant in Jane Austen's *Mansfield Park*, as they discussed an espaliered tree on the stable wall: "Sir, it is a Moor Park, we bought it as a Moor Park and it cost us—that is it was a present from Sir Thomas, but I saw the bill, it cost seven shillings and was charged as a Moor Park." Dr. Grant responded, "You were imposed on ma'am, these potatoes have as much the flavour of Moor Park apricot as the fruit of that tree." William Prince, Jr., was the first nurseryman to offer it in the United States, in 1790, and soon all the major eastern fruit growers listed it. John Hartwell Cocke cultivated it at Bremo, and by 1848 A. J. Downing referred to the Moor Park as "a fine old variety," a status it continues to hold today.[7]

Moor Park is a vigorous tree requiring, according to most early fruit writers, the shortening-in method of pruning. The large, roundish fruit has a bright golden orange color with very firm orange flesh. The stone of the Moor Park, which parts easily from the flesh, has a peculiar longitudinal passage through which a pin may be passed.[8]

PEACH ("German," "peach-apricot")

The Peach apricot was Jefferson's favorite, "the finest fruit which grows in Europe," and after numerous frustrating efforts to establish it at Monticello, he finally succeeded in 1809, mostly through the diligence of John Threlkeld. Philip Mazzei, "at beginning of 1804," included two Peach (which he called "German") apricot grafts ("they should have there, as they do here and in Languedoc, better flavor than those in the vicinity of Paris") and a "greater quantity" of seeds among his shipment of twenty-six fruit varieties (pl. 34). Despite his assertion that "they came in perfect order, so that I doubt if one will be lost," Jefferson reported that "the single plant of the Peach Apricot [was] stolen by the way," in transit to Monticello. Mazzei, after hearing of this, responded by reminding Jefferson that two trees had been sent ("that means that both were stolen or lost"), and that the variety was irreplaceable. Alexander Hepburn, who had been propagating the stones, successfully reared eight Peach apricot trees, which were also forwarded from Washington to Monticello in 1806 and apparently also "lost" during the journey.[9]

John Threlkeld, however, had fortuitously snipped scions from the young trees while visiting Hepburn's nursery in Washington. In 1807 he sent "six Peach Apricots Mr. Jefferson had at Hepburn marked no. 1" and again in 1809 forwarded to Monticello five more young trees he had personally propagated. It is unclear whether the propagating material for this last shipment derived from the Hepburn trees, or whether they were stones he had received from France himself, "from a Lady near Bourdeaux." In 1810 Jefferson recorded planting three trees in row *g*, probably from the second shipment, and also noted sowing twenty-four stones harvested from a flourishing tree in row *f*, likely from the 1807 shipment. The final irony to Jefferson's struggle with the Peach apricot was that the Mazzei scions and stones probably were misidentified. When Jefferson described the Mazzei apricot stones to Charles Clay, he said that the Peach apricot was "distinguishable from all others by a sheath in the side, through which you may thrust a pin," a characteristic of Moor Park.[10]

Confusion reigned among fruit authorities about the synonymity of the two varieties, suggesting that the Peach was perhaps the parent of Moor Park, but by the middle of the nineteenth century the differences became more apparent: the fruit of the Peach is larger than the Moor Park, about two and a half inches in diameter, and the skin and flesh yellower; the skin is often a fawn yellow in the shade, and the flesh a saffron yellow. The Peach was also considered juicier with a more "peculiar"-tasting pulp.[11]

OTHER JEFFERSON APRICOT VARIETIES

Besides the Moor Park, Jefferson received four trees of the Brussels and four of the Large Early apricot from the William Prince nursery in 1791. They were planted "in the vacant places of the same kind of fruit trees in the orchard. Where there are no vacancies of the same kind they may be planted in those of any other kind." The Mazzei shipment of 1804 also included the Angelica (two grafted trees, three seedlings, and numerous stones) and seeds of Large Red, which apparently failed to germinate in the hands of Alexander Hepburn. Jefferson recorded planting two of the five trees of Angelica in 1805; although Hepburn successfully propagated one tree from the stone, and it was carried to Monticello, there is no record of its planting. John Threlkeld also sent two trees in both March and November of a variety "that derive their origin from the Bishop of Bourdeaux's Garden. The fruit is said to be large, fine and of the cling stone kind." Jefferson, in turn, sent the trees from Washington to William Meriwether,

a neighbor, to await his arrival home from the presidency. They were planted at Monticello in 1810.[12]

Angelica, according to Philip Mazzei, was named or "baptized" by himself. Mazzei said the fruit was medium-sized, straw-colored, with "a very delicate flavor," and it probably was unknown in the United States at the time. Giorgio Gallesio illustrated and described Angelica in 1817.[13]

Brussels, an ancient apricot probably dating from classical Rome and introduced into England in 1702, was the most popular cultivar before the appearance of Moor Park. Brussels was Batty Langley's favorite apricot for its hardiness and "fine brisk high flavoured juice." While William Coxe and Kenrick agreed with Langley that it was the hardiest and most dependable sort, Downing said the Brussels was "not a fine fruit in this country."[14]

Large Early was listed as early as 1771 by William Prince, then by McMahon and Landreth, but the descriptions by early writers varied.[15]

"Melon" was first mentioned by Jefferson in a letter to Richard Cary from Paris in 1787: "I will send you also some plants of the melon apricot, a variety of fruit obtained in France only 8 or 10 years ago & as yet known no where else. It is an Apricot with the high flavor of a mushmelon, & is certainly the best fruit in this country." Jefferson returned home in 1789 with "4. melon apricots." The next February he planted three grafted and three seedling trees in the apricot row, g, and also "3 dozen among vacancies in the peach trees."[16]

Nectarines

THE "ARTIFICIAL PLANT"

Jefferson planted thirty-three nectarine trees at Monticello, including two varieties, Red Roman and Yellow Roman, that were purchased from the William Prince nursery, the "plumb," or clingstone, nectarine probably obtained from George Wythe of Williamsburg, and the "Kaskaskia soft" received from James Taylor of Norfolk in 1810. Only five trees propagated from the Taylor scion wood were reported in the mature 1811 orchard. The nectarine (*Prunus persica* var. *nucipersica*) is simply a hairless peach, and most early fruit writers astutely considered them the same species. While the characters of the two trees are identical, the nectarine fruit is smaller, firmer, more fragrant, richer in flavor, and, at least with modern varieties, has a darker, more reddish skin. U. P. Hedrick described the nectarine as an "artificial plant" because it does not appear in the wild and never escapes from cultivation. Except for the gardening-wise gentry, most Virginians around 1800 probably had never heard of the nectarine. As late as 1820 William Cobbett said that the nectarine "is not grown, or but very little in America."[1]

It is uncertain where and when nectarines were first noticed by garden writers. Pliny noted the "duracinus," possibly an allusion to the fruit, but it was not until 1629 that John Parkinson first provided a version of the nectarine's modern name, "nectorin," a change from the more common seventeenth-century appellation, "nucipersica," which was derived from the nectarine's internal similarity to the outer rind of the walnut. John Banister, late in the seventeenth century, was probably the first Virginian to record the nectarine's presence in the New World, and he, like Robert Beverley twenty years later, associated "plum nectarines" with "plum peaches." John

Lawson said, "We have likewise very fair Nectarines, especially the red, that clings to the Stone; the other yellow Fruit, that leaves the Stone. Of the last, I have a Tree that most Years brings me fifteen or twenty Bushels. I see no Foreign Fruit like this." William Byrd described the "nectarine peach" similarly, but both he and John Bartram confided to Peter Collinson that their nectarines were "worm-eaten before they are ripe." After hearing of their problems, Collinson, perhaps gloating over his own success with the fruit, acclaimed the nectarine "one of the most delicious fruits in the universe, and much exceeds a Peach, in a rich vinous flavoured juice." Richard Parkinson also reported on his insect-riddled nectarines, and the "American Farmer" wrote, *Nectarines* scarcely ever ripen in the parts of America where the editor has been. An insect punctures the green fruit, and *gum* flows from it, till the fruit drops without ripening." Even William Coxe, early America's foremost fruit grower, "abandoned the full cultivation of them" because of "the various species of Aphides" and probably also the curculio.[2]

Nevertheless, nectarines are not impossible to grow. Philip Fithian reported eating nectarines in the fruit garden at Lee Hall in Westmoreland County. George Washington, Charles Carroll, St. George Tucker, John Hartwell Cocke, and the Skipwiths all grew either seedling trees propagated at home or else nursery-grown European varieties purchased from England or the Prince nurseries. These included the standard cultivars such as Red Roman, Newington, and Elruge, an anagram named for an eighteenth-century English nurseryman, Captain Gurle (fig. 88). Nectarine varieties were rarely listed by Virginia nurseries. In 1792 Richard Warren sold Fairchild's Early and Franklin, probably an American seedling named in

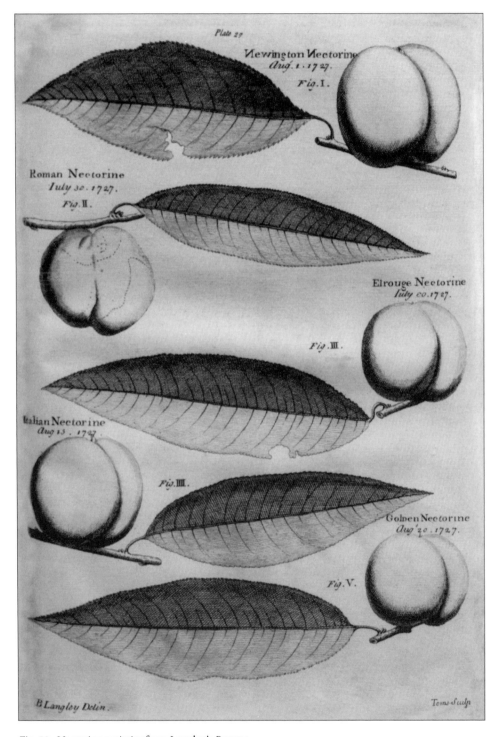

Fig. 88. Nectarine varieties from Langley's *Pomona*

honor of Benjamin Franklin, and Philip Walten sold Red Roman and Yellow Roman at his Baltimore nursery in 1788. William Prince offered twelve varieties in 1771, many more than were listed by Booth in 1810 or Landreth in 1811.[3]

RED ROMAN

The Red Roman is an ancient variety that was praised by Parkinson ("of an excellent good taste"), Langley ("full of a fine delicious sugar'd juice"), and Miller ("a large fair fruit of an excellent flavour"). It was widely cultivated by Virginia fruit lovers such as Tucker, Washington, the Skipwiths, and John Hartwell Cocke and was a standard item on the lists of early American nurseries. William Coxe thought it was "most hardy in our climate" among all the nectarine cultivars available in 1817, and Downing said it was "still esteemed" in 1849. The fruit is large, roundish, and somewhat flattened on the bottom. The skin is dark brownish-red on the sun side of the fruit but yellow in the shade. The clingstone flesh is firm, greenish-yellow, and deep red at the pit with a rich, vinous, juicy flavor.[4]

Almonds

A FUTILE EXPERIMENT

Jefferson returned from Paris in 1789 with twenty-six pounds of French-grown almonds. Such extravagance suggests his affection for this delicacy, considered a nut by the consumer but a tree fruit to the horticulturist. Perhaps the burden and investment of importing the nuts reinforced a passion for growing his own trees at Monticello. Unfortunately, Jefferson failed at cultivating this delicate species, *Prunus dulcis*, the earliest blooming of all fruit trees and the most likely to succumb to frost damage. Despite sowing 167 almond kernels of at least seven different types on five different occasions and securing scion wood and seeds from at least six different sources, Jefferson recorded planting only four almond trees at Monticello: three in 1778 and one in the nursery in 1812. The "almond row" in the 1811 south orchard had no almond trees, only peaches, apples, and one cherry. Jefferson acknowledged, "The almond tree is so precarious, that none can depend for subsistence on its produce, but persons of capital," and in his inventory of Mediterranean fruits he wrote that "the almond, the hardiest, loses its fruit the oftenest, on account of its forwardness." Jefferson's ordeal with the almond, though, probably arose from his inability to get the 167 seeds to germinate and produce orchard-ready seedling trees, rather than frost or freeze damage to the flowers or infant fruit. In his log of the bloom dates through the season, his Monticello almond trees flowered at nearly the same time as the peach, suggesting that frost damage was no worse to the almond than to any other tree fruit. Although temperamental and sensitive to the vagaries of a cold, damp, continental climate, the species will survive as far north as the peach. Jefferson was a planter, not a cultivator. Nowhere is this distinction more apparent than in his growing of the almond tree.[1]

Almonds and peaches, like nectarines and peaches, have striking similarities. The almond is the pit, stone, or kernel of a peachlike fruit that has a dry, woolly flesh which splits open when mature. The trees have similar leaves, although the habit of the almond is more upright, broad-topped like an apple, and the species flowers one to three weeks earlier than the peach. Jefferson grew both the hard- and soft-shelled sweet almond (*Prunus dulcis* var. *dulcis*), the commercial nut, and the bitter almond (*Prunus dulcis* var. *amara*) used in flavoring extracts and to make prussic acid. Although an ancient fruit commonly associated with the southern Mediterranean, almond trees were not documented in England until the sixteenth century. John Parkinson felt that "the almond also [like the nectarine] may be reckoned unto the stock or kindred of the Peaches" and mentioned the variations—bitter, sweet, long, thick-shelled, soft-shelled, thin-shelled—later recorded by Jefferson and nineteenth-century American fruit writers. Philip Miller suggested the almond tree, "cultivated in all the Nurseries," was appreciated primarily as an ornamental because of its uncertain fruitfulness.[2]

William Byrd's *Natural History* included what was probably the first mention of Virginia-grown almonds: "There are *almonds,* but only in the gardens, and only a few. They grow to be large, beautiful, and good. Only a little trouble is needed therefore to plant them." Although no Virginian planted almonds as diligently and enthusiastically as Jefferson, St. George Tucker sowed almond kernels in 1784, George Washington imported trees from England, and John Hartwell Cocke purchased trees from Benjamin Prince in

1815. Northern nurserymen did not begin to sell almond trees until the nineteenth century, when William Booth of Baltimore offered four varieties in 1810. Many of the major fruit writers of the mid-nineteenth century failed even to mention the almond, although A. J. Downing wondered why: "There is no apparent reason why the culture of the Almond should not be pursued to a profitable extent in the warm and favourable climate of some of the southern states."[3]

ALMOND VARIETIES

Jefferson planted as many as seven distinct forms of almond. In 1774 he sowed eighty-two kernels of six varieties provided by Philip Mazzei. These included "a Virginian Almond," probably a native nut like the bitternut (*Juglans cinerea*) or indigenous hazelnut (*Corylus americana*); "Almonds from the Streights," likely the Straits of Gibraltar where almond culture was extensive; "sweet almonds with smooth rinds"; "sweet almonds with hairy rinds"; "sweet almonds with hard shells"; and "bitter almonds." In 1810 he planted in his nursery "52. hardshelled sweet almonds from Cadiz. from Harriet Hackley," who was Thomas Mann Randolph's sister then residing in southern Spain, and "10. Kernels of the hard shelled bitter almond in a box," one of which germinated and was transplanted to the nursery in 1812. He also collected twenty-four sweet almonds from George Divers's tree the same year and planted them in the nursery. Jefferson knew the almond in many of its variations. The bitter almond has large pale blossoms and a bitter-tasting seed, suitable only for the fragrant and medicinal extract. The most esteemed almond was the soft-shelled sweet, also known as the Lady almond. The forms of the sweet that Jefferson was sowing—the hard-shelled and those with smooth and hairy rinds—were hardier but probably not so delicately flavored or textured. Booth in 1810 sold Bitter-fruited, Large sweet-fruited hard-shelled, Sweet-fruited tender-shelled, and Lady, or Parchment. In his earliest plantings at Monticello, Jefferson used peaches as a rootstock—a practice generally endorsed by fruit authorities —for a "bitter almond from Blenheim," a nearby estate, that was budded in July 1777 and then transplanted into the orchard the following March.[4]

Quinces

HUMBLE AND FORGOTTEN

The quince (*Cydonia oblonga*) was more popular before 1800 than it is today, when these trees are rarely found in fruit gardens or orchards. A relic of early American fruit culture, its decline coincided with the flagging interest in food preservation and the surging preference for soft dessert fruits like strawberries and tropical oranges and bananas. The quince is a small, crooked tree (twelve to fifteen feet) with a dense, rounded crown, handsome white and pale pink blossoms, and oval leaves with a whitish bloom underneath. The mid-season golden yellow fruit, often compared to an orange, apple, or pear, is rarely palatable when fresh off the tree. Varietal names of the eighteenth century, Apple quince or Pear quince, suggests the association the quince had with its more familiar pomological cousins. The culinary range of the quince, however, is more specific: from jellies and marmalades to quince juices and syrups to preserves with pickled or baked fruit. John Parkinson said, "There is no fruit growing in this Land that is of so many excellent uses," and the variety of quince-based recipes in Mary Randolph's *Virginia House-wife* suggests the culinary diversity of the quince was still cherished two hundred years later. Jefferson recorded only two plantings of quince trees in the south orchard, in 1769 and 1778, yet five trees survived to be included in the 1811 plan. In 1782 he marveled over a quince weighing nearly eighteen ounces, certainly a weighty harvest, yet only a bantam compared to William Coxe's boast in 1817 of a twenty-three-and-a-half-ounce champion.[1]

L. H. Bailey observed in 1900 that "few fruits play a more important part in ancient history than the quince, and yet there is hardly a fruit with equal or poorer merit that in recent years has not received more attention." Although the tree

is native to the Mideast—Persia, Turkestan, and the Caucasus—the quince's genus name, *Cydonia*, is derived from a Greek city on Crete. Highly regarded by ancient writers such as Pliny, who discussed the Sparrow-apple, Golden quince, and Must apple, the quince was a standard medieval fruit that was cherished for pies and jellies and for its preserving qualities. It was grown in England by the thirteenth century, and Parkinson evaluated six varieties in 1629, including the English or Apple quince: "No man can endure to eate it rawe, but either boiled, stewed, roasted or baked; all of which says it is very good." Parkinson's Portugal Apple, later known as Orange, was the only cultivar suitable for eating off the tree (fig. 89). William Forsyth's and Miller's favorite variety was the Portugal, "the most valuable, the pulp of it turning a fine purple when stewed or baked, and becomes much softer and less austere than the others, so is much better for making of marmalade." Forsyth was another quince enthusiast; he suggested the harvested fruit be stored with apples, which would release the distinctive, piquant quince flavor when made into pies and puddings.[2]

It is not surprising that such a highly regarded, diversely functional fruit should be found in the earliest narratives of the Virginia landscape. New World quince culture was observed in 1649 by Sir William Berkeley, by Nathaniel Shrigley in 1669, and by John Joyce who said in 1676, "Here are also a great store of Quinces, which are larger and fairer than those of England, and not so harsh in taste; of the juice of these they also make Quince-drink." John Lawson noted three varieties in the Carolinas—Brunswick, Portugal, and Barbary—and agreed with Joyce that "no place has better relish." Lawson also praised the quince wine, "which I approve of beyond

Fig. 89. Portugal Apple quince,
from Langley's *Pomona*

any drink which that country affords, though a great deal of cider and perry is there made. The Quince-Drink most commonly purges and cleanses the body very well." William Byrd commented further: "One finds here six species of *quinces,* namely Indian, Spanish, Portugese, Italian, Barbary, and Brunswickian, which are all very sweet and good either raw or cooked. One makes also many sweetmeats and electuaries from them, as also a wine or quince drink, a drink which is made far more than all others in this land, disregarding many kinds of apple juice and pear juice. It is a little less [strong] than wine. It opens up the body for those who drink it for the first time, and purifies the bowels very well, whereby the opinion of the medical gentlemen about constipation is refuted, unless it be that the climate can produce the change."[3]

The quince's utilitarian functions and relative ease of cul-

ture, its common familiarity, perhaps explain its comparative rarity in the fruit gardens of wealthy Virginia horticulturists. George Washington had only one quince tree in his garden, and St. George Tucker and John Hartwell Cocke used it as a dwarfing and rugged rootstock for more cherished pear varieties. The quince was no prize but rather a simple and useful addition most common in the farmyards of the middle class. The "American Farmer" defined its place when he said, "A few *quinces,* for preserves, are in a corner of the American apple-orchard or garden," and democratic William Coxe reported the species "in most of our gardens." L. H. Bailey suggested the species' ultimate rank in the fruit world was reflected by the places where it was most commonly observed, "in back yards and fence corners and often in the lowest dampest fruit land on the farm."[4]

Part
III

Grapes

THE SPECIES OF UTOPIA

homas Jefferson's knowledgeable and enduring fascination with wine and his pioneering experiments in grape growing at Monticello have endowed him with the reputation of America's "first distinguished viticulturist." Volumes have been composed on Jefferson's appreciation of Europe's classic vintages, and from the early nineteenth century to the present, American viticulturists have recalled the Jeffersonian grape legacy to promote their own experiments with vine growing and wine making. Jefferson advised George Washington, John Adams, James Monroe, and James Madison on suitable wines for the White House cellars, imported extravagant quantities of France's most esteemed wines for his own cellars in Washington and at Monticello, and kept detailed and often-quoted notes on his wine-tasting travels through Provence, northern Italy, and Germany. His own vibrant refrains on wine animate the story: such remarks as, "No nation is drunken where wine is cheap," or, "Wine from long habit has become an indispensable for my health," provide inspiration for the oenologist and viticulturist alike. Perhaps most importantly, Jefferson's promotion of American-made wine and his association with other pioneering grape growers—Philip Mazzei, Peter Legaux, Bernard McMahon, John Adlum, Jean David, S. W. Johnson, and John James Dufour—stimulated experimental viticulture in the New World.[1]

A study of viticulture at Monticello is a study of the ambiguities, contradictions, and even the elusiveness of Jefferson himself. The story is fragmented by documentary gaps and unanswerable puzzles. Jefferson recorded numerous, and at times detailed, vine plantings at Monticello, yet unlike the orchard record, reports on harvest dates or the state of the vineyard are missing. The continual replanting of the Monticello vineyards suggests a perennial and losing struggle with grape cultivation. But Jefferson was not alone; there were few successful ventures in grape growing in eastern North America until after his death. The successful cultivation of *Vitis vinifera*, the classic European wine species, was virtually impossible outside of California and before the development of modern pesticides to control such destructive pests as black rot, powdery mildew, downy mildew, and phylloxera, the deadly root and leaf aphid. Many of the numerous native grape species were more effectively grown, yet the quality of the resultant wine (as well as an inherent prejudice against native plants) impeded the development of an established industry until the late 1820s.

Just as a study of the evolution of American fruit-tree cultivation reveals a tension between the imported fruits of Europe and those native to North America, so does the history of grape culture at Monticello suggest Jefferson's unrelenting oscillation between a desire to grow the difficult yet rewarding *vinifera* and an awareness of the possibilities of New World alternatives: *Vitis labrusca*, the fox grape, and the Scuppernong variety of the muscadine grape, *Vitis rotundifolia*. Although Jefferson probably never made a Monticello-grown wine, his tireless enthusiasm and the diverse collection of varieties he assembled were worthy accomplishments in themselves. Jefferson should be remembered as an influential advocate of New World viticulture, as an enthusiastic promoter of both American-grown *Vitis vinifera* and the possibilities of native grapes for wine, yet his own trials at Monticello, promising in their vision, were perfunctory in their execution. Thomas Pinney, whose *History of Wine in America* is the most comprehensive study of the evolution of this country's grape growing, acknowledged Jefferson's own frustrated attempts: "But he cared much that others should succeed, and, by virtue of his zeal and his eminence, can be called the greatest patron of wine and winegrowing that this country has yet had."[2]

THE GRAPE AT MONTICELLO

By 1778 Jefferson had mapped his vineyard in the heart of the fruitery just below the vegetable garden and garden pavilion —a prime location that suggests its leading role (fig. 90). Although the orchard plan for this year shows that the 90-by-100-foot vineyard contained 561 vines spaced three feet apart

(fig. 91), the earlier plantings recorded in the Garden Book, before 1800, were sporadic, haphazard, and casually experimental. An exception was in 1774, when Philip Mazzei's vignerons planted 30 vines in one vineyard row, including Spanish raisins from Colonel Richard Bland of Williamsburg and wild grapes from Monticello. Jefferson's 1774 description of the planting process in his own vineyard, performed by Mazzei's vignerons, was the most detailed and exhaustive elucidation of any horticultural practice at Monticello.[3]

Philip Mazzei had a profound influence on the earliest plantings at Monticello, not only because his Italian workers planted the earliest vines but because the conclusions drawn from his experimental vineyard nearby at Colle undoubtedly shaped Jefferson's own trials (fig. 92). Mazzei was born in 1739

Fig. 90. The restored northeast (*foreground*) and southwest (*background*) vineyards, with the "berry squares" of currants, raspberries, gooseberries, and figs between

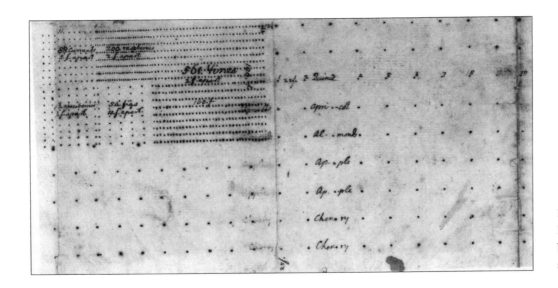

Fig. 91. Detail of the first Monticello vineyard and berry squares from Jefferson's 1778 orchard plan

Fig. 92. Philip Mazzei, by Joseph Amelio Finelli

at Poggio-a-Caiano, near Florence, and after an abbreviated career as a physician moved to London, where he imported Italian wines and befriended Benjamin Franklin and the American merchant Thomas Adams, both of whom encouraged the loquacious Italian to move to Virginia. Although his original grand concept of a London-based Virginia wine company failed, Mazzei recruited ten Tuscan vine dressers and enough Italian capital to sail to the colony in 1773. The Mazzei party, burdened with tools, vines, and grandiose visions of a Mediterranean paradise on the Virginia frontier, set off from Williamsburg for land in the Shenandoah Valley. They were waylaid at Monticello where Jefferson, smitten with the project and the ebullient Italian, offered them 2,000 acres of an adjacent property Mazzei was later to enlarge and name Colle, "hill" in Italian, perhaps as a response to Monticello, or "little mountain." Mazzei's enthusiasm arose, in part, because of the abundance of "200 varieties of wild grapes" at Colle—a typically hyperbolic rendering of the prolific, variable, and confusing native grape flora. Mazzei succinctly expressed the universal, yet ultimately flawed, argument for the success of American viticulture when he said: "Especially in Virginia, nature seems to favor vineyards. I have never seen such perfect, varied, and abundant wild grapes." He wrote George Washington that "this country is better calculated than any other I am acquainted with for the produce of wine," and he later forecast, "The best wine in the world will be made here." The one lesson the history of grape growing in eastern North America reveals is that the abundant native grape flora did not translate into a profitable wine industry, at least until well into the nineteenth century.[4]

In order to revive Mazzei's wine company in 1774, a "subscription of 2,000 pounds sterling" was solicited from numerous prominent Virginians, including Jefferson, Washington, Peyton Randolph, and George Mason. A killing May frost in 1774 was an immediate setback for the first Colle plantings of what were probably native vines, but 1,500 *vinifera* vines were set out in June 1775, and 2,000 more wild grape cuttings were planted in the spring of 1776. Mazzei reported that the Tuscan vines "produced grapes with more flavor and substance than those grown in Italy," and he also compared the wines made from wild grapes favorably with those of Italy and France. Mazzei's experiments were generally inconclusive as the outbreak of the Revolutionary War diverted attention from grape growing and dispersed many of the Tuscan vignerons. The rental of Colle as barracks for Hessian soldiers sealed the fate of Mazzei's vine experiments in Albemarle County and, according to Jefferson, "destroyed the whole labor of three or four years; and thus ended an experiment which, from every appearance, would in a year or two have established the practicality of that branch of culture in America."[5]

Despite the initial 1774 plantings of the easier-grown wild grape, there is no evidence that these vines were successful. In 1782 Jefferson recorded in the Garden Book that "seventeen bushels of winter grapes made 40 gallons of vinegar," yet these "winter" grapes, probably *Vitis vulpina*, or frost grape, probably were harvested from wild vines rather than from the vineyard. In 1786, while Jefferson was in Paris, Antonio Giannini, a horticultural survivor of the Mazzei experiment, was hoping to revive the Monticello vineyard. He wrote Jefferson that "the vines are improving marvelously but no wine has been made because each year the grapes are picked before they are ripe, which is very harmful to the vine. He [Giannini] has begged Mr. Lewis [an overseer] to stop people

from taking grapes. When the grapes are ripe he will make wine and send it to Paris in the autumn. . . . The location is well adapted to a vineyard." Surely the vineyard should have yielded bountifully by this time, at least eight years from planting, yet the raiding by workmen and slaves seems to indicate that vine culture at Monticello was not considered a serious venture.[6]

Jefferson's lengthy travel log of his journey through the vine-growing regions of southern France and Italy in the spring of 1787 reveals his unbounding curiosity about viticulture. But Jefferson was sobered by the impact of vine-growing on the social fabric of Provence; seeing it probably tempered his own experiments at Monticello. He wrote Williamsburg's George Wythe, his law school professor and mentor, that the vine "is the parent of misery. Those who cultivate it are always poor." Nevertheless, Jefferson promised a friend, Archibald Cary, to make "a collection of vines for wine and for the table" and then assembled numerous grape varieties for his Parisian garden at the Hôtel de Langeac. He obtained what were probably Chardonnay and Pinot Noir from the celebrated vineyards of Burgundy—Montrachet, Clos de Vougeot, Chambertin, and Romanée—through his wine agent and occasional tour guide, Etienne Parent. He also cultivated cuttings of Riesling collected during his study tour of vineyards along the Rhine. He wrote Major von Geismar, a Hessian officer once confined at Charlottesville but then living in Frankfurt, "The vines which I took from Hochheim and Rudesheim are now growing luxuriously in my garden here, and will cross the Atlantic next winter, and that probably, if you ever revisit Monticello, I shall be able to give you there a glass of hock or Rudesheim of my own making." Jefferson certainly aspired to bring these *vinifera* vines home to Monticello, yet no grapes were itemized on his list of baggage in 1789 along with the French pears, apricots, and figs, nor were there subsequent notations of plantings at Monticello. However, a 1794 entry in the Garden Book, "Objects for the garden this year," includes "vines Malesherb." among a list of fruits, vegetables, and herbs Jefferson hoped to plant that year. In 1785 Jefferson had written the Reverend James Madison that Chrétien-Guillaume de Lamoignon de Malesherbes, a French acquaintance and fellow plantsman, was collecting for him "vines from which the Burgundy, Champagne, Bourdeaux, Frontignac, and other of the most valuable wines of this country are made," and perhaps the Malesherbes grape cuttings had finally arrived nine years later. In 1821 John W. Eppes asked Jefferson for "15 or 20 slips of your purple grapes which you brought from France." Eppes's request suggests that *vinifera* grapes had thrived for some thirty years at Monticello.[7]

Jefferson obtained more grapevines from Benjamin Hawkins of Warrenton, North Carolina, in 1796, but they perished soon after being set out. "The vines you were so kind as to send me by mr. Chiles were delivered to me alive. Every one budded after it was planted. Yet every one died immediately after. It was certainly not for want of care." John James Dufour, Swiss-born author of *The American Vine Dresser's Guide* (1826), leader of a doomed Kentucky colony of vine experimenters and an itinerant observer and proponent of New World viticulture, visited Monticello in 1799. He said the vineyard "had been abandoned, or left without any care for three of four years before, which proved, evidently, that it had not been profitable." Perhaps motivated, or even embarrassed, by Dufour's visit, Jefferson instructed his overseer, Richard Richardson, to have John, a gardening slave, "espalier the rest of the vines" later in the same year.[8]

The next Garden Book reference to viticulture at Monticello was in 1802, when Jefferson planted seventy rooted grape cuttings from Peter Legaux in the southwest vineyard. Antonio Giannini set out the vines on May 11, too late in the growing season to expect success with rooted cuttings. Legaux, a Frenchman who established a relatively successful vineyard at Spring Mill just outside of Philadelphia, has been described as "the most intelligent and public-spirited grape grower which the country had known." Legaux's shipment to Monticello was only a sample of the thousands of grapes he had disseminated to "my fellow citizens possessing pecuniary means" throughout the country; Legaux could be called the Johnny Appleseed of the vine. The varieties he sent to Monticello were mostly identified by the classic French provinces (Bordeaux, Champagne, and Burgundy) where they were grown. But the legitimacy of such noble appellations is doubtful because the shipment also included the so-called

Cape of Good Hope grape, a controversial variety popularized by Legaux himself. He hoped to promote the naturally occurring *vinifera* × *labrusca* hybrid Alexander grape, discovered about 1740 by James Alexander, gardener to a son of William Penn, by associating this indigenous variety with the more exotic shores of South Africa. Although the misnaming of the grape, "foisted on the public as the Cape of Good Hope grape," failed as a public relations ploy, Jefferson praised the wine from it; he said it was "as good as the best Burgundy and resembling it" and "was worthy of the best vineyards in France." These innocent endorsements stimulated the Alexander's cultivation by early viticultural pioneers like Legaux, John Adlum, and John James Dufour.[9]

While president, Jefferson began assembling European, particularly Italian, varieties, culminating in 1807 in the most important and completely documented vineyard planting at Monticello. In 1801 he requested *"eating* grapes" from Philip Mazzei, who responded in 1803 with a shipment of six Italian table varieties: 6 bearing vines; 5 "barbartelle," or root cuttings; and 97 "magliuoli," or stem cuttings. Mazzei also sent 322 barbartelle, which he said would "root well and will produce fruit quickly," in 1805. Thomas Appleton, the American consul at Livorno, also collected various dry Italian wine varieties from the Florence Botanical Garden and forwarded them to Jefferson in "a barrel containing 225. Vine-Cuttings of 9 different qualities." These cuttings probably were propagated by Alexander Hepburn, the Washington nurseryman who cared for the Mazzei fruit-tree varieties.[10]

The March 25, 1807, vineyard plan, jotted down in Jefferson's Weather Memorandum Book, detailed the planting of 287 rooted vines or cuttings of twenty-four *vinifera* grape varieties not only from Mazzei and Appleton but also from the Thomas Main nursery of Washington (fig. 93). The northeast vineyard, on the site of the original 1778 vineyard, was arranged into seventeen terraces carved into the steep hillside, with an eighteenth "occupied chiefly by trees." The newer southwest vineyard was larger, 16,000 square feet compared to 9,000, and was reserved for the eight varieties shipped by Main and "6 plants of Purple Syrian grape from Twickenham" sent by Timothy Matlack. Although terraces were reserved for specific varieties, planting occurred only in "va-

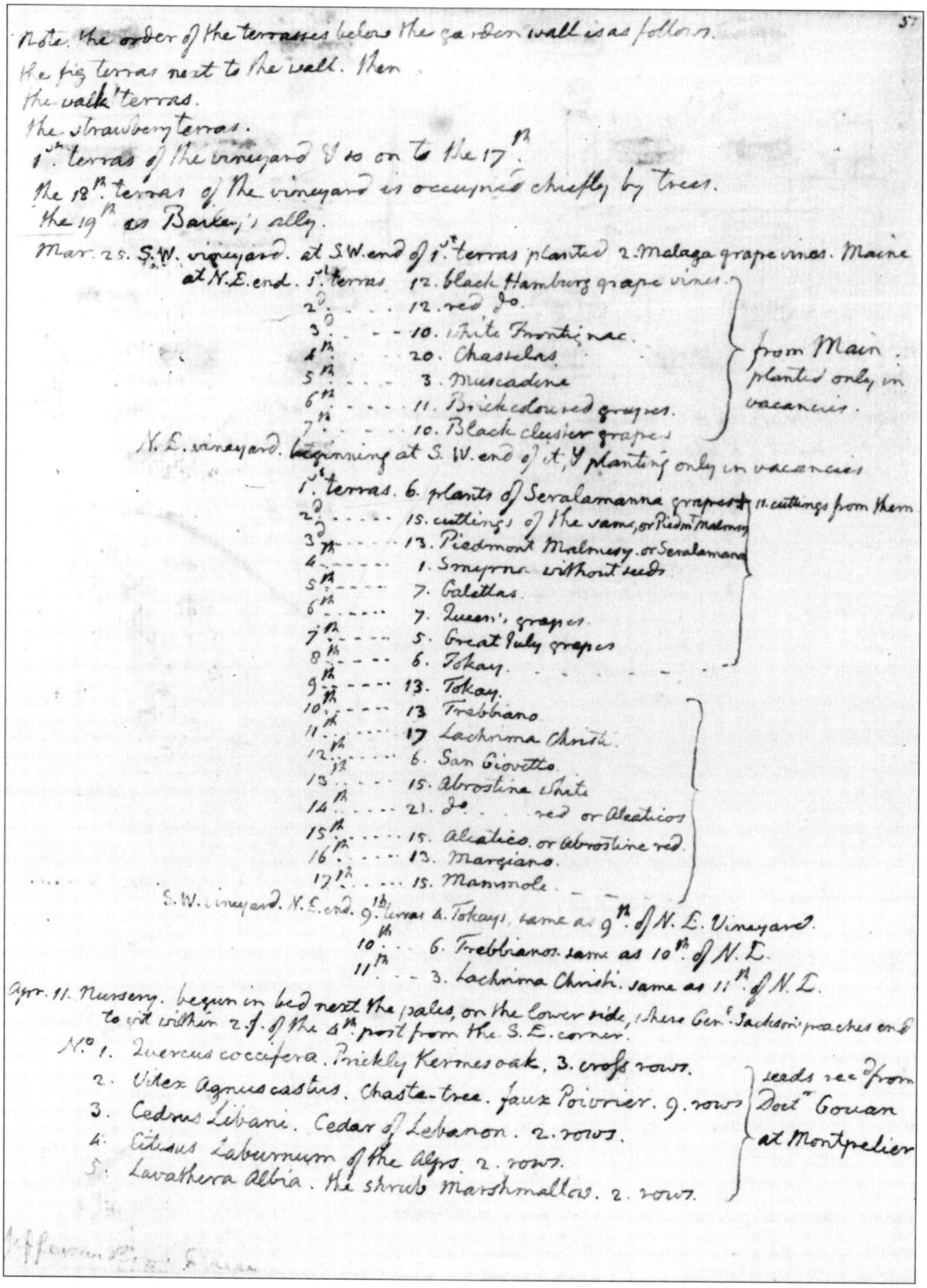

57

Note. the order of the terrasses below the garden wall is as follows.
the fig terras next to the wall. then
the walk terras.
the strawberry terras.
1st. terras of the vineyard & so on to the 17th
the 18th terras of the vineyard is occupied chiefly by trees.
the 19th is Barley's alley.
Mar. 25. S.W. vineyard. at S.W. end of 1st terras planted 2. Malaga grape vines. Maine
        at N.E. end. 1st terras   12. black Hamburg grape vines.
            2d . . . . 12. red do.
            3d . . . . 10. White Frontignac.
            4th . . . . 20. Chasselas   } from Main.
            5th . . . . 3. Muscadine   planted only in
            6th . . . . 11. Brick coloured grapes.   vacancies.
            7th . . . . 10. Black cluster grapes
    N.E. vineyard. beginning at S.W. end of it, & planting only in vacancies
            1st. terras. 6. plants of Seralamanna grapes } 11. cuttings from them
            2d . . . . 15. cuttings of the same, or Piedm Malmsy
            3d . . . . 13. Piedmont Malmsey. or Seralamanna
            4th . . . . 1. Smyrna without seeds
            5th . . . . 7. Galettas.
            6th . . . . 7. Queen's grapes
            7th . . . . 5. Great July grapes
            8th . . . . 6. Tokay.
            9th . . . . 13. Tokay.
            10th . . . . 13. Trebbiano
            11th . . . . 17. Lachrima Christi.
            12th . . . . 6. San Giovetto.
            13th . . . . 15. Abrostine White
            14th . . . . 21. do . . . red or Aleaticos
            15th . . . . 15. Aleatico. or Abrostine red
            16th . . . . 13. Marqiano.
            17th . . . . 15. Mammole.
        S.W. vineyard. N.E. end. 9th terras 4. Tokays. same as 9th of N.E. Vineyard.
            10th . . . 6. Trebbianos. same as 10th of N.E.
            11th . . . 3. Lachrima Christi. same as 11th of N.E.
Apr. 11. Nursery. begun in bed next the pales, on the lower side, where Genl. Jackson's peaches are &
        to wit within 2f. of the 4th post from the S.E. corner.
    No. 1. Quercus coccifera. Prickly Kermes oak, 3. cross rows.
        2. Vitex agnus castus. Chaste-tree. faux Poivrier. 9. rows } seeds recd from
        3. Cedrus Libani. Cedar of Lebanon. 2. rows.   Docr Gouan
        4. Citisus Laburnum of the Alps. 2. rows.   at Montpelier
        5. Lavathera Albia. the shrub Marshmallow. 2. rows.

Fig. 93. March 25, 1807, vineyard plan in Jefferson's Weather Memorandum Book

cancies," so it is difficult to ascertain whether Jefferson continued to space his vines three feet apart as he did in 1778. Many of these *vinifera* cultivars probably had never before been cultivated in the New World; such a varietal rainbow of grapes, so awkward to blend into a harmonious vintage, represented the garden of a plant collector, an experimenter rather than a wine maker.[11]

Indeed, the vines never became established. Although 1807 was a favorable growing season, Jefferson's correspondence indicated he was more involved with the planting of the hawthorn hedge and a McMahon shipment of Lewis and Clark plants. Three years later, in 1810, the "11. uppermost terrasses of the E. [Northeast] vineyard" were replanted with "165. cuttings of a native winegrape recd. from Major Adlum of Maryland. . . . I have drunk the wine. it resembles the Comartin Burgundy." These Alexander grapes from John Adlum, called the "Father of American Viticulture" for his discovery and promotion of the Catawba grape and his publication of the first book on grapes in the United States, were immediate replacements for the failed Italian *vinifera* varieties and reflect Jefferson's failure and swift (but only temporary) disenchantment with the Old World grape. That Jefferson's Italian grapes did not last two years suggests they were dead on arrival, dried out and perished soon after planting, or perhaps were unprotected and killed during the next winter.[12]

If Jefferson's judgment on the suitability of the *vinifera* was based on the 1807 planting, he was guilty of blaming a relatively innocent species for his own neglect. In requesting the Alexander from Adlum, who had originally received it from Peter Legaux, Jefferson said, "I think it would be well to push the culture of that grape, without losing our time & efforts in search of foreign vines, which it will take centuries to adapt to our soil and climate." But the Alexander grapes from Adlum died as well. Jefferson wrote him the day after planting: "Their long passage gives them a dry appearance, tho I hope that out of so many some will live and enable me to fill my ground. Their chance will be lessened because living on the top of a mountain I have not yet the command of water, which I hope to obtain this year by *cisterns*." Grape cuttings generally present a dry appearance when dormant; not a reflection of their viability, this feature makes them most suit-

able for surviving long-distance transportation, the planting process, and their sensitive infancy. Moreover, Jefferson's meteorological record shows the spring of 1810 was only slightly drier than usual. Nevertheless, he wrote to William Thornton on May 24 that Monticello was in the throes of "the most calamitous drought which had been known for 55 years." In 1816 Jefferson tried again. He wrote Adlum requesting more cuttings of the Alexander, still apparently not realizing that the "Cape" grape was the same. He commented that he had been so "disheartened" by the failure of 1810 and so much at a loss because of the lack of a skilled vigneron, that "I never troubled you again on the subject." Jefferson's excuses—the absence of water and of a trained gardener—do not seem to explain the fourth consecutive vineyard failure, or the three that followed.[13]

The failure of the Adlum shipment likely returned the Monticello vineyard to viticultural limbo. In 1812 Jefferson planted it with experimental grasses ("sweet scented grass," ryegrass), field crops (oats, barley), and vegetables (cabbage, kale, parsnips), treating it essentially like he did his nursery. That year Jefferson received another shipment, the third, of Alexander grapes, still misidentified as the "Cape grape," from Bernard McMahon, secretary of the Philadelphia Society for the Promotion of Viticulture. McMahon felt the Cape "is the variety of grape most to be depended on for giving wine to the United States." Giovannini da Prato, part of the Mazzei legacy, was paid for work in the vineyard, and perhaps because of the dismal success rate so far, he was entrusted with the McMahon shipment. This particular planting had everything going for it: the early spring season was a good time to receive what were probably cuttings, the best means of propagating and establishing this variety; a trained Italian was doing the planting; the season proved favorable for other crops; and because only fourteen cuttings were set out, the planting would have been easily manageable. Yet there is no record that these grapes succeeded.[14]

Another hope for the revival of the Monticello vineyards was Jean David, an ambitious French viticulturist then traveling through the United States who, at least temporarily, rekindled Jefferson's interest in grape growing. David contacted Jefferson late in 1815 with a convincing outline for the development of an American wine industry and a request for employment. Jefferson responded positively and urged David to visit at Monticello. On the same day, December 25, Jefferson wrote Louis Hue Girardin, a mutual acquaintance, reviewing his own failures at Monticello and summarizing his views on the possibilities of American viticulture:

> I have formerly been eager to introduce the culture of the vine and sunk a good deal of money in the endeavor. Altho' unsuccesful, I would still persevere were I younger, but I would do it on a small scale. I would engage a laboring vigneron from France, skilled in the culture of the vine & manipulation of the wine, try only so much ground as he with one or two common laborers could cultivate in ordinary [soil], having occasional assistance when there was great pressure. Let them raise their own provisions of every kind, and to meet the other expences proceed at once to making wine from the wild grape. I have seen too many instance of good wine made from the woods to doubt its success. There is a wild grape [Alexander] so remarkable for the quality of its wine that it ought to be tried. The vigneron should have a liberal interest in the success of the vineyard. Such an experiment would expose one to little loss, and admit of enlargement according to it's success, but this would be too small a scale for the talents of Mr. David. He should if possible be engaged on a larger one; and should the opportunity occur I should not fail to recommend his employment.[15]

While ostensibly denying any intention of hiring David, Jefferson nonetheless purchased vines in anticipation of the Frenchman's arrival. "I have now an opportunity of renewing the trial under a person brought up to the culture of the vine & making wine from his nativity." Jefferson baited the Frenchman with secondary enticements, including possible employment with James Monroe or John Hartwell Cocke, who was described as "rich, liberal, patriotic, judicious & persevering." But David, disenchanted with his failure to get a government subsidy, pessimistic about the potential mone-

tary rewards, and even expressing mock concern that a David-inspired American industry would subvert the economy of his native land, never came to Monticello.[16]

The flurry over David isolates one of the central issues involved in Jefferson's grape-growing failures: his oscillation between the easier-grown though oenologically flawed native grapes versus the more desirable and prestigious *vinifera*. Jefferson wrote David and at first endorsed the European cultivars, noting that "the trial had better be made with one or two kinds of grape only, & these of the wines known to be preferred in this country, as the Madeira Bordeaux Champagne." Two weeks later Jefferson wrote Adlum, "I am so convinced that our first success will be from a native grape, that I would try no other." As he anticipated the possible employment of David, Jefferson ordered cuttings of the native Alexander from John Adlum on January 13, then three days later asked James Monroe for cuttings of his "fine collection of vines which he had selected & brought with him from France." Jefferson recorded paying one shilling to Monroe's gardener for these *vinifera* vines later in April; as well, he paid the postage for a "box of vines" that were probably Adlum's Alexander. No documents survive on their fate despite Jefferson's zeal to consider every varietal possibility.[17]

With his characteristic indefatigable optimism, Jefferson soon turned his attention to another native grape, the Scuppernong. On March 27, 1817, John Hartwell Cocke sent him Scuppernong wine made in eastern North Carolina in exchange for cuttings and young plants of Monticello's renowned Marseilles fig and paper mulberry trees. Cocke remarked on the wine's "delicious flavor, resembling Frontignac," and Jefferson agreed. He wrote North Carolina's William Johnson in May: "I am not without hope that thro' your efforts and example, we shall yet see it [North Carolina] a country abounding in wine and oil. North Carolina has the merit of taking the lead in the former culture, of giving the first specimen of an exquisite wine, produced in quantity, and established in its culture beyond the danger of being discontinued. Her Scuppernon[g] wine, made on the Southside of the Sound [Albemarle], would be distinguished on the best tables of Europe, for its fine aroma, and chrystalline transparence." Jefferson planted fifteen cuttings of the Scuppernong in the "lowest terras of Vineyard" in 1817. They perished because the Scuppernong, unique among grape species, will not root from slips but requires the layering of branches during the growing season. The vine cuttings perhaps came from Bremo, where an ancient twelve-inch trunk of Scuppernong still thrives. In 1822 Jefferson provided Samuel Maverick of South Carolina still another statement on the possibilities of the native grape in the New World:

> Age, debility and decay of memory have for some time withdrawn me from attention to matters without doors. The grape you inquire after as having gone from this place is not now recollected by me. As some in my vineyard have died, others have been substituted without noting which, so that at present all are unknown. That as good wines will be made in America as in Europe the Scuppernon[g] of North Carolina furnishes sufficient proof. The vine is congenial to every climate in Europe from Hungary to the Mediterranean, and will be bound to succeed in the same temperatures here wherever tried by intelligent vignerons. The culture however is more desirable for domestic use than profitable as an occupation for market. In countries which use ardent spirits drunkeness is the mortal vice; but in those which make wine for common use you never see a drunkard.[18]

It seems odd that the cosmopolitan, discriminating Jefferson, so enamored of the classic wines of France, would praise such an inelegant, harshly flavored, sweet wine as is made from the lowly Scuppernong. He expressed a similar sentiment in 1823 after John Adlum sent him a bottle of Catawba wine made from the fox grape Adlum himself discovered and referred to as "Tokay." Jefferson said it was "truly a fine wine, of high flavor, and, as you assure me there was not a drop of brandy or other spirit in it, I may say it is a wine of a good body of its own." Adlum sent a copy of Jefferson's letter to the *American Farmer* and also printed a facsimile as the frontispiece to the 1828 second edition of his book, *A Memoir on the Cultivation of the Vine in America*. Jefferson's enthusiasm for a wine of such questionable quality represents one side of the contradiction that defined his grape-growing and wine-tasting ventures, and indeed, his flirtation with the various Old and New World species of grapes was not unlike his changeable wine preferences. Some historians have described Jefferson as a "faddist" when it came to wine choices. According to Thomas Pinney, "This propensity may help to explain some of the remarkable things that he had to say about American wines." Jefferson's puzzling wide-eyed endorsement of wine made from native Scuppernong, Catawba, and Alexander grapes, however, was typical of the patriotic advocacy he showed toward the horticultural products of the New World—from the currant, bean, and corn varieties brought back by the Lewis and Clark expedition to the seeds of native forest trees he had forwarded to him in Paris to the wildflowers he sowed in his oval flower beds at Monticello. Such a curious enthusiasm reflects the tradition of natural historians since the early seventeenth century—including John Smith, William Byrd, Robert Beverley, and John Lawson—writers who glorified the natural products of the New World in order to justify its exploration and settlement.[19]

THE SPECIES OF UTOPIA: THE VINE IN VIRGINIA

The themes found in Jefferson's experience with grape growing at Monticello—his optimism about its potential, his perennial wavering between the desirability of native versus *vinifera* species, his consistent failures—also defined his heritage as a Virginia viticulturist. Beginning with the trials of government-sponsored, French vignerons at Jamestown in 1622 and continuing through the eighteenth century, promising experiments by the patriarchs of Virginia history—the colonial governors William Berkeley and Alexander Spotswood and such powerful landowners as Robert Beverley, William Byrd, Charles and Landon Carter, Robert Bolling, George Washington—and by experienced European growers like Mazzei and Frenchman Andrew Estave failed to prove that the European grape could find an amenable home in the New World or that the native grapes, so abundant and prolific in the forest, were worth the effort of serious cultivation. The massive amount of documentation and the ensuing discussion of modern historians about these viticultural experiments are a testament to the universality of the vision often associated with Jefferson himself—a pastoral, New World paradise of gentle vine dressers creating an alternative form of classical agrarianism. The grape was the species of utopia.[20]

Optimism about the potential of *Vitis vinifera* continued well into the nineteenth century because carefully tended vines may bear beginning in their third year and continue for years. Many of the earliest pioneers experienced some initial success only to die or move away before their vines were given a legitimate test. The native vines failed because their selection from the wild was haphazard, and unlike the earliest apple or peach varieties and with the exception of notable hybrids like the Alexander or Bland, the cultivation of these choices failed to produce improvements. As well, frontier wine making was not sophisticated enough to provide an appealing rendering of the fox grape, a name of uncertain origin and indefinite meaning that probably refers to its distinctive "foxy" taste. Certain characteristics familiar from Jefferson's experience defined the experiments of eighteenth-century gentlemen gardeners: an unrelenting optimism based on the prolific indigenous grape; patriotic, public-spirited commitment on behalf of the country's welfare; some intitial success harvesting the European grape and making wine from the native species; a multitude of excuses for failure; and an inability to realize the fundamental problem with *vinifera*—disease. Ironically, it was the native vine's dazzling omnipresence that ultimately subverted American efforts at cultivating *Vitis vinifera*. Although a majority of our fruit-tree pests were imported from other continents, the most serious grape disease and insect problems were already here; breeding, thriving, but not crippling the wild grapes in the forest. These same pests devastate the *vinifera* so fatally that a twentieth-century horticulturist as astute as U. P. Hedrick would emphatically state, "We have seen that it is an absolute impossibility to grow the Old World grape in eastern America."[21]

No native species—plum, cherry, even the naturalized peach—promised so much as the native grape; few seventeenth- and eighteenth-century landscape descriptions failed to include lavish images of wild vines twisting through and smothering the loftiest forest trees, a description so universal that it became a central symbol for the natural bounty of the American forest (fig. 94). Inevitably, few natural historians failed to jump the gap between the rampant and unaided success of the wild grape and the inherent possibilities of viticulture in the New World. John Smith in 1612, apparently borrowing from the prose of William Strachey, described how grapes "climbe the toppes of the highest trees" and, where exposed full to the sun, "are covered with fruit, though never manured or pruned." Smith claimed twenty gallons of wine were produced from these native grapes between 1607 and 1609, "neare as good as your French Brittish wine [French wine sold in Britain?], but certainly they would prove good were they well manured." Another reporter from Jamestown in 1619 observed: "Vines here are in such abundance, as where soever a man treads, they are ready to embrace his foote. I have tasted here of a great black grape as big as a Damascen, that hath a true Muscatell-taste; the vine whereof now spending itselfe to the topps of high trees, if it were reduced into a vineyard, and there domesticated, would yield incomparable fruite." Edward Williams, a Londoner who composed essays on mulberry and grape culture in 1650, opened his "Treatise of the Vine" with an elegant tribute to the New World grape: "That the use of the Vine is really intended by nature for Virginia, those infinite store of Grapes which crowne the forehead of that happy Countrey are so many speaking Testimonies." The plain-speaking William Hugh Grove also thought the native grape "might be Improved and good Wine made but all their [colonists'] Care is for Tobacco and Little else minded Except Corn." In 1676 Thomas Glover reported on "the abundance of native vines, which twine about the Oaks and Poplars, and run to the top of them. . . . If some of these vines were planted in convenient vine-yards, where the Sun might have a more kindly influence on them, and kept with diligence and seasonable pruning, they might afford as good grapes as the Claret-grapes of France."[22]

Ultimately these North American grapes have had only a limited impact on the world's wine industry, and certainly they occupy a relatively lowly position on the viticultural hierarchy of grape species. One historian has remarked,

Fig. 94. Wild grapes, *Vitis vulpina*, in the woodlands of Monticello

"Wine from the unadulterated native grape is not wine at all by the standards of *Vitis vinifera*," and the distinctively acidic, musky taste and foxy odor associated with American grapes often elicit disdain from wine connoisseurs. The grapes of *vinifera*, the grape of antiquity that has defined the agriculture of the Mediterranean, are solider, have a higher sugar level, are more delicately flavored, and when properly grown, produce larger berries. On the other hand, the positive qualities of the New World grape have justified repeated, and ultimately economically successful, alternative efforts at its cultivation. North American grapes adapt to cold and humid climates and heavy soils unsuited to *vinifera*, the sweet and flavorful juice made from the cultivars of the fox grape as well as the muscadine and Scuppernong is delicious when unfermented, and the species' resistance to disease and phylloxera and their resultant use as a rootstock for the *vinifera* rescued the late nineteenth-century European industry from extinction. The continuing possibilities of hybrid American grapes and the welcome establishment of French-American hybrid grapes still offer hope for superior varieties in the future.[23]

Experimental vineyards using both the American and European grape were common from the founding of Jamestown.

In 1619 the London Company, eager to foster agricultural diversity in the colonies, sent eight French vignerons from Languedoc as well as *vinifera* grape cuttings, which, according to Robert Beverley, bore fruit remarkably in a year and a half from planting: "They had not heard of the like in any other Country." The Virginia assembly passed a statute requiring "every householder" to plant vines "under penalty of Law," and there were reports of vineyards with 10,000 vines. In 1622 the company sent to every Jamestown householder a manual on grape cultivation written by the Frenchman who recruited the Languedoc vine dressers, John Bonoeil. The failure of the French experiments was attributed to the Indian massacre of 1622, tensions in the English community, poor wine-making techniques, and browsing deer. Nevertheless, the tradition of government-sponsored experiments continued through the next 150 years. In 1623 the assembly passed another law requiring that for every four men in the colony a garden should be planted that included grape cuttings, in 1639 premiums were offered, and in 1658 a reward of 10,000 pounds of tobacco was given for "two tunne of wine."[24]

Robert Beverley reviewed a few of the more notable Virginia viticultural experiments before 1700, including Governor William Berkeley's trials of 1650 using mulberry trees as supporting espaliers for native vines, the French Huguenots' efforts to make wine in 1699 at Manakin just west of Richmond, and the vineyard of Isaac Jamart, also on the James River. His own three-acre hillside vineyard at the head of the Mattaponi River thirty miles north of Richmond may have included French varieties. Hugh Jones, in *The Present State of Virginia*, reported that Beverley "bragged much of it in Publick, but being bantered by several Gentlemen, he proposed to give each of them a Guinea down, if they would give him Ten, if he made a certain number of Gallons of pure Wine." Beverley put down 100 guineas, won his wager, which he invested further in vines, "and would have brought it to very high Perfection, had he lived some years longer." Jones himself also saw great possibilities for Virginia grape culture, especially in the hilly western lands, "which at present lye waste."[25]

The number of explanations for the failure of Virginia grape growing equaled the number of experiments, yet the promise and possibilities for a Virginia wine industry continued for generations. William Byrd tried to grow twenty *vinifera* cultivars at Westover in an attempt to find alternatives to Virginia corn and tobacco culture. He stumbled upon one solution to the failure of the European grape—a solution that when commonly practiced two centuries later helped to establish successful *vinifera* growing in eastern North America —when he wrote, "the way to succeed, in a vineyard, is to graft choice vines, on stocks of our wild ones, to naturalize them better to our soyl & Clymate." Between 1759 and 1765 the Virginia assembly offered cash prizes, some as large as £500, for the best wine and the largest planting of grapevines. One recipient of the premium was the assembly's chairman, Charles Carter of King George County, whose vineyard included 1,800 bearing *vinifera* vines planted at six-foot intervals. Charles's brother Landon Carter of Sabine Hall planted peach trees in his vineyard. He soon discovered, however, that their shade invited moisture-loving diseases and so removed them. Carter's homemade wine was concocted from wild vines and was described as "pleasant" and "admired by everybody," yet his cultivated grapes probably were not so successful.[26]

Virginia's two most ambitious pre-Revolutionary vineyard experiments, the public vineyard in Williamsburg and Robert Bolling's piedmont trials with *vinifera* grapes, demonstrated the tensions between the grape of the Old World and the New, an issue that for the first time became the subject of a public debate in Williamsburg's *Virginia Gazette*. The culmination of state-endorsed viticulture occurred in 1770 when the Virginia assembly passed another act encouraging grape growing, although this time the investment was significantly more substantial and included the allocation of £450 from the state treasury to a subsidized Williamsburg vineyard. The trustees of the project were authorized to purchase as many as 100 acres of land, build a dwelling, purchase three black slaves as laborers, and hire three apprentice vine dressers. Andrew Estave, a Frenchman from Bordeaux who was then working in Williamsburg as a baker, was asked to direct the experiment, and if he succeeded in producing ten hogsheads of salable wine in six years, the property and slaves were to be his reward. Estave endorsed the New World vine and planted it exclusively once his *vinifera* varieties were decimated by what was most likely disease. In 1774, the year Philip

Pl. 44. Gallesio's "Fico Albo," Jefferson's Marseilles fig, from *Pomona italiana*

Pl. 45. Fig harvest at Monticello in 1991

Pl. 46. Strawberries from George Brookshaw's *Pomona Brittanica*, 1817: Golden Drop (*top*); Hautboy (*center left*); Chili (*middle*); Pine (*center right*); Scarlet-fleshed Pine (*bottom*)

Pl. 47. White Antwerp raspberry from Hooker's *Pomona Londinensis*

Pl. 48. White Dutch currant from Hooker's *Pomona Londinensis*

Pl. 49. *Ribes aureum*, the yellow-flowering currant, at Monticello

Mazzei lost his grapes to cold, Estave requested more funds for his vineyard to offset drought and frost. The request was rejected and in 1777 the vineyard land and slaves were sold for £560.[27]

At the same time Colonel Robert Bolling, Jr., of Chellow, a remote location in the red-hill piedmont of Buckingham County fifty miles south of Monticello, began ambitious experiments with the Old World grape. Bolling's writings advocating American, particularly piedmont Virginia ("our poorer lands"), viticulture appeared in the *Gazette* and, posthumously, Baltimore's *American Farmer*. His "Essay on the Utility of Vine Planting in Virginia" publicly chastised the Estave trials for their reliance on the native grape, which "wants fire"; the Williamsburg vineyard's lowland situation, which resulted in grapes that were "too pulpy . . . whence a thin acid Liquor"; and the wasteful expense of public moneys for a venture he suggested had an undemocratic bias. Bolling championed the possibilities of frontier viticulture as the best alternative for poor, western-migrating tobacco farmers. He blamed past failures on a misguided selection of *vinifera* cultivars and recommended late-season, northern Italian varieties, which he felt ripened during a suitable time between the hot August and the cool, rainy October of the piedmont. Bolling posed the argument, often repeated by early New World vine advocates, that plant species, particularly grapes, indigenous or acclimated to a particular latitude in Europe, should adapt to the same latitude in America. Virginia does have about the same latitude as southern France and northern Italy, but the climatic disparity is extreme in terms of rainfall, humidity, and temperature variations.[28]

Estave gently rebuked ("We ought not to blame his Endeavors . . . but I doubt their Success") both of Bolling's 1773 *Gazette* essays by defending the more resilient native grape, which he felt was maligned because past trials had neglected vigorous cultural practices: "Has any one transplanted the Vines, enclosed, cultivated, and dressed them? No one has a Right to condemn it [the public vineyard] until the Experiment has been fairly made." Estave said, "I can affirm, from Experience, that Vines, planted and cultivated, bear a Fruit one third at least larger that what is found on the spontaneous Growth of the Woods; and that the Juice of the former is in-

finitely richer, and more spiritous." Estave insisted that European varieties were too susceptible to insects, disease, and late-season rain and also ripened too early in the season. He requested more time for his experiments to mature: "I beseech them [critics like Bolling] to suspend for a While their Judgment, and to consider a little the unlucky Seasons we have had for the two last Years; nothing being more contrary to fresh planted Vines than excessive Droughts."[29]

Bolling's skepticism apparently fueled efforts to abandon the Williamsburg public vineyard. Like Robert Beverley, Bolling died, in July 1775, before his four-acre vine planting had produced sufficiently to confirm his opinions. One modern grape historian has remarked, "One can also be thankful that he died while the vineyard was still young and promising." After Edward Antill of New Jersey, Bolling was the second American writer on grape cultivation, and sections of his compilation of traditional European advice on grape growing, "A Sketch of Vine Culture," were published in the *American Farmer* in 1829 and 1830 (fig. 95). Despite his Old World, classical bias, Bolling could be acutely on the mark. He pinpointed the absence of economically important native plants in eastern North America when he said, "The Country has unhappily a great Partiality for native Vines, the only Native Production to which it was ever partial." He also suggested the potential of hybrid grapes uniting the hardiness, disease resistance, and vigor of the native species with the flavor and wine-making qualities of *vinifera*. Not only did Bolling define a way for doing this, involving the interplanting of both species, but he predicted the future development of French-American hybrids now popular in eastern North American vineyards: "It is probable we may obtain varieties better adapted to our soils and climates, and better for wine or table, than either of those kinds from whence they sprang."[30]

George Washington's experiments in grape culture were typical and surprisingly similar to Jefferson's. His vineyard, ambitiously planted with 55 cuttings of "Madeira" in 1755 and 2,000 cuttings of the native "winter" grape in 1771, was later abandoned to fruit-tree culture, unusual and promising vegetables, and nursery activities. He blamed its failure on his extended absence from Mount Vernon. Washington said he

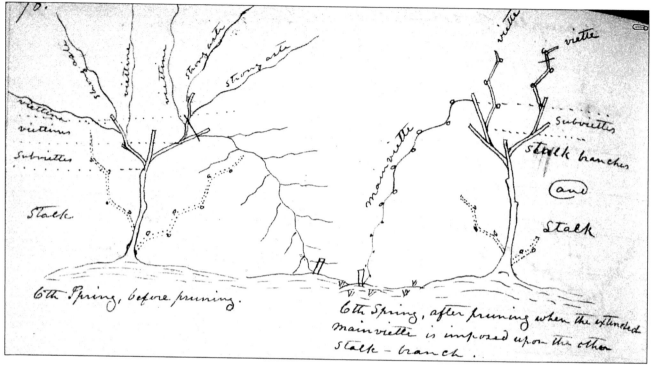

Fig. 95. Sketches of pruning techniques from copy of Robert Bolling's manuscript, "A Sketch of Vine Culture"

"never contemplated" growing the European species but hoped that "by a happy choice of the [native] species I might succeed better than those who had attempted the foreign vine," yet he frequently ordered *vinifera* grapes. Like Estave, he also stated that ripening in "our Summer and Autumnal heats," resulting in excessive fermentation of the fruit, had caused earlier failed experiments in *vinifera* grape culture. Washington supported Philip Mazzei's trials: "I have long been of opinion from the spontaneous growth of the vine, that the climate and soil in many parts of Virginia were well fitted for Vineyards and that Wine, sooner or later would become a valuable article of produce." Like Jefferson, he sought vines from M. de Malesherbes of France in 1784 and was among the first to experiment with European table grapes. Similarly, many of the vines Washington ordered died in transit or were planted casually in his fruit garden.[31]

GRAPE CULTURE

Sporting with the long branches, bending them in
festoons, and marking the growth of the fine clusters
from the upper buds . . . has the happiest effect on
the human mind—such as Bonaparte never felt.
These are the proper play things of great men; and
had George Washington lived to this day, I would
have said to him, "One thing lackest thou yet, in that,
after saving the world from a political deluge, thou
hast not yet planted a vineyard."

—*Timothy Matlack, "On the Cultivation of the Vine"*

The viticultural history of seventeenth- and eighteenth-century America, the promise and the ensuing failure of virtually every dedicated experiment, should have banished any illusions about grape growing as an easy and simple matter.

Yet the dream persisted. An experimental vineyard was acknowledged as a difficult, expensive, and labor-intensive investment; the success of future experiments hinged on a grower's rigorous adherence to stringent rules of site and soil selection, planting, pruning and training, and the use of manures. Timothy Matlack summed up the uneasy American fascination with grape culture: "So much has been said about raising vines, as to have frightened people with the ghosts of difficulties that never existed."[32]

The importance of the possibilities of grape culture in America before 1830 was reflected by the abundant technical advice provided by writers and growers like Edward Antill, Robert Bolling, Peter Legaux, James Mease, Bernard McMahon, S. W. Johnson, John Adlum, and John James Dufour, the creators of Matlack's "ghosts." Grape literature before 1830 not only presented the state of the art of American horticulture, but these writers and growers provide another chapter in the viticultural biography of Thomas Jefferson. Although their viticultural directions were mostly culled from earlier European authorities, their advice on grape growing was significantly more comprehensive than the directions given for any other horticultural crop. Jefferson, like most of the early viticultural experts, failed to develop new techniques of grape culture suited to the American situation. Ironically, at the same time, his grapes died in part because he never read anything at all about grape culture. When Jefferson wrote John Adlum in 1823 to thank him for two bottles of wine and a copy of his book, A Memoir on the Cultivation of the Vine in America, he admitted his ignorance of the subject and explained his unremitting failure as a grape grower: "Of your book on the culture of the vine it would be presumptious in me to give any opinion, because it is a culture of which I have no knowledge either from practice or reading."[33]

Like many later viticultural writers, Edward Antill (1700–1770) of New Jersey prefaced his eighty-page "Essay on the Cultivation of the Vine, and the Making of Wine, Suited to the Different Climates in North-America" with patriotic, public-spirited sentiment: "Nothing but the love of my country and the good of mankind could have tempted me to appear and expose myself to public views." Antill fancied himself as the "father" leading his "children by the hand" through

the process, and his rambling essay, published in the Transactions of the American Philosophical Society a year after his death, was often cited and copied by later writers. James Mease, in the 1803 American edition of the Domestic Encyclopedia, reprinted large portions of Antill's "Essay," reinforcing its continuing influence on this country's earlier viticulture. Robert Bolling's "Sketch of Vine Culture for Pennsylvania, Maryland, Virginia, and the Carolinas" was written in 1773 or 1774. It also relied on contemporary European writers like Miller and Forsyth, as well as Antill himself. The primary inspiration for Bolling's "Sketch," however, was the writings of classical writers like Virgil and Columella.[34]

While Peter Legaux never published a treatise comparable to Antill's "Essay" or Bolling's "Sketch," the example of his Spring Mill vineyard inspired the ample practical directions given by Bernard McMahon in his Calendar and by another New Jersey vine grower, S. W. Johnson, whose Rural Economy, 1803, was dedicated to Jefferson and included thirty-one pages "On the Culture of the Vine." McMahon touted the possibilities of using the hardy native grape as a rootstock for the more delicate vinifera. In as dramatic a move as William Coxe's definition of a New World form of pomology, John Adlum (1759–1836) of Georgetown decisively rejected European sources ("throw them in the fire") and championed native grapes and New World know-how: "With the use of a little common sense, an American will raise a bushel of grapes where a foreigner will not have a gallon" (fig. 96). He permanently altered the character of American viticulture through frequent writings in the American Farmer, distribution of the Catawba and other native grapes, and his public advocacy of an experimental national vineyard (fig. 97). Adlum's discovery of the Catawba grape, the first native species to adapt to commercial wine making, coincided with the publication of his Memoir on the Cultivation of the Vine in America, and the Best Mode of Making Wine.[35]

Why did Jefferson's grapes die? Perhaps too hot for European apples, plums, and pears, the Monticello fruitery nonetheless provided grapes, both native and exotic, an ideal setting for their fullest expression. Jefferson's vineyards were inspired by the Mediterranean example—terraced, elevated and exposed to the southeast, and overhung by a massive

Fig. 96. John Adlum, portrait attributed to
Charles Willson Peale, c. 1794

Both the northeast and southwest vineyards were terraced when Jefferson's ambitious 1807 scheme was planted, and the terracing may have evolved from the massive earthmoving performed by Mazzei's vignerons in 1774, when four-foot-deep, four-foot-wide trenches were excavated as planting holes—an ancient Mediterranean technique similar to the horticultural practice of double digging. Such thorough preparation was the best way to mellow the heavy clay soil, an excellent alternative to the frequent deep plowing recommended by Miller and most early American writers.[36]

Perhaps another reason for the early optimism about the success of *Vitis vinifera* was that before the foliage is disfigured by mildew, anthracnose, and black rot, the vines grow more robustly in eastern North America than in the arid Mediterranean and therefore require more space. The fox grape and its related New World species such as the Scuppernong, which can easily cover a thirty-foot-square arbor, are also more vigorous than the Old World vine. Most writers, however, provided a general recommendation that grapes be planted three to six feet apart. This substantially limited the success of grape growing in America, and Jefferson as well was guilty of blind obedience to traditional sources. His 1774 planting included a two-to-three-foot spacing, the 1778 plan shows vines three feet apart, and his 1807 scheme suggests that the plants were distanced no more than four and a half feet.[37]

While Jefferson's grapes may have suffered because they were planted too close in a heavy, sticky soil, most of the later plantings—in 1796, 1802, 1807, 1810, 1812, 1815, and 1817—probably perished because they were not set out properly. Rooted vines were not watered during the planting process, and rootless, dormant cuttings were not covered sufficiently to protect the topmost buds from dessicating April winds or late May frost. In 1796 when Jefferson wrote Benjamin Hawkins, "Every one budded after it was planted. Yet every one died immediately after," he showed his ignorance of the lessons provided by his horticultural library. The planting advice of vine authorities was specific and a crucial key to success: cuttings, eventually trimmed to a length of twelve to eighteen inches, were to be taken from parent vines during the autumn pruning and stored in soil-covered ditches over the winter. Unrooted cuttings were preferred unanimously because of their

stone wall—and their conception was ideal. Monticello's heavy red clay soil, on the other hand, has traditionally been regarded as an inhospitable soil medium, especially for the European species, and lean, stony, light, well-drained soils as most suitable. Johnson, for example, said, "The soil of the vineyard should be so light, that in digging the foot need not be put on the spade." Nevertheless, Jefferson said the rocky, red land at Mazzei's Colle vineyard, only two miles away, resembled "extremely the Cote of Burgundy from Chambertin to Montrachet where the famous wines of Burgundy are made. I am inclined to believe he [Mazzei] was right in preferring the South Eastern face of this ridge of mountains."

Fig. 97. Catawba grape from C. L. Fleischmann, *Grapes of America*

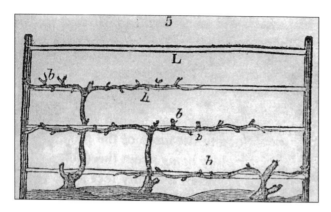

Fig. 98. John James Dufour's sketches of vine-training systems in *The American Vine Dresser's Guide*, 1826

ability to adapt to their new situation and resist the damaging effects of dryness or cold. Ditches, such as those dug by Mazzei's vignerons in 1774, or deep holes twelve to eighteen inches deep, at times made with a long, stout, three-inch-wide iron bar, were dug in well-pulverized, occasionally amended soil during the late winter or spring months. Cuttings were dipped in dung water, as was done at Monticello in 1774, and planted so that their topmost bud was from two inches above to level with the ground surface. The key step of the process involved covering that top bud with loose soil, hay, or other litter to prevent damage from frost or drying spring winds. It was imperative that the cuttings be buried enough that they were protected during their delicate infancy, and even today in modern vineyards the young foliage that emerges from the leaf bud (often before the roots develop) is covered with melted wax to prevent transpiration.[38]

Training and pruning were the topics most discussed by the earliest writers. When in 1799 Jefferson left a memorandum requesting that one of his slaves "espalier" the grapes in the vineyard, he provided a hint that his vines were trained on a permanent trellis system (fig. 98). In 1809 two terraces of the northeast vineyard were planted with gourds — a sprawling, twining vine requiring support—suggesting that the espalier structure may still have been intact ten years later, outlasting the vines. The more common training system, adapted from European sources by Antill, Bolling,

Legaux, Johnson, McMahon, and Adlum, involved the use of four- to six-foot poles, usually two to four for each vine, stuck in annually and segregating the bearing shoots from "the branches of reserve," which would bear fruiting clusters the following year. The purpose of this system was to allow the cold-climate grower to bury his bearing buds every winter to protect them from injury, yet the labor-intensive process of annually renewing the poles seems complicated and time-consuming. Similarly tedious, the columnar growth habit of each shoot had to be encouraged with intensive summer pruning of suckers, loose, horizontal branches, and any foliage growing above the four-to-five-foot poles (fig. 99).[39]

The alternative method, perhaps used at Monticello, was recommended for warmer climates and fruit-garden walls and, according to Antill, was adapted from the classical "Roman frame," essentially a rail fence built to accommodate twining grape vines. Six-foot-high posts were placed six feet apart, and three horizontal poles or rails at four, five, and six feet above the ground connected them (fig. 100). Vines were trained to the lowest rail, pruned every autumn to create a "head" of bearing and reserve buds, or "eyes," and formed during the growing season into a fan shape (fig. 101). Variations depended upon which European authority was mimicked. Although their techniques were derivative, American growers used local materials to tie up the vines. Jefferson mentioned that the 1774 planting involved the use of "bear grass,"

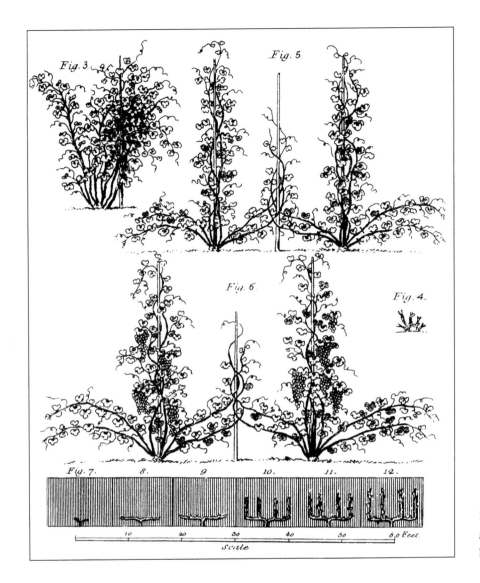

Fig. 99. S. W. Johnson's illustration of grape training, with the use of temporary poles, in *Rural Economy*, 1806

or yucca leaves, to temporarily tie up the vines during the planting process. Other American writers found similar native products: Antill suggested dried leaves of the sweet flag, *Acorus calamus*, a water-loving native herb; Johnson endorsed dried rushes; and McMahon recommended planting willows in order to harvest the young, flexible branches—ideal for securing grapevines.[40]

Peaches thrived in the New World because there were no native peaches, and therefore no peach pests. Although a majority of our fruit-tree pests were imported from other continents, the most serious grape disease and insect problems were already here, breeding, thriving, but not crippling the wild grapes in the forest. In contrast, *vinifera* vines imported to *Vitis*-free areas such as Chile, Australia, and South Africa thrive relatively unencumbered by pests. Black rot (*Guignardia bidwellii*) is the most widespread and crippling grape pest

Fig. 100. The design for the vine-
yard espalier system at Monticello
is based on Edward Antill, "An
Essay on the Cultivation of the
Vine," American Philosophical
Society, *Transactions*, 1771.

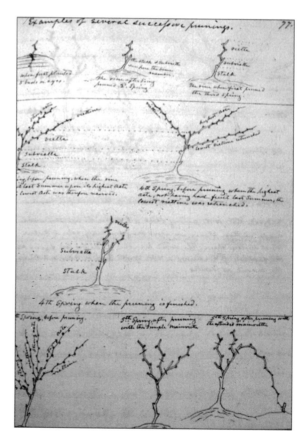

Fig. 101. Sketches of pruning techniques from
Bolling's "Sketch of Vine Culture"

Fig. 102. Black rot on grapes

in Virginia, infecting young growth in the spring and then spreading to the ripening berries, which are transformed into black, hard, shriveled mummies (fig. 102). Downy mildew (*Plasmopara viticola*) can defoliate an entire plant of *vinifera* by autumn, while powdery mildew (*Uncinula necator*), well known for the characteristic grayish-white, powdery growth on the leaves, can both defoliate the vine and inhibit the maturation of the grapes. These diseases were introduced from North America into Europe, "where they have wrought widespread havoc," in the latter half of the nineteenth century. Native grapes such as the Catawba are by no means immune to mildew and black rot, both of which devastated the grape industry that evolved around Cincinnati, "the Rhineland of America," in the middle of the nineteenth century. Phylloxera, an aphidlike louse that sucks nourishment from both the roots and the leaves, became notorious late in the nineteenth century when, after an accidental introduction into Europe in 1863, it nearly destroyed that continent's wine economy (fig. 103). By using American species rootstock, a tougher and denser wood, and grafting the *vinifera* cultivar onto it, phyl-

Fig. 103. Phylloxera attack on grape leaves. Root damage by this same insect is especially deadly to *Vitis vinifera* vines.

loxera has been controlled. Systemic fungicides, more effective than the Bordeaux mix (lime, sulfur, and copper) used as a spray in the late nineteenth century, have also controlled the mildews and black rot to such an extent that, beginning in the 1970s and growing through the 1980s and 1990s, a wine industry based on *vinifera* grapes has become established in Virginia.[41]

Most of Virginia's eighteenth-century grape-growing ventures—those by Beverley, Byrd, Spotswood, Bolling, Estave, Mazzei—were abandoned before these indigenous diseases became well established. Despite suggesting their presence, few early growers acknowledged disease, or insects for that matter, as a serious problem. One exception was John James Dufour, who often alluded to the "sickness" afflicting grapes and described "mildew" in his list of the "different diseases that I have seen afflicting vines." Dufour's "mildew" was probably anthracnose, a European import. Miller remarked that he had heard that grapes "burst" before ripening in America, probably a symptom of powdery mildew. Antill mentioned "vine fretters," possibly a caterpillar, which could be picked off by hand. McMahon and other writers implied that clean cultivation methods would reduce mildew on the vines, and James Mease's *Domestic Encyclopedia* recommended cutting a two-centimeter ring around the bark to prevent "rot," perhaps black rot. The focus of writers' discussion about pests concerned relatively trivial nuisances—birds, wasps, mammalian intruders, and rose bugs—which the "astonished" William Cobbett blamed for the general neglect of grape culture in America. Molasses or honey-filled traps were standard recommendations for troublesome bees. Birds were warded off by cutting down nearby attractive vegetation like pokeweed or wild cherries. Antill suggested the vigneron be given a gun, or at least "a smart watchful dog," to keep out animals, and Mease argued that the "numerous insects [that] prey upon the vine" could be controlled with frequent waterings, three times a week—a standard Forsyth technique. By 1823 a Massachusetts grape grower was alarmed by a yellow insect with brown stripes ("the labour and care of cultivation is lost"). His remedy involved covering his vines with movable tents, twelve feet long, and smoking tobacco leaves within.[42]

ALEXANDER ("Cape," "Cape of Good Hope")

The Alexander grape at least temporarily answered the riddle to successful grape cultivation in eastern North America (fig. 104). Jefferson planted this grape as the "Cape of Good Hope" grape in 1802 from Peter Legaux; as the "native wine-grapes rec'd from Major Adlum of Maryland" in 1810; and as the "Cape grape" in 1812 from McMahon. It seems doubtful any of these plantings thrived at Monticello. In 1809 Adlum forwarded a sample of wine made from the Alexander to Jefferson, who acclaimed it three times over the next year. In October 1809 he said, "This was a very fine wine, & so exactly resembling the red Burgundy of Chambertin . . . the company could not distinguish the one from the other." In January 1810 he pronounced it "as good as the best Burgundy," and in April he wrote, "The quality of the bottle you sent before satisfies me that we have at length found one native grape, inured to all accidents of our climate, which will give us a wine worthy of the best vineyards of France." Jefferson's praise had far-reaching consequences, unquestionably encouraging Adlum to pursue grander viticultural projects, which led to his role as "Father of American Viticulture." Adlum, as well as Dufour, quoted from Jefferson's October letter in his *Memoir* and even tried to reprint the 1809 letter in the *American Farmer* in 1822.[43]

The Alexander was discovered around 1740 by James Alexander, the gardener to Thomas Penn, a son of William Penn, and seems to have been a hybrid between a *vinifera* cultivar surviving from the elder Penn's 1685 vineyard and a *Vitis labrusca* growing wild in the nearby forest. The variety of synonyms for Alexander—Tasker's, Constantia, Schuykill, Cape, and others—suggests its importance to, and widespread distribution among, the pioneers in American grape culture. Colonel Benjamin Tasker, Jr., of Maryland, for example, successfully grew and made wine from the Alexander as early as 1759. Peter Legaux is credited with popularizing the Alexander by distributing thousands of vines to grape growers throughout the United States in the first years of the nineteenth century. Legaux advertised the "Cape" grape as an exotic *vinifera*, thereby boosting its attractiveness yet beginning a controversial argument that was waged for the next century:

Schuylkill.

Fig. 104 Alexander grape, known as the "Cape" grape to Jefferson and Schuykill or Tasker's to others,
from Fleischmann, *Grapes of America*

William Bartram suggested it was a pure native, McMahon argued for mixed blood, and others such as John James Dufour abided by Legaux's claim. Still others like Constantine Rafinesque, author of *American Manual of Grape Vines and the Method of Making Wine* (1830), accused Legaux of creating a public relations hoax. Nevertheless, when planted by early viticulturists alongside *vinifera* varieties, the Alexander thrived in comparison because of its hardiness and pest resistance.[44]

In defending the black, thick-skinned "Cape" grape, Dufour compared it to the Hewes Crab apple: although inedible out of hand, the Hewes is delicious when made into juice. On the other hand, William Bartram found the Cape "as sweet as any grape. Many persons think them too luscious." Downing, as he often did, found middle ground when he said it was "quite sweet when ripe, and makes a very fair wine, but is quite too pulpy and coarse for table use." Writers also debated the degree of foxiness inherent in Alexander wine, a key clue to its native heritage. The Alexander's season of ripening (quite late in autumn) and the shape of its berries (oval) suggest European blood. Despite the contention about its origin and the arguments about its qualities, the Alexander inspired tangible hope for American viticulture until the introduction in 1823 of Adlum's Catawba, which proved to be more resistant to disease, conveniently earlier, and of higher quality. Jefferson's highly publicized but mild endorsement of Catawba wine, reprinted both in Adlum's *Memoirs* and the *American Farmer*, stimulated its ascendance as the premier American grape. The Alexander is probably extinct today.[45]

GRAPES SENT BY THOMAS MAIN

"Black cluster" was, confusingly, Pinot Gris to Philip Miller, Cabernet Sauvignon to William Robert Prince, and McMahon's and Downing's Pinot Noir, traditionally associated with Burgundian wine and seemingly the top choice for trials in the New World.[46]

Black Hamburg, like many of the Muscat and Chasselas grapes popular in the eighteenth century (and therefore sold by Thomas Main and other American nurserymen), was considered first choice as a table or dessert grape when cultivated under glass. Miller and McMahon both praised this large,

nearly black, oval grape for its size, flavor, and attractiveness. Black Hamburg, like most of its European cousins, has larger, more uniform berries, a richer, more delicate flavor, and the potential to be more productive than any American grape. This was the only *vinifera* ranked among "Major Varieties" in U. P. Hedrick's *Grapes of New York*.[47]

Chasselas Doré, or Golden Chasselas, was the original and most commonly cultivated of the Chasselas grapes in the early nineteenth century and once ranked as the most widely disseminated grape variety in the world. It was typical of the English hothouse varieties distributed by early nineteenth-century American nurserymen. A synonym, Chasselas de Fontainebleau, suggests its association with the royal court of France, a central point for its distribution throughout Europe in the sixteenth through eighteenth centuries. Once highly regarded as a dessert variety and useful in some vintages when low acidity was important, Chasselas Doré is renowned for its earliness, August 11 in Charlottesville. The cluster and berry are above medium size; the spherical grapes yellowish-green, translucent, juicy, tender, and sweet.[48]

Chasselas Rosé ("brick-coloured," "Chaselas of Fountainbleau"). This was the grape Jefferson described to Benjamin Hawkins in 1796: "I have also a grape from Italy, of a brick dust color, coming about a fortnight later than the sweetwater and lasting till frost, the most valuable I ever knew. It deserves this character for its flavor, its quantities, and its hardiness. I take it to be the Chasselas of Fontainebleau." This is the only reference to the successful harvest of *Vitis vinifera* at Monticello. Jefferson was close in his identification, yet "brick-colored" aptly describes the Chasselas Rosé rather than Chasselas Doré, the genuine Chasselas of Fontainebleau. McMahon described the Brick grape: "The berries of this kind are small, inclining to an oval figure, and of a pale red or brick color. This is a very sweet grape, though not much admired." A review in 1917 by a New York proponent of *vinifera* culture reported, "It is better eating than most of our native grapes and ripens so early for a Vinifera that it is quite desirable." Chasselas Rosé, although a traditional table variety, is still grown as a wine grape in Germany, where it is blended with Muscat of Hamburg to create Schoenburger.[49]

"Malaga" (Muscat of Alexandria? Malaga Rosada?). The

Fig. 105. White Frontinac, or Muscat Blanc, from Langley's *Pomona*

Fig. 106. Muscat Blanc from Duhamel's *Traité*

1807 planting scheme identified a number of vines by the wines they produced rather than the grape variety itself. Malaga wine, common in Virginia as early as 1623, is usually made from Pedro Ximénes, a Spanish variety. The "Malaga" grape has had numerous alternative names, including Cinsaut, Gros Semillon, and Muscat of Alexandria. Malaga Rosada, a more recent development, is still in cultivation and known as Grec Rouge.[50]

"Muscadine" (Chasselas Blanc?). Thomas Main's "Musca-

dine" grape was perhaps Chasselas Blanc, considered a variant of the Doré by modern ampelographers. McMahon described White Muscadine as "a large white berry" that bore abundantly early in the season—a quality of the Chasselas tribe.[51]

Muscat Blanc ("white Frontignac") is considered the grandfather of the aromatic race of muscat grapes, which produce a syrupy dessert wine: Moscato in Italy, Moscatel in Spain, Muscatel in France (figs. 105, 106, pl. 41). Muscat wine was a favorite of Jefferson's, popular in the colonies, and intimately associated with the culture of the ancient Mediterranean. Ripening soon after the Chasselas, Muscat Blanc has thickly clustered, round, greenish-white berries. McMahon declared it "a high flavoured grape [with] a peculiar rich juice," and Downing pronounced it "a very favorite."[52]

Fig. 107. Cornichon Blanc from Duhamel's *Traité*

Red Hamburg may be synonymous with the more common Black Hamburg. McMahon described its berries as "dark red, with thin skins and juicy delicate flesh." According to J. C. Loudon, this is the famous Hampton-Court vine, planted 250 years ago and still thriving in its own individual greenhouse outside London.[53]

TABLE GRAPES SENT BY PHILIP MAZZEI FROM TUSCANY

Galletta, Olivette Blanche, or Cornichon Blanc ("Galettas"). Jefferson's "Galettas" was the Galletta grape, the Tuscan name for Cornichon Blanc, which means "the spur of the cock" in French (fig. 107). Today it is known as Olivette Blanche ("olive-shaped white grape"), a reference to the curious fingerlike shape of the grape itself. Widely distributed in France and Italy as a decorative novelty and once common in Rome markets, the berries are white with thick skin and firm sweet flesh.[54]

Luglienga, or Lignan Blanc ("Great July"; "Lugliola grossa" to Mazzei), an ancient northern Italian table variety, was esteemed throughout Europe as the first table grape of the season. This may have been widely distributed in England and the colonies as "White Sweetwater." Although they considered it inferior to Chasselas Doré, twentieth-century New York horticulturists proclaimed the Luglienga, or Lignan Blanc, "excellent in quality" and "far superior to the first native grapes." The berries are amber yellow and quite sweet.[55]

"Piedmont Malmsey," "Malvagia di Piemonte" to Mazzei (Malvasia Bianca?). Jefferson transcribed Mazzei's "Malvagia di Piemonte" as "Piedmont Malmsey," "Malmsey" being a traditional English corruption of Malvasia and a reference to a strong, sweet wine. There are numerous Malvasia grapes, some with a flavor resembling that of a muscat, others with a simpler taste. A commonly cultivated Tuscan Malvasia, Malvasia Bianca del Chianti, is a white grape used to add fragrance to Chianti.[56]

Regina ("Queen's grape") is a familiar table variety in Italy, where its vigorous habit is often supported by arbors. The large, oval, amber grapes possess a simple yet pleasing flavor.[57]

Seralamanna (Muscat of Alexandria?) was introduced from

Fig. 108. Muscat of Alexandria, synonymous, some have argued, with Seralamanna, from Duhamel's *Traité*

Greece to Italy in the sixteenth century by the Florentine Ser (or Monsieur) Alamanno Salviati, and the name was soon corrupted: Uva di Ser Alamanno became abbreviated to Sera la manna, Uva Seralamanna, or Salamanna (fig. 108, pl. 40). For centuries ampelographers have debated its synonymity with the more universally known Muscat of Alexandria. Seralamanna belongs among the muscat family, used primarily as a table grape or for raisins. The yellow-gold grapes were proclaimed the most beautiful and valuable of all dessert varieties by Giorgio Gallesio. Mazzei wrote Jefferson that although it was "the worst for making wine, [it] is the best for eating fresh that I have tasted anywhere in the world, not excepting Asia Minor."[58]

"Smyrna grape without seeds." Jefferson had observed "a small dried grape from Smyrna without a seed" in Marseilles in 1787, possibly the same variety sent by Mazzei as "di Smirne senza vinaccioli." The oval-berried Sultanina and the small round Sultana (from which we are indebted for Thompson's Seedless today) are two ancient seedless grapes, a quality relatively uncommon in the early nineteenth century.[59]

"Tokay" ("Toccai" to Mazzei and Appleton) (Tocai Rosso?) is a Hungarian wine made from the Furmint grape. Some Italian ampelographers claim the Furmint ("Tocai Friulano" to them) was taken from northern Italy in the seventeenth century to form the basis of the Hungarian Tokay wine industry. However, Mazzei's table grape ("Toccai") was more likely Tocai Rosso while Appleton's wine "Toccai" was apparently Furmint.[60]

DRY WINE GRAPES FROM THE FLORENCE BOTANICAL GARDEN

"Abrostine Red" (Colorino?). "Abrosti" was a Tuscan term used to refer to large-fruiting seedlings of the Colorino grape, often added to wines to provide color and strength (pl. 37). Today, the Red Colorino is still a regional grape, occasionally added (5%) to Chianti.[61]

"Abrostine White" (Picolit?) is also a generic name for a race of grapes, the most common being Picolit, a small, oval-shaped, white grape that turns amber when ripe (pl. 38). A sweet dessert wine made from Picolit is currently enjoying a revival in Friuli.[62]

Aleatico produces a very sweet, muscat-flavored wine (pl. 39). Although grown in Tuscany since the fourteenth century, Aleatico is believed to be a mutation of Muscat Blanc. Like many of the other Italian grapes planted in 1807, it was possibly a Jefferson introduction into North America.[63]

Furmint ("Tokay"). Appleton wrote Jefferson that this particular variety had been "transplanted into Etruria with the utmost success, and the wine so perfectly similar to the finest of Hungary that the most intelligent cannot discover the smallest difference. Mr Lastri [who had procured the vines for Appleton] is therefore decidedly of the opinion, that it depends on the process observed in making the wine, and not on the soil on which it grows." Appleton's "Tokay" was apparently the Hungarian Furmint, which produces Tokay wine.[64]

"Lachrima Christi" is most widely known as the clear, dry, white Neapolitan wine; however, the synonyms for the grape variety Lachrima Christi are varied and confusing. Lacrima Bianca was the source for the Naples wine, while Lacrima Dolce and Lacrima Forte were Tuscan varieties (pl. 36).[65]

Mammolo Toscano, or Rafojone Nero ("Mammole"), a flowery, heavily scented red grape, is still an optional ingredient of Chianti. An ancient Tuscan variety, the spreading, vigorous vines produce medium-sized, suboval, purplish-black grapes.[66]

Morgiano ("Margiano"), from Tuscany, has a long, black berry which makes a colorful wine.[67]

Sangiovese ("San Giovetto"), in all its clonal variety, is the basic ingredient of Chianti (pls. 42, 43). It is a hardy vine, producing abundant quantities of bluish-black grapes distinguished by high levels of sugar, tannin, and acidity. Sangiovese Grosso was the form most associated with seventeenth- and eighteenth-century Tuscany.[68]

Trebbiano, first described in 1302 (White Trebbiano), is used in more wine than any other grape variety: Trebbiano and Soave in Italy, Ugni Blanc in Provence, and St. Emillion in Cognac. Also blended into Chianti, Trebbiano is popular for its high acidity, late fruiting, frost resistance, and productivity. The Trebbiano Toscano (from Tuscany) is recognizable for its large leaves and grape cluster.[69]

OTHER GRAPE VARIETIES

Bland, seemingly another *labrusca × vinifera* cross, was sent to Jefferson in 1822 by James Wallace. The Bland was accidentally discovered before the Revolution as a seedling by Colonel Theodorick Bland on the Eastern Shore of Virginia. It was given to William Bartram, who described it in the 1803 edition of the *Domestic Encyclopedia*: "This excellent grape bids fairest, next to the bull-grape [Scuppernong], to afford a good wine." Along with the Alexander, the Bland may have been one of the two grapes John James Dufour succeeded with in his ill-fated Kentucky experiment. Adlum also praised "Bland's Madeira": "It is a great bearer, and a good Grape for the table, and makes a very fine Wine." The round berries, formed on a long, loose cluster, turn a pale red or rose color

Pl. 36. Lachrima dolce grapes, possibly Jefferson's "Lachrima Christi," from Gallesio's *Pomona italiana*

Pl. 37. Colorino, the likely synonym for Jefferson's "Abrostine Red," from Gallesio's *Pomona italiana*

Pl. 38. Picolit, possibly Jefferson's "Abrostine White," from Gallesio's *Pomona italiana*

Pl. 39. Aleatico from Gallesio's *Pomona italiana*

Pl. 40. Seralamanna from Gallesio's *Pomona italiana*

Pl. 41. Muscat Blanc grapes ripening in the northeast vineyard

Pl. 42. Sangiovese from Gallesio's *Pomona italiana*

Pl. 43. Sangiovese grapes in the southwest vineyard

Fig. 109. Norton's Virginia, or Norton's Seedling, from Fleischmann, *Grapes of America*

when ripe. Although widely distributed in the first half of the nineteenth century and offered by commercial nurseries, the Bland diminished in importance by the 1840s.[70]

Norton's Seedling? In 1824 Jefferson was sent "a Box of Grape cuttings" by his Richmond agent, Bernard Peyton. The vines originated with Dr. Daniel N. Norton, who developed Norton's Seedling, "perhaps the greatest stimulus to Virginia viticulture" and, according to one modern authority, "the best of all native hybrids so far for the making of red wine" (fig. 109). Norton deliberately hybridized vines of Bland (*Vitis aestivalis*) and Meunier (*V. vinifera*) in his vineyard outside Richmond around 1815. Norton, known also as Virginia Seedling, became the basis for the booming wine industry that evolved in and around Charlottesville, "the Wine Belt of Virginia," after the Civil War. Norton received national recognition when sold by the Robert Prince nursery in 1823 and was prominent throughout the nineteenth century, even in California, as a commercial wine variety. Norton is distinguished by its hardy, robust, disease-free growth, nine-inch-long bunches of small, black, and round berries, and unfailing productivity.[71]

"Purple Syrian grape from Twickenham," sent by Timothy Matlack of Pennsylvania and included in the 1807 planting, was considered a coarse-flavored English greenhouse variety, famous for the size of its twenty-pound bunches. Although the Syrian is universally described as a white grape, Matlack evidently obtained a purple variant or sport from a greenhouse grower in England.[72]

Scuppernong is usually considered the white-fruiting form of the southern muscadine grape, *V. rotundifolia*. Although they never rooted, Jefferson planted cuttings in 1817 after expressing enthusiasm for Scuppernong wine sent to him from the coastal plain of North Carolina, where numerous gentlemen growers were making significant quantities of the wine. George E. Spruel of Plymouth had an arbor-laden vine that reputedly covered an acre of ground. Another grower, L. Sawyer of Elizabeth City, described his Scuppernong wine as "somewhat sweet, but remarkably rich, luscious, and oily." By the early years of the twentieth century, Virginia Dare, made from North Carolina–grown *rotundifolia*, was the most popular wine in the United States, and there are still commercial Scuppernong plantings today.[73]

The Scuppernong, named after a North Carolina river, grows wild from southern Delaware to Florida, most prominently along the coastal plain. It is easily distinguished from the European and other native grapes by its small, round, glossy, pale green leaf, slender shoots, and smooth, nonflaking bark. Bartram referred to it as the Bull grape, in reference to the bulletlike shape of the fruit. He also said, "This undoubtedly is the first American grape which merits attention and cultivation for wine."[74]

Figs

"VULGAR" FRUIT OR "WHOLESOME" DELICACY

The fig tree (*Ficus carica*) has long been a symbol of heavenly contentment on earth. Margaret Bayard Smith, the romantic and chatty chronicler of nineteenth-century Washington society, described her visit in 1809 to Monticello, where Jefferson escorted her through the garden, discussing his future plans and plucking "really fine" figs: "As we walked, he explained his future designs of cultivation and improvement, 'for my long absence from this place, (said he) has made a wilderness around me.' 'But you have now returned,' I replied, 'and the *wilderness shall blossom like the rose*, and you I hope, will long sit *beneath your own vine and your own fig tree.*'" Jefferson's figs were located in a prime sheltered location in the "submural beds" below the stone wall at the southwestern end of the vegetable garden. Although it is doubtful the Monticello figs grew so high that he could "sit beneath" them—winter temperatures below twenty degrees convert the natural fig tree to a shrub of dense, suckering branches—Jefferson achieved success with this tender species, often recording harvesting dates and regularly passing on his favorite variety, Marseilles, to friends and neighbors. Monticello figs were renowned for their flavor and abundance.[1]

Jefferson planted figs as early as 1769, when two rows of trees were set out as standards (tree-shaped) in the young orchard. In the 1774 plan of the Monticello south orchard, fifty-four figs planted ten feet apart were assigned a large quarter of the Monticello "berry squares." Jefferson's tour of the Mediterranean marked a turning point in his devotion to fig culture. He returned from France in 1789 with three fig varieties: white Angelic, "white" (Marseilles), and "large fig." They were planted at the base of the vegetable garden wall,

just above the northeast vineyard, alongside what Jefferson called the "ancient fig," an intriguing reference suggesting the plant was at Monticello before he arrived in 1769. Jefferson immediately propagated new plants, particularly of the "white" variety he was later to identify as Marseilles, "the most delicious I ever tasted in any country" (fig. 110). The "fig terras next to the wall" was extended to the "submural beds" at the base of the southwest end of the vegetable garden, where in 1809 and 1810 additional figs from Dr. William Thornton were planted. The success of later fig harvests depended on the severity of the winter and Jefferson's dedication to providing protective covering to his plants. Jefferson freely gave fresh figs and fig plants to his friends Thornton, John Hartwell Cocke, Isaac Coles, and others—a reflection of his esteem for the Marseilles and the species in general.[2]

Jefferson was considered a pioneer grower of the fig. John Hartwell Cocke recalled in 1865 that figs were "first successfully cultivated by Mr. Jefferson at Monticello after his return from his mission to France." Ignorance of an earlier American fig-growing tradition was also expressed by A. J. Downing, who erroneously stated that it was not until 1790 that William Hamilton of Philadelphia first introduced figs into this country. Jefferson was closer to the truth when he wrote South Carolina's William Drayton in 1787, "The fig and mulberry are so well known in America that nothing be said of them." In contrast to the Deep South where the species was easily and often grown as an evergreen tree unfazed by fruit-killing temperatures, Virginia's eighteenth-century kitchen gardens at least occasionally included figs.[3]

The fig, regarded as a tree in the south and a shrub in the north, prospered as a dooryard ornament or yard specimen,

Fig. 110. White fig from Langley's *Pomona*

esteemed for its large, tropical, mitten-shape leaves and vigorous habit. Even if cold temperatures destroy its fruit, the fat, lush fig is a happy, thriving, decorative shrub in Virginia. Jefferson himself included it as a desirable addition to the shrubberies he planned in "the open ground on the West" at Monticello in 1774. But figs were, and still are, particularly glamorous to northern gardeners because they represent a kind of Holy Grail of fruit. The tempting sweetness of a ripe fig, universally and curiously described as "wholesome" by nineteenth-century fruit writers but probably too rich for eighteenth-century middle-class tastes, enhanced the fruit's status as an exotic treasure suitable for only the most refined connoisseurs. The romance of the fig—the classical associations of its discovery by Dionysus and the thunderbolts of Jupiter; its biblical tradition as the tree of knowledge and as a symbol of the fallen innocence and sensual pleasures of Paradise—further endeared the fruit to gentlemen gardeners, who could serve fresh figs as culinary trophies. Finally, because of their sensitivity to cold, figs are a precious crop in central Virgina—their fruition hardly more certain than that of the almond tree, their harvest a testament to a gardener's skill and diligence.[4]

Native to western Asia and the eastern Mediterranean from Afghanistan to Syria and cultivated in Egypt as early as 2700 B.C., the fig was mentioned by all the ancient writers on natural history as an essential part of the Mediterranean diet, especially when dried. Theophrastus first described "caprification," the curious process by which an insect mysteriously fertilizes the minute fig flowers within the shell of the "fruit," botanically a syncarp. The introduction of the species into England did not occur, according to tradition, until 1525 when Cardinal Pole planted a Marseilles fig at Lambeth, the London palace of the archbishop of Canterbury. This tree was fifty feet tall in 1834, one of the many witnesses to the longevity of the species. Nevertheless, as a garden plant the fig was slow to become established in cool, cloudy England. Philip Miller, a fig devotee amid a phlegmatic populace who "were not lovers of this fruit," introduced many new fig varieties from Venice and described fourteen varieties in *The Gardener's Dictionary*, 1768. These included types still prominent today: Brown Ischia, "the largest fruit of any I have yet seen"; Marseilles, or "small white early"; and the long, pyramidal-shaped Brunswick.[5]

Numerous accounts document the introduction of the fig into Spanish America and Florida in the sixteenth century. The species' longevity also provided clues to its common presence in the Deep South. John Bartram described in 1766 how the English had ransacked the Spanish fruit gardens of St. Augustine, Florida; however, they left fig trees unmolested: "As for the Figs, the English are not very fond of them." William Bartram, between 1773 and 1776, observed figs "of the shape of pears, and as large, and of a dark bluish purple color," near Mobile, Alabama, around "ancient habitations" built by the Spanish; on the abandoned St. Simons Island town of Frederica, the first English settlement in Georgia; and at Indian settlements in Florida where they were cultivated. The fig was first reported in Virginia in 1621. John Smith said figs "prospered exceedingly" after being brought to Jamestown from Bermuda. According to Smith, Jane Pierce, wife of Captain William Pierce, planted a three- or four-acre fruit and vegetable garden and harvested one hundred bushels of "excellent figges" in the summer of 1629. Thomas Glover in 1676 observed that Virginia figs were equal to those in Spain, "but there are few planted yet." Robert Beverley, thirty years later, was more specific when he said "there are not ten People in the Country, that have any of them in their Gardens."[6]

Other accounts also suggest that the species may have been relatively unfamiliar to gardeners around 1800. McMahon, for example, justified his lengthy discussion of fig culture by noting the species was "not as well known in the United-States, as other kinds of fruit-trees." The "American Farmer" suggested figs were not only uncommon but somewhat of a controversial item in 1803. He said this "fine wholesome fruit, though not an American favourite, is highly esteemed in countries where it ripens, and is everywhere deemed *wholesome* and *delicious* when eaten ripe from the tree. The editor knows that at first his neighbors in America who disliked their flavor, soon were fond of them, and they are in truth a wholesome and valuable fruit, as in his Maryland garden was often attested from experience." The "American Farmer"'s defense of the fig, his repeated use of the adjective "wholesome," reminds one of a modern public relations campaign for some suspiciously unsavory product. Fresh figs were perhaps too rich for uncultivated palates. Middle-class gardeners like Annapolis craftsman William Faris, who around 1800 grew nearly every fruit possibly suited to a temperate climate, never mentioned the fig in his extensive garden diary. At the same time, figs were advertised by only about one-fourth of Chesapeake commercial nurseries that sold fruit trees and berries, and they were never sold by variety name, only as generic "Figs."[7]

Appreciation of the taste of the fig may have depended on one's place in the economic pyramid, and even then, reactions to the fruit were strong and varied. Henry Phillips, whose *Pomarium Brittanicum* was reprinted in the *American Farmer* in 1822, said that in Sussex "I have known it not only neglected by the middle and lower classes, but even mentioned with derision in their disputes." In Great Britain, to give someone "the fig" consisted "in thrusting the thumb between two of the closed fingers or into the mouth" and was considered a contemptuous gesture. In 1835 Margaret Bayard Smith reported a conversation with Henry Orr, "the most experienced and fashionable waiter in the city," about the menu for a sophisticated Washington dinner party. When she suggested a dessert that included figs, Orr responded, "Oh no, ma'am, they are quite vulgar." The tutor for an aristocratic Virginia family, Philip Fithian, who also could not "endure them," gathered figs from the garden at Nomini Hall with the more appreciative "Ladies." Landon Carter was surprised at how "prodigious" summer rains had rendered Colonel John Tayloe's usually "remarkably fine and luscious" figs "tasteless" in 1775 at Mount Airy on the Northern Neck between the Potomac and Rappahannock rivers. At Stratford Hall not far away, Lucinda Orr reported how in 1782 she and her cousin "walked in the Garden, sat about two hours under a butiful shade tree, and eat as many figs as we could." William Cobbett found figs "a mawkish thing at best."[8]

Although consistently killed to the ground during cold winters (temperatures below 15° F), the fig is uniquely long-lived among all temperate climate fruits. The species' unrelenting persistence around the historic sites associated with the Virginia gentry suggest they may have been more common than the documentation implies, and they often provide graphic confirmation of the location of a historic garden. A visitor in 1882 to George Washington's birthplace at Wakefield, where the house had long been in ruins, found "a dense thicket of shrubby fig trees covering a circular space of nearly fifty feet in diameter." In the 1920s members of Richmond's James River Garden Club compiled descriptions of well-known gardens associated with famous Virginians in *Historic Gardens of Virginia*. They described "great hedges" of figs at Brandon along the James River below Richmond, "some upshoots of the original fig" at Mount Vernon, and old plantings at Landon Carter's Sabine Hall and Lady Jean Skipwith's Prestwould. In 1957 centuries-old fig bushes were still thriving at Mount Vernon, Stratford Hall, Jamestown, Williamsburg, and other historic sites in Virginia. Few garden plants can rival the fig for its central role in the tradition of southern gardens.[9]

The crucial concern regarding fig culture in piedmont Virginia is how to protect the plants during the winter (fig. 111). In frost-free or even moderate climates like the Virginia tidewater, where 257,057 pounds of commercial figs were harvested in 1909, fig trees will produce two crops a season; the first, which ripens in midsummer, is produced on the previous year's growth; the second on young summer shoots in late summer or early fall. The first crop on unprotected plants is usually damaged when winter temperatures fall below 25 degrees. In 1762 John Bartram drew a line 120 miles north and west of Charleston and said figs grown outside the line were killed to the ground while those within it were more treelike and fruitful. The second crop, hopeless in England and the northern states, fails when a cool or short growing season inhibits ripening. Jefferson unknowingly defined the two harvest seasons when he said that at Monticello "the fig, protected by a little straw, begins to ripen in July; if unprotected, not till the 1st of September." John Hartwell Cocke said he preferred his personal method of protecting figs by covering them with earth to Jefferson's technique involving a covering of "a thatch of corn stalks." In 1806 Jefferson directed Wormley, a slave gardener, to cover the figs with "straw rope," a twine made from twisted straw.[10]

Fig. 111. Figs growing in the submural beds

MARSEILLES

When Jefferson said the Marseilles fig was "incomparably superior to any fig I have ever seen," he implicitly ranked it with his great favorites of the fruit world (figs. 112, pls. 44, 45). Apparently he had sampled the Marseilles before bringing plants home from France: he sent some to William Drayton of South Carolina in 1789 and said, "The Marseilles-Fig is admitted to be the best in the world." However, Jefferson's enthusiasm was not shared by many fruit writers. John Parkinson's "white ordinary kind" was the Marseilles, and Miller said the "small white early" was "sweet, but not high flavoured." George Brookshaw, London author of *The Horti-*

cultural Repository, 1823, said the Lambeth Palace Marseilles, was "inferior to many varieties," and William White of Georgia thought it "worthless" in 1859. Although tapioca sweet, the Marseilles is not so fruity as other fig varieties. The small (two inches in diameter), turban-shaped fruit has a slightly ribbed skin, which turns yellowish-white when ripe. The white pulp is rich yet often rather dry. The Marseilles, often named Early White in reference to its bearing season (ripe as early as July 12 for Jefferson), seems to be hardier and more productive than other fig varieties. The absence of Marseilles from American fruit lists of the early nineteenth century might lead one to presume that Jefferson introduced it into the United States; however, an ancient and prospering Mar-

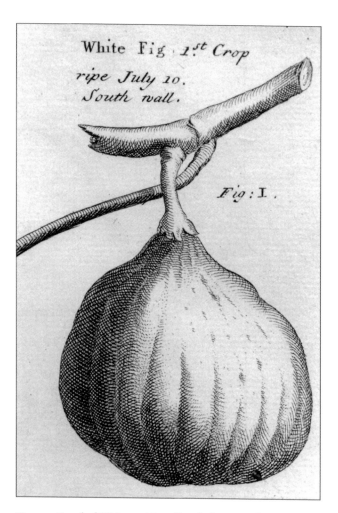

Fig. 112. Detail of White, or Marseilles, fig from Langley's *Pomona*

seilles fig tree was thriving in 1957 near Cape Charles, Virginia, on the property of gardening enthusiast John Custis, who died in 1754.[11]

ANOTHER FIG VARIETY

Angelique ("white Angelic"). After planting it below the garden wall in February 1790, Jefferson made no further mention of "white Angelic," perhaps because he preferred the Marseilles. "Angelic" or "Angelica" is undoubtedly the French variety Angelique, a popular market fig grown outside Paris and described by late eighteenth-century European fruit writers. Absent from American nursery and pomological lists until later in the nineteenth century, it was described by Downing ("only tolerably sweet") and Kenrick ("of excellent flavor"). The small, yellow-skinned, pyramidal-shaped Angelique has white flesh with a fruity, red center.[12]

Strawberries

ARCADIAN DAINTIES

Arcadian dainties with a true paradisiacal flavor.

—A. J. Downing

In 1767, when Jefferson harvested strawberries from his garden at Shadwell, he noted in his Garden Book that "100 fill half a pint," a remarkable testament to the petite berries and the humble state of the garden strawberry in the eighteenth century. Jefferson knew the berries that Downing called "Arcadian dainties" in the infant stage of their modern development, as the indigenous species of three continents—the Scarlet (*Fragaria virginiana*) from North America and the Chili (*F. chiloensis*) from the Pacific coasts of North and South America—were first being selected and accidentally hybridized into the strawberry we know today, *Fragaria* × *ananassa* (*Fragaria* from the fruit's fragrance; *ananassa* from the berry's resemblance to the shape, aroma, and flavor of the pineapple, *Ananas comosus*). Because of the quantity of references in his Garden Book, the strawberry ranks with the peach, apple, grape—perhaps the cherry and fig—as one of Jefferson's favorite fruits. Cultivated strawberries abounded at Monticello at a time when they were surprisingly infrequent in Virginia kitchen gardens. They were planted in a remarkable variety of sites: the northwest border of his vegetable garden, "squares" in the garden itself, a special submural terrace below the garden wall, the mysterious "circular" beds at the southwestern end of the vegetable garden, the "new nursery," and earthen troughs reserved for special curiosities. Jefferson even proposed planting fields of the everbearing but small-fruiting Alpine strawberry. He provided friends strawberries from his garden,

forwarded surplus plants to Poplar Forest, and occasionally remarked that his berries survived the vagaries of spring weather when other fruits perished—all indications of success. With his typical unabated zeal for the latest horticultural novelty, Jefferson repeatedly requested the newest strawberries from Philadelphia nurserymen John Bartram, Jr., and Bernard McMahon. The range of species Jefferson eventually planted at Monticello reflected the diverse bloodlines that formed one of the most interesting chapters in North American horticulture.[1]

Infrequently mentioned by ancient commentators on agriculture, and then only as a cherished wild plant of meadows and fields, strawberries were not brought into European gardens until after the fourteenth century. They are a relatively recent development compared to, for example, pears, grapes, or apples; as we know it today, the garden strawberry is the youngest of all cultivated temperate-climate fruits except for blueberries and cranberries. Old World species and cultivars included the Alpine (*F. vesca*), cherished because its small, highly flavored fruit ripens throughout the growing season; the rich, musky-flavored Hautboy (*F. moschata*), an English corruption of the French word *hautbois*; the Capiton (*F. vesca*, sometimes *moschata*), the seventeenth-century progenitor of the Hautboy and "the goodliest and greatest" according to Parkinson in 1629; and finally, the commonly cultivated Wood strawberry of western Europe and England (also *F. vesca*; fig. 113). When compared to the European species, the New

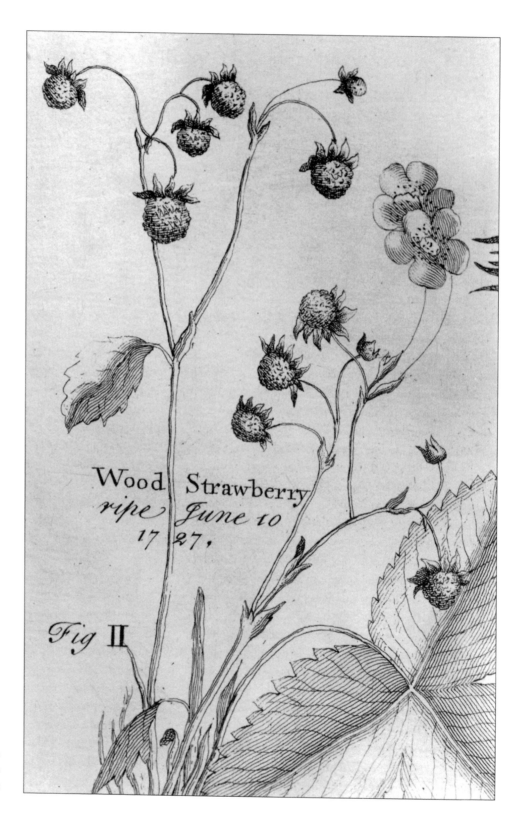

Wood Strawberry
ripe June 10
17 27,

Fig II

Fig. 113. Wood strawberry,
Fragaria vesca, from
Langley's *Pomona*

World *F. virginiana* has admirable qualities: the perfumed fragrance and rich scarlet color of its ripe berry, its comparative earliness, the plant's vigor and productivity, and, most conveniently, the species' hermaphroditic sexuality which eliminates the necessity of providing both male and female flowers for pollination. The consensus among horticultural taxonomists is that *F. virginiana* has imparted the vivid scarlet color, an early harvest season, hardiness, and certain vigorous leaf and leaf runner qualities to modern varieties. By the early twentieth century L. H. Bailey estimated that over eighteen hundred cultivars of American origin had been introduced into cultivation. One wonders if any other native eastern North American plant has made such an important contribution to the world's horticulture.[2]

Eight years before Jefferson harvested his petite Shadwell berries, in the seventh edition of *The Gardener's Dictionary*, 1759, Philip Miller described a large fruiting strawberry he had obtained from George Clifford, director of the Netherlands East India Company and owner of a respected botanic garden near Haarlem. The question of the identity of "Miller's strawberry" sparked a fierce debate that persisted for two centuries, but most horticultural taxonomists now concur that it was a cross between the flavorful, fragrant, yet comparatively small *virginiana* and the large-berried *chiloensis*, which had been introduced into France from the Pacific coast of Chile in 1714 by Amédée François Frézier. The two species were growing side by side in Clifford's Dutch garden when the accidental hybridization occurred. Antoine Duchesne, author of the landmark work *Histoire naturelle des fraisiers*, 1766, correctly identified Miller's strawberry as a chance hybrid and named it the "Pine" (short for pineapple), or *Fragaria ananassa*. Duchesne was the first to argue that a new race of fruit could arise by the crossing of two species, in this case *F. chiloensis* and *F. virginiana*, while Philip Miller has been credited with discovering the progenitor of the modern strawberry, the Pine—both monumental events in the history of horticulture (fig. 114, pl. 46). No longer an "Arcadian dainty" but a fat, juicy, vividly red, and delicately perfumed fruit the size of a small plum, the genetic potential of the new Pine strawberry seemed limitless. Curiously, the Pine reflected a new and unique internationalism in garden plants: species from two

Fig. 114. Pine strawberries in the vegetable garden

continents, North and South America, were hybridized accidentally in a third, Europe.[3]

Like the naturalized peach or native grape, the Scarlet, or Virginia, strawberry, "the softest and juiciest of all the species" according to Duchesne, provided still another deliciously sensuous item for the native American table of fruit. In 1608 one of the first Virginia colonists, George Percy, said the wild *Fragaria virginiana*, plentiful in open woodlands and fields, was "foure times bigger and better than ours in England [*Fragaria vesca*, Wood strawberry]." Another report noted that "it was impossible to direct the foot without dying it the blood of this fruit." Although Canadian-collected *virginiana* probably were grown earlier in French botanical gardens, Thomas Hariot, the scientific adviser and narrator for the Sir Walter Raleigh expedition in 1585, may have been the first to relay the Virginia strawberry, "as good and as great as those which we have in our English gardens," to England. It was soon described as the "greene strawberrie" (partly because of abbreviated ripening) by John Gerard in 1597 and illustrated in European herbals such as Basilius Besler's *Hortus Eyestettensis* in 1613. John Parkinson, who thought the inability to ripen the American species in London was due to "the want of skill, or industry to order it aright," included the Virginia strawberry among his "Kitchen Garden" items. The Large Early Scarlet, or simply Scarlet, a selected large-berried form of *Fragaria virginiana*, was introduced into European gardens by 1613 and renewed interest in the quality of the New World strawberry. It was first illustrated in England by Batty Langley, and Miller, who praised the earliness as well as the flavor of the Scarlet strawberry in 1768, said that "the fruit is so good, as by many persons of good taste to be preferred to most other sorts."[4]

Wild strawberries thrived with the conquest and settlement of North America: as a pioneer species when Indians or Europeans cleared or burned the forests, or when exhausted tobacco fields were abandoned. Like all wild fruits, the strawberry responded to the additional light that resulted from the disturbance of the native forest by bearing more and larger berries on a rich green carpet of leaves. Richard Peters described an 800-acre indigenous strawberry garden, "in most extraordinary profusion," that emerged following the burning of a pine forest outside Philadelphia in the late eighteenth century: "The people of the towns . . . from distances of more than 20 miles were accustomed to gather and carry off these strawberries, in quantities almost incredible." The strawberries, however, disappeared as the forest returned and shaded out the plants. William Bartram often alluded to natural "strawberry beds" and strawberry fields that dyed the legs and feet of his horses in his botanical journeys through the Southeast in 1776. In one such "Elysian field" in western North Carolina, Bartram reported in perhaps the most sensuously lyrical passage of his *Travels*, "companies of young, innocent Cherokee virgins, some busily gathering the rich fragrant fruit, others having already filled their baskets, lay re-

clined under the shade of floriferous and fragrant native bowers of Magnolia, Azalea, Philadelphus, perfumed Calycanthus, sweet Yellow Jessamine and cerulian Glycine frutescens, disclosing their beauties to the fluttering breeeze, and bathing their limbs in the cool fleeting streams; whilst other parties, more gay and libertine, were yet collecting strawberries or wantonly chasing their companions, tantalising them, staining their lips and cheeks with the rich fruit." Wild strawberries are still abundant in grasslands, open woods, and old orchards throughout eastern North America, but it would be difficult to find spontaneous strawberry gardens as opulent as those depicted by Bartram. Even by 1900 L. H. Bailey questioned whether a "few pints" of wild strawberries could be harvested in an entire day of picking and concluded that the abundance and size of the native species had deteriorated because of the historical depletion of the soil.[5]

Writers differed in their reports on how extensively the strawberry was cultivated before the Revolution. Robert Beverley noted strawberries "as delicious as any in the World, and growing almost every where in the Woods, and Fields. They are eaten almost by all Creatures; and yet are so plentiful, that very few Persons take care to transplant them, but can find enough to fill their baskets . . . in the deserted old Fields." Modern horticultural historians have questioned the extent of colonial strawberry cultivation. S. W. Fletcher believed eighteenth-century gardeners "considered strawberry-growing an exceedingly difficult and uncertain matter" because of confusion about the need for cross-pollination: some strawberry plants, particularly the European Hautboy and Chili, are imperfect, or "blind"—bearing flowers with only female (pistillate) or male (staminate) parts—and require another plant with sexually compatible flowers for pollination. This feature inevitably resulted in sterile strawberry plantings and an aversion to bringing such plants into the garden. In addition, while the size of Virginia strawberries is usually increased when they are cultivated, the flavor of those harvested from forests and fields is often considered superior, in the same way that wild game has a stronger and more vivid taste than its domesticated cousins. Allusions to garden strawberries are relatively infrequent in the diaries and records of Jefferson's contemporaries.[6]

As early as the 1600s New England's Roger Williams marveled at the quantity of wild strawberries cultivated in Indian gardens: "I have many times seen as many as would fill a good ship." Nonetheless, plants were introduced into kitchen gardens by Virginia gardeners who considered the strawberry a prestigious item and by gardeners in towns without access to "strawberry fields." William Byrd said, "All the woods, fields and gardens are full of strawberries, which grow exceedingly well in this beautiful and lovely land." John Lawson observed, "Strawberries, not Foreign, but those of the Country, grow here in great Plenty. Last April I planted a Bed of two hundred Foot in Length, which bore the same year." Directions for strawberry culture were included in the only Virginia colonial treatise on kitchen gardening, written by John Randolph of Williamsburg and owned by Jefferson. Cultivated strawberries were observed by William Hugh Grove as "garden stuff" around 1710 and by Philip Fithian in the garden at Nomini Hall in 1774. John Custis of Williamsburg, beginning in 1736, was repeatedly sent the recently discovered and much treasured Chili strawberry, as well as the European Hautboy, by Peter Collinson. If the transported plants survived the perilous transatlantic journey and were not killed by overwatering ("Captain Friend killed them with kindness giving them so much water that rotted them"), they perished during the heat and droughts of the Williamsburg summer. Landon Carter also had problems nursing the European Hautboy through the droughts of a Virginia summer in 1772 and was determined to water them day and night. Around 1770 John Randolph, relying on Philip Miller's dictionary, said the Wood, Hautboy, and also the Scarlet, or Virginia, were the "three sorts chiefly propagated," presumably in Williamsburg. Randolph mentioned the Pine strawberry but said it had not yet been introduced into American gardens. Although listed by 1803 in James Mease's American version of Willich's *Domestic Encyclopedia*, it was not until around 1806, when David Hosack was credited with growing it in New York's Elgin Botanic Gardens (now the site of Rockefeller Center), that the Pine was successfully grown in America.[7]

Continuing the pattern of offering fashionable European fruit rather than the acclimated natives, most urban nurseries sold only exotic strawberries before 1820. However, limited commercial strawberry culture arose around large cities like Boston, Philadelphia, and New York in the early years of the nineteenth century, mostly based on strains of the native Scarlet. Growing strawberries for the market proved that most of the exotic species—Hautboy, Alpine, Pine, and Chili—were fickle curiosities rather than reliably productive sorts. Despite its *virginiana* parents, the Pine, or Carolina Pine, strawberry of Europe demanded milder temperatures and attentive cultural nursing to make it profitable. The Chili was not hardy in the North; the species suffered in the hot, humid South; and its imperfect flowering proved inconvenient in cultivation. An exception was the hermaphroditic Wood strawberry, which thrived and was sold around Boston by 1820. Otherwise, Early Hudson, Hudson's Bay, Large Early Scarlet, Methven Scarlet, and Crimson Cone proved most suitable because their hardiness and productivity—essential qualities for a commercial variety—were based on the bloodlines of an indigenous species, *Fragaria virginiana*. As McMahon noted in 1806, the Scarlet was "so good as to be generally preferred to most others."[8]

In theory, a native strawberry brought into the garden from the neighboring fields should be superior to its wild cousins due to the careful selection of vigorous plants, high-flavored berries, or heavy-bearing plants. Proper spacing in well-prepared, irrigated, and manured soil and the judicious removal of wayward runners usually will result in larger and tastier fruit. Jefferson provided some cultural advice to his granddaughter Anne Cary Randolph in 1808: "I am sorry our strawberries are so unpromising; however, I trust they will put out soon. If some sand and stable manure were put on the earth, the waterings would carry both down into the clay & loosen & enrich it." Historically there has been a prejudice against garden-grown strawberries. Duchesne's assertion that the strawberry's "size is obtained by cultivation, but [the] liveliness of its taste is diminished," has been, and still is, verified by committed gardeners. In 1790 Samuel Dean, whose *New England Farmer* was among the first American books to discuss strawberry culture, acknowledged that "our grass fields often produce strawberries in plenty" but then argued that garden-grown plants would be larger and better flavored. Reserving strawberries for the garden also would eliminate the "trampling" of precious hayfields. The issue continued to be discussed in 1823 when a writer in the *American Farmer* disputed the value of intensively managed strawberry plants, believing instead they should be left to grow up in fields, surrounded by tall grasses as they are in nature: "This may be considered a slovenly mode of culture; I merely state how I have obtained fine fruit, when the *secundum artem* system gave me none." Another writer to the *American Farmer* regretted preparing raised beds, mulching, and pruning runners, believing instead the more natural approach would diminish the insect problems he had encountered. One popular technique that evolved in New York and New England in the 1820s was a deliberate attempt to imitate the prolific resurrection of wild strawberries after the burning of the native forest: garden strawberries were covered with one inch of dry straw and set

on fire in the early spring. This helped control insects, weeds, and diseases and hastened flowering and fruiting by weeks.[9]

Philip Miller in 1768 said the strawberry was so common that few English gardeners bothered to care for cultivated plants, a concern shared by Duchesne, who said that only a few French commercial growers manured, pruned, or mulched strawberries in the mid-eighteenth century. While Miller's discussion of strawberry culture was relatively brief, its influence was widespread and is still evident in the way, for example, many gardeners prepare raised beds. One of the suggested derivations of the word strawberry is that it comes from the shredded straw mulches used as winter protection and to prevent spring rains from splashing dirt on the ripening fruit, a practice as old as the cultivation of the fruit itself. Mulching also helps to control weeds, an aggravating problem with strawberries because of their rambling runners and one that troubled Landon Carter, whose gardener struggled to clean out a weed-choked strawberry bed at Sabine Hall in 1777.[10]

ALPINE (*F. vesca*), "MONTHLY"

Jefferson obtained seeds of the Alpine, or "Monthly," from Philip Mazzei in 1774 ("Fragole Alpine") and 1807 ("the genuine Alpine strawberry") and from James Worthington, the governor of Ohio, in 1805 and 1808 (fig. 115). He also purchased plants from the Philadelphia nurseries of both John Bartram, Jr., and Bernard McMahon. Jefferson had high expectations for the Alpine; he described it as "immensely valuable" to his son-in-law Thomas Mann Randolph. In a letter to James Monroe in 1795 he included it with the skylark and red-legged partridge as one of "the three objects which you should endeavor to enrich our country with." The prolific Alpine flourished at Monticello and was so successful that Jefferson offered baskets of plants to friends like George Divers. But Jefferson was ultimately disappointed at the yield of this highly flavored, everbearing, yet tiny (the size of a fingernail) fruit. He wrote General John Mason, "I think it would take acres to yield a dish," and decided by 1812 to banish his Alpine strawberries to the "truck patch, as I cannot afford them room enough in the garden."[11]

The fruit of the Alpine is pointed rather than round, and

Fig. 115. Alpine strawberry from Duhamel's *Traité*

the robust plants flower and bear almost continually from April to November. Miller noted in 1768 that the Alpine only recently had been introduced into England, where, at least initially, a pinch of seed was reputedly worth up to one guinea. While McMahon mentioned four varieties of Alpine in his *Calendar*, he had trouble securing eight plants of the common Scarlet Alpine for Jefferson in 1807—suggesting the actual scarcity of the Alpine in American gardens at that time. The heaven-sent promise of strawberries in November never justified the disadvantages of the tiny fruit, eventually limiting cultivation of the Alpine to the home gardens and greenhouses of the curious.[12]

CHILI

The Chili strawberry was never successfully established at Monticello (fig. 116, pl. 46). Jefferson tried; he sent nursery-grown plants to Charlottesville from Philadelphia in 1798, but his ensuing persistent requests of Bartram and McMahon for this "immensely valuable" species suggest the plants never arrived or else died soon after planting. Amédée Frézier came across this species with the largest berries of any *Fragaria* while monitoring Spanish activities in South America. Frézier was so impressed by its large berries, "the size of hen's eggs," that on the long journey home he sacrificed his personal supply of drinking water to keep the sample plants alive. The five survivors of the transoceanic journey were distributed to botanic gardens in France; however, they were all pistillate, and so the species received a reputation for being unproductive. This imperfect propensity, however, provided the ideal match for staminate Virginia strawberries, and when the two species were grown side by side in George Clifford's Dutch botanic garden in the 1760s, the resultant marriage produced the famous Pine.[13]

Fragaria chiloensis is one of the few species indigenous to both North and South America, growing along the Pacific coast from Alaska to Patagonia. Admired for its enormous fruit rather than a flavor William Cobbett said was "little superior to the potato," the Chili differs dramatically from the Virginia strawberry: the very large, firm fruit is brownish-red with a whitish (rather than pale scarlet) flesh, and the leaves

are thick, leathery, and shiny, obviously adapted to xerophytic beach conditions. The Chili, because it is native to a mild, oceanic climate, is neither reliably cold hardy in the North nor adapted to the heat and humidity of the eastern North American summer. Although McMahon said, "I have none nor have I seen any in America," the Chili was a standard offering in commercial nurseries from 1771. So few important cultivars emerged from this species, and so many competing cultivars sprang up with improved Pine characteristics, that by 1845 Kenrick included the entire race of Chili strawberries among his "outcasts."[14]

Fig. 116. Chili strawberry from Duhamel's *Traité*

HUDSON

Jefferson wrote George Divers in 1812 that he had spent "20 yrs. trying unsuccessfully" to obtain the Hudson strawberry for his garden at Monticello. After repeated requests of McMahon, who said the Hudson was "the best kind we have here," Jefferson finally established "flourishing" plants in the submural beds below the vegetable garden wall. Some au-thorities feel Hudson was a selected form of the Scarlet and the "first named variety listed in North America." Others be-lieve Hudson was a hybrid seedling of *virginiana* and *chiloense* that occurred in a Rhode Island garden around 1780. What-ever the Hudson's muddled origins, it was a pioneer Ameri-can cultivar, "very large, fine flavor, and great bearers" ac-cording to the 1790 William Prince catalog.[15]

Currants, Gooseberries, and Raspberries

Currants and gooseberries are often lumped together because they belong to the same genus, *Ribes*, and are traditional, Old World bush fruits linked to the English fruit garden, where they were commonly planted on the edges of garden squares, trimmed into ornamental balls and pyramids, or espaliered on walls. While the garden gooseberry (*Ribes uva-crispa*) has thorny branches and bears its green, red, or yellow fruit singularly, the red currant (*Ribes sativum*) has smooth branches and bears its fruit in bunches. When planted in the New World, European gooseberries and currants were the emblem of civilized society, but like the quince they have become fruits of the past in eastern North America, more popular in 1800 than today. In fact, cultivation of either species is legally forbidden in some states because they are the alternate host of the white-pine blister rust and therefore threaten the timber industry. On the other hand, hybrid cultivars of the European raspberry (*Rubus idaeus*) have become much more popular in home gardens, especially because modern breeding has combined the hardiness and adaptability of the New World species, *Rubus occidentalis* and *Rubus strigosus*, with the large, sweet, and flavorful fruiting characteristics of the Old World raspberry. Although the blood of American species has been introduced to some extent into today's currants and gooseberries, neither fruit—for any of its dessert, culinary, or liquor qualities—has captured the imagination of American growers like the raspberry.

Jefferson grew currants, gooseberries, and raspberries in the Monticello "berry squares," first mapped in his 1778 or-chard plan. The eighty-eight currants, planted five feet apart in eleven rows, and sixty-three gooseberries, set out at seven-foot intervals in nine rows, occupied the two westernmost of four quadrants, or "squares." Two hundred raspberry plants were planted two feet apart in the eight rows of the upper easternmost quadrant. By 1811 the entire 10,000-square-foot plot was organized into seventeen terraces between the northeast and southwest vineyards. Jefferson's siting of these three northern European fruits was critical: although the currants may have survived the hot blasts of the summer sun, one wonders how his gooseberries could withstand such an exposed site on the southern slope of Monticello. The documentary record also suggests that Jefferson's prized cultivars of European raspberry, which like his grapes were planted again and again, never flourished at Monticello.[1]

Although currants, gooseberries, and raspberries were minor fruits in Jefferson's pomological cosmos, each had its spurt of glory. Jefferson played a pioneering role in preserving two New World currant species initially discovered by the Lewis and Clark expedition: *Ribes aureum*, the yellow currant of the Rocky Mountains, and *Ribes odoratum*, the sweet-scented, or buffalo, currant of the western plains. Jefferson passed on seed of these species to Bernard McMahon and then later successfully cultivated the plants at Monticello. As well, Jefferson's recipe for currant jelly in 1782 was one of the few culinary notations in the Garden Book. Even though he admitted that European-grown gooseberries were "better," Jefferson's continued enthusiasm for the species as late as 1812, after forty-five years of inevitable struggle with its cultivation, suggests he was not just mimicking a standard European tradition. His repeated plantings of the latest and most fashionable raspberry varieties, White and Red Antwerp ("It has the reputation of being among the finest fruits in the world") and an everbearing "Monthly" sort procured from George Divers, reflect his unrelenting drive to assemble a quality fruit collection. European gooseberries, and to some extent raspberries, are difficult to grow in a southern climate, yet Jefferson mentioned the need to "trim" and weed them in winter — indications that these fragile Old World species, if not prospering, were at least growing at Monticello.[2]

CURRANTS

The currant of gardens, native to northern Europe and therefore absent from the records of ancient fruit commentators, was named for its association with a dried grape commonly exported from the Greek city of Corinth: "currant" is a corruption of that place-name. Dutch growers have been credited with domesticating and improving the wild currant in the late sixteenth century, and the names of the most commonly cultivated varieties, Red and White Dutch, suggest Holland's leading role in improving the small-fruiting and unattractive wild species (pl. 48). Parkinson, Langley, and Miller either suggested or stated outright that the introduction of these improvements stimulated the currant's popularity in the gardens of England, where it was cherished for preserves, jellies, and especially for wine. The reputation of currant wine earned this bush fruit equal respect with fancy dessert berries like strawberries and raspberries. William Forsyth, for example, said it was "the most useful of the small fruits." Curiously, just as fruit connoisseurs preferred white strawberries and white raspberries to red-skinned varieties, Parkinson said white currants possessed "a more pleasant winie taste . . . more daintie and less common [than the Red]." Unlike gooseberries, however, there was no proliferation and therefore little improvement of currant varieties before 1840: the Red and White Dutch, along with the pale-skinned Champagne and few others, were the only varieties listed by writers and nurserymen both in England and the United States.

The Red Dutch was still the "standard" variety cultivated in Virginia in 1903.[3]

Currants probably were brought to Virginia in the seventeenth century despite Thomas Glover's assertion in 1676 that he had never seen any in gardens. In 1706 Robert Beverley said, "There grow naturally Two Sorts of Currants, one red and the other black, far more pleasant than those of the same Colour in England," but it is unclear whether he was referring to native shrubs that looked like currants or to the European garden species. William Byrd said the various currants were "very good in taste. . . . Many of them are dried and kept for winter. Also many fancy cakes are made from them, which are excellent." John Randolph adapted the currant-growing advice of Philip Miller, and the "American Farmer" included them among his "sure and perfect crops" in 1803. Richard Parkinson, in an unusual endorsement, acknowledged that the American-grown currant was "equally good as in England."[4]

Currant bushes were commonly found in gentlemen's fruit gardens before 1820, partly because they were "raised with ease and preserved with little labor." *Ribes sativum* (as well as *R. nigrum*) escaped from cultivation in the early nineteenth century so successfully that it is still found naturalized in abandoned fields, pastures, and along fence lines. John Custis was sent the White currant in 1738 by Peter Collinson and was promised the same by John Bartram, Jr., when the Philadelphia botanist visited him in Williamsburg. Landon Carter, George Washington, Lady Jean Skipwith, and John Hartwell Cocke, whose Scottish gardener arrived from Europe with "Red" and "White" currants, all grew currants in their gardens, as did middle-class craftsman William Faris of Annapolis. Before 1820 they were universally listed generically, as "currants," by Chesapeake nurseries. Northern urban nurseries in Philadelphia and New York usually specified the common and Dutch varieties, as well as Jefferson's "Lewis' Fragrant [*Ribes odoratum*]" sold by A. McMahon and the American Black offered by Benjamin Prince. There was little discussion of the value of currant wine until 1822, when the *American Farmer* published a recipe for its concoction by currant proponent "Cincinnatus," who urged his readers to reserve "a portion of the garden" for this "wholesome" fruit.[5]

GOOSEBERRIES

The name gooseberry is derived from the fruit's use as a sauce traditionally served with young geese. Even more than the currant, the gooseberry is identified with the fruit gardens of England (fig. 117). Although a native of eastern Europe, gooseberry bushes were introduced into England as early as the thirteenth century, and by the seventeenth it was more diligently fussed over, and therefore developed, than any other small fruit. A peculiar gooseberry madness overtook English gardeners as Gooseberry Clubs emerged late in the eighteenth century that focused on competitions for the fattest fruit and the acquisition of the latest fashionable variety. The weights of champion gooseberries gradually increased, and the number of varieties exploded: in 1826 the Horticultural Society of London listed 185 gooseberry varieties; in 1831, 360 varieties.[6]

In the climatically harsh New World, however, the gooseberry quickly became a casualty of severe winters; hot, humid summers; and powdery mildew. Thomas Glover was uncharacteristically subdued when he said, "Those that take the pains to plant Goose-berries, have them," and natural his-

Tom. I.ᵉʳ   Pl. II.   Pag. 272.

L.B. del.   Eᵗᵉ Bouvard Sculp.

Groseillier Epineux.

Fig. 117. Gooseberries from Duhamel's *Traité*

torians like Robert Beverley and William Byrd never mentioned them. John Lawson explained the species' lackluster performance ("they do not do so well as in England") when he said, "Want of Dressing may be some Reason for this." The "American Farmer" agreed: "*Gooseberries* are not such certain or perfect productions; unless it may be in the cooler, more northern parts: but yet they answer culinary purposes, and bottle well. This is with scarcely any attention to their cultivation." James Mease attributed the gooseberry's problems in Philadelphia to the "great heat of our summers" and recommended a shady site. For Richard Parkinson, the gooseberry was among those many fruits that, at least in America, "dwindle away before they are ripe." Although William Cobbett found rhubarb a more pleasing culinary alternative for sauces, he was puzzled by the gooseberry's relative scarcity in American gardens: "Various are the sorts and not one that is not good."[7]

The gooseberry was nevertheless an integral part of the British fruit garden heritage. It was planted as enthusiastically and as commonly as currants by gentlemen gardeners like John Custis and Landon Carter, who had "a great plenty" in 1766. Philip Fithian reported "great plenty" at Nomini Hall in 1774. George Washington's secretary, Tobias Lear, ordered gooseberry plants from England, and John Hartwell Cocke planted a variety in 1810 that had been imported many years earlier by his father. Surprisingly, while nurserymen rarely bothered to offer named varieties of the thriving currant, they sold hundreds of English varieties of the unreliable gooseberry, usually named for the gentleman who first raised the seed. Growers like Benjamin Prince and McMahon, who listed 119 gooseberry varieties in his *Calendar* compared to only 5 currants, made emphatic statements about the need to care for this "most delicious and very valuable fruit" carefully and vigorously by choosing the proper varieties, planting them in the most fertile soil in the garden, keeping weeds from around the shrubs, and manuring and pruning them annually. Otherwise, according to McMahon, "it will be in vain to expect fine fruit." In the mid-nineteenth century a wave of New World gooseberries were developed into garden plants, including Houghton, a seedling of the native *Ribes oxycanthoides*. Nevertheless, U. P. Hedrick in 1950 summed up the

fate of the American gooseberry thus: "In Great Britain, the gooseberry is a choice dessert fruit; in the United States, it is used always for culinary purposes. The fruits of the American varieties are not nearly so large and handsome as those of the English sorts, but they are just as palatable. Like the blackberry, the gooseberry awaits a genius in plant breeding. . . . Meanwhile it is less and less grown."[8]

RASPBERRIES

Jefferson reported planting, or else sent home, raspberry plants or seeds seven times between 1774 and 1812. Philip Mazzei, Bartram's and McMahon's nurseries, George Divers, and Margaret Bayard Smith were among the sources for eight separate plantings, some of which involved as many as 200 plants. In 1782 Jefferson observed, "Raspberries come and last a month," and in 1798 Martha Randolph reported that "there will be more than common" at Monticello. However, later there were more ominous hints of problems with raspberry cultivation. In 1807 Jefferson noted planting ninety plants of McMahon's Antwerp raspberries in the "6. upper raspberry terraces" of the berry squares, yet in 1812 the second and third terraces were abandoned to the planting of the Lewis and Clark currant species. In his 1815 calendar of the dates upon which six select fruit and vegetable species were brought to the Monticello table, Jefferson omitted any dates for the raspberry. Again, the raspberry at Monticello was another example of how a fancy European garden species was unable to survive either probable horticultural neglect or the hot, humid climate.[9]

The European red raspberry (*Rubus idaeus*), native to northern Europe from Great Britain to Siberia, was given its common name from *raspis*, a reference to its thorny, prickly canes, and its botanical species name *idaeus*, from an association with the ancient Mount Ida of the Greeks. Jefferson cultivated raspberries, like the strawberry, at their infant stage of development as a garden plant. Historically they were considered more a medicinal or culinary plant easily collected from forests rather than a cultivated dessert fruit. As late as 1629 John Parkinson failed to mention any significant horticultural improvements and dismissed the "Raspisberrie" as "nothing so pleasant as the Strawberrie." Considering our esteem for raspberries today, Philip Miller's discussion of them as garden plants was also surprisingly brief. However, the introduction into England late in the eighteenth century of the Red and White Antwerp—like the Red and White Dutch currant, an improvement with more vigor, hardiness, and larger and sweeter berries—stimulated interest in what was once considered a rather ordinary wild bramble. The species quickly rose up the hierarchical ladder of fruit: new varieties were elegantly illustrated in works such as George Brookshaw's *Pomona Brittanica*, 1812, and also featured in the displays and competitions of the London Horticultural Society.[10]

North American raspberries, just as conspicuously prolific as the native strawberry or woodland grape, at first suffered in comparison to those grown in Europe. Beverley said, "The wild Raspberry is by some there, preferr'd to those, that were transplanted thither from *England;* but I cannot be of this opinion." In 1768 Philip Miller dismissed the "Virginian Raspberry": "The fruit has little flavour; so the plants are never cultivated for their fruit here." Once it was established in his garden, Carolina historian John Lawson had difficulty rooting out the aggressive and rather weedy native species, which could have been the black raspberry (*R. occidentalis*), the native red *R. strigosus* with botanical similarities to *idaeus*, or the American dewberry (*R. flagellaris*). Although William Byrd found the natives "as good as European [ones], if not better," he also observed, "When they are planted, they increase extremely vigorously." Many nineteenth-century fruit breeders concentrated on *Rubus strigosus*, and between 1850 and 1950 over one thousand raspberry varieties were developed in the United States, mostly based on New World bloodlines. Farther north in the mid-Atlantic colonies, Peter Kalm also found the wild raspberry to be an aggressive weed: "The American brambles (*Rubus occidentalis*) are here in great abundance. When a field is left uncultivated they are the first plants to appear on it. They are not easily extirpated. . . . On some old land which had long been uncultivated there were so many bushes of this kind that it was very troublesome and dangerous walking among them. A wine is made of the berries."[11]

Jefferson, like most nineteenth-century Virginians, undoubtedly planted only the European raspberry because the native brambles were considered such unappealing garden bullies. As well, just as with the strawberry, native berries were so easily harvested from wild brambles that cultivation of the New World species, and to some extent the European, was not worth the effort. Although included among "garden stuff" by William Hugh Grove in 1732, covered in John Randolph's *Treatise* of around 1770, and among the "American Farmer"'s "very sure and perfect crops," raspberries were rare in gardens before 1800, perhaps also because the quality of American-grown raspberries, whether native or European, was questionable. Richard Parkinson in 1799 said garden raspberries he had tasted in Maryland were "very inferior," while William Cobbett in 1821 said, "I have never seen them fine in America." Compared to his contemporaries, Thomas Jefferson was a leader in raspberry growing.[12]

BERRY CULTURE

Although Jefferson rarely recorded any sort of active cultivation in his fruitery, there are a few Garden Book allusions to plans to weed and prune his currants, gooseberries, and raspberries. Gooseberries, in particular, were acknowledged by American writers as the one species of fruit requiring special care: "requisite skill, patience, and industry to rear and perfect it," according to John Skinner, editor of the *American Farmer*. Some writers suggested gooseberries be planted under trees or on the north side of walls, but all unanimously recommended they be planted in the most fertile soil in the garden. Currants, and sometimes gooseberries, were referred to by pomological writers as "trees" because of the way gardeners would prune them into decorative standards with wineglass-shaped heads. Both were easily propagated by stem cuttings, which would then be trained into upright, miniature trees by eliminating side branches in the nursery, with the heads beginning one to three feet from the ground. McMahon adamantly insisted that they be constantly weeded to prevent an invasion of powdery mildew, an indigenous North American disease that, like grape pests such as black rot and phylloxera, was introduced into Europe in the late nineteenth century after crippling European species in the New World.[13]

RIBES AUREUM AND RIBES ODORATUM

Although not documented specifically, seeds of the western currant species *Ribes aureum* and *R. odoratum* were apparently among the packet of Lewis and Clark material sent by Jefferson to McMahon in 1807: "They are the fruits of his (Lewis') journey across the continent, and will I trust add some useful or agreeable varieties to what we now possess." Jefferson added, "I am in too indifferent a situation to take the care of them which they merit." McMahon immediately reported positively on the progress of various currants and gooseberries and in 1812 forwarded to Monticello "Ribes odoratissimum (mihi). this is one of Capt. Lewis's and an important shrub, the fruit very large, of a dark purple colour, the flowers yellow, showey, & *extremely fragrant.*" Also included were plants of "The yellow Currant of the river Jefferson; this is specifically different from the others, but I have not yet given it a specific botanical name." On March 12 Jefferson recorded planting one "Lewis' sweetscented Currant. Odoratissima" and one "L's Yellow currant" in special boxes and twenty more plants in the currant terraces of the berry squares. Jefferson later wrote that the plants were "flourishing" and passed on cuttings of the "sweetscented" to his son-in-law John Wayles Eppes.[14]

Both currants were commonly confused. The "yellow" currant is probably *Ribes aureum*, called the golden or buffalo currant and native to the Rocky Mountains and westward (pl. 49). It has yellow flowers with a spicy fragrance and purplish-black fruit. The "sweetscented" currant is *Ribes odoratum*, commonly called buffalo or Missouri currant, and grows wild in the plains east of the Rockies. Its yellow flowers are larger than *aureum,* the plant has a more spreading habit, and its berries are black. Meriwether Lewis preferred this species to the other *Ribes* discovered on their adventure. At least one, or perhaps both, currants soon found their way into general cultivation. The A. McMahon nursery sold "Lewis' Fragrant" around 1820, Bartram's garden contained "Lewis's Missouri ornamental Currant" in 1828, and Downing mentioned the "ornamental" Missouri currant, what he identified as *Ribes aureum*. In 1888 R. W. Crandall of Newton, Kansas, discovered a promising wild seedling of *Ribes odoratum* with large,

firm, and handsome fruits on a vigorous, hardy, and productive shrub. Although today both species are considered more ornamental than edible, the Crandall is occasionally cultivated.[15]

RED AND WHITE ANTWERP RASPBERRIES

In 1798 Jefferson sent home from Philadelphia "twenty odd plants" of the Antwerp raspberry purchased from the Bartram nursery (pl. 47). He noted, "It has the reputation of being among the finest fruits in the world." Jefferson also received plants of both the White and Red Antwerp in 1807, 1808, and 1812 from McMahon and Margaret Bayard Smith. The cultivars were the standards of raspberry excellence throughout the nineteenth century; however, it seems unlikely either prospered at Monticello. In 1806 McMahon described the Antwerps as "excellent fruits, and less hardy than other varieties," perhaps explaining the apparent demise of the Jefferson plantings. In 1848 A. J. Downing said, "Red Antwerp is the standard variety for size, flavour, and productiveness; wherever it is grown," while White Antwerp was "indispensable to every good garden."[16]

BERRY VARIETIES PLANTED AT MONTICELLO

Except for the Lewis and Clark currant species, there is no documentation to identify the types of currants—red, white, or black—grown by Jefferson. Documentary obscurity also clouds the early gooseberry plantings. Later, in 1809, Bernard McMahon sent Jefferson sample fruit of a "red" gooseberry. Jefferson measured the "wonderful" fat, three-inch-round fruit and repeatedly requested nursery stock from Philadelphia. In 1812 he obtained six European gooseberries from James Ronaldson, a Scotsman who had emigrated from Edinburgh to Philadelphia, and, finally, "4 small plants Gooseberries, large red fruit & the best I have ever seen" from McMahon. One plant of this "red" gooseberry was planted in a special twelve-inch planter, and the rest were set out in the gooseberry terraces.[17]

APPENDIX

NOTES

BIBLIOGRAPHY

CREDITS

INDEX

Appendix

FRUIT VARIETIES GROWN BY THOMAS JEFFERSON AT MONTICELLO

KEY

Gro = Virginia growers contemporary with Jefferson
Washington = George Washington (1732–1799)
Skipwith = Lady Jean Skipwith (1748–1826)
Tucker = St. George Tucker (1752–1827)
Cocke = John Hartwell Cocke (1780–1862)

Nur = Commercial nurseries offering Jefferson variety
Smith = William Smith nursery, Surry County, 1755
Sorsby = William Sorsby nursery, Surry County, 1763
Stratchan & Maury = Stratchan and Maury nursery, Spotsylvania
    County, 1798
Prince, 71, 90 = William Prince nursery, Flushing, N.Y., 1771, 1790
Lithen = John Lithen nursery, Philadelphia, c. 1800
Booth = William Booth nursery, Baltimore, 1810
Landreth = David and Cuthbert Landreth nursery, Philadelphia,
    1811
B. Prince, 1815 = Benjamin Prince nursery, Flushing, N.Y., 1815
A. MM = A. McMahon & Co. nursery, Philadelphia, c. 1819
Prince & Mills = Prince and Mills nursery, Flushing, N.Y., 1822

Lit = Literature in which variety is mentioned or described
Langley = Batty Langley, *Pomona*, 1729
Miller = Phillip Miller, *Gardener's Dictionary*, 8th ed., 1768
Forsyth = William Forsyth, *Treatise on the Culture and Management
    of Fruit Trees*, 2d ed., 1803
MM = Bernard McMahon, *American Gardener's Calendar*, 1806
Coxe = William Coxe, *View of the Cultivation of Fruit Trees*, 1817
Gallesio = Giorgio Gallesio, *Pomona italiana*, 1817
R. Prince = William Robert Prince, *Pomological Manual*, 1832
Kenrick = William Kenrick, *New American Orchardist*, 1845
Downing = Andrew Jackson Downing, *Fruits and Fruit Trees of
    America*, 9th ed., 1849; 2d rev., C. Downing, 1900
Hooper = E. J. Hooper, *Hooper's Western Fruit Book*, 1857
Thomas = John J. Thomas, *American Fruit Culturist*, 1867
Fitz = James Fitz, *Southern Apple and Peach Culturist*, 1872

ALMOND (*Prunus dulcis* var. *dulcis*)

"Almonds from the Streights"

"bitter almonds"

"hard shelled bitter almond"

"hardshelled sweet almonds from Cadiz. from Harriet Hackley"

"sweet almonds with hairy rinds"

"sweet almonds with hard shells"

"sweet almonds with smooth rinds"

"a Virginian Almond," perhaps bitternut (*Juglans cinerea*) or
    hazelnut (*Corylus americana*)

APPLE (*Malus pumila*)

Calville Blanc d'Hiver ("Calvite")
    Nur: Booth, Landreth, B. Prince, A. MM, Prince & Mills.
    Lit: Langley, Miller, Forsyth, Coxe, Downing, Hooper.
Clarke Pearmain (possibly synonymous with Golden Pearmain)
    Gro: Tucker, Cocke.
    Nur: Smith, Sorsby.
"Detroit large white" (probably synonymous with White Bell-
    flower)
    Lit: Hooper.
Detroit Red ("Detroit large red")
    Lit: Downing, Fitz.
Early Harvest ("Large early harvest")
    Gro: Tucker, Cocke.
    Nur: Prince 71, 90, Booth, Landreth, B. Prince, Prince &
    Mills.
    Lit: MM, Coxe, Kenrick, Downing, Hooper, Thomas, Fitz.
English Codling ("Codlin")
    Gro: Cocke.
    Nur: Smith, Prince 71, 90, Booth, Landreth, B. Prince, A. MM,
    Prince & Mills.

Lit: Langley, Miller, Forsyth, MM, Downing, Hooper, Thomas, Fitz.

Esopus Spitzenburg
Gro: Skipwith, Tucker, Cocke.
Nur: Prince 71, 90, Lithen, Booth, Landreth, B. Prince, A. MM, Prince & Mills.
Lit: MM, Coxe, Kenrick, Downing, Hooper, Thomas, Fitz.

Golden Wilding
Gro: Cocke.

Hewes Crab ("red Hughes," Hughes's Crab, Virginia Crab)
Gro: Tucker, Cocke.
Nur: Smith, Sorsby, Stratchan & Maury, Prince 90, Booth, Landreth, B. Prince, A. MM, Prince & Mills.
Lit: MM, Coxe, Kenrick, Downing, Hooper, Thomas, Fitz.

"iron wilding"

"mammoth" (possibly Gloria Mundi)

Medlar Russetin
Gro: Washington.
Nur: Stratchan & Maury.

Newtown Pippin
Gro: Washington, Tucker, Cocke.
Nur: Smith, Sorsby, Stratchan & Maury, Prince 71, 90, Lithen, Booth, Landreth, B. Prince, A. MM, Prince & Mills.
Lit: Forsyth, MM, Coxe, Kenrick, Downing, Hooper, Thomas, Fitz.

"ox-eye striped" (either Vandevere or Newtown Spitzenburg)

Pomme Gris ("pumgray")
Nur: B. Prince, Prince & Mills.
Lit: Forsyth, Downing, Hooper, Thomas.

"russetin" (likely Golden Russet or Roxbury Russet)

Taliaferro (Robinson, "Robertson")
Gro: Cocke.
Nur: Stratchan & Maury, Booth, A. MM.
Lit: Kenrick, Fitz.

White, Virginia White, or Bray's White ("white")
Nur: Smith, Sorsby.

APRICOT (*Prunus armeniaca*)

Angelica
Lit: Gallesio.

"Bordeaux"

Brussels
Gro: Tucker.
Nur: Prince 71, 90, Booth, Landreth, B. Prince, A. MM, Prince & Mills.

Lit: Langley, Miller, Forsyth, MM, Coxe, Kenrick, Downing, Hooper.

Large Early
Gro: Skipwith, Tucker, Cocke.
Nur: Prince 71, 90, Landreth, B. Prince.
Lit: MM, Coxe, Kenrick, Downing, Hooper, Thomas.

Large Red

"Melon"

Moor Park
Gro: Cocke.
Nur: Prince 90, Booth, Landreth, B. Prince, A. MM, Prince & Mills.
Lit: MM, R. Prince, Kenrick, Downing, Hooper, Thomas.

Peach ("peach-apricot," "German")
Gro: Cocke.
Nur: Prince 90 ("Moor Park or Peach"), Booth, Landreth, B. Prince, Prince & Mills.
Lit: Forsyth, Coxe, R. Prince, Kenrick, Downing.

CHERRY (*Prunus cerasus, Prunus avium*)

"August"
Nur: Prince & Mills.

Black Heart ("forward" and "latter")
Gro: Washington, Skipwith, Tucker, Cocke.
Nur: Smith, Prince 71, 90, Booth, Landreth, B. Prince, A. MM, Prince & Mills.
Lit: Langley, Miller, Forsyth, MM, Coxe, R. Prince, Kenrick, Downing, Hooper, Thomas.

Bleeding Heart
Gro: Cocke.
Nur: Prince 71, 90, Landreth, B. Prince, A. MM, Prince & Mills.
Lit: Langley, Miller, Forsyth, MM, Coxe, B. Prince, Downing, Thomas.

"Broadnax"

Carnation
Gro: Washington, Skipwith, Tucker, Cocke.
Nur: Smith, Prince 71, 90, Booth, Landreth, B. Prince, A. MM, Prince & Mills.
Lit: Forsyth, Miller, MM, Coxe, R. Prince, Downing, Hooper, Thomas.

Cornus mas ("Ciriege corniole")

Early May ("May," *Prunus fruticosa*)
Gro: Washington, Cocke.
Nur: Booth, Landreth, B. Prince, A. MM, Prince & Mills.
Lit: Langley, Miller, MM, R. Prince, Downing, Thomas.

English Morello ("Myrilla," "large Morella")
　　Gro: Washington, Skipwith, Tucker, Cocke.
　　Nur: Smith, Prince 71, 90, Booth, Landreth, B. Prince, A. MM,
　　　　Prince & Mills.
　　Lit: Langley, Miller, Forsyth, MM, Coxe, R. Prince, Kenrick,
　　　　Downing, Thomas.

"Kentish" (Early Richmond and/or Late Kentish)
　　Gro: Tucker, Cocke.
　　Nur: Smith, Prince 71, 90, Booth, Landreth, B. Prince, Prince &
　　　　Mills.
　　Lit: Miller, MM, Coxe, Kenrick, Downing, Hooper, Thomas.

"May" (Early Richmond?)

May Duke ("Duke")
　　Gro: Washington, Skipwith, Tucker, Cocke.
　　Nur: Smith, Prince 71, 90, Booth, Landreth, B. Prince, A. MM,
　　　　Prince & Mills.
　　Lit: Langley, Miller, Forsyth, MM, Coxe, R. Prince, Kenrick,
　　　　Downing, Hooper, Thomas.

"Tuckahoe grey heart"

White Heart
　　Gro: Washington, Skipwith, Tucker, Cocke.
　　Nur: Smith, Prince 71, 90, Booth, Landreth, B. Prince, Prince &
　　　　Mills.
　　Lit: Langley, Miller, Forsyth, Coxe, R. Prince, Downing,
　　　　Thomas.

CURRANT (*Ribes* sp.)

European red currant (*Ribes sativum*)

Sweet-scented or buffalo currant (*Ribes odoratum*)
　　Nur: A. MM, Prince & Mills.
　　Lit: Kenrick.

Yellow currant (*Ribes aureum*)
　　Lit: Thomas.

FIG (*Ficus carica*)

"ancient"

Angelique ("white Angelic")
　　Lit: Langley, Miller, Forsyth, Kenrick, Downing.

"large"

Marseilles ("white")
　　Gro: Cocke.
　　Nur: "large white": B. Prince, Prince & Mills.
　　Lit: "small early white": Miller, Forsyth, MM; Kenrick, Down-
　　　　ing.

"purple"

GOOSEBERRY (*Ribes uva-crispa*)

"Red"

GRAPES
(*Vitis vinifera*, *Vitis rotundifolia*, *Vitis vulpina*, etc.)

"Abrostine red" (Colorino?)
　　Lit: Gallesio.

"Abrostine white" (Picolit?)
　　Lit: Gallesio.

Aleatico
　　Lit: Gallesio.

Alexander ("Cape," "Cape of Good Hope grape")
　　Nur: Prince & Mills.
　　Lit: MM, Kenrick, Downing, Thomas.

"Black cluster" (Pinot Noir?)
　　Nur: A. MM.
　　Lit: Langley, Miller, Forsyth, Downing, Hooper, Thomas.

Black Hamburg
　　Nur: Booth, A. MM, B. Prince.
　　Lit: Miller, Forsyth, MM.

Bland
　　Nur: B. Prince, A. MM, Prince & Mills.
　　Lit: MM, Kenrick, Downing, Hooper, Thomas.

Chasselas Doré ("Chasselas")
　　Gro: Cocke.
　　Nur: B. Prince, A. MM, Prince & Mills.
　　Lit: "Royal Muscadine": Miller, Forsyth, MM; Kenrick, Down-
　　　　ing, Thomas.

Chasselas Rosé ("Brick coloured")
　　Gro: Cocke.
　　Nur: B. Prince.
　　Lit: "Red Chasselas": Miller, Forsyth, MM; "Brick": Langley,
　　　　Kenrick, Downing, Thomas.

Furmint ("Tokay")

"Lachrima Christi" (Tinto di Spagna?)
　　Lit: Gallesio.

Luglienga ("Great July," "Lugliola grossa," Lignan Blanc)
　　Lit: Langley, Miller, MM.

"Malaga" (Muscat of Alexandria?)
　　Gro: Cocke.
　　Lit: Miller, Forsyth, Kenrick, Downing, Thomas.

Mammolo Toscano ("Mammole")

Morgiano ("Margiano")

"Muscadine" (Chasselas Blanc?)
　　Lit: Langley, Miller, Forsyth, MM.

Muscat Blanc ("white Frontignac")
    Nur: Booth, A. MM, Prince & Mills.
    Lit: Langley, Miller, Forsyth, MM, Kenrick, Downing, Hooper.

Norton's Seedling
    Lit: Kenrick, Downing, Hooper.

Olivette Blanche ("Galettas")
    Lit: Miller, Forsyth, MM.

"Piedmont Malmsey" ("Malvagia di Piemonte," Malvasia Bianca?)

"Purple Syrian"

Red Hamburg
    Lit: Miller, Forsyth, MM, Thomas.

Regina ("Queen's grape")

Sangiovese ("San Giovetto")
    Lit: Gallesio.

Scuppernong (*Vitis rotundifolia*)
    Gro: Cocke.
    Lit: Kenrick, Downing, Thomas.

Seralamanna (Muscat of Alexandria?)
    Lit: Gallesio.

"Smyrna grape without seeds"

"Spanish raisins"

"Toccai" or "Tokay" (Tocai Rosso?)

Trebbiano
    Lit: Gallesio.

"White Sweet Water"
    Gro: Cocke.
    Nur: Booth, A. MM, Prince & Mills.
    Lit: Langley, Forsyth, Kenrick, Downing, Thomas.

NECTARINE (*Prunus persica* var. *nucipersica*)

"Kaskaskia soft"

Red Roman
    Gro: Skipwith, Tucker, Cocke.
    Nur: Prince 71, 90, Booth, Landreth, B. Prince, A. MM, Prince & Mills.
    Lit: Langley, Miller, Forsyth, MM, Coxe, R. Prince, Kenrick, Downing, Thomas.

Yellow Roman
    Nur: Prince 71, 90, Landreth.

PEACH (*Prunus persica*)

Alberges
    Nur: Prince & Mills.
    Lit: Langley, Miller, Forsyth, Gallesio, R. Prince, Downing,

    Hooper, Thomas.

Algiers Yellow ("yellow clingstone of October")
    Nur: Prince 90, B. Prince, Prince & Mills.
    Lit: R. Prince, Thomas.

Apple ("Pesca Mela," "Melon")
    Lit: Gallesio.

"Balyal's white, red, & yellow plumb peaches"

"General Jackson's"

Green Nutmeg
    Gro: Tucker, Cocke.
    Nur: Prince 71, 90, Lithen, Booth, Landreth, B. Prince, Prince & Mills.
    Lit: Langley, Miller, Forsyth, MM, Coxe, R. Prince, Kenrick, Downing, Hooper, Thomas.

Heath Cling
    Gro: Washington, Tucker, Cocke.
    Nur: Prince 90, Lithen, Booth, Landreth, B. Prince, A. MM, Prince & Mills.
    Lit: MM, Coxe, R. Prince, Kenrick, Downing, Hooper, Thomas, Fitz.

Indian Blood Cling ("black Georgia plumb peach")
    Gro: Cocke.
    Nur: Prince 71, 90, Booth, Landreth, B. Prince, Prince & Mills.
    Lit: Langley, Miller, Forsyth, MM, Coxe, R. Prince, Kenrick, Downing, Hooper, Thomas, Fitz.

Indian Blood Free ("black soft peaches from Georgia," Blood)
    Gro: Cocke.
    Nur: Booth, Prince & Mills.
    Lit: Coxe, Downing, Hooper.

"Lady's favorite"

Lemon Cling ("Lemon," "Carolina Canada," Kennedy Carolina)
    Gro: Tucker, Cocke.
    Nur: Prince 71, 90, Lithen, Booth, Landreth, B. Prince, A. MM, Prince & Mills.
    Lit: MM, Coxe, R. Prince, Kenrick, Downing, Hooper, Thomas, Fitz.

Maddelena
    Lit: Gallesio, Thomas.

"Magdalene"

Malta
    Gro: Cocke.
    Nur: B. Prince, Prince & Mills.
    Lit: Forsyth, Miller, R. Prince, Kenrick, Downing, Hooper, Thomas, Fitz.

"mammoth"

Morris's Red Rareripe ("Italian red-freestone")

Nur: Landreth.

Lit: Coxe, R. Prince, Kenrick, Downing, Hooper, Thomas.

Morris's White Rareripe ("Italian White-freestone")

Nur: Landreth.

Lit: Coxe, R. Prince, Kenrick, Downing, Hooper, Thomas.

"October," "yellow clingstone of October" (Algiers Yellow?)

Nur: Prince 70, 91, B. Prince, Prince & Mills.

Oldmixon Cling

Nur: Landreth, B. Prince, A. MM, Prince & Mills.

Lit: MM, Coxe, R. Prince, Kenrick, Downing, Hooper,
Thomas, Fitz.

Oldmixon Free

Nur: Landreth.

Lit: Coxe, R. Prince, Kenrick, Downing, Hooper, Thomas, Fitz.

"plumb"

Poppa di Venere ("Teat," Breast of Venus)

Nur: Booth, Landreth, B. Prince, A. MM, Prince & Mills.

Lit: Langley, Miller, Forsyth, MM, Coxe, Kenrick, Downing,
Hooper.

Portugal

Gro: Washington.

Lit: Miller, Forsyth, B. Prince.

San Jacopo (St. James)

"soft" ("October soft," "November soft," "Timothy Lomax's
soft," "large white soft," "fine white soft," "large yellow
soft," "early soft," etc.)

Vaga Loggia Cling

Lit: Gallesio.

Vaga Loggia Free

Lit: Gallesio.

"White blossomed"

Nur: Prince & Mills.

Lit: Forsyth, Downing.

PEAR (*Pyrus communis*)

Beurré Gris ("Bursé," Brown Beurré)

Gro: Washington, Skipwith, Tucker, Cocke.

Nur: Prince 71, 90, Booth, Landreth, B. Prince, A. MM, Prince
& Mills.

Lit: Langley, Miller, Forsyth, MM, Coxe, R. Prince, Kenrick,
Downing, Hooper, Thomas.

Crassane

Nur: Prince 71, 90, Booth, Landreth, B. Prince, Prince & Mills.

Lit: Langley, Miller, Forsyth, MM, Coxe, R. Prince, Kenrick,
Downing, Thomas.

"English" ("3 kinds")

"fine late large"

"forward"

Meriwether

Lit: C. Downing (1900).

Royal (Winter Royal)

Nur: B. Prince, A. MM.

Lit: Langley, Miller, Coxe, Kenrick, Downing, Thomas.

Seckel

Nur: Landreth, A. MM, Prince & Mills.

Lit: Coxe, R. Prince, Kenrick, Downing, Hooper, Thomas.

St. Germaine, or Richmond

Gro: Washington, Cocke.

Nur: Prince 71, 90, Booth, Landreth, B. Prince, A. MM, Prince
& Mills.

Lit: Langley, Miller, Forsyth, MM, Coxe, R. Prince, Kenrick,
Downing, Hooper, Thomas.

"Sugar"

Virgouleuse

Gro: Tucker, Cocke.

Nur: Prince 71, 90, Booth, Landreth, B. Prince, A. MM, Prince
& Mills.

Lit: Langley, Miller, Forsyth, MM, Coxe, R. Prince, Kenrick,
Downing, Hooper, Thomas.

PLUM (*Prunus* sp.)

Apricot (*Prunus domestica*)

Gro: Tucker, Cocke.

Nur: Prince 71, 90, B. Prince, Prince & Mills.

Lit: Miller, Forsyth, MM, R. Prince, Kenrick, Downing,
Thomas.

Boccon del Re (*Prunus insititia*)

Lit: Gallesio.

Brignole (*Prunus domestica*)

Nur: Prince 71, 90.

Lit: Miller, Forsyth, MM, R. Prince, Downing.

Chickasaw (*Prunus angustifolia*, "Cherokee")

Gro: Washington, Tucker.

Nur: B. Prince, Prince & Mills.

Lit: MM, Downing, Hooper.

Cooper's Large (*Prunus domestica*)

Nur: Lithen, Landreth.

Lit: MM, Coxe, Kenrick, Downing.

Damson (*Prunus insititia*, "Damascene")

Gro: Washington, Cocke.

Nur: Smith, Prince 71, 90, Booth, Landreth, B. Prince, A. MM,
    Prince & Mills.
Lit: MM, Coxe, Kenrick, Downing, Hooper, Thomas.
Drap d'Or (*Prunus insititia*)
    Gro: Skipwith, Cocke.
    Nur: Prince 71, 90, B. Prince, A. MM, Prince & Mills.
    Lit: Langley, Miller, Forsyth, Coxe, R. Prince, Kenrick, Down-
        ing, Thomas.
"Florida" (probably *Prunus umbellata*)
Green Gage (*Prunus domestica*, Reine Claude, "Regina Claudia")
    Gro: Washington, Skipwith, Tucker, Cocke.
    Nur: Smith, Prince 71, 90, Lithen, Booth, Landreth, B. Prince,
        A. MM, Prince & Mills.
    Lit: Langley, Miller, Forsyth, MM, Coxe, R. Prince, Kenrick,
        Downing, Hooper, Thomas.
"Horse" (*Prunus americana* or Damson, *P. insititia*)
    Lit: Kenrick, Downing, Thomas.
Imperatrice, Blue Imperatrice (*Prunus domestica*)
    Nur: Smith ("Blue Imperial"), Prince 71, 90, Landreth.
    Lit: Langley, Forsyth, Coxe, R. Prince, Kenrick, Downing,
        Thomas.
"Large Blue"
"Large white sweet"
Magnum Bonum, Mogul, Yellow Egg, White Imperial (*Prunus do-
    mestica*)
    Gro: Washington, Tucker.
    Nur: Smith, Prince 71, 90, Lithen, Booth, Landreth, B. Prince,
        A. MM, Prince & Mills.
    Lit: Langley, Miller, Forsyth, MM, Coxe, R. Prince, Kenrick,
        Downing, Hooper, Thomas.
Mirabelle (*Prunus insititia*)
    Lit: Langley, Miller, Forsyth, MM, Downing, Thomas.
Muscle (*Prunus domestica*)
    Nur: Prince & Mills.
    Lit: Miller, R. Prince.
Orleans (*Prunus domestica*)
    Gro: Washington, Skipwith, Tucker, Cocke.
    Nur: Smith, Prince 71, 90, Booth, Landreth, B. Prince, A. MM,
        Prince & Mills.
    Lit: Langley, Miller, Forsyth, MM, Coxe, R. Prince, Kenrick,
        Downing, Hooper, Thomas.
Red Imperial (*Prunus domestica*)
    Gro: Tucker, Cocke.
    Nur: Prince 71, 90, Landreth, B. Prince, Prince & Mills.
    Lit: Miller, Forsyth, Coxe, Downing, Thomas.
"Regina" (possibly Queen Mother, or Damas Violet)

"Purple prune" (*Prunus domestica*)
Royal (*Prunus domestica*)
    Nur: Prince 71.
    Lit: Langley, Miller, Forsyth, MM, B. Prince, Downing.
"Small green plum"
White Imperial (*Prunus domestica*)
    Nur: Prince 71, 90, Booth.
    Lit: Downing, Thomas.

POMEGRANATE (*Punica granatum*)

QUINCE (*Cydonia oblonga*)

RASPBERRY (*Rubus idaeus*)

"Common"
"Monthly"
Red Antwerp
    Gro: Cocke.
    Nur: Lithen, Booth, Landreth, B. Prince, A. MM, Prince &
        Mills.
    Lit: Forsyth, Kenrick, Downing.
White Antwerp
    Gro: Cocke.
    Nur: Booth, Landreth, B. Prince, A. MM.
    Lit: Forsyth, MM, Kenrick, Downing, Thomas.

STRAWBERRY (*Fragaria* sp.)

Alpine (*Fragaria vesca*)
    Gro: Cocke.
    Nur: Lithen, Booth, B. Prince, A. MM.
    Lit: MM, R. Prince, Kenrick, Downing, Hooper.
Chili (*Fragaria chiloensis*)
    Gro: Cocke.
    Nur: Prince 71, 90, Booth, B. Prince, A. MM.
    Lit: MM, R. Prince, Downing, Hooper, Thomas.
Hudson (*Fragaria × ananassa?*)
    Gro: Cocke.
    Nur: Lithen, B. Prince, A. MM.
    Lit: Downing, Hooper, Thomas.
"large garden" ("Fragoloni di giardino")
"May" ("Fragoloni Mazzese")
Scarlet (*Fragaria virginiana*)
    Nur: Booth, A. MM.
    Lit: Langley, Miller, Forsyth, MM, R. Prince, Kenrick, Hooper.
"White" (*Fragaria vesca* or *Fragaria moschata*)

Notes

ABBREVIATIONS

AF	*American Farmer*
FB	*Farm Book*
GB	*Garden Book*
VMHB	*Virginia Magazine of History and Biography*
VSHS	Virginia State Horticultural Society

INTRODUCTION

1. Bailey, *Cyclopedia* 2:1522, 1572 ("The influence of Downing's *The Fruits and Fruit Trees of America* has been greater than all others in extending a love of fruit and a critical attitude toward varieties"); Downing, *Fruits*, v; see also Hedrick, *History*, 485–86, where another titan of American horticulture, Ulysses P. Hedrick, said of Downing's *Fruits*: "At once it became the standard pomological authority."

2. "Jefferson's plan for laying off lots for minor articles of husbandry," probably from the 1790s, CSmH. See also Beiswanger, "The Temple in the Garden," for the *ferme ornée*.

3. See appendix; Bailey, *Cyclopedia* 2:1523–52, for a list of American horticultural works published before 1900; Woodburn, "Books Published from 1861–1920," 528–40; Hedrick, *History*, 30, 35, on the first American apples; Ayres, "Fruit Culture," 18–29, for a compilation of apple varieties grown in Virginia before 1800.

4. See Bailey, *Evolution*, vii–x.

5. Fitz, *Southern Apple and Peach Culturist*, 65; Coxe, *View*, 1, 58; Janson, "William Coxe," i–xxiv, Coxe, "On Orchards"; Coxe, "The Gloucester White, Taliaferro, or Robertson Apple"; Coxe, "View," 699, 783, 810; see also Laudrum, "Fruit Trees," 268, and Fitz, *Southern Apple and Peach Culturist*, 79, praising Coxe.

6. Entry for Aug. 3, 1767, *GB*, 352, 6; see also Kalm, *Travels* 1:86, who was "frequently surprised at the prudence of the inhabitants" of Pennsylvania whose "first care" upon establishing a homestead, even before the construction of the house, was the planting of an apple orchard.

7. Entry for Mar. 19, 1814, *GB*, 54.

8. Fletcher, *Pennsylvania Agriculture*, 206 ("Fruit growing was by far the most important phase of colonial horticulture, mainly because fruits could be converted to 'comfortable drinks'"), 210; see

also Bailey, *Cyclopedia* 2:1513: "It was not well into the past century that people seem to have escaped the European notion that fruit is to be drunk"; Hedrick, *Peaches*, 48; Ayres, "Fruit Culture," 101–28.

9. TJ to James Madison, May 15, 1794, *GB*, 219: "It turns out that our fruit has not been as entirely killed as was at first apprehended; some later blossoms have yielded a small supply of this precious refreshment."

10. TJ to James Barbour, Mar. 5, 1816, *GB*, 516: "My collection of fruits went to entire decay in my absence and has not been renewed."

11. Bear, *Jefferson at Monticello*, 47; TJ to James Mease, June 29, 1814, Mease, "Account of the Virginia Cyder Apple."

12. Malone, *Jefferson the President*, 291; 1807 vineyard plan, from Weather Memorandum Book, PHi.

THE FARM ORCHARD AND THE FRUIT GARDEN

1. Fletcher, "History," 4–5; "Newport's Virginia Discoveries," *VMHB* 14 (1907): 375; Ayres, "Fruit Culture," 4; Michel, "Journey," 33; Banister, *History*, 355–56.

2. Beverley, *History*, 314; Lawson, *History*, 110–15; Eddis, *Letters from America*, 67; Parkinson, *Tour*, 212.

3. Michaux, "Travels to the West," 215; Pryor, "Orchard Fruits," 12; "American Farmer," *Epitome*, 134; see also Bordley, *Essays*, 497; McMahon, *Calendar*, 133.

4. Ayres, "Fruit Culture," 103–4; Parkinson, *Tour*, 623. See also Pryor, "Orchard Fruits," 7, on similar advertisements in Maryland; Banister, *History*, 355, Beverley, *History*, 291–92, and Lawson, *History*, 110, on the use of seedling trees.

5. Miller, *Dictionary*, s.v. "Garden," "Kitchen Garden"; McMahon, *Calendar*, 16–17, 100, 103.

6. Notations for Mar. 11, June 29, 1786, *1786 Almanac*, and for Mar. 17, 1787, *1787 Almanac*, Tucker-Coleman Papers, ViW; see also Martin, *Pleasure Gardens*, 177–81.

7. Notation for Feb. 16, Mar. 17, 1787, Mar. 19, [1788?], *1787 Almanac*, Tucker-Coleman Papers.

8. Notations for Mar. 17, Mar. 22, 1787, *1787 Almanac*, Apr. 1, 1784, *1784 Almanac*, Aug. 25, 1783, *1783 Almanac*, ibid.

9. Niemcewicz, *Under Their Vine,* 98; Miller, *Dictionary,* s.v. "Kitchen Garden"; Washington, *Diaries* 1:295 (Mar. 22, 24, 1762), 315–17 (Mar. 21, 1763), 327–29 (Mar. 29, 1764), 336 (Mar. 6, 1765), 338 (May 30, 1765), 4:113 (Apr. 4, 1785), 286–87 (Feb. 27, 1786); "Weekly Reports of George Washington's Gardener," Jan. 6, 1797, Jan. 26, 1799, Mount Vernon; Leighton, *American Gardens,* 223–24.

10. Washington, *Diaries* 1:128 (Mar. 1760), 4:222 (Nov. 12, 1785); Pryor, "Orchard Fruits," 42; Fletcher, "History," 17.

11. Morison and Commager, *Growth of the American Republic,* 338–39; see also Coyner, "John Hartwell Cocke."

12. Cocke, "On Peach Trees"; Coyner, "John Hartwell Cocke," 238–39; Joseph C. Cabell and John Hartwell Cocke to Benjamin Prince, Sept. 20, 1815, "John Hartwell Cocke's records pertaining to fruit tree 'association,'" 1815, Benjamin Prince to John Hartwell Cocke and Joseph C. Cabell, Sept. 4, 1815, "List of books in library at Bremo c. 1920," Ann Barraud Cocke to the Barrauds, Mar. 2, 1803, Ann Barraud Cocke to Ann B. Barraud, Mar. 12, 1815, "Contract between John Hartwell Cocke and Archibald Blair, gardener," 1816; John Hartwell Cocke Diary, 1816–18, Nov. 20, 1817, Cocke Papers, NiU.

13. Entries for Mar. 8, 29, 1810, Gardening Memoranda, 1810–12, John Hartwell Cocke Diary, June 25, 1817, Ann Barraud Cocke to John Hartwell Cocke, Jan. 30, 1815, "Memorandum of Orchard Plantings and Graftings," Mar. 1816, Louisiana B. Cocke to John Hartwell Cocke, Jr., April 4, 1817, Cocke Papers; Jane Nicholas Randolph to Mrs. N. P. Trist (Virginia Randolph Trist), June 24, 1827, Nicholas Trist Papers, NcU.

14. "Kinds of Fruit planted at U. B. 15 Dec. 1815," Charles Ellis to John Hartwell Cocke, Mar. 9, 1818, "Memo of Trees Grafted in the year 1810," Ro. Sampson to John Hartwell Cocke, Nov. 20, 1808, Benjamin Anderson to John Hartwell Cocke, Mar. 4, 1817, Nicholas Faulcon to John Hartwell Cocke, Nov. 30, 1814, July 17, 1815, Cocke Papers; Coyner, "John Hartwell Cocke," 306.

15. Castiglioni, *Viaggio,* 185, 194; Ayres, "Fruit Culture," 115; Fithian, *Journal,* 43–44, 78–79; Spooner, "A Topographical Description of Prince George County, 1793," 8; see also Sarudy, "Eighteenth-Century Gardens"; Martin, *Pleasure Gardens,* 79–99.

FRUIT-TREE CULTURE AT MONTICELLO

1. TJ to Philip Tabb, June 1, 1809, *GB,* 413.

2. Langley, *Pomona,* vii–ix; Henrey, *British Botanical Literature* 2:470–71; Sowerby, *Catalogue* 4:368.

3. Sowerby, *Catalogue* 4:364; Henrey, *British Botanical Literature* 1:211, 215–19; Swem, *Brothers,* 164n; Stetson, "American Garden Books"; entry for July 27, 1769, TJ to John Bartram, Jr., Jan. 17, 1786, to John Taylor, Dec. 29, 1794, to James Madison, Feb. 5, 1795, *GB,* 16, 109, 221, 231; Miller, *Dictionary,* s.v. "Persica."

4. Sowerby, *Catalogue* 4:368; Bailey, *Cyclopedia* 2:1568, 1522, 1533; "An Epitome of Mr. Forsyth's Treatise on the Culture and Management of Fruit Trees," in *From Seed to Flower,* 51. William Cobbett is the most logical candidate to be the "American Farmer," although there are other possibilities: see Manks, "Some Early American Horticultural Writers."

5. Sowerby, *Catalogue* 4:369; TJ to Anne Cary Randolph, Feb. 16, 1808, McMahon to TJ, Mar. 10, 1811, entry for Oct. 19, 1819, *GB,* 363, 453, 583; McMahon, *Calendar,* iii, 38, 72, 133, 138.

The Monticello library included other horticultural works dealing with fruit culture. John Abercrombie's *Every Man His Own Gardener* (York, Eng. 1767) was imitated by numerous English writers and by McMahon. Abercrombie, the most successful of all eighteenth-century English nurseryman-authors, published the book under the name of Thomas Mawe, at the time a more recognizable figure. John Gardiner and David Hepburn's *American Gardener,* 1804, was described by Jefferson as an "excellent gardening book" (TJ to Martha Jefferson Randolph, *GB,* 299). Hepburn's brother, Alexander, a Washington nurseryman, propagated Italian peaches sent by Philip Mazzei to Jefferson in 1804. A relatively unknown work published in 1793, *The Practical Farmer* by John Spurrier, was dedicated to Jefferson. Spurrier, an Englishman transplanted to Wilmington, Delaware, included extensive directions for fruit-tree culture, particularly fruit propagation. Although primarily an agricultural work, John Bordley's *Essays and Notes on Rural Affairs* (Philadelphia, 1799) included detailed directions on fruit cultivation. See Sowerby, *Catalogue* 4:329, 333, 366, 368; Henrey, *British Botanical Literature* 2:364–71.

6. Parkinson, *Paradisi,* 571; TJ to William Prince, July 6, 1791, to Edmund Bacon, Nov. 24, 1807, Alexander Hepburn to TJ, June 12, 1806, *GB,* 166–67, 355, 319.

7. "Method of distinguishing or designating the terrasses below the garden wall," Dec. 24, 1813, entry for Mar. 21, 1810, *GB,* 498, 420–23; "Directions, Oct 1783," MHi; Beiswanger, "Report," s.v. "Nurseries." See also Spivey, "Thomas Jefferson's Nurseries," for a compilation of plants grown in the Monticello nurseries.

8. Memorandum to Mr. Perry, Sept. 24, 1804, ViU; entries for Apr. 29, 1804, Apr. 11, 17, 1807, Mar. 21, June 6, 1810, May 15, 1811, TJ to Thomas Mann Randolph, Dec. 16, 1790, *GB,* 4, 291, 334–35, 422, 425, 447, 155; Forest, *Gardens at Mount Vernon,* 79–81.

9. McMahon, *Calendar,* 43–45, 241; Miller, *Dictionary,* s.v. "Nursery"; Peters, "On Orchards," 213; Capron, "Planting Trees"; John S. Skinner, editorial note, *AF* 4 (1824): 244; see also Coxe, *View,* 14–17.

10. According to Ayres, "Fruit Culture," 17, only 8 of 369 property advertisements in the *Virginia Gazette* before 1780 that gave orchard descriptions mentioned grafted trees.

11. TJ to Ferdinand Grand, Dec. 28, 1786, *GB,* 119; TJ to Isaac Coles, June 10, 1811, MHi.

12. Beiswanger, "Report," s.v. "Enclosures"; 1778 orchard plan;

insurance plat from Stanton, "Interim Compilation"; TJ to Martha Jefferson Randolph, Mar. 10, 1793, Betts and Bear, *Family Letters*, 113.

13. Betts's note on the hawthorn hedge, and Thomas Main to TJ, Mar. 13, 1805, Feb. 24, 1806, TJ to Edmund Bacon, Jan. 26, 1807, Mar. 22, 1808, "Thomas Main sold to TJ," Mar. 7, 1807, TJ to J. P. Reibelt, Aug. 12, 1807, to William Hamilton, Mar. 1, 1808, *GB*, 299, 300, 316, 339, 367, 342, 350–51, 365; Jefferson's plan of the mountaintop, 1806, Jefferson Papers, CtY; 1811 orchard plan, ViU; Cobbett, *American Gardener*, no. 33.

14. "Directions for Mr. Watkins," Sept. 27, 1808, *GB*, 377; Isaac in Bear, *Jefferson at Monticello*, 12; Thomas Mann Randolph to TJ, Apr. 9, 1792, ViU; TJ to Martha Jefferson Randolph, June 6, 1814, Stanton, "Interim Compilation"; William Hooper, "Visit to Thomas Jefferson and Monticello," in "Descriptions, 1780–1826." See also Edmund Bacon to TJ, Feb. 24, 1809, Stanton, "Interim Compilation," for what may have been another ha-ha at Monticello.

15. Fletcher, *History*, 5; William Fitzhugh to Ralph Smith, Apr. 22, 1686, "Letters of William Fitzhugh," 395; Ayres, "Fruit Culture," 120–21; Bruce, *Economic History* 1:317; Parkinson, *Tour*, 49; see also Jacocks, "On the Use of Juniper Rails," 10; Carter, *Diary* 1:589 (July 9, 1771), describing a woven wattle fence.

16. Bear, *Jefferson at Monticello*, 87–88.

17. Anburey in Morrison, *Travels in Virginia*, 28; Kalm, *Travels* 1:324; Parkinson, *Tour*, 31; Cobbett, *American Gardener*, no. 33.

18. Thomas Mann Randolph to TJ, Mar. 27, 1792, MHi; Bear, *Jefferson at Monticello*, 47. See also entry for Apr. 19, 1795, and TJ to James Madison, Apr. 16, 1810, *GB*, 226, 435, for Jefferson's self-satisfied comments on comparative frost damage.

19. Dickson in Pryor, "Orchard Fruits," 11–13; Grove, "Diary," 1, ViU; Coxe, *View*, 30–31; Skipwith in Leighton, *American Gardens*, 277.

20. 1778 orchard plan; entries for Mar. 21, 1810, Mar. 17, 18, 1811, Mar. 19, 1812, *GB*, 421, 475, 524; William Prince to Mr. Love, 1799 ("Nothing is more customary here than Planting Peach trees when in Bloom"), to G. M. Forman, Feb. 24, 1799 ("Pears are in so great a demand that I cannot keep them long enough more than two years old from the graft"), Prince Collection, NAL; "Oct. 6, 1816 order'd from Prince," handwritten list of trees "lost in transplanting" from Benjamin Prince catalog, Cocke Papers; notation for Mar. 19, [1788?], *1787 Almanac*, Tucker-Coleman Papers; Coxe, *View*, 6–7; Washington, *Diaries* 4:214 (Oct. 26, 1785); John Custis to Peter Collinson, "Believed to be before July 18, 1738," Swem, *Brothers*, 53. Garden writers were generally neutral on the best planting season; see Miller, *Dictionary*, s.v. "Malus," "Planting"; McMahon, *Calendar*, 327.

21. TJ to Thomas Mann Randolph, Mar. 22, 1798, MHi; Miller, *Dictionary*, s.v. "Orchard"; McMahon, *Calendar*, 224–26; Coxe, *View*, 46; Collin, "Remarks on the Damage to Apple Trees," 201; Kelso, "Report," 42; TJ to Jeremiah A. Goodman, May 12, 1812, entry for Apr. 6, 1774, *GB*, 487, 53; Washington, *Diaries* 4:111 (Apr. 1, 1785).

22. Miller, *Dictionary*, s.v. "Planting," "Orchards"; Matlack, "On Peach Trees," 1:278; Cobbett, *American Gardener*, no. 285; "Visit of Iwan Alexiowitz to John Bartram," in Darlington, *Memorials*, 50–51; John Custis to Peter Collinson, July 18, 1738, Swem, *Brothers*, 71.

23. Duc de La Rochefoucauld-Liancourt in *GB*, 243; TJ to Nicholas Lewis, Apr. 4, 1791, Boyd, *Papers* 20:103; entries for Apr. 30, 1794, Apr. 28, 1810, entry for Jan. and Feb. 1795 from Farm Book, TJ to John Freeman, Feb. 7, 1806, to Edmund Bacon, Oct. 19, 1806, Mar. 8, 1808, entry for May 1, 1807, from Weather Memorandum Book, *GB*, 211, 424, 227, 318, 327, 336, 366.

24. Ayres, "Fruit Culture," 118; Carter, *Diaries* 2:668 (May 6, 1772), 700 (June 4, 1772), 1034 (May 4, 1776); notation for June 29, 1786, *1786 Almanac*, Tucker-Coleman Papers; Coxe, *View*, 49; entry for Apr. 22, 1817, Garden Diary of John Hartwell Cocke, Cocke Papers; "Journal of Col. James Gordon," 191; TJ to Nicholas Lewis, Apr. 4, 1791, Boyd, *Papers* 20:103; Coxe, *View*, 49; Wynkoop, "Account of a Crab Apple Orchard"; Peters, "On the Injurious Effects of Clover"; "Fruit," *AF* 11 (1829): 5; *Southern Planter*, Feb. 1842, 35. See also Fletcher, *Pennsylvania Agriculture*, 214, and Cobbett, *American Gardener*, nos. 291–98, on cultivation in orchards.

25. McMahon, *Calendar*, 134, 222; *Southern Planter*, Feb. 1842, 42; Fitz, *Southern Apple and Peach Culturist*, 243; John Gates, "Extract from *Massachusetts Agricultural Repository and Journal*," in *Central Gazette* (Charlottesville), May 11, 1821. On manures, see also Fletcher, *Pennsylvania Agriculture*, 214; Preston, "On Fruit and Fruit Trees," 82; Phillips, "On Peach Trees." On mulching, see also William Prince to Mr. Love, 1799, Prince Collection; Bordley, *Essays*, 504.

26. Extract from Account Book, 1767–70, and "Calendar for this year," *GB*, 21, 474; Forsyth, *Treatise*, 17, 33–35, 44, 59, 75, 229–32, pls. 1–9; "American Farmer," *Epitome*, 100–101, 184.

27. Coxe, *View*, 40–43; Coxe, "View," 810; "American Farmer," *Epitome*, 127; Forsyth, *Treatise*, 278. See also McMahon, *Calendar*, 210, 38; Spurrier, *Practical Farmer*, 244–46; and Bordley, *Essays*, 501–2, providing their own wound-healing compounds in response to Forsyth. See also Thomas, "On the Preservation of Peach Trees"; "Rusticus," "Planting Apple Orchards"; Fitz, *Southern Apple and Peach Culturist*, 22, 247, for examples of Forsyth's influence.

28. Martha Jefferson Randolph to TJ, May 16, 1793, Betts and Bear, *Family Letters*, 118; TJ to Martha Randolph, July 21, 1793, to Thomas Mann Randolph, May 1, 1791, *GB*, 198, 163.

29. Fletcher, "History," 7; Hedrick, *History*, 104, 149; Bailey, *Cyclopedia* 2:1515; Cobbett, "List of Fruits," 385; Cobbett, *American Gardener*, no. 318.

30. Peter Collinson to John Bartram, Apr. 26, 1746, Darlington, *Memorials*, 177; Crèvecoeur, *Letters*, 269; Clinton, "Extracts," 109; Martha Jefferson Randolph to TJ, June 26, 1793, Betts and Bear, *Family Letters*, 121.

31. Anon., "Culture of the Peach Tree"; Richter, "Description."

32. Barton, "Of the Usefulness of Birds," 157–63; Clinton, "Extracts," 109; Worth, "Observations on Insects," 394–95; Peter Collinson to John Bartram, Apr. 26, 1746, Darlington, *Memorials*, 178; Peter Collinson to John Custis, Jan. 31, 1739, Swem, *Brothers*, 65; Coxe, *View*, 5. See also Worth, "On the Hessian Fly."

33. TJ to Thomas Mann Randolph, Aug. 11, 1793, *GB*, 203; Peters, "On Peach Trees," 16, 21–22.

34. "Veritas," "Orchards"; Anon., "Culture of the Peach Tree"; "Rusticus," "Planting Apple Orchards."

35. Noelden, "Some Further Observations"; Wellington, "Ringing Fruit Trees"; W. G. C., "Queries on Barking Fruit Trees"; Anon., "Peeling and Barking Fruit Trees"; P. L., "Concerning Fruit Trees"; Willis, "A Wash for Fruit Trees"; Falconer, "Soap Suds as a Manure"; N. Hammond, "Soft Soap Undiluted," 402; Cobbett, *American Gardener*, no. 298. See also Forsyth, *Treatise*, 175–210, for the most complete description of fruit pests and their control around 1800.

36. Hedrick, *History*, 104; Ayres, "Fruit Culture," 121; Pryor, "Orchard Fruits," 32–33; Preston, "On Fruit and Fruit Trees," 87 (editorial note by Richard Peters); Anon., "Method of Securing the Blossoms of Fruit Trees."

37. TJ to William Strickland, Mar. 23, 1798, to Charles W. Peale, Apr. 17, 1813, entry for Sept. 30, 1771, and entry from *Notes*, *GB*, 263, 509, 23, 648; Elmore, "Weed Survey"; Dirr, "Most Common Weeds"; Brosten and Simmonds, "Crops Gone," 26; Anon., *AF* 4 (1823): 412; Randolph, "Transactions of the Agricultural Society of Albemarle."

38. Dirr, "Most Common Weeds," 145; Parkinson, *Tour*, 159–60; Smith and Josslyn references in Crosby, *Ecological Imperialism*, 155–56; John Bartram to Philip Miller, June 16, 1758, Darlington, *Memorials*, 382–88; Kalm, *Travels* 1:81; Cobbett, *American Gardener*, no. 219; Hold, "Mount Clare Orchard Floral Analysis."

39. John Bartram to Philip Miller, June 16, 1758, Darlington, *Memorials*, 383; Roberts, "Extirpation of Wild Garlic," 120; Peters, "On Tough Sod, Star of Bethlehem, and Blue Bottle," 178–79; Boulster, "Wild Garlic"; Armstrong, "Wild Garlic."

THE SOUTH ORCHARD

1. Jefferson, *Notes*, 110. The pre-Jefferson Monticello landscape is a puzzle. It seems unlikely Jefferson would "level" the top of Monticello mountain (and its accompanying vegetation) if the original forest was still in place because of his sensitivity, expressed in later years, to the preservation of native trees and their welcoming shade. Also, many visitors to Monticello remarked on the mature forest that clothed the mountain on three sides almost to the top. See also Goodwin, "Italians in the Monticello Orchard," 1–9; TJ to William Hamilton, July 1806, *GB*, 322–24; "Visitor's descriptions, 1780–1826"; and Maxwell, "The Use and Abuse of Forests by the Virginia Indians."

2. Entries for Mar. 14, 1769, Oct. 8, 1772, *GB*, 15, 34; see also TJ to Angelica Church, Feb. 17, 1788, ibid., xv.

3. Goodwin, "Italians in the Monticello Orchard," 1–9; entry for Mar. 31, 1774, Thomas Mann Randolph to TJ, Aug. 14, 1793, *GB*, 50, 203; TJ to Thomas Mann Randolph, Sept. 2, 1793, MHi.

4. 1778 orchard plan, MHi.

5. Ibid.; "State of fruit trees. Nov. 1778," ibid.; entries for Mar. 31, 1773, Mar. 9–14, 1778, *GB*, 39–40, 76.

6. "Directions, 1783," MHi.

7. "Revisal of my Fruit, 1783," ViU. I have substituted parentheses for Jefferson's brackets in the transcription of this planting memorandum.

8. TJ to Rev. James Madison, Oct. 28, 1785, *GB*, 106 (the letter to Madison was reprinted in Boyd, *Papers* 8:681–83, without the mistranscription as "Redtown pippin"); see also TJ to Ferdinand Grand, Dec. 28, 1786, *GB*, 119, for a similar letter on the comparative quality of American and European fruit.

9. TJ to Antonio Giannini, Feb. 5, 1786, *GB*, 632–33; Giannini to TJ, June 9, 1786, Boyd, *Papers* 9:624.

10. Beiswanger, "Report," s.v. "Orchard"; "Feb. 1790 planted," ViU; "Plants from France," undated packing list of ornamental and fruit trees, MHi; "List of Baggage Shipped by Jefferson from France," c. Sept. 1, 1789, Boyd, *Papers* 15:376; TJ to William Prince, July 6, 1791, *GB*, 166; "Prince Wm 1791," planting memorandum, ViU; Thomas Mann Randolph to TJ, Mar. 27, 1792, MHi.

11. TJ to Thomas Mann Randolph, Jan. 1, 1792, *GB*, 175; "Peach trees planted Dec. '94," "Orchards," Sept. 4, 1796, *FB*, 38, 96; unpublished Garden Book entry, Mar. 19–23, 1805, NjP.

12. John Armstrong to TJ, Feb. 20, 1804, entry for May 26, 1802, *GB*, 294–95, 277; unpublished Garden Book entry, Mar. 19–23, 1805.

13. TJ to Mazzei, Mar. 17, 1801, Mazzei to TJ, Sept. 28, 1801, Goodwin, "Fruits from Mazzei"; entries for May 26, 1802, Mar. 17–20, 1810, *GB*, 277, 420.

14. "Mazzei's list of plants etc. sent TJ 'at beginning of 1804'" and TJ to Mazzei, July 18, 1804, May 4, 1805, to Charles Clay, Mar. 1, 1806, Goodwin, "Fruits from Mazzei"; unpublished Garden Book entry, Mar. 19–23, 1805.

15. TJ to John Freeman, Feb. 7, 26, June 28, 1806, *GB*, 314, 316, 320; TJ to William Meriwether, Nov. 24, 1807, John Threlkeld to TJ, Mar. 8, 1809, Goodwin, "Fruits from Mazzei."

16. Entry for Apr. 21, 1807, Timothy Matlack to TJ, Feb. 25, Oct. 19, 1807, TJ to Edmund Bacon, Nov. 24, 1807, TJ to Charles W. Peale, Aug. 20, 1811, and "Memorandums," *GB*, 335–36, 340–41, 352, 354–55, 461, 358.

17. Entries for Mar. 17–Apr. 26, 1810, TJ to Threlkeld, Mar. 26, 1807, *GB*, 420–23, 345; Threlkeld to TJ, Mar. 25, Nov. 23, 1807, Goodwin, "Fruits from Mazzei."

18. 1811 orchard plan, Betts Collection, ViU.

19. Entries for Mar. 17–21, 1812, Apr. 10, Oct. 6, 1813, Mar. 19, 1814, TJ to James Barbour, Mar. 5, 1816, *GB*, 475, 497, 523, 556.

20. TJ to Barbour, Mar. 5, 1816, ibid., 556.

21. "Descriptions of Monticello, 1780–1826" (other brief allusions to the orchard and fruit garden were by Isaac Weld in 1796, John Edwards Caldwell in 1808, and Margaret Bayard Smith in 1809); Castiglioni, *Viaggio*, 185; Loudon, *Encyclopædia*, 331; Beiswanger, "Report," s.v. "The South Orchard"; *Central Gazette,* Mar. 27, 1827; Adams, *Jefferson's Monticello*, 245.

APPLES: "OUR DEMOCRATIC FRUIT"

1. TJ to Mary Walker Lewis, Dec. 25, 1813, MHi; *The Saga of a City: Lynchburg, Virginia*, 58, for reminiscence of the granddaughter of James Steptoe, Jefferson's Bedford County neighbor; entry for Mar. 14, 1769, *GB*, 15; 1778 orchard plan; 1811 orchard plan; entry for Sept. 4, 1796, *FB*, 96. Recipes for apple fritters and apple pudding are among the few surviving in the Jefferson family papers.

2. Ayres, "Fruit Culture," 162–63; Pryor, "Orchard Fruits," 54–55; "American Farmer," *Epitome*, 131; Bailey, *Cyclopedia* 2:1513; Hooker in Robbins, *David Hosack*, 47.

3. Ragan, *Nomenclature*; Rouché, "One Hundred Thousand Varieties," 33; Hedrick, *History*, 105; Fitz, *Southern Apple and Peach Culturist*, 198; see also Downing, *Fruits*, 57.

4. Bailey, *Cyclopedia* 1:323–25; Hedrick, *History*, 105; Bruce, *Economic History* 1:214; Chastellux, *Travels in North America*, 390; Taylor, *Arator*, 231, 33; Kalm, *Travels* 1:86; Rouché, "One Hundred Thousand Varieties," 35; "Pomona," "Cider."

5. Fletcher, "History," 4, 6; Fitzhugh in Glover, "An Account of Virginia," in Swem, *Brothers*, 34; Bruce, *Economic History* 1:469; Troubetzkoy, "Big Business"; Hedrick, *History*, 104; Lawson, *History*, 110–11; Byrd, *Natural History*, 43–44; Michel, "Journey," 33.

6. Lawson, *History*, 110–11; Beverley, *History*, 314; Beach, *Apples*, 7; Michel, "Journey," 33.

7. *Virginia Gazette*, Sept. 26, 1755, Nov. 4, 1763; Colden list from McGann, "Apple Cultivars," 154; *Virginia Gazette and General Advertiser*, Oct. 9, 1798; *Virginia Gazette*, Jan. 15, 1799; *Virginia Argus*, Oct. 6, 1804.

8. Bailey, *Cyclopedia* 2:1514; Walten list in Hedrick, *History*, 159; William Prince nursery catalogs, 1771, 1790, DLC; David and Cuthbert Landreth nursery catalog, 1811, NAL; Booth nursery catalog, 1810, DLC; see also McMahon, *Calendar*, 584–85; Coxe, *View*, 126, 142; Beach, *Apples*, 15.

9. Benjamin Prince to John Hartwell Cocke, Nov. 12, 1815, and "List of shipment of trees and other articles," Nov. 1815, Cocke Papers; see also Hooper, *Western Fruit Book*, 11–117.

10. Bailey, *Apple Tree*, 62; Durand of Dauphiné in Ayres, "Fruit Culture," 130–31; Byrd in Troubetzkoy, "Big Business," 28.

11. Hedrick, *History*, 215; Bruce, *Economic Life* 1:469; Bruce, *Social Life* 1:169; Parkinson, *Tour*, 219; Rush in Martin, *Apples*, 48; "Pomona," "Cider"; Samuel L. Mitchell to David Hosack, *AF* 6 (1823): 226; "General R. G. Harper's Address, 1824," *AF* 6 (1824): 297 ("ardent spirits"); see also Nichols, "Rating the Golden Oldies."

12. TJ to Dr. Vine Utley, Mar. 21, 1819, DLC; Peterson, *Visitors to Monticello*, 58; Bear, *Jefferson at Monticello*, 13, 100; entry for Nov. 1, 1799, *FB*, 96; Farm Book Addenda, Mar. 22, 1810, "Statement of cyder made in November last" (175 gallons of cider produced 532 bottles), MHi; Wynkoop, "Account of a Crab Apple Orchard," 192.

13. Martha Jefferson Randolph to TJ, June 26, 1793, Betts and Bear, *Family Letters*, 121; TJ to Thomas Mann Randolph, Feb. 4, 1800, to Thomas Newton, Nov. 20, 1802, *FB*, 17, 415.

14. Spurrier, *Practical Farmer*, 252; TJ to Edmund Bacon, Nov. 15, 1817, *GB*, 574–75; entry for Sept. 4, 1796, *FB*, 96; Evans in Fletcher, *Pennsylvania Agriculture*, 208.

15. Tayloe, "On Virginia Husbandry," 102; Peters, "Remarks," 103; "American Farmer," *Epitome*, 131–32; Rusticus, "Planting Apple Orchards"; "Orchard Conditions," VSHS, *Report*, Jan. 1902, 86. For pruning, see also Langley, *Pomona*, 33; Miller, *Dictionary*, s.v. "Malus"; McMahon, *Calendar*, 39; Coxe, *View*, 40–43; Collin, "Remarks"; Knight, *Culture of the Apple and Pear*, 86–88.

16. Fitz, *Southern Apple and Peach Culturist*, 65; Taylor, *Arator*, 231; White, *Gardening*, 374. See also Downing, *Fruits*, 69, and Coxe, *View*, 9, on the apple's southern limit.

17. Van Deman, "Modern Apple Culture," 108; Coxe, *View*, 175; Richter, "Description of Coxe's 'View,'" vi–vii; Keith, "Scab of Apples," 646; "Extracts from the Diary of General John Hartwell Cocke," July 26, 1817, *GB*, 637; see also Preston, "On Fruit," 82–88; McMahon, *Calendar*, 134; "American Farmer," *Epitome*, 96; Forsyth, *Treatise*, 351–58.

18. Worth, "Observations on Insects," 394; Coxe, *View*, 44; Parkinson, *Tour*, 363; Kalm, *Travels* 1:304–5; *Insect Pests of Virginia*, 6–13; Taylor, *Arator*, 230; Horsfall, "Pine Mouse"; Banks, "Notes Relative to Aphis lanigera"; Mosley, "On the *Aphis lanigera*," 54; Leach, "Note on the Insect"; Fitz, *Southern Apple and Peach Culturist*, 191, 167; Van Alsteyn, "Care of Apple Orchards"; Downing, *Fruits*, 62–67; Bailey, *Cyclopedia* 1:1047–48; Byrd, "History of the Dividing Line," 205–6; Catesby, *Natural History* 2:11, describing how the parrot would destroy apples and wild crabs in order to eat the seeds.

19. Fitz, *Southern Apple and Peach Culturist*, 143; Beach, *Apples* 1:272; *Virginia Herald*, Oct. 4, 1799; *Virginia Argus*, Oct. 6, 1804; *Virginia Advocate*, Apr. 7, 1819; Hooper, *Western Fruit Book*, 75, 105–17; Kenrick, *New American Orchardist*, 85; Stipp, "Apple of Our Eye"; see also Hatch, "Thomas Jefferson, Citizen Genet, and the Fuji Apple"; Triolo, "Probable Origin of 'Ralls'"; Byram, "Description of Three Fine Western Apples"; Springer, "Raul's Gennetting Apple."

20. TJ to Rev. James Madison, Oct. 28, 1785, Boyd, *Papers* 8:681–83; 1778 orchard plan; 1811 orchard plan; "Directions, 1783"; entries for Mar. 14, 1769, Mar. 21, 1810, Mar. 17, 18, 1812, Mar. 19, 1814, *GB*, 15, 421, 475, 524.

21. Beach, *Apples* 1:148; Ayres, "Fruit Culture," 18; Washington, *Diaries* 1:314 (Mar. 29, 1764); notation for Mar. 17, 1787, *1787 Almanac*, Tucker-Coleman Papers; "List of fruit trees grafted at Prestwould 16 March, 1784," Skipwith Papers; Ro. Sampson to John Hartwell Cocke, Nov. 20, 1808, "Mrs. Paulina Legrand's List of Fruit Trees," n.d., "List of trees purchased from Benjamin Prince," Nov. 25, 1816, Cocke Papers; Parkinson, *Tour*, 613.

22. Benjamin Prince to John Hartwell Cocke, Sept. 4, 1815, Cocke Papers; Coxe, *View*, 142; Downing, *Fruits*, 118; see also Hooper, *Western Fruit Book*, 102; Kenrick, *New American Orchardist*, 74.

23. Hench, "Albemarle Pippin," 21; Hedrick, *History*, 279; Fitz, *Southern Apple and Peach Culturist*, 141; Anon., "Apple in Piedmont"; Thomas, *American Fruit Culturist*, 177; Beach, *Apples* 1:149; Otey, "Best Varieties"; Alwood, "Notes."

24. Beach, *Apples* 1:148–49.

25. Hedrick, *History*, 83, 89; Peter Collinson to John Bartram, Oct. 10, 1759, Darlington, *Memorials*, 220; Biggs, "An Account"; Beach, *Apples*, 1:111; Wardlaw, "Young Victoria"; Hench, "Albemarle Pippin"; Downing, *Fruits*, 48; Van Deman, "Modern Apple Culture," 108; Rouché, "One Hundred Thousand Varieties," 35.

26. "Prince Wm 1791," planting memorandum; Thomas Main to TJ, Nov. 20, 1807, TJ to Edmund Bacon, Nov. 24, 1807, entries for Mar. 17–21, 1810, Mar. 17, 18, 1812, Mar. 19, 1814, *GB*, 353, 355, 421, 475, 524; unpublished Garden Book entry, Mar. 19–23, 1805; 1811 orchard plan.

27. "List of grafted Fruit Trees of different Kinds planted at Prestwould 16 Mar 1792," Skipwith Papers; "Kinds of fruit planted at U.B. [Upper Bremo] 15 Dec. 1815," Cocke Papers; Thomas, *American Fruit Culturist*, 222; Coxe, *View*, 127; Downing, *Fruits*, 139; Beach, *Apples* 1:121; Alwood, "Paris Exposition, 1900."

28. "Directions, 1783"; TJ to Edmund Bacon, Nov. 15, 1817, *GB*, 574; entries for Sept. 4, 1796, Nov. 1, 1799, April 22, 1810 (from Memorandum Book), *FB*, 96; Mease, "Account of the Virginia Cyder Apple"; Pickering, "Some Account"; Ayres, "Fruit Culture," 133; TJ to Martha Jefferson Randolph, Feb. 28, 1797, Betts and Bear, *Family Letters*, 138; entry of Nov. 21, 1817, Cocke Garden Diary, Cocke Papers; Coxe, *View*, 150–51. Kenrick, *New American Orchardist*, 83; Hooper, *Western Fruit Book*, 44; Fitz, *Southern Apple and Peach Culturist*, 153.

29. Carter, *Diary* 2:673 (Apr. 25, 1772); Wynkoop, "Account of a Crab Apple Orchard," 189–93; Coxe, *View*, 151; Wynkoop, "On Cyder Making," 46.

30. TJ to James Mease, June 29, 1814, to James Barbour, Mar. 5, 1816, to Ellen Randolph Coolidge, Mar. 19, 1826, entries for Mar. 21, 1810, Mar. 17, 18, 1812, Mar. 19, 1814, *GB*, 535, 556, 618, 421, 475, 524; 1778 orchard plan; 1811 orchard plan; "Gardening memoranda," July

12, 1812, Cocke Papers.

31. TJ to James Mease, June 29, 1814, *GB*, 533.

32. Kenrick, *New American Orchardist*, 82; *Virginia Gazette*, Jan. 15, 1799; Booth catalog; A. McMahon catalog; Fitz, *Southern Apple and Peach Culturist*, 163.

In the Philadelphia Society for Promoting Agriculture *Memoirs* 4(1818): 49–51, William Coxe and James Mease discussed the identity of the Taliaferro. Mease printed Jefferson's remarks on its discovery while Coxe submitted his description of the Gloucester White, which at that time he considered synonymous with Taliaferro. Coxe, in the unpublished second edition of "View," listed the Taliaferro as a synonym for Gloucester White; however, Coxe later crossed out the name "Taliaferro." The first edition of *View* (1817), 116–17, denies any synonymity.

33. John Armstrong to TJ, Feb. 20, 1804, entry for Mar. 21, 1810, *GB*, 265, 421; 1811 orchard plan; Coxe, *View*, 136; Downing, *Fruits*, 102; Hooper, *Western Fruit Book*, 22.

34. Entry for Sept. 4, 1796, *FB*, 96; Ro. Sampson to John Hartwell Cocke, Nov. 20, 1808, Cocke Papers; Thomas, *American Fruit Culturist*, 225.

35. John Armstrong to TJ, Feb. 20, 1804, *GB*, 294; unpublished Garden Book entry, Mar. 19–23, 1805; Hooper, *Western Fruit Book*, 29, 98. Beach, *Apples* 2:244, listed thirty-two synonyms for Ortley.

36. Unpublished Garden Book entry, Mar. 19–23, 1805; John Armstrong to TJ, Feb. 20, 1804, I. A. Coles to TJ, Mar. 13, 1811, *GB*, 294, 454; Downing, *Fruits*, 106; Beach, *Apples* 2:47. Fitz, *Southern Apple and Peach Culturist*, 51, recommended Detroit Red, "a large, productive, and excellent variety."

37. TJ to William Prince, July 6, 1791, William Prince to TJ, Nov. 8, 1791, *GB*, 167–68; Ayres, "Fruit Culture," 21; "List of trees purchased from Benjamin Prince," Nov. 25, 1816, Cocke Papers; "Prince Wm 1791," planting memorandum; Benjamin Prince catalog, 1815, Cocke Papers; Coxe, *View*, 101; Downing, *Fruits*, 72; Beach, *Apples* 2:51.

38. 1778 orchard plan; entries for Mar. 17–19, 1794, Mar. 21, 1810, *GB*, 209, 422; Miller, *Dictionary*, s.v. "Malus"; Lawson, *History*, 111; Coxe, *View*, 105; conversation with Harry Baker, curator of fruit at Wisley Gardens outside of London.

39. 1778 orchard plan; "Directions, 1783"; entries for Feb. 12, 1782, Sept. 4, 1796, *FB*, 94, 96; Benjamin Anderson to John Hartwell Cocke, Mar. 4, 1817, Cocke Papers; *Virginia Argus*, Oct. 6, 1804; Ragan, *Nomenclature*, 125; Charles Downing, *Fruits*, 197.

40. Mar. 21, 1810, *GB*, 422; Ragan, *Nomenclature*, 154.

41. TJ to Dr. James W. Wallace, Feb. 28, 1809, *GB*, 408. Beach, *Apples* 2:76–77, recorded the use of the synonym Mammoth Pippin twenty-one times by nineteenth-century writers.

42. Entry for Mar. 25, 1771, *GB*, 22; "Revisal of my Fruit, 1783"; 1778 orchard plan; *Virginia Herald*, June 24, 1800. See also Washington, *Papers* 4:286 (Feb. 27, 1786). Troubetzkoy, "Big Business," 28, ob-

served that Lord Fairfax requested the "Medlar apple" from George Fairfax in the late eighteenth century.

43. John Armstrong to TJ, Feb. 20, 1804, *GB*, 295; unpublished Garden Book entry, Mar. 19–23, 1805. See also Ragan, *Nomenclature*, 223; Downing, *Fruits*, 110, 141; Coles, *American Fruit Book*, 122; Hooper, *Western Fruit Book*, 65, for links between "ox-eye striped," Vandevere, and Newtown Spitzenburg.

44. John Armstrong to TJ, Feb. 20, 1804, *GB*, 295; unpublished Garden Book entry, Mar. 19–23, 1805; Downing, *Fruits*, 124; Thomas, *American Fruit Culturist*, 229.

45. Entry for Feb. 12, 1782, *GB*, 94; Hedrick, *History*, 35. See Lawson, *History*, 110, and Byrd, *Natural History*, 43, on the Golden Russet.

46. 1778 orchard plan; entry for Mar. 9–14, 1778, *GB*, 75; Byrd, "Progress to the Mines," 373. See also Ayres, "Fruit Culture," 19–20.

THE LUXURY OF THE PEACH

1. Lawson, *History*, 112; 1811 orchard plan; entry for Dec. 1794, *FB*, 38.

2. Entry for Dec. 1794, *FB*, 38; Hedrick, *Peaches*, 50–51; TJ to Ferdinand Grand, Dec. 28, 1786, *GB*, 119.

3. Hedrick, *Peaches*, 4; Crosby, *Ecological Imperialism*, 156–57.

4. Hedrick, *Peaches*, 39–46; Byrd, "Occaneechee Island"; 122; Bartram, *Travels*, 16, 40, 193, 211, 218, 257, 260; Banister, *Natural History*, 367n; Fletcher, *Pennsylvania Agriculture*, 206; Castiglioni, *Viaggio*, 115; Catesby, *Natural History* 2:xx; Harvill, *Atlas of Virginia Flora*, 130; Lawson, *History*, 112–13.

5. Beverley, *History*, 315; Peter Collinson to John Custis, Dec. 5, 1737, Swem, *Brothers*, 49; Grove, "Diary," 11; Quincy in Ayres, "Fruit Culture," 4, 107–8; Hedrick, *History*, 184; White, *Gardening for the South*, 304.

6. Fithian, *Journal*, 113–14, 175; Castiglioni, *Viaggio*, 305; entry for Oct. 22, 1782, *GB*, 95; entry for Sept. 1, 1795, *FB*, 47; Byrd, *Natural History*, 48; see also Hazard, "Journal," 420; Kalm, *Travels* 1:51.

7. Mayo, "Virginia Council Journals, 1726–1753"; Oldmixon in Hedrick, *Peaches*, 50; Carter, *Diary*, 897 (Dec. 14, 16, 1774); Byrd, *Natural History*, 47–48; Randolph, *Virginia House-wife*, 192–94; TJ to Martha Randolph, Aug. 31, 1815, *GB*, 547; see also Ayres, "Fruit Culture," 148.

8. TJ to Thomas Mann Randolph, Mar. 30, 1792, entry for Mar. 17–19, 1794, *GB* 175, 209; Hedrick, *History*, 184.

9. Unpublished Garden Book entry, Mar. 19–23, 1805; Nicholas P. Trist to Virginia R. Trist, Oct. 1829, Trist Papers; entry for Dec. 1794, *FB*, 38; La Rochefoucauld-Liancourt, *Travels*, in *GB*, 243; Grove, "Diary," 12.

10. Bartram, *Travels*, 23; Beverley, *History*, 315; Banister, *Natural History*, 367; anon. letter to *AF* 1 (1819): 223; Kenrick, *New American Orchardist*, 192; TJ to Martha Randolph, Aug. 31, 1815, *GB*, 547; "Jour-

nal of Benjamin Smith Barton," 94; Cobbett, "Introduction," in Forsyth, *Treatise*, v; Peters, postscript to Garrigues, "Observations on Fruit Trees," 185.

11. Peters, "On Peach Trees," 21; Downing, *Fruits*, 461; White, *Gardening for the South*, 304.

12. TJ to Thomas Mann Randolph, May 1, 1791, *GB*, 163; McMahon, *Calendar*, 136–38; Muse, "Address"; Powel, "On the Cultivation of Peach Trees," 401.

13. Unpublished TJ memorandum, May 9, 1798, DLC; entry for Apr. 1824, *FB*, 96; Coxe, *View*, 216–17; Downing, *Fruits*, 461; Cocke, "On Peach Trees"; Peters, "On Peach Trees," 19; Coles, "On the Culture of Peach Trees"; *Southern Planter*, Apr. 1841, 64–65, June 1841, 97. See also Mease, *Domestic Encyclopedia*, 30; Worth, "An Account of the Insect."

14. Brevard, "On the Practicability of Retarding the Flowering of the Peach Tree"; Say, "On the Peach Tree Insect"; Powel, "On the Cultivation of Peach Trees," 401; "On the Use of Charcoal," *AF* 6 (1825): 346; see also letter from Samuel Martin to *AF* 3 (1821): 302, on the use of the brine from a pickle barrel on ailing peach trees.

15. Peters, "On Peach Trees," 184–85; Mease, *Domestic Encyclopedia*, 31–32.

16. Peters, "On Peach Trees," 17–19; see also Phillips, "On Peach Trees," 14; "American Farmer," *Epitome*, 130–31; Downing, *Fruits*, 454; Bailey, *Encyclopedia* 2:1515; Pryor, "Orchard Fruits," 12. For peach pruning and fertilization, see also McMahon, *Calendar*, 59, 134; Kenrick, *New American Orchardist*, 240; Downing, *Fruits*, 457; Thomas, *American Fruit Culturist*, 281–82.

17. "Journal of Benjamin Smith Barton," 94; George Mason to TJ, Oct. 6, 1780, *GB*, 91. For site selection, see also Coxe, *View*, 217; McMahon, *Calendar*, 221, 224; "American Farmer," *Epitome*, 14; Kenrick, *New American Orchardist*, 201; Swem, *Brothers*, 166; Pryor, "Orchard Fruits," 27.

18. Ayres, "Fruit Culture," appendixes 2A, 2B; Washington, *Diaries* 4:286 (Feb. 27, 1786); "Peach stones buried at Prestwould Octo 1791," "List of grafted Fruit Trees . . . 16 Mar. 1792," Skipwith Papers, ViW; Cobbett, *American Gardener*, no. 318; Peter Collinson to John Custis, Dec. 25, 1736, Custis to Collinson, May 1740, Swem, *Brothers*, 41, 68; Ayres, "Fruit Culture," 37; "List of trees brought up by Wm. Kirby, Nov. 1815," Cocke Papers; Coxe, *View*, 216–28; *Southern Planter*, Feb. 1841, 30; Hedrick, *Peaches*, 57–58.

19. TJ to Ferdinand Grand, Dec. 28, 1786, *GB*, 119; TJ to William Short, Nov. 25, 1791, Boyd, *Papers* 22:334; Mayo, "Virginia Council Journals."

20. Hedrick, *Peaches*, 58.

21. Hedrick, *Peaches*, 58; "American Farmer," *Epitome*, 130; Downing, *Fruits*, 453, 489–95.

22. McMahon, *Calendar*, 587; Booth catalog, 1810; Downing, *Fruits*, 452–99; Hedrick, *Peaches*, 60.

23. Entry for Oct. 6, 1813, *GB*, 497; "American Farmer," *Epitome*, 130; Coxe, *View*, 228; Downing, *Fruits*, 494; Hedrick, *Peaches*, 225; Prince, *Pomological Manual* 2:30.

24. Coxe, *View*, 228; Hedrick, *Peaches*, 225; Hooper, *Western Fruit Book*, 222; Kenrick, *New American Orchardist*, 192; Downing, *Fruits*, 494; Prince, *Pomological Manual* 2:30; entry for Mar. 17, 1812, Cocke Garden Diary, Cocke Papers; notation for Feb. 16, 1787, *1787 Almanac*, Tucker-Coleman Papers; Washington, *Diaries* 3:24 (Feb. 27, 1786).

25. Timothy Matlack to TJ, Feb. 25, 1807, entry for Apr. 21, 1807 from Weather Memorandum Book, *GB*, 340, 335; Hedrick, *Peaches*, 254; Coxe, *View*, 228; Downing, *Fruits*, 494; Hooper, *Western Fruit Book*, 228; Kenrick, *New American Orchardist*, 188.

26. Timothy Matlack to TJ, Feb. 25, 1807, Isaac Coles to TJ, Mar. 9, 1816, entry for Apr. 21, 1807, from Weather Memorandum Book, *GB*, 340, 556, 335; Prince, *Pomological Manual* 2:17; Hedrick, *Peaches*, 401, 40; Downing, *Fruits*, 495; Coxe, *View*, 224.

27. Thomas Main to TJ, Nov. 20, 1807, entries for Mar. 21, 1810, Apr. 10, 1809, Apr. 10, 1804, *GB*, 353, 421, 385, 291; Miller, *Dictionary*, s.v. "Persica"; Coxe, *View*, 230; Downing, *Fruits*, 493–94; Hedrick, *Peaches*, 187; Hooper, *Western Fruit Book*, 214.

28. Philip Mazzei to TJ, Sept. 28, 1801, Sept. 28, 1807, and "Mazzei's list of plants 'at beginning of 1804,'" Goodwin "Fruits from Mazzei"; TJ to John Freeman, Feb. 26, 1806, entries for May 26, 1802, May 17–20, 1810, *GB*, 316, 277, 420; Coxe, *View*, 227; Hedrick, *Peaches*, 478; Miller, *Dictionary*, s.v. "Persica"; Kenrick, *New American Orchardist*, 210; Gallesio, *Pomona italiana* 1: s.v. "Pesca Poppa di Venere," pl. 19; Hooper, *Western Fruit Book*, 231. Poppa di Venere was first described in the United States by Coxe in 1817.

29. "Mazzei's list of plants 'at beginning of 1804,'" Goodwin, "Fruits from Mazzei"; TJ to John Freeman, Feb. 26, 1806, *GB*, 326; Gallesio, *Pomona Italiana* 1: s.v. "Pesca Alberges," pl. 7; see also Prince, *Pomological Manual* 1:183–84; Hedrick, *Peaches*, 293; Miller, *Dictionary*, s.v. "Persica"; Hooper, *Western Fruit Book*, 212, for differing evaluations of Alberges.

30. TJ to William Prince, July 6, 1791, *GB*, 167; William Prince catalog, 1790; Prince, *Pomological Manual* 2:16.

31. Entry for May 26, 1802, *GB*, 277; Mazzei to TJ, Sept. 28, 1801, Goodwin, "Fruits from Mazzei"; Gallesio, *Pomona italiana* 1: s.v. "Pesca Mela," pl. 28.

32. Entry for Apr. 11, 1807, from Weather Memorandum Book, *GB*, 335.

33. William Prince invoice, 1791, ViU; Hedrick, *Peaches*, 298; Downing, *Fruits*, 474–75; Thomas, *American Fruit Culturist*, 315; Prince, *Pomological Manual* 1:173.

34. Entry for Apr. 21, 1807, from Weather Memorandum Book, Timothy Matlack to TJ, Feb. 25, 1807, *GB*, 335, 341.

35. Entries for May 26, 1802, Mar. 17–20, 1810, *GB*, 277, 420; unpublished Garden Book entry, Mar. 19–23, 1805; TJ to John Freeman, Feb. 26, 1807, Mazzei to TJ, Sept. 28, 1801, Hepburn invoice, Goodwin, "Fruits from Mazzei"; Gallesio, *Pomona italiana* 1: s.v. "Pesca Maddelena," pl. 15.

36. James Taylor to TJ, Feb. 3, 1803, entries for Mar. 21, 26, 1810, *GB*, 314, 421, 423; Coxe, *View*, 219, 226; Downing, *Fruits*, 481; Prince, *Pomological Manual* 1:185.

37. Entry for April 10, 1813, *GB*, 497; Miller, *Dictionary*, s.v. "Persica"; Downing, *Fruits*, 482; Hedrick, *Peaches*, 412; Thomas, *American Fruit Culturist*, 316; Kenrick, *New American Orchardist*, 190.

38. Entry for Apr. 21, 1807, from Weather Memorandum Book, Timothy Matlack to TJ, Feb. 25, 1807, *GB*, 355, 341.

39. Timothy Matlack to TJ, Feb. 25, 1807, *GB*, 341; Downing, *Fruits*, 480–81; Coxe, "View," 736; Hedrick, *Peaches*, 421; Hooper, *Western Fruit Book*, 225–26; Coxe, *View*, 222. See also Prince, *Pomological Manual* 2:14, 26, disputing the Morris association and arguing that the White Rareripe was discovered by his grandfather and the Red had been imported to Long Island by the French early in the eighteenth century.

40. Thomas Main to TJ, Nov. 20, 1807, TJ to Edmund Bacon, Nov. 24, 1807, *GB*, 353, 355.

41. Entry for Oct. 8, 1772, TJ to Anthony Giannini, Feb. 5, 1786, to Rev. James Madison, Oct. 28, 1785, *GB*, 34, 632, 106.

42. George Mason to TJ, Oct. 6, 1780, Thomas Main to TJ, Nov. 20, 1807, *GB*, 91, 353; Prince, *Pomological Manual* 2:21–22; Miller, *Dictionary*, s.v. "Persica"; Washington, *Diaries* 2:249 (Mar. 11, 1785).

43. Mazzei to TJ, Sept. 28, 1801, and Hepburn invoice, Goodwin, "Fruits from Mazzei"; Alexander Hepburn to TJ, June 12, 1806, *GB*, 319; Parkinson, *Paradisi*, 580.

44. 1778 orchard plan; entries for Mar. 17–20, 1810, Mar. 17, 18, 1812, *GB*, 420–21, 475; Downing, *Fruits*, 496.

45. "Mazzei's list of plants sent TJ 'at beginning of 1804,'" TJ to John Freeman, Feb. 26, 7, 1806, Mazzei to TJ, Sept. 28, 1801, Goodwin, "Fruits from Mazzei"; Gallesio, *Pomona italiana* 1: s.v. "Pesca Vaga Loggia," pl. 33, 34.

CHERRIES: FOR USE OR DELIGHT

1. Randall, *Life of Jefferson* 3:349; 1811 orchard plan; Ayres, "Fruit Culture," 103.

2. Entries for Apr. 1, 1777, Mar. 23, 1794, entry for Apr. 4, 1795, from Farm Book, TJ to Martha Jefferson, Apr. 11, 1791, Mar. 13, 1799, to Thomas Mann Randolph, Mar. 23, 1797, "Jefferson's Summary of His Meteorological Journal for the Years 1810 through 1816 at Monticello," *GB*, 71, 210, 228, 162, 297, 254, 627.

3. Entry for June 6, 1810, ibid., 425; Miller, *Dictionary*, s.v. "Cerasus"; Downing, *Fruits*, 163; Washington, *Diaries* 1:329 (Mar. 29, 1764);

Byrd, "A Progress to the Mines, 1732," 335; "The Recollections of John Mason," 43–46, Gunston Hall, Lorton, Va.; John Adams in Sarudy, "Eighteenth-Century Gardens of the Chesapeake," 125; Kalm, *Travels*, 324; Prince, *Pomological Manual* 2:110; Hedrick, "Cherry," in Bailey, *Cyclopedia* 1:739; see also Martin, *Pleasure Gardens of Virginia*, 124–27; and Fletcher, *Pennsylvania Agriculture*, 208, recounting observation of Pennsylvanian Lewis Evans, who said, "We adorn our Avenues with Black Heart cherries." Hedrick, *History*, 65, alluded to a 300-yard-long avenue of Morello cherries in upstate New York in 1758. Downing, *Fruits*, 163, said, "The larger growing sorts of black cherry are the finest of all fruit trees for shade, and are, therfore, generally chosen by farmers, who are always desirous of combining the useful and ornamental."

4. Kelso, "Report," 73–74; Noël Hume, *Food*, 42–43; Byrd, *Diary*, 103 (Nov. 11, 1709); "Cherries dried," undated (probably after 1809) MS in unverified hand (probably Virginia J. Randolph Trist, Jefferson's great-granddaughter), Trist Papers, ViU.

5. Noël Hume, *Food*, 39; Michel, "Journey," 33; Randolph, *Virginia House-wife*, 212–14, 40, 151, 197; Carter, *Diary* 2:620 (Aug. 26, 1771); TJ to Rev. James Madison, Oct. 28, 1785, *GB*, 425; "American Farmer," *Epitome*, 128; Byrd, *Diary*, 185 (May 31, 1710); see also Kenrick, *New American Orchardist*, 232; Downing, *Fruits*, 163.

6. Hedrick, *Cherries*, 39–50; Bailey, *Cyclopedia* 1:739; Parkinson, *Paradisi*, 571–75; Miller, *Dictionary*, s.v. "Cerasus"; Langley, *Pomona*, 85; Forsyth, *Treatise*, 41–44; Glover in Ayres, "Fruit Culture," 4; Michel, "Journey," 33; Jones, *Present State*, 78; Byrd, *Diary*, 298–99 (Feb. 8, 1711); Beverley, *History*, 129; *Virginia Gazette*, Sept. 26, 1755. See also Hedrick, *Cherries*, describing 1,145 cherry varieties, 75 percent of which originated in Europe; most of the approximately 275 American cultivars were developed with the burgeoning cherry industry after 1880.

7. Entries for Aug. 1, 3, 1767, Mar. 14, 1769, Mar. 31, 1773, Mar. 9–14, 1778, *GB*, 6, 15, 39, 75; 1778 orchard plan (nine references to "inoculation" of cherries); "Revisal of my Fruit, 1783"; TJ to Isaac A. Coles, June 10, 1811, MHi; "Extracts from an account of the travels of George Ellicott, 1841," "Descriptions, 1826–Present." There were only three documented cherry plantings at Monticello after 1783: in 1790, 1807, and 1811 ("Feb. 1790 planted"; entry for Apr. 20, 1807, from Weather Memorandum Book, *GB*, 335; 1811 orchard plan).

8. Jones, *Present State*, 78; White, *Gardening for the South*, 324; Worth, "Some Observations"; "American Farmer," *Epitome*, 128; see also Prince, *Pomological Manual* 2:143.

9. TJ to James Barbour, Mar. 5, 1816, entries for Mar. 31, 1773, Mar. 12, 1782, June 6, 1810, Mar. 17, 18, 1812, *GB*, 556, 39, 94, 425, 475; 1778 orchard plan; "Revisal of my Fruit, 1783"; Hedrick, *History*, 157; Ayres, "Fruit Culture," 54; notation for Mar. 17, 1787, *1787 Almanac*, Tucker-Coleman Papers; Washington *Diaries* 1:295 (Mar. 24, 1762); *Virginia Gazette*, Sept. 26, 1755; Nicholas Faulcon to John Hartwell Cocke, Mar.

15, 1812, Cocke Papers; Coxe, *View*, 251; Mease, *Domestic Encyclopedia*, 105; Downing, *Fruits*, 194; Hedrick, *Cherries*, 114; Prince, *Pomological Manual* 2:138–39.

10. "Directions, Oct. 1783"; Mease, *Domestic Encyclopedia*, 105.

11. 1778 orchard plan; entries for Mar. 12, 1782, June 6, 1810, *GB*, 94, 425; Prince, *Pomological Manual* 2:115; Coxe, *View*, 250; Downing, *Fruits*, 169; *Virginia Gazette*, Sept. 26, 1755; notation for Mar. 17, 1787, *1786 Almanac*, Tucker-Coleman Papers; Ayres, "Fruit Culture," 53; Washington, *Papers* 2:179 (Mar. 10, 1775); Nicholas Faulcon to John Hartwell Cocke, Mar. 15, 1812, Cocke Papers; Mease, *Domestic Encyclopedia*, 442; Hedrick, *Cherries*, 106.

12. "Directions, Oct. 1783"; Hedrick, *Cherries*, 109; Parkinson, *Paradisi*, 571–72; Coxe, *View*, 248; Prince, *Pomological Manual* 2:120. Downing, *Fruits*, 174; Nicholas Faulcon to John Hartwell Cocke, Mar. 15, 1812, Nov. 30, 1814, Cocke Papers.

13. 1778 orchard plan; "Broadnax Family," *VMHB* 24 (Oct. 1916): 418.

14. Entry for Mar. 31, 1774, *GB*, 50; Miller, *Dictionary*, s.v. "Cornus"; see also Eppler, "The Cornelian Cherry Dogwood."

15. 1778 orchard plan; entries for Mar. 9–14, 1778, Mar. 12, 1782, *GB*, 75, 94; "Revisal of my Fruit, 1783"; Parkinson, *Paradisi*, 572; Coxe, *View*, 252; Noël Hume, *Food*, 43; Hedrick, *Cherries*, 139; Ayres, "Fruit Culture," 53; Washington, *Diaries* 1:310 (Mar. 6, 1765); "List of shipment of fruit trees, Nov., 1815," Cocke Papers; *Virginia Gazette*, Sept. 26, 1755; Prince, *Pomological Manual* 2:143; Downing, *Fruits*, 198.

16. 1778 orchard plan; "Revisal of my Fruit, 1783"; entry for Mar. 12, 1782, *GB*, 94; Prince, *Pomological Manual* 2:142; Mease, *Domestic Encyclopedia*, 105; Downing, *Fruits*, 197; Hedrick, *Cherries*, 132, 157; Coxe, *View*, 249; Ayres, "Fruit Culture," 54; "List of shipment of fruit trees, Nov., 1815," Cocke Papers; *Virginia Gazette*, Sept. 26, 1755.

17. Entries for Aug. 1, 1767, June 6, 1810, *GB*, 6, 425; "Feb. 1790 planted," ViU; Hedrick, *Cherries*, 128, 133, 164; Parkinson, *Paradisi*, 571; Langley, *Pomona*, 40; Washington, *Diaries* 1:327 (Mar. 29, 1764); "List of shipment of fruit trees, Nov., 1815," Cocke Papers; Prince, *Pomological Manual* 2:131; Downing, *Fruits*, 195.

18. Coxe, *View*, 246–47; Downing, *Fruits*, 191; Hedrick, *Cherries*, 164; Prince, *Pomological Manual* 2:134–35; *Virginia Gazette*, Sept. 26, 1755; Ayres, "Fruit Culture," 54; Washington, *Diaries* 1:199 (Mar. 21, 1764), 3:319 (Mar. 10, 1775); Nicholas Faulcon to John Hartwell Cocke, Mar. 15, 1812, Nov. 30, 1818, Cocke Papers; 1778 orchard plan; "Revisal of my Fruit, 1783"; entry for April 20, 1807, from Weather Memorandum Book, entry for June 6, 1810, *GB*, 335, 425.

19. 1811 orchard plan.

20. Hedrick, *Cherries*, 197; Ayres, "Fruit Culture," 53; Washington, *Diaries* 4:113 (Apr. 4, 1785); Nicholas Faulcon to John Hartwell Cocke, Mar. 15, 1812, Cocke Papers; Mease, *Domestic Encyclopedia*, 105; Prince, *Pomological Manual* 2:115; 1778 orchard plan; entry for Feb. 12, 1782, *GB*, 94.

PEARS: LEISURE-CLASS FRUIT

1. TJ to Rev. James Madison, Oct. 28, 1785, to George Divers, Mar. 10, 1812, to Ferdinand Grand, Dec. 28, 1786, entry for Mar. 17, 18, 1812, *GB*, 106, 483–84, 119, 475; 1811 orchard plan. See also Ayres, "Fruit Culture," 103; Silsbee, "Pruning Fruit Trees," 392.

2. Byrd, *Natural History*, 44–46; Washington, *Diaries* 1:327–29 (Mar. 29, 1764), 4:89 (Feb. 12, 1785), 111–12 (Apr. 1, 1785), 113 (Apr. 4, 1785), 222 (Nov. 12, 1785), 286 (Feb. 27, 1786); gardening memorandum, Mar. 3, 1810, "Kinds of fruit planted at U. B. [Upper Bremo], Dec. 1815," the Barrauds to Ann Barraud Cocke, Dec. 24, 1809, Charles Ellis to John Hartwell Cocke, July 11, 1817, "Memorandum of Orchard Plantings and Graftings," Mar. 1816, Cocke Papers; Hedrick, *Pears*, 27, 215; TJ to Timothy Matlack, Oct. 19, 1807, *GB*, 352; Coxe, *View*, 24; Downing, *Fruits*, 415.

3. Bailey, *Cyclopedia* 3:2515; Hedrick, *Pears*, 39, 51; Knight, *Treatise on the Apple and Pear*, 155, 139; Roach, *Cultivated Fruits*, 140; Byrd, *Natural History*, 45, 91; "American Farmer," *Epitome*, 132; Ayres, "Fruit Culture," 44; see also, Hedrick, *History*, 281–83. On the other hand, William White, *Gardening for the South*, 355, felt the pear was more adaptable to the heat of the South than the apple.

4. Glover in Ayres, "Fruit Culture," 4; Michel, "Journey," 33; Byrd, *Natural History*, 44–46; William Byrd to Mr. Warner in England, July 1729, *VMHB* 36 (1928): 116; Lawson, *History*, 111–12; Parkinson, *Paradisi*, 586–89; *Virginia Gazette*, Sept. 26, 1755; *Virginia Argus*, July 17, 1795. See also *Richmond Enquirer*, Dec. 8, 1804, for an example of a Virginia nurseryman who avoided listing the names of pear varieties.

5. See above, note 2, for Washington and Cocke pear citations; notation for Mar. 17, 1787, *1787 Almanac*, Tucker-Coleman Papers; see also William Prince catalog, 1771 (42 varieties), 1790 (35); Benjamin Prince catalog, 1815 (45); John Lithen catalog, c. 1800 (7); Booth catalog, 1810 (41), Landreth catalog, 1811 (66); A. McMahon catalog, c. 1820 (28), for European varieties of pear.

6. "American Farmer," *Epitome*, 132; Kalm, *Travels* 1:334; Parkinson, *Tour*, 219; Hedrick, *Pears*, 40–49.

7. Hedrick, *Pears*, 51, 111–13; Peters, "On Peach Trees," 21; Coxe, *View*, 117; Forsyth, *Treatise*, 364; "Horticulture in Early Philadelphia," *From Seed to Flower*, 26; Downing, *Fruits*, 322–27; see also Anon., "On Pear Trees," recommending that trees be planted in shade or else very close together to shield the roots from "the reflection of the sun's rays."

8. Timothy Matlack to TJ, Feb. 25, Oct. 19, 1807, entry for Apr. 21, 1807, *GB*, 341, 352, 336.

9. Coxe, *View*, 189; Prince, *Pomological Manual* 1:139; Downing, *Fruits*, 415–16; "Report on Fruit List for Virginia," *VSHS*, *Report*, Dec. 1902, 244; Hedrick, *Pears*, 215.

10. Downing, *Fruits*, 415–16; Prince, *Pomological Manual* 1:140; Hedrick, *Pears*, 215.

11. Hedrick, *Pears*, 215; Coxe, *View*, 189; Downing, *Fruits*, 415–16.

12. Entries for Mar. 31, 1773, Mar. 24, 1810, Mar. 17, 18, 1812, TJ to George Divers, Mar. 10, 1812, *GB*, 39, 422, 475, 483–84; 1778 orchard plan; "Directions, Oct. 1783."

13. TJ to William Prince, July 6, 1791, *GB*, 166; "Prince Wm 1791," planting memorandum; Washington, *Diaries* 4:89 (Feb. 12, 1785); "Kinds of fruit planted at U.B. [Upper Bremo] 15 Dec. 1815," Cocke Papers; Leighton, *American Gardens*, 223; Coxe, *View*, 188; Downing, *Fruits*, 357; Prince, *Pomological Manual* 1:49; Kenrick, *New American Orchardist*, 121; Hedrick, *Pears*, 296.

14. "List of Baggage Shipped by Jefferson from France," c. Sept. 1, 1789, Boyd, *Papers* 15:377; "Feb. 1790 planted," ViU; Hedrick, *Pears*, 350; Miller, *Dictionary*, s.v. "Pyrus"; Forsyth, *Treatise*, 69; Coxe, *View*, 194–95; Downing, *Fruits*, 375; Kenrick, *New American Orchardist*, 122.

15. 1778 orchard plan; "Extracts from the Diary of John Hartwell Cocke," July 26, 1817, *GB*, 638; Charles Downing, *Fruits*, 866.

16. Coxe, *View*, 202; Hedrick, *Pears*, 532; Kenrick, *New American Orchardist*, 124.

17. Timothy Matlack to TJ, Feb. 25, 1807, entry for April 21, 1807, *GB*, 340, 336; Charles Downing, *Fruits*, 850; Washington, *Diaries* 4:89 (Feb. 12, 1785); the Barrauds to Ann Barraud Cocke, Dec. 24, 1809, Cocke Papers; Coxe, *View*, 197; Downing, *Fruits*, 447; Hedrick, *Pears*, 535; Forsyth, *Treatise*, 69; Prince, *Pomological Manual* 1:96; Kenrick, *New American Orchardist*, 124.

18. 1778 orchard plan; entry for Mar. 9–14, 1778, *GB*, 75; Coxe, *View*, 193, describing Green Sugar; Downing, *Fruits*, 330, describing Early Sugar.

19. Forsyth, *Treatise*, 69; Hedrick, *Pears*, 573; Coxe, *View*, 196; Prince, *Pomological Manual* 1:87; Downing, *Fruits*, 378; Kenrick, *New American Orchardist*, 124.

PLUMS OF THE OLD WORLD AND NEW

1. 1778 orchard plan; entries for Mar. 17, 18, 1812, Apr. 16, 1814, excerpt from "Notes on the State of Virginia," *GB*, 475, 534, 645; Bailey, *Evolution*, iii–iv, 173–92; see also White, *Gardening for the South*, 350.

2. 1811 orchard plan; Ayres, "Fruit Culture," 55; Pryor, "Orchard Fruits," 100; TJ to Rev. James Madison, Oct. 28, 1785, *GB*, 106; 1778 orchard plan; "Revisal of my Fruit, 1783."

3. Hedrick, *Plums*, 27–33; Roach, *Cultivated Fruits*, 142–44; Bailey, *Cyclopedia* 3:2716.

4. Bailey, *Evolution*, 170–72; Peattie, *Natural History of Trees*, 573–74; Beverley, *History*, 130; Lawson, *History*, 108; see also Byrd, *Natural History*, 36–37, 49.

5. Glover in Swem, *Brothers*, 165n, 34; Michel, "Journey," 33; Lawson, *History*, 113; John Custis to Peter Collinson, July 29, 1736, Swem, *Brothers*, 34; Byrd, *Natural History*, 48; John Bartram to Peter

Collinson, May 1738, Collinson to Bartram, Aug. 28, 1736, Darlington, *Memorials*, 120, 81; William Byrd II to Peter Collinson, [c. 1730?], Tinling, *Correspondence of the Three Byrds*, 427–28; Catesby, *Natural History* 2:xx; Parkinson, *Tour*, 219; "American Farmer," *Epitome*, 133; McMahon, *Calendar*, 38, 136; Cobbett, *American Gardener*, no. 320; Castiglioni, *Viaggio*, 194; Coxe, *View*, 232.

6. Dutton, *Plants of Colonial Williamsburg*, 11; notation for Mar. 17, 1787, *1787 Almanac*, Tucker-Coleman Papers; "List of trees purchased from Benjamin Prince," Nov. 25, 1816, and entry for Mar. 20, 1812, Cocke Garden Diary, Cocke Papers; Hedrick, *Plums*, 23–24; Roach, *Cultivated Fruits*, 155; Landreth catalog, 1811, Lithen catalog, c. 1800; Downing, *Fruits*, 263.

7. Byrd in Pryor, "Orchard Fruits," 101; TJ to William Drayton, May 7, 1789, *GB*, 143–44; Hedrick, *Plums*, 38; Parkinson, *Paradisi*, 578; Carter, *Diaries* 1:529 (Dec. 9, 1770), 531 (Dec. 24, 1770), 2:901 (Dec. 23, 1774), 1087 (Feb. 27, 1777); Randolph, *Virginia House-wife*, 151, 200; "American Farmer," *Epitome*, 133.

8. 1778 orchard entry for Mar. 20, 1812, plan; "Memorandum of Orchard Plantings and Graftings Mar. 1816," and Cocke Garden Diary, Cocke Papers; notations for Feb. 16, Mar. 22, 1787, *1787 Almanac*, Tucker-Coleman Papers; "American Farmer," *Epitome*, 145–46; Miller, *Dictionary*, s.v. "Prunus"; Langley, *Pomona*, 33; Peter Collinson to John Custis, Feb. 6, 1743, Swem, *Brothers*, 83; Collinson to William Byrd II, c. 1730, Tinling, *Correspondence of the Three Byrds*, 428; Collinson to John Bartram, Feb. 12, 1736, Darlington, *Memorials*, 71; see also Downing, *Fruits*, 264; Thomas, *American Fruit Culturist*, 336; White, *Gardening for the South*, 350; Hedrick, *Plums*, 115; Beverley, *History*, 314.

9. Collinson to William Byrd II, c. 1730, Tinling, *Correspondence of the Three Byrds*, 428; "Agricola," "Growth of Fruit Trees"; Hackney, "Culture of the Peach Tree"; P. L., "Concerning Fruit Trees"; Worth, "On the Insects Which Injure Plums"; Downing, *Fruits*, 263–69; White, *Gardening for the South*, 349–50; Thomas, *American Fruit Culturist*, 337; Kenrick, *New American Orchardist*, 30; Miller, *Dictionary*, s.v. "Prunus."

10. Entry for Mar. 17–18, 1812, and excerpt from *Notes on the State of Virginia*, *GB*, 475, 645; Beverley, *History*, 130; Lawson, *History*, 13; Hedrick, *Plums*, 83; Bailey, *Evolution*, 193; Harvill, *Atlas of the Virginia Flora*, 130.

11. Washington, *Diaries* 4:354 (June 29, 1786); notation for Mar. 22, 1787, *1787 Almanac*, Tucker-Coleman Papers; McMahon, *Calendar*, 588; White, *Gardening for the South*, 350; Downing, *Fruits*, 263; Hooper, *Western Fruit Book*, 243; Bailey, *Evolution*, 193; Hedrick, *Plums*, 85.

12. "Revisal of my Fruit, 1783"; "Directions, Oct. 1783"; "Mazzei's list of plants etc. sent TJ 'at beginning of 1804,'" TJ to John Freeman, Feb. 26, 1806, Goodwin, "Fruits from Mazzei"; Hedrick, *Plums*, 28; Roach, *Cultivated Fruits*, 155; Parkinson, *Paradisi*, 576; Langley, *Pomona*, 93–94; Dutton, *Plants of Colonial Williamsburg*, 11; *Virginia*

Gazette, Sept. 26, 1755; notation for July 29, 1784, *1784 Almanac*, Tucker-Coleman Papers; entry for Mar. 20, 1812, Cocke Garden Diary, Cocke Papers; "List of Grafted Fruit Trees of different Kinds, or planted, at Prestwould 16 Mar 1792," Skipwith Papers; Washington, *Diaries* 4:354 (June 29, 1786).

13. "American Farmer," *Epitome*, 8; Coxe, "View," 610; Downing, *Fruits*, 276; Prince, *Pomological Manual* 2:48–49; Hedrick, *Plums*, 327–28.

14. 1778 orchard plan; "Revisal of my Fruit, 1783"; entries for June 6, 1810, Mar. 9–14, 1778, John Armstrong to TJ, Feb. 20, 1804, *GB*, 425, 76, 294–95.

15. Hedrick, *Plums*, 387; Langley, *Pomona*, 95; Miller, *Dictionary*, s.v. "Prunus"; *Virginia Gazette*, Sept. 26, 1755; notation for Mar. 17, 1787, *1787 Almanac*, Tucker-Coleman Papers; Washington, *Diaries* 1:328 (Mar. 29, 1764); Randolph, *Virginia House-wife*, 155; Coxe, "View," 233; Downing, *Fruits*, 286; Hooper, *Western Fruit Book*, 239; Forsyth, *Treatise*, 20; Prince, *Pomological Manual* 2:57–58.

16. "Revisal of my Fruit, 1783"; "Mazzei's list of plants etc. sent TJ 'at beginning of 1804,'" Goodwin, "Fruits from Mazzei."

17. Notation for Mar. 17, 1787, *1787 Almanac*, Tucker-Coleman Papers; "Memorandum of Orchard Plantings and Graftings Mar 1816," Cocke Papers; Parkinson, *Paradisi*, 578; Miller, *Dictionary*, s.v. "Prunus"; Forsyth, *Treatise*, 20; McMahon, *Calendar*, 587; Coxe, "View," 646; Downing, *Fruits*, 272; Prince, *Pomological Manual* 1:70.

18. TJ to William Prince, July 6, 1791, Prince to TJ, Nov. 8, 1791, TJ to William Drayton, May 7, 1789, *GB*, 166–67, 168–69, 143–44; Parkinson, *Paradisi*, 578; Miller, *Dictionary*, s.v. "Prunus"; Prince, *Pomological Manual* 2:67; Downing, *Fruits*, 290; Hedrick, *Plums*, 409; Forsyth, *Treatise*, 20.

19. Miller, *Dictionary*, s.v. "Prunus"; Langley, *Pomona*, 94; Forsyth, *Treatise*, 20; Coxe, *View*, 233; Hedrick, *Plums*, 195; Prince, *Pomological Manual* 2:75–76.

20. Timothy Matlack to TJ, Feb. 25, 1807, *GB*, 341; Hedrick, *History*, 432–33; Hedrick, *Plums*, 423; Coxe, *View*, 236; Prince, *Pomological Manual* 2:97; Downing, *Fruits*, 291.

21. 1778 orchard plan; "Revisal of my Fruit, 1783"; Parkinson, *Paradisi*, 578; Hedrick, *Plums*, 35–36; Leighton, *American Gardens*, 241; Nicholas Faulcon to John Hartwell Cocke, Mar. 15, 1812, Cocke Papers; Downing, *Fruits*, 297.

22. Entry for Apr. 16, 1814, *GB*, 524.

23. 1778 orchard plan; "Revisal of my Fruit, 1783"; Thomas, *American Fruit Culturist*, 50, 339; Hooper, *Western Fruit Book*, 246–47; Hedrick, *Plums*, 59, 464; Downing, *Fruits*, 301.

24. Coxe, *View*, 236; Downing, *Fruits*, 290; Prince, *Pomological Manual* 2:60; Hedrick, *Plums*, 249; *Virginia Gazette*, Sept. 26, 1755.

25. William Prince catalog, 1771.

26. "Mazzei's list of plants etc. sent TJ 'at beginning of 1804,'" TJ to John Freeman, Feb. 26, 1806, Goodwin, "Fruits from Mazzei"; Alexander Hepburn to TJ, June 12, 1806, *GB*, 319; McMahon, *Calen-*

dar, 588; Downing, *Fruits*, 282; Hedrick, *Plums*, 284; Forsyth, *Treatise*, 20.

27. Entry for Apr. 2, 1767, *GB*, 4; Parkinson, *Paradisi*, 576–77; Miller, s.v. "Prunus"; Prince, *Pomological Manual* 2:105; Hedrick, *Plums*, 501.

28. *Virginia Gazette*, Sept. 26, 1755; notation for Mar. 17, 1787, *1787 Almanac*, Tucker-Coleman Papers; Leighton, *American Gardens*, 241; "Memorandum of Orchard Plantings and Graftings Mar 1816," Cocke Papers; Langley, *Pomona*, 91; Miller, *Dictionary*, s.v. "Prunus"; Forsyth, *Treatise*, 19; Coxe, *View*, 234; Downing, *Fruits*, 304; Hedrick, *Plums*, 302; Prince, *Pomological Manual* 2:67.

29. Hedrick, *Plums*, 326; Miller, *Dictionary*, s.v. "Prunus"; Downing, *Fruits*, 312; Forsyth, *Treatise*, 19; William Prince order, *1787 Almanac*, Tucker-Coleman Papers; "Memorandum of Orchard Plantings and Graftings Mar 1816," Cocke Papers.

30. "Mazzei's list of plants etc. sent TJ 'at beginning of 1804,'" TJ to John Freeman, Feb. 26, 1806, Goodwin, "Fruits from Mazzei"; Parkinson, *Paradisi*, 576–77; Langley, *Pomona*, 94; Miller, *Dictionary*, s.v. "Prunus"; Downing, *Fruits*, 310; Hedrick, *Plums*, 522.

31. "Mazzei's list of plants etc. sent TJ 'at beginning of 1804,'" TJ to John Freeman, Feb. 26, 1806, Goodwin, "Fruits from Mazzei"; Parkinson, *Paradisi*, 576–77; Langley, *Pomona*, 94; Miller, *Dictionary*, s.v. "Prunus"; Downing, *Fruits*, 310; Hedrick, *Plums*, 522.

32. "Mazzei's list of plants etc. sent TJ 'at beginning of 1804,'" TJ to John Freeman, Feb. 26, 1806, Goodwin, "Fruits from Mazzei"; entry for Mar. 21, 1810, Timothy Matlack to TJ, Feb. 25, 1807, *GB*, 422, 341; 1778 orchard plan.

APRICOTS: PRECIOUS BUT PRECARIOUS

1. 1778 orchard plan; "Revisal of my Fruit, 1783"; "Feb. 1790 planted," ViU; TJ to Ferdinand Grand, Dec. 28, 1786, to Richard Cary, Aug. 13, 1787, entry for Apr. 4, 1809, *GB*, 119, 130, 385; TJ to Charles Clay, Mar. 1, 1806, Goodwin, "Fruits from Mazzei"; 1811 orchard plan.

2. Ayres, "Fruit Culture," 162; notation for Mar. 17, 1787, *1787 Almanac*, Tucker-Coleman Papers; Washington, *Diaries* 1:295 (Mar. 24, 1762), 4:87 (Feb. 9, 1785). See also Bailey, *Cyclopedia* 1:333; Hedrick, *History*, 156.

3. Fletcher, "History," 4–5; Ayres, "Fruit Culture," 4; Banister, *Natural History*, 355; Beverley, *History*, 314; Lawson, *History*, 113; Grove, "Diary," 13; Byrd, *Natural History*, 48; Fithian, *Journal*, 79; "Memo of peach stones etc. set out in Nov. near the stable door" and notation for Mar. 17, 1787, *1787 Almanac*, Tucker-Coleman Papers; Leighton, *American Gardens*, 224; Washington, *Diaries* 1:295 (Mar. 24, 1762), 4:87 (Feb. 9, 1785); *Virginia Gazette*, Aug. 3, 1792; Pryor, "Orchard Fruits," 135; "Memo of Orchard Plantings & Graftings, Mar 1816," Nicholas Faulcon to John Hartwell Cocke, Nov. 30, Apr. 26, 1814, "Account of trees etc. brought up by Wm. Kirby, Nov. 1816," Charles Ellis to John Hartwell Cocke, July 11, 1817, Cocke Papers; Hedrick, *History*, 454.

4. Glover in Ayres, "Fruit Culture," 4; William Byrd to Mr. Warner, July 1729, *VMHB* 36 (1928): 117; John Bartram to Peter Collinson, May 1738, Darlington, *Memorials*, 120; Forsyth, *Treatise*, ed. Cobbett, 17; Parkinson, *Tour*, 219; Mease, *Domestic Encyclopedia* 1:86.

5. Langley, *Pomona*, 45; Miller, *Dictionary*, s.v. "Armeniaca"; Coxe, *View*, 240; Downing, *Fruits*, 153; White, *Gardening for the South*, 319; Hooper, *Western Fruit Book*, 241; Forsyth, *Treatise*, 4; Peter Collinson to John Bartram, Apr. 26, 1746, Darlington, *Memorials*, 178; Thomas, *American Fruit Culturist*, 331.

6. "American Farmer," *Epitome*, 128; Peter Collinson to John Bartram, Feb. 3, 1736, Darlington, *Memorials*, 85; Bailey, *Cyclopedia* 1:334.

7. William Prince to TJ, Nov. 8, 1791, Timothy Matlack to TJ, Feb. 25, 1807, *GB*, 168, 341; Jane Austen, *Mansfield Park*, in Roach, *Cultivated Fruits*, 195; "Memo of Orchard Plantings & Graftings, Mar 1816," Cocke Papers; Downing, *Fruits*, 195.

8. Downing, *Fruits*, 195; Prince, *Pomological Manual* 1:161.

9. TJ to Charles Clay, Mar. 1, 1806, "Mazzei's list of plants etc. sent TJ 'at beginning of 1804,'" Philip Mazzei to TJ, July 20, Sept. 12, 1805, TJ to Mazzei, July 18, 1804, Goodwin, "Fruits from Mazzei"; Threlkeld to TJ, Nov. 23, 1807, Alexander Hepburn to TJ, June 12, 1806, *GB*, 353–54, 319.

10. Threlkeld to TJ, Mar. 25, Nov. 23, 1807, TJ to Threlkeld, Mar. 26, 1807, TJ to Charles Clay, Mar. 1, 1806, Goodwin, "Fruits from Mazzei"; Threlkeld to TJ, Mar. 8, 1809, entries for Mar. 17–20, 21, 1810, *GB*, 409, 420, 421.

11. Coxe, *View*, 241; Kenrick, *New American Orchardist*, 215; White, *Gardening for the South*, 320; Downing, *Fruits*, 157; Mease, *Domestic Encyclopedia*, 85; see also Forsyth, *Treatise*, 4.

12. "Prince Wm 1791," planting memorandum; "Mazzei's list of plants etc. sent TJ 'at beginning of 1804,'" Goodwin, "Fruits from Mazzei"; unpublished Garden Book entry, Mar. 19–23, 1805; William Prince to TJ, Nov. 8, 1791, Alexander Hepburn to TJ, June 12, 1806, John Threlkeld to TJ, Mar. 25, Nov. 23, 1807, TJ to Captain William Meriwether, Nov. 24, 1807, entry for Mar. 17–20, 1810, *GB*, 168, 319, 344, 353, 354, 420.

13. Mazzei to TJ, July 20, 1805, Goodwin, "Fruits from Mazzei"; Gallesio, *Pomona* 1: s.v. "Albicocca Angelica."

14. Loudon, *Encyclopædia*, 719; Roach, *Cultivated Fruits*, 192; Miller, *Dictionary*, s.v. "Armeniaca"; Forsyth, *Treatise*, 14; Langley, *Pomona*, 89; Coxe, *View*, 241; Kenrick, *New American Orchardist*, 213; Downing, *Fruits*, 155.

15. Prince catalog, 1771; McMahon, *Calendar*, 585; Landreth catalog, 1811; Langley, *Pomona*, 88; Miller, *Dictionary*, s.v. "Armeniaca"; Coxe, *View*, 240; Downing, *Fruits*, 155; Kenrick, *New American Orchardist*, 214; Hooper, *Western Fruit Book*, 240.

16. TJ to Richard Cary, Aug. 13, 1787, *GB*, 140; "List of Baggage Shipped by Jefferson from France," c. Sept. 1, 1789, Boyd, *Papers* 15:376; "Feb. 1790 planted," ViU.

NECTARINES: THE "ARTIFICIAL PLANT"

1. 1778 orchard plan; "State of Fruit Trees, Nov. 1778," MHi; "Revisal of my Fruit, 1783"; George Wythe to TJ, Mar. 9, 1769, TJ to William Prince, July 6, 1791, William Prince to TJ, Nov. 8, 1791, James Taylor to TJ, Feb. 3, 1806, entries for Mar. 17–20, Mar. 21, 1810, *GB*, 20, 167, 168, 314, 420, 421; 1811 orchard plan; Hedrick, *Peaches*, 84; Cobbett, *American Gardener*, no. 316.

2. Hedrick, *Peaches*, 81–84; Parkinson, *Paradisi*, 582–83; Langley, *Pomona*, 98, 102–3; Miller, *Dictionary*, s.v. "Nectarine"; Forsyth, *Treatise*, 38–39; Banister, *Natural History*, 335; Beverley, *History*, 314–15; Lawson, *History*, 112; Byrd, *Natural History*, 47; William Byrd II to Peter Collinson, June 23, 1729, Tinling, *Correspondence of the Three Byrds*, 409; Collinson to Bartram, Apr. 26, 1746, Darlington, *Memorials*, 177; Forsyth, *Treatise*, 40; Parkinson, *Tour*, 219; "American Farmer," *Epitome*, 131; Coxe, *View*, 244; see also *Southern Planter*, July 1842, 160–61.

3. Fithian, *Journal*, 175; Leighton, *American Gardens*, 224; Pryor, "Orchard Fruits," 125; "Set a nectarine among the Canada peaches," July 29, 1784, *1784 Almanac*, notations for Mar. 17 and Nov. 15, 1787, *1787 Almanac*, Tucker-Coleman Papers; "Account of Trees brought up by Wm. Kirby, Nov. 1815," Charles Ellis to John Hartwell Cocke, July 11, 1817, Cocke Papers; "Peach stones buried at Prestwould, Octo 1791," "List of grafted Fruit Trees, Mar. 16, 1792," Skipwith Papers; *Virginia Gazette*, Aug. 3, 1792; Hedrick, *History*, 160; Prince catalog; Booth catalog; Landreth catalog.

4. Parkinson, *Paradisi*, 583; Langley, *Pomona*, 102; Miller, *Dictionary*, s.v. "Nectarine"; notation for Nov. 15, 1787, *1787 Almanac*, Tucker-Coleman Papers; Leighton, *American Gardens*, 224; "List of Grafted Fruit Trees, Mar. 16, 1792," Skipwith Papers; Charles Ellis to John Hartwell Cocke, July 11, 1817, Cocke Papers; Coxe, *View*, 244; Downing, *Fruits*, 508; Prince, *Pomological Manual* 1:45. Roach, *Cultivated Fruits*, 184, states that Red Roman is still grown in England.

ALMONDS

1. "List of Baggage Shipped by Jefferson from France," c. Sept. 1789, Boyd, *Papers* 15:376; entries for Mar. 31, 1773, Mar. 12, 31, 1774, Mar. 21, Apr. 25, 1810, Mar. 21, 1812, TJ to William Drayton, July 30, 1787, "Jefferson's Summary of His Meteorological Journal for the Years 1810 through 1816 at Monticello," *GB*, 39, 47, 50, 421, 423, 475, 127–29, 627; 1811 orchard plan; 1778 orchard plan.

2. Hedrick, *Peaches*, 69–70; Roach, *Cultivated Fruits*, 177; Downing, *Fruits*, 149; Sturtevant, *Edible Plants*, 456; Roach, *Cultivated Fruits*, 28; Parkinson, *Paradisi*, 583; Miller, *Dictionary*, s.v. "Amygdalus."

3. Byrd, *Natural History*, 51; notation for July 29, 1784, *1784 Almanac*, Tucker-Coleman Papers; Leighton, *American Gardens*, 224; "Account of trees brought up by Wm. Kirby, Nov., 1815," "Memo-

randum of Orchard Plantings and Graftings, Mar 1816," Cocke Papers; Booth catalog, 1810; "American Farmer," *Epitome*, 146; Downing, *Fruits*, 150.

4. Entries for Mar. 12, 31, 1774, Mar. 21, Apr. 25, 1810, Mar. 21, 1812, *GB*, 47, 50, 421, 423, 475; Downing, *Fruits*, 150–51; 1811 orchard plan.

QUINCES: HUMBLE AND FORGOTTEN

1. Hedrick, *History*, 115, 154–55; Roach, *Cultivated Fruits*, 221; Bailey, *Cyclopedia* 3:2891; Miller, *Dictionary*, s.v. "Cydonia"; Parkinson, *Paradisi*, 589; Randolph, *Virginia House-wife*, 176–77, 194–96; entries for Mar. 15, 1769, Sept. 11, 1782, *GB*, 15, 95; 1778 orchard plan; "State of fruit trees, Nov. 1778," MHi; Coxe, *View*, 214.

2. Bailey, *Cyclopedia* 3:2891; Roach, *Cultivated Fruits*, 221; Parkinson, *Paradisi*, 589; Miller, *Dictionary*, s.v. "Cydonia"; Forsyth, *Treatise*, 104–5.

3. Berkeley and Shrigley in Sturtevant, *Edible Plants*, 475; Joyce in Ayres, "Fruit Culture," 4; Lawson, *History*, 114–15; Byrd, *Natural History*, 46–47.

4. Washington, *Diaries* 1:313 (Aug. 26, 1763); notation for Mar. 22, 1787, *1787 Almanac*, Tucker-Coleman Papers; "Memorandum of Orchard Plantings and Graftings, Mar 1816," Cocke Papers; "American Farmer," *Epitome*, 132; Coxe, *View*, 214; Bailey, *Cyclopedia* 3:2891.

GRAPES: THE SPECIES OF UTOPIA

1. TJ to Baron Hyde de Neuville, Dec. 13, 1818, Bergh, *Writings* 15:178; TJ to John Oliveira Fernandes, Dec. 16, 1815, DLC.

2. Pinney, *History*, 129.

3. 1778 orchard plan; George Wythe to TJ, Mar. 9, 1770, entries for Mar. 8, 1771, Apr. 2, 1773, Apr. 1, 6, 1774, *GB*, 20, 22, 40, 52–54.

4. H. Christopher Martin, "Jefferson's Italian Vigneron: Philip Mazzei, Revolutionary Patriot," Treville Lawrence, *Jefferson and Wine*, 18–31; Goodwin, *Italians in the Monticello Orchard*, 4–7; Pinney, *History*, 77–81.

5. Martin, "Jefferson's Italian Vigneron: Philip Mazzei, Revolutionary Patriot," Treville Lawrence, *Jefferson and Wine*, 18–31; Pinney, *History*, 77–81; TJ to Albert Gallatin, Jan. 25, 1793, *GB*, 63.

6. Entry for Oct. 22, 1782, *GB*, 95; Antonio Giannini to TJ, June 9, 1786, Boyd, *Papers* 9:624.

7. "Notes of a Tour into the Southern Parts of France, etc.," TJ to George Wythe, Sept. 16, 1787, to William Drayton, July 30, 1787, to Archibald Cary, Jan. 7, 1786, to Etienne Parent, Mar. 13, 1787, Parent to TJ, Feb. 3, 1788, TJ to Major von Geismar, July 13, 1788, Boyd, *Papers* 11:415–62, 12:127, 11:646–47, 9:158, 11:211–13, 12:360, 13:356–57; TJ to Rev. James Madison, Oct. 28, 1785, "Objects for the garden this year," 1792, *GB*, 106, 208; TJ to John W. Eppes, Dec. 8, 1821, ViU.

8. TJ to Benjamin Hawkins, Mar. 22, 1796, *GB*, 248–49; Dufour, *American Vine Dresser's Guide*, 22–23; Jefferson's instructions to

Richard Richardson, probably c. Dec. 24, 1799, *New York Times*, Apr. 15, 1923; see also Pinney, *History*, 117–26.

9. Entries for May 11, 1802, June 13, 1822, Apr. 18, 1810, Mar. 12, 1812, TJ to John Adlum, Jan. 13, 1816, *GB*, 277, 604, 423, 475, 554; TJ to John Adlum, in Mary M. Bowes, "The Spirit of Jefferson Wine-Growing: The Adlum Letters," in Treville Lawrence, *Jefferson and Wine*, 231; Hedrick, *History*, 435; Bailey, *Evolution*, 19, 25, 43–44; Pinney, *History*, 110–20.

10. TJ to Mazzei, Mar. 17, 1801, Mazzei to TJ, Mar. 18, 1805, Thomas Appleton to TJ, Mar. 15, 1804, Stanton, "Grapes from Italy."

11. 1807 vineyard plan, in Weather Memorandum Book, PHi; Timothy Matlack to TJ, Feb. 25, 1807, *GB*, 341; Mazzei to TJ, Oct. 25, 1803, Stanton, "Grapes from Italy."

12. Entry for Apr. 20, 1810, TJ to John Adlum, Oct. 7, 1809, *GB*, 423, 415. For Adlum, see also Pinney, *History*, 139–49.

13. TJ to John Adlum, Apr. 20, 1810, and Jan. 13, 1816, "Jefferson's Summary of his Meteorological Journal for the Years 1810 through 1816 at Monticello," TJ to William Thornton, May 24, 1810, *GB*, 436, 554–55, 625, 439.

14. Entries for Mar. 26, 11, 12, 1812, McMahon to TJ, Feb. 28, 1812, entry for Mar. 19, 1812, from Account Book, *GB*, 474, 475, 481, 493.

15. Jean David to TJ, Nov. 26, 1815, TJ to David, Dec. 25, 1815, to L. Girardin, Dec. 25, 1815, Stanton, "Correspondence."

16. TJ to John Adlum, Jan. 13, 1816, to Jean David, Jan. 13, 1816, to James Monroe, Jan. 16, 1816, *GB*, 554–55; David to TJ, Feb. 1, 1816, Stanton, "Correspondence."

17. TJ to David, Dec. 25, 1815, Stanton, "Correspondence"; TJ to John Adlum, Jan. 13, 1816, to James Monroe, Jan. 16, 1816, entry for Apr. 8, 1816, from Account Book, *GB*, 554–55, 562.

18. "Extracts from the diary of General John Hartwell Cocke," Mar. 27, 1817, TJ to William Johnson, May 10, 1817, to Samuel Maverick, May 12, 1822, entry for Apr. 4, 1817, *GB*, 637, 572, 600, 565; Francis W. Eppes to TJ, Oct. 31, 1822, Bear and Betts, *Family Letters*, 447.

19. James A. Bear, Jr., "Quality No Matter the Wine," in Treville Lawrence, *Jefferson and Wine*, 14–15; Pinney, *History*, 127.

20. For the early history of American grape culture, see also Ayres, "Fruit Culture," 61–100; Hedrick, *Grapes*, 1–68; Bailey, *Evolution*, 1–49; Pinney, *History*; McGrew, "Some Untold Episodes," 82–85, 102.

21. Hedrick, *Grapes*, 29. See also Pinney, *History*, 443–47, on "Fox Grapes and Foxiness."

22. Pinney, *History*, 13; McGrew, "Some Untold Episodes," 82; "Smith's Description of Virginia," in Tyler, *Narratives of Early Virginia*, 91; Strachey, *Historie of Travail*, 131–32; "John Pory to Sir Dudley Carleton," ibid., 284; Edward Williams in Raphael, *Oak Spring Sylva*, 84; Grove, "Diary," 11; Glover in Ayres, "Fruit Culture," 64. See also Hedrick, *Grapes*, 26–36; Bailey, *Evolution*, 1–9; Pinney, *History*, 1–39; Beverley, *History*, 133–36; Lawson, *History*, 104, 114–17; and Byrd, "History of the Dividing Line," 244.

23. Pinney, *History*, 6.

24. Beverley, *History*, 136; Hedrick, *Grapes*, 7; "Proceedings of the Virginia Assembly, 1619," "The Virginia Planters' Answer to Captain Butler, 1623," in Tyler, *Narratives of Early Virginia*, 265, 416; Pinney, *History*, 15–24; McGrew, "Some Untold Episodes," 82.

25. Beverley, *History*, 135–36; Jones, *Present State of Virginia*, 128–29; Hedrick, *Grapes*, 40; Ayres, "Fruit Culture," 64–66.

26. Hedrick, *Grapes*, 38; William Byrd to Mr. Warner, July 1729, to Peter Collinson, July 18, 1736, *VMHB* 36 (1928): 116–17, 353–55; Charles and Landon Carter's experiments in Ayres, "Fruit Culture," 70–78; Pinney, *History*, 70; McGrew, "Some Untold Episodes," 83.

27. Bolling's and Estave's experiments in Ayres, "Fruit Culture," 78–89; Pinney, *History*, 71–73.

28. Bolling, "Essay on Vine Culture," *Virginia Gazette*, Feb. 25, 1773; Bolling, "To the Friends," ibid., July 29, 1773; Pinney, *History*, 73–77.

29. *Virginia Gazette*, Mar. 18, Sept. 2, 1773.

30. Ayres, "Fruit Culture," 87–89; McGrew, "Some Untold Episodes," 84.

31. Forest, *Grounds and Gardens of Mount Vernon*, 83–85; see also Ayres, "Fruit Culture," 88–92; McGrew, "Some Untold Episodes," 84.

32. Matlack, "On the Cultivation of the Vine."

33. TJ's letter to John Adlum, Apr. 11, 1823, was published as a frontispiece in the reprint edition of *Memoir*.

34. Antill, "Essay," 180, 182, 227, 237–38, 341; Pinney, *History*, 91–92; Hedrick, *Grapes*, 15; Mease, *Domestic Encyclopedia* 5:285–325; Hedrick, *Grapes*, 15; Bolling, "A Sketch of Vine Culture," 341, NAL.

35. Johnson, *Rural Economy*, 156–96; McMahon, *Calendar*, 41, 227–35, 488; Pinney, *History*, 116, 139–49; Adlum, letter to *AF* 6 (1825): 297, and 4 (1822): 256; Manks, "John Adlum," introduction to *Memoir*; see also Amoureux, *A Short and Practical Treatise*; Cobbett, *American Gardener*, no. 310; Dufour, *American Vine Dresser's Guide*.

36. Johnson, *Rural Economy*, 195; TJ to John Dortie, Oct. 1, 1811, entry for Apr. 6, 1774, *GB*, 463, 52. For site selection and soils, see also Antill, "Essay," 187–91; Bolling, "A Sketch of Vine Culture," 3–4; McMahon, *Calendar*, 235; Adlum, *Memoir*, 25; Mease, *Domestic Encyclopedia*, 299.

37. Entry for Apr. 6, 1774, *GB*, 53; 1778 orchard plan; 1807 vineyard plan. For spacing, see also Antill, "Essay," 28, 109–11, 195, 233, 261; Bolling, "A Sketch of Vine Culture," 34; Amoureux, *A Short and Practical Treatise*; Johnson, *Rural Economy*, 174; McMahon, *Calendar*, 236.

38. TJ to Benjamin Hawkins, Mar. 22, 1796, entry for Apr. 6, 1774; *GB*, 248, 52–54. For planting directions, see also Miller, *Dictionary*, s.v. "Vitis"; Antill, "Essay," 192–94; Bolling, "A Sketch of Vine Culture," 9; Johnson, *Rural Economy*, 174–76; Mease, *Domestic Encyclopedia* 5:300–10; McMahon, *Calendar*, 237–40; Adlum, *Memoirs*, 8–9, 31; Amoureux, *A Short and Practical Treatise*.

39. Jefferson's instructions to Richard Richardson, probably c.

Dec. 24, 1799, *New York Times*, Apr. 15, 1923; entry for May 2, 1809, *GB*, 387; Antill, "Essay," 201–10, 237; Bolling, "A Sketch of Vine Culture," 56–67; Amoureux, *A Short and Practical Treatise*; Mease, *Domestic Encyclopedia*, 301–12; Johnson, *Rural Economy*, 176–79; McMahon, *Calendar*, 41, 139–40, 236, 522; Adlum, *Memoirs*, 10–19, 41–45.

40. Antill, "Essay," 237–38; Mease, *Domestic Encyclopedia*, 308, 312; McMahon, *Calendar*, 140–41; "American Farmer," *Epitome*, 34; entry for Apr. 6, 1774, *GB*, 53; Johnson, *Rural Economy*, 190; McMahon, *Calendar*, 522.

41. Hedrick, *Grapes*, 29; Drake, *Diseases of Grapes*, 4–7; Bailey, *Evolution*, 90–93.

42. Dufour, *American Vine Dresser's Guide*, 203–16; Miller, *Dictionary*, s.v. "Vitis"; Antill, "Essay," 230–32; McMahon, *Calendar*, 459; Johnson, *Rural Economy*, 196; Mease, *Domestic Encyclopedia*, 286–88, 314; Cobbett, *American Gardener*, no. 310; Anon., "On the Culture of Grape Vines," *AF* 4 (1823): 387.

43. Entries for May 11, 1802, Apr. 10, 1810, Mar. 11, 12, 1812, McMahon to TJ, Feb. 28, 1812, TJ to Adlum, Jan. 13, 1810, *GB*, 277, 423, 475, 481, 554; TJ to Adlum, Oct. 9, 1809, Apr. 20, 1810, Adlum to TJ, June 5, 1822, in Mary M. Bowes, "The Spirit of Jefferson Wine-Growing, The Adlum Letters," Treville Lawrence, *Jefferson and Wine*, 224–32; Hedrick, *Grapes*, 16–19; Pinney, *History*, 141–43; Adlum, *Memoir*, 30; Dufour, *American Vine Dresser's Guide*, 25. See also McGrew, "'Alexander' Grape."

44. Hedrick, *Grapes*, 16–19, 160–63; Pinney, *History*, 84–85, 109–20, 127; McGrew, "'Alexander' Grape"; Bartram, "Description," 91; McMahon, *Calendar*, 235; Dufour, *American Vine Dresser's Guide*, 5, 25.

45. Dufour, *American Vine Dresser's Guide*, 25; Bartram, "Description," 91; Downing, *Fruits*, 251–53; Hedrick, *Grapes*, 160–63. See also Pinney, *History*, 139–47, for Adlum's acknowledgment that the wine sent to Jefferson in 1809 was the result of a fortuitous accident, and also for the early history of Catawba.

46. McMahon, *Calendar*, 229–31; Downing, *Fruits*, 236, 240; John McGrew, personal correspondence, Dec. 2, 1983; Miller, *Dictionary*, s.v. "Vitis"; Prince, *Treatise*, 121.

47. Hedrick, *Grapes*, 186–88; Miller, *Dictionary*, s.v. "Vitis"; McMahon, *Calendar*, 230; Robinson, *Vines*, 211.

48. McGrew, personal correspondence, Dec. 2, 1983; Viala, *Ampélographie* 1:6; Robinson, *Vines*, 254–55; McMahon, *Calendar*, 229; Miller, *Dictionary*, s.v. "Vitis" (Miller used "Chasselas" to refer to Royal Muscadine); Wellington, *Vinifera Grapes*, 5; Anthony, *Vinifera Grapes*, 93.

49. TJ to Benjamin Hawkins, Mar. 22, 1796, *GB*, 249; Viala, *Ampélographie* 2:15; McGrew, personal correspondence, Dec. 2, 1983; McMahon, *Calendar*, 229; Miller, *Dictionary*, s.v. "Vitis"; Anthony, *Vinifera Grapes*, 94; Robinson, *Vines*, 254.

50. Pinney, *History*, 19; Robinson, *Vines*, 119, 143; Downing, *Fruits*, 243; Prince, *Treatise*, 85; Viala, *Ampélographie* 3:108, 277.

51. Miller, *Dictionary*, s.v. "Vitis"; McMahon, *Calendar*, 229. Dr. John McGrew suggests another interpretation of "Muscadine": "Muscadine seems to be a term then used for any of the large fruited, muscat flavored glasshouse grapes in England, according to Antill, 'An Essay,' pp. 190–91." A "muscadine" today, especially in the southern United States, is a form of *Vitis rotundifolia*.

52. Pinney, *History*, 128; Robinson, *Vines*, 183–84; Miller, *Dictionary*, s.v. "Vitis"; McMahon, *Calendar*, 229; Downing, *Fruits*, 244.

53. McGrew, personal correspondence, Dec. 2, 1983; Galet, *Cépages et Vignobles de France* 4:3186; Miller, *Dictionary*, s.v. "Vitis"; Loudon, *Encyclopedia*, 752; McMahon, *Calendar*, 230.

54. Viala, *Ampélographie* 4:315–19; McMahon, *Calendar*, 234.

55. Mazzei to TJ, Dec. 28, 1803, Stanton, "Correspondence"; Viala, *Ampélographie* 3:69–74; Dalmasso, *Uve de tavola*, 38; Miller, *Dictionary*, s.v. "Vitis"; McMahon, *Calendar*, 229; Anthony, *Vinifera Grapes*, 95; Wellington, *Vinifera Grapes*, 5.

56. Mazzei to TJ, Dec. 28, 1803, Stanton, "Correspondence"; Viala, *Ampélographie* 3:211; Robinson, *Vines*, 194–96.

57. Dalmasso, *Uva da tavola*, 57.

58. Viala, *Ampélographie* 3:108; McGrew, personal correspondence, Dec. 2, 1983; Gallesio, *Pomona italiana* 2: s.v. "Seralamanna"; Mazzei to TJ, Oct. 25, 1803, Goodwin, "Fruits from Mazzei."

59. Mazzei to TJ, Dec. 28, 1803, Stanton, "Correspondence"; McGrew, personal correspondence, Dec. 2, 1983.

60. Robinson, *Vines*, 240. "Tokay" was initially the word Adlum used to describe what became known as Catawba.

61. Gallesio, *Pomona italiana* 2: s.v. "Uva del Friuli"; Viala, *Ampélographie* 7:10; Robinson, *Vines*, 151.

62. Gallesio, *Pomona italiana* 2: s.v. "Uva del Friuli"; Robinson, *Vines*, 241.

63. Appleton to TJ, Mar. 15, 1804, Stanton, "Grapes from Italy"; Robinson, *Vines*, 189.

64. Appleton to TJ, March 15, 1804, Stanton, "Grapes from Italy"; Robinson, *Vines*, 240.

65. Molon, *Ampelografia*, 678–91; Viala, *Ampélographie* 7:201; Gallesio, *Pomona italiana* 2: s.v. "Uva Lacrima."

66. Viala, *Ampélographie* 3:213; 4:157–58; Robinson, *Vines*, 211.

67. Rovasenda, *Saggio di ampelografia universala*, 125; Trinci, *L'agricoltore sperimentato*, 52; Viala, *Ampélographie* 7:228.

68. Hazan, *Italian Wines*, 30–31; Robinson, *Vines*, 150–52.

69. Robinson, *Vines*, 189–92.

70. James W. Wallace to TJ, Apr. 5, 1822, *GB*, 602; Bartram, "Description," 29; McMahon, *Calendar*, 229; Pinney, *History*, 119; Adlum, *Memoir*, 139; Downing, *Fruits*, 253–54; Hedrick, *Grapes*, 441.

71. Bernard Peyton to TJ, Mar. 22, 1824, *GB*, 613; McGrew, "Some Untold Episodes," 85; Pinney, *History*, 82; Kenrick, *New American Orchardist*, 259–60; Downing, *Fruits*, 256.

72. Entry for Apr. 21, 1807, *GB*, 336; Viala, *Ampélographie* 7:310.

73. Entry for Apr. 4, 1817, *GB*, 565; Francis W. Eppes to TJ, Oct. 31, 1822, Bear and Betts, *Family Letters*, 447; Hedrick, *Grapes*, 109–12; Sawyer, "Scuppernong Grapes"; Pinney, *History*, 415–19.

74. Hedrick, *Grapes*, 109–12; Bartram, "Description," 29; Downing, *Fruits*, 258–59; White, *Gardening for the South*, 396.

FIGS: "VULGAR" FRUIT OR "WHOLESOME" DELICACY?

1. Smith, *First Forty Years*, 69; see also Smith, "Recollections of a Visit to Monticello."

2. 1778 orchard plan; "List of Baggage Shipped by Jefferson from France," c. Sept. 1, 1789, Boyd, *Papers* 15:376–77; "Feb. 1790 planted," ViU; entries for Mar. 14, 1769, Sept. 5, 1809, May 14, 1810, TJ to Benjamin Hawkins, Mar. 22, 1796, William Thornton to TJ, May 5, 1810, TJ to Thornton, May 24, 1810, Martha Randolph to TJ, May 12, 1798, Isaac Coles to TJ, Oct. 11, 1814, TJ to John W. Eppes, Mar. 6, 1817, "fig terras next to the wall," from Weather Memorandum Book, "Kalendar, 1813," calendar of harvest dates, 1816–25, "Extracts of garden diary of John Hartwell Cocke," May 28, 1817, *GB*, 15, 387, 425, 249, 437, 438–39, 264, 534, 569, 332, 497, 537, 637; TJ to [Mary Walker?] Lewis, July 12, 1811, ViU.

3. Coyner, "John Hartwell Cocke," 240 n. 171; Downing, *Fruits*, 207; TJ to William Drayton, July 30, 1787, *GB*, 127.

4. "The Open Ground on the West—a shrubbery," *GB*, 27; Downing, *Fruits*, 207; White, *Gardening for the South*, 332; Kenrick, *New American Orchardist*, 323; Phillips, "Figs."

5. Sturtevant, *Edible Plants*, 268; Roach, *Cultivated Fruits*, 197–201; George Brookshaw, *Horticultural Repository* 1:105; Condit, "Fig History," 19; Parkinson, *Paradisi*, 566–67; Langley, *Pomona*, 118; Miller, *Dictionary*, s.v. "Ficus." See also McMahon, *Calendar*, 210–11; Forsyth, *Treatise*, 204–6, for fig variety descriptions copied from Miller.

6. John Bartram to Peter Collinson, Aug. 26, 1766, Darlington, *Memorials*, 284; Bartram, *Travels*, 40, 193, 258, 268; John Smith in Condit, "Fig History," 19; Jane Pierce in Dutton, *Plants of Colonial Williamsburg*, 21, and Bruce, *Economic History* 2:200; Glover in Ayres, "Fruit Culture," 4; Beverley, *History*, 316. See also Lawson, *History*, 113; Byrd, *Natural History*, 49.

7. McMahon, *Calendar*, 212; "American Farmer," *Epitome*, 143–44. See also Sarudy, "Eighteenth-Century Gardens of the Chesapeake," 141–49; Booth catalog, 1810.

8. Phillips, "Figs," 190; Smith, *First Forty Years*, 359–60; Fithian, *Journal*, 178 (Aug. 26, 1774); Carter, *Diaries* 2:946 (Sept. 20, 1775); Lee, *Journal*, 25; Cobbett, *American Gardener*, no. 307.

9. Condit, "Fig History," 21, 24; Sale, *Historic Gardens of Virginia*, 11, 35, 89, 103, 136, 151, 187, 268.

10. Bailey, *Cyclopedia* 2:2217; John Bartram to Peter Collinson, Dec. 3, 1762, Darlington, *Memorials*, 242–43; TJ to Jean Baptiste Say, Mar.

2, 1815, *GB*, 543; Coyner, "John Hartwell Cocke," 240 n. 171; TJ to Edmund Bacon, Sept. 29, 1806, Bear, *Jefferson at Monticello*, 62. See also Langley, *Pomona*, 33–34, 119; Forsyth, *Treatise*, 210; Miller, *Dictionary*, s.v. "Ficus"; McMahon, *Calendar*, 210; Downing, *Fruits*, 209; Kenrick, *New American Orchardist*, 327; Thornton to TJ, May 7, 1810, TJ to Thornton, May 10, 1810, *GB*, 437–39.

11. TJ to Thornton, Oct. 11, 1809, 416, to William Drayton, May 7, 1789, *GB*, 416, 143; Parkinson, *Paradisi*, 566; Miller, *Dictionary*, s.v. "Ficus"; Brookshaw, *The Horticultural Repository* 1:105; White, *Gardening for the South*, 334; TJ to [Mary Walker?] Lewis, July 12, 1811, ViU; Downing, *Fruits*, 212; Kenrick, *New American Orchardist*, 326; Condit, "Fig History," 24.

12. "List of Baggage Shipped by Jefferson from France," c. Sept. 1, 1789, Boyd, *Papers* 15:376–77; "Feb. 1790 planted," ViU; TJ to Benjamin Hawkins, Mar. 22, 1796, *GB*, 249; Downing, *Fruits*, 211–12; Kenrick, *New American Orchardist*, 324.

STRAWBERRIES: ARCADIAN DAINTIES

1. Downing, *Fruits*, 521; entries for May 27, Apr. 7, 1767, Mar. 1, 12, 1812, Apr. 29, 1807, Apr. 13, 1809, Feb. 12, 1782, "Arrangement of the Garden," 1812, TJ to Bartram, June 11, 1801, to Thomas M. Randolph, Mar. 22, 1798, to McMahon, Feb. 8, 1809, Jan. 13, 1810, Apr. 8, 1811, Feb. 16, 1812, to George Divers, Mar. 10, 1812, Martha Randolph to TJ, May 12, 1798, McMahon to TJ, Mar. 10, 1811, *GB*, 5, 473, 336, 385, 94, 475, 275, 261, 406, 431, 455, 480, 483, 264, 452; Otterbacher, "Derivation of the Binomial *Fragaria*"; Fletcher, *Strawberry*, 1.

2. Duchesne, "Natural History," 7–9; Parkinson, *Paradisi*, 528; Wilhelm, *History*, 20–22, 30–47, 120–28; Fletcher, *Strawberry*, 106, 147–56; Otterbacher, "Derivation of the Binomial *Fragaria*."

3. Otterbacher, "Derivation of the Binomial *Fragaria*"; 637–39; Fletcher, *Strawberry*, 109–13; Duchesne, "Natural History," 123–31; see also Wilhelm, *History*, 122–26; Leach, "Colonial Berries," 39.

4. Duchesne, "Natural History," 137, 149; Wilhelm, *History*, 50–84; Fletcher, *Strawberry*, 2, 5; Dutton, *Plants of Colonial Williamsburg*, 154; Leighton, *American Gardens*, 245; Parkinson, *Paradisi*, 526; Langley, *Pomona*, 120; Miller, *Dictionary*, s.v. "Fragaria."

5. Fletcher, *Strawberry*, 2–3; Maxwell, "The Use and Abuse of the Virginia Forest," 88; Peters, "Herbage and Shrubs," 237; Bartram, *Travels*, 224–26; Bailey, *Evolution*, 425–26.

6. Beverley, *History*, 131; Hedrick, *History*, 39; Fletcher, *Strawberry*, 2, 4–5, 9–10, 19.

7. Williams in Bailey, *Evolution*, 426; Byrd, *Natural History*, 38; Lawson, *History*, 114; Randolph, *Treatise*, 45–46; Grove, "Diary," 10; Fithian, *Journal*, 110 (May 29, 1774); Swem, *Brothers*, 32, 37, 40, 42, 62, 86; Carter, *Diaries* 2:1088 (Apr. 17, 1777), 695 (May 28, 1772); Mease, *Domestic Encyclopedia*, 56; Wilhelm, *History*, 141–42.

8. William Prince catalog; Booth catalog; Benjamin Prince cata-

log; A. McMahon catalog; Wilhelm, *History*, 140; Fletcher, *Strawberry*, 12–21; McMahon, *Calendar*, 476.

9. TJ to Anne Cary Randolph, Mar. 22, 1808, *GB*, 368; Duchesne, "Natural History," 155; Dean in Fletcher, *Strawberry*, 8; Gibbes, "The Vine"; Worth, "Strawberries"; Wilhelm, *History*, 149.

10. Miller, *Dictionary*, s.v. "Fragaria"; Duchesne, "Natural History," 163–97; Carter, *Diaries* 2:1088 (Apr. 17, 1777). See also Banks, "On the Revival of an Obsolete Mode of Managing Strawberries"; Phillips, "Strawberries"; McMahon, *Calendar*, 476–78; Randolph, *Treatise*, 46–47; Mease, *Domestic Encyclopedia*, 56–59; Cobbett, *American Gardener*, no. 323.

11. Entries for Mar. 31, 1774, Apr. 29, 1807, Apr. 13, 1809, TJ to Thomas M. Randolph, Mar. 22, 1798, to James Monroe, May 26, 1795, to John Bartram, Jr., June 11, 1801, to Bernard McMahon, Jan. 6, 1807, McMahon to TJ, Apr. 2, 29, 1807, Anne Cary Randolph to TJ, Apr. 15, 1808, TJ to General John Mason, June 22, 1809, to George Divers, Mar. 10, 1812, 1813 Calendar, Dec. 24, 1813, *GB*, 51, 336, 385, 261, 235, 275, 337, 346, 369, 439, 483, 497; unpublished 1805 Garden Book entry, Mar. 19–23, 1805.

12. Fletcher, *Strawberry*, 139–47; Miller, *Dictionary*, s.v. "Fragaria"; McMahon, *Calendar*, 476–78; McMahon to TJ, Apr. 2, 1807, *GB*, 346.

13. TJ to Thomas M. Randolph, Mar. 22, 1798, to Bartram, June 11, 1801, to McMahon, Feb. 8, 1809, Jan. 13, 1810, Apr. 8, 1811, Feb. 16, 1812, entries for Mar. 1, 12, 1812, Apr. 29, 1807, Apr. 13, 1809, Apr. 7, 1767, *GB*, 261, 275, 406, 431, 455, 480, 473, 336, 385, 5; Fletcher, *Strawberry*, 115, 151; Leach, "Colonial Berries," 38–39; Duchesne, "Natural History," 109–22; Wilhelm, *History*, 125–29.

14. Cobbett reference in Fletcher, *Strawberry*, 119–20; McMahon to TJ, Feb. 13, 1809, *GB*, 107; William Prince catalog, 1771; Kenrick, *New American Orchardist*, 303.

15. TJ to George Divers, Mar. 10, 1812, to McMahon, Feb. 16, 1809, Jan. 13, 1810, Apr. 8, 1811, Feb. 16, Oct. 11, 1812, McMahon to TJ, Feb. 28, 1812, entry for Mar. 1, 1813, *GB*, 483, 406, 431, 455, 480, 490, 481, 499; TJ to Joel Yancey, Mar. 15, 1816, MHi; William Prince catalog, 1790. See also Fletcher, *Strawberry*, 7; Wilhelm, *History*, 140, 148–49; Darrow, *Strawberry*, 133, 177; "Mr. Longworth and the Strawberry Question," *Horticulturist* 1 (1846): 81–84; Thomas, *American Fruit Culturist*, 423; Hooper, *Western Fruit Book*, 290; Downing *Fruits*, 527.

CURRANTS, GOOSEBERRIES, AND RASPBERRIES

1. 1778 orchard plan; 1811 orchard plan.

2. Entries for May 6, 1782, Apr. 2, 1768, TJ to McMahon, Mar. 12, 20, 1807, Oct. 11, Feb. 16, 1812, McMahon to TJ, Apr. 10, 1807, Mar. 21, 1810, Mar. 12, Feb. 28, 1812, TJ to Rev. James Madison, Oct. 28, 1785, to George Divers, Mar. 10, 1812, to Maria Jefferson, Mar. 31, 1791, "Calendar for this year," 1812, "Agenda," 1813, *GB*, 94, 4, 490, 480, 343,

347, 422, 474, 481, 106, 483, 161, 474, 500; see also True, "Some Neglected Botanical Results."

3. Roach, *Cultivated Fruits*, 295–303; Parkinson, *Paradisi*, 558–59; Langley, *Pomona*, 124; Miller, *Dictionary*, s.v. "Ribes"; Forsyth, *Treatise*, 233; William Prince catalog, 1771, 1790, Booth catalog, 1810; Landreth catalog, 1811, Benjamin Prince catalog, 1815; "Report," *VSHS, Report* 4 (Dec. 2–3, 1902): 244.

4. Ayres, "Fruit Culture," 4; Beverley, *History*, 131; Byrd, *Natural History*, 49–50; Randolph, *Treatise*, 20–21; "American Farmer," *Epitome*, 128; Parkinson, *Tour*, 219. See also Catesby, *Natural History* 2:xxi; Lawson, *History*, 114; Grove, "Diary," 10.

5. Hedrick, *History*, 446; Leach, "Colonial Berries," 11; John Custis to Peter Collinson, Jan. 25, 1739, Swem, *Brothers*, 58–60; Carter, *Diary* 1:294 (May 1, 1766); Washington in Leighton, *American Gardens*, 231; "Prestwould 1807," memorandum of seasonal fruit calendar, Skipwith Papers; "Invoice of Sundry Seeds etc. furnished Arch[ibald] Blair," 1817, Cocke Papers; Sarudy, "Eighteenth-Century Gardens of the Chesapeake," 159, 154–55; A. McMahon catalog; Benjamin Prince catalog; "Cincinnatus," "Currants."

6. Roach, *Cultivated Fruits*, 311–21; Parkinson, *Paradisi*, 560–61; Forsyth, *Treatise*, 220–23, 227.

7. Glover in Ayres, "Fruit Culture," 4; Lawson, *History*, 114; "American Farmer," *Epitome*, 128; Mease, *Domestic Encyclopedia* 2:254; Parkinson, *Tour*, 219; Cobbett, *American Gardener*, no. 309.

8. John Custis to Robert Carey, 1726, Swem, *Brothers*, 22; Carter, *Diary* 1:294 (May 1, 1766); Fithian, *Journal*, 110 (May 29, 1774); Washington in Leighton, *American Gardens*, 232; notation for May 10, 1810, Cocke Garden Diary, Cocke Papers; Benjamin Prince catalog; McMahon, *Calendar*, 130, 516–17, 586; Bailey, *Evolution*, 393–99; Hedrick, *History*, 446.

9. 1778 orchard plan; TJ to Thomas Mann Randolph, Mar. 22, 1798, McMahon to TJ, Apr. 2, 1807, Sept. 23, 1812, George Divers to TJ, Mar. 17, 1811, Samuel Harrison Smith [Margaret Bayard] to TJ, Mar. 26, 1808, TJ to Ellen Randolph Coolidge, Feb. 6, 1809, Martha Jefferson Randolph to TJ, May 12, 1798, entries for Mar. 31, 1774, June 2, 1782, Mar. 12, 1812, 1815 "Kalendar," *GB*, 261, 346, 489, 368, 406, 454, 264, 51, 94, 475, 537. See also ibid., 646, for the three native raspberry species Jefferson included under the "esculent" species in *Notes on the State of Virginia*.

10. Bailey, *Evolution*, 274–75; Roach, *Cultivated Fruits*, 263–69; Parkinson, *Paradisi*, 557.

11. Beverley, *History*, 131; Miller, *Dictionary*, s.v. "Rubus"; Lawson, *History*, 106, 114; Byrd, *Natural History*, 37; Kalm, *Travels* 1:86.

12. Leach, "Colonial Berries," 9–10; Grove, "Diary," 10; Randolph, *Treatise*, 43; "American Farmer," *Epitome*, 128; Parkinson, *Tour*, 219; Cobbett, *American Gardener*, no. 322.

13. "Calendar for this year, 1812," Poplar Forest memorandum, "Agenda," 1813, TJ to Edmund Bacon, May 13, 1807, *GB*, 474, 488, 500,

348; Randolph, *Treatise*, 20–21, 24–25; Skinner, "Culpable Neglect of Fruit Trees"; McMahon, *Calendar*, 25, 130, 214, 516–17; Mease, *Domestic Encyclopedia* 1:568–69; 2:256; Cobbett, *American Gardener*, no. 322; Downing, *Fruits*, 213–15. See also Langley, *Pomona*, 124; Miller, *Dictionary*, s.v. "Grossularia," "Ribes," and "Rubus"; Forsyth, *Treatise*, 225–30, 255–56, 568–69;. McMahon, *Calendar*, 131, 214, 517; "American Farmer," *Epitome*, 61–63; Randolph, *Treatise*, 43.

14. TJ to McMahon, Mar. 22, 1807, Oct. 11, 1812, McMahon to TJ, Mar. 27, Apr. 2, 10, 1807, June 28, 1808, Feb. 28, 1812, TJ to John W. Eppes, Mar. 6, 1817, entries for Mar. 12, 1812, Mar. 17–20, 1810, *GB*, 344, 490, 345, 346, 347, 373, 481, 568, 474, 422.

15. *Hortus Third*, 969–70; Stanton, "Plants from Lewis and Clark," s.v. "Golden currant," "Sweetscented currant"; A. McMahon catalog; Kenrick, *New American Orchardist*, 287, 386; Downing, *Fruits*, 205; Bailey, *Evolution*, 402.

16. TJ to Thomas Mann Randolph, Mar. 22, 1798, McMahon to TJ, Apr. 2, May 1, 1807, Sept. 23, 1812, Samuel Harrison Smith to TJ, Mar. 26, 1808, *GB*, 261, 346, 336, 489, 368; McMahon, *Calendar*, 552; entry for May 18, 1812, Cocke Garden Diary, Cocke Papers; Downing, *Fruits*, 514–15.

17. McMahon to TJ, June 28, 1808, Feb. 28, 1812, TJ to George Divers, Mar. 10, 1812, to McMahon, Feb. 8, 1809, Jan. 13, 1810, "Calendar for this year, 1812," entry for Mar. 12, 1812, *GB*, 372, 481, 483, 406, 431, 476, 474–75. See also McMahon, *Calendar*, 585–86, for list of fifty-one red-fruited gooseberry cultivars.

Bibliography

MANUSCRIPTS

College of William and Mary, Williamsburg, Va., Swem Library
  (ViW)
  Skipwith Papers
  Tucker-Coleman Papers
Gunston Hall Plantation, Lorton, Va.
  Mason, John. "Recollections of John Mason"
The Henry E. Huntington Library, San Marino, Calif. (CsmH)
  Jefferson Papers
Historical Society of Pennsylvania, Philadelphia (PHi)
  Dreer Collection: Letters and Papers of Thomas Jefferson, in-
    cluding Weather Memorandum Books and 1807 vineyard
    plan
  John Lithen nursery catalog, c. 1800
Library of Congress, Washington, D.C. (DLC)
  William Booth nursery catalog, 1810
  Jefferson Papers ("Revisal of my Fruit, July 1783")
  David and Cuthbert Landreth nursery catalog, 1811
  William Prince nursery catalog, 1771
  William Prince nursery catalog, 1790
Massachusetts Historical Society, Boston (MHi)
  Jefferson Papers (Garden Book, 1778 orchard plan,
    "Directions, Oct. 1783," 1811 orchard plan)
Monticello, Thomas Jefferson Memorial Foundation, Inc.,
    Charlottesville, Va.
  "Descriptions of Monticello, 1780–1826"
  "Descriptions of Monticello, 1826–Present"
  Spivey, Rosa. "Thomas Jefferson's Nurseries," 1979
Mount Vernon Ladies' Association, Mount Vernon, Va.
  "Weekly Reports of George Washington's Gardener," 1797–99
National Agricultural Library, Beltsville, Md. (NAL)
  Bolling, Robert. "A Sketch of Vine Culture for Pennsylvania,
    Maryland, Virginia, and the Carolinas." 1773 or 1774. Manu-
    script at Huntington Library, San Marino, Calif. Copy pre-
    pared by Robert Bolling, Jr., Prince Family Papers.
  Coxe, William. "A View of the Cultivation of Fruit Trees and
    the Management of Orchards and Cider." Manuscript for 2d
    edition.

A. McMahon nursery catalog c. 1819
Prince Family Letters
Princeton University Library, Princeton, N.J. (NjP)
  Jefferson Papers (unpublished Garden Book entry, Mar. 19–23,
    1805)
University of North Carolina, Chapel Hill (NcU)
  Southern Historical Collection: Nicholas Trist Papers
University of Virginia, Charlottesville (ViU)
  Barrett Collection ("Prince Wm 1791," planting memorandum)
  Edwin M. Betts Collection ("Feb. 1790 planted")
  John Hartwell Cocke Papers
  Diary of William Hugh Grove, 1698–1732
  Jefferson Papers
Yale University Library, New Haven (CtY)
  Jefferson Papers (1806 plan of the mountain)

NEWSPAPERS AND SPECIALIZED PERIODICALS

American Farmer (Baltimore), 1819–29
Central Gazette (Charlottesville), 1820, 1827
Southern Planter (Richmond), 1841–44
Virginia Advocate (Charlottesville), 1819
Virginia Argus (Richmond), 1804
Virginia Gazette (Williamsburg), 1736–1800
Virginia Gazette and General Advertiser (Richmond), 1798
Virginia Herald (Fredericksburg), 1799–1800

PUBLISHED SOURCES, RESEARCH REPORTS, AND DISSERTATIONS

[Abercrombie, John] Thomas Mawe. *Every Man His Own Gardener.*
  York, Eng., 1767.
Adams, William Howard. *Jefferson's Monticello.* New York, 1983.
Adlum, John. Letter to *American Farmer* 4, no. 32 (Nov. 1, 1822): 256.
———. Letter to *American Farmer* 6, no. 2 (Mar. 4, 1825): 297.
———. *A Memoir on the Cultivation of the Vine in America, and the
  Best Mode of Making Wine.* Washington, D.C., 1823. Rept.
  Hopewell, N.J., 1971.

"Agricola." "Growth of Fruit Trees." *American Farmer* 4, no. 11 (June 7, 1822): 84.

Alwood, William B. "Letter on American Apples at the Paris Exposition, 1900." Virginia State Horticultural Society, *Report*, Nov. 20, 21, 1900, 139.

——. "Notes on the Behavior of Standard and Newer Varieties at Blacksburg." Virginia State Horticultural Society, *Report*, Jan. 15, 16, 1900, 43.

"An American Farmer." *An Epitome of Mr. Forsyth's Treatise on the Culture and Management of Fruit Trees*. Philadelphia, 1803.

Amoureux, Pierre Joseph. *A Short and Practical Treatise on the Culture of Wine-Grapes in the United States of America*. Washington, D.C., 1800. Broadside at Library of Congress, Washington, D.C.

Anon. "The Apple in Piedmont: Its Capabilities and Culture." Virginia State Horticultural Society, *Report*, Nov. 20, 21, 1900, 51.

——. "Culture of the Peach Tree." *American Farmer* 6, no. 10 (May 7, 1824): 75.

——. "Fruit." *American Farmer* 11, no. 2 (Mar. 27, 1829): 5.

——. "Method of Securing the Blossoms of Fruit Trees against Destruction by Late Frosts." *American Farmer* 6, no. 28 (Oct. 22, 1824): 247.

——. "On Pear Trees." *American Farmer* 3, no. 3 (Apr. 13, 1821): 23.

——. "On the Culture of Grape Vines." *American Farmer* 4, no. 49 (Feb. 28, 1823): 387.

——. "On the Use of Charcoal for the Preservation of Peach Trees." *American Farmer* 6, no. 44 (Jan. 21, 1825): 346.

——. "Peeling and Barking Fruit Trees." Rep. from London *Farmer's Journal*. *American Farmer* 4, no. 20 (Aug. 9, 1822): 158–59.

——. "Peeling and Barking Fruit Trees." *American Farmer* 4, no. 26 (Sept. 20, 1822): 205.

Anthony, R. D. *Vinifera Grapes in New York*. Bulletin no. 432. New York Agricultural Experiment Station, Geneva, N.Y., 1917.

Antill, Edward. "An Essay on the Cultivation of the Vine, and the Making of Wine, Suited to the Different Climates in North-America," American Philosophical Society, *Transactions* 1 (1771; 2d ed., 1789): 180–341.

Armstrong, John. "Wild Garlic." *American Farmer* 1, no. 11 (May 28, 1819): 70.

Ayres, Edward, "Fruit Culture in Colonial Virginia." Research report for Colonial Williamsburg, Williamsburg, Va., Apr. 1973.

Bailey, Liberty Hyde. *The Apple Tree*. New York, 1922.

——. *Sketch of the Evolution of Our Native Fruits*. New York, 1898.

——. *The Standard Cyclopedia of Horticulture*. 2d rev. ed. 3 vols. New York, 1939.

Banister, John. *Natural History of Virginia, 1678–1692*. Ed. Joseph and Nesta Ewan. Urbana, Ill., 1970.

Banks, Sir Joseph. "Notes Relative to the First Appearance of the *Aphis lanigera*, or the Apple-Tree Insect in This Country." Horticultural Society of London, *Transactions* 2 (1818): 162.

——. "On the Revival of an Obsolete Mode of Managing Strawberries." Horticultural Society of London, *Transactions* 1 (1815): 54.

Barton, Benjamin. "Journal of Benjamin Smith Barton on a Visit to Virginia, 1802." Ed. W. L. McAtee. *Castanea* 3, nos. 7, 8 (Nov., Dec. 1938): 85–117.

——. "Of the Usefulness of Birds," partially reprinted in "An American Farmer." *An Epitome of Mr. Forsyth's Treatise on the Culture and Management of Fruit Trees*. Philadelphia, 1803.

Bartram, William. "Description of the Species and Varieties of Vines in North America." In A. F. M. Willich, *Domestic Encyclopedia*. 1st American ed. by James Mease. 5 vols. Philadelphia, 1803–4.

——. *The Travels of William Bartram*. Ed. Francis Harper. New Haven, 1958.

Beach, S. A. *The Apples of New York*. 2 vols. Albany, 1905.

Bear, James A., Jr., ed. *Jefferson at Monticello*. Charlottesville, Va., 1967.

Beiswanger, William. "Report on Research and a Program for the Restoration of the Monticello Vegetable Garden Terrace, Orchard, Vineyard, Berry Patches, and Nursery." Research report for Thomas Jefferson Memorial Foundation, Nov. 1978.

——. "The Temple in the Garden: Thomas Jefferson's Vision of the Monticello Landscape." In *British and American Gardens in the Eighteenth Century*, ed. John Dixon Hunt. Williamsburg, Va., 1984. Pp. 170–88.

Bergh, Albert, and Andrew A. Lipscomb, eds. *The Writings of Thomas Jefferson*. 15 vols. Washington, D.C., 1907.

Betts, Edwin Morris, ed. *Thomas Jefferson's Farm Book*. Charlottesville, Va., 1953.

——, ed. *Thomas Jefferson's Garden Book, 1766–1824*. Philadelphia, 1944.

Betts, Edwin Morris, and James A. Bear, Jr., eds. *The Family Letters of Thomas Jefferson*. Columbia, Mo., 1966.

Beverley, Robert. *The History and Present State of Virginia*. 1705. Ed. Louis B. Wright. Chapel Hill, N.C., 1947.

Biggs, Arthur. "An Account of Some New Apples." London Horticultural Society, *Transactions* 1 (1815): 67.

Bolling, Robert. "Essay on the Utility of Vine Planting in Virginia." *Virginia Gazette*, Feb. 25, 1773.

——. "To the Friends to Vine Planting." *Virginia Gazette*, July 29, 1773.

Bordley, John Beale. *Essays and Notes on Husbandry and Rural Affairs*. Philadelphia, 1799.

Boulster, John. "Wild Garlic: Can It Be Advantageously Cultivated?" *American Farmer* 4, no. 47 (Feb. 14, 1823): 376.

Boyd, Julian P., et al., eds. *The Papers of Thomas Jefferson.* 26 vols. to date. Princeton, N.J., 1950—.

Brevard, John F. "On the Practicability of Retarding the Flowering of the Peach Tree, and Thereby Saving That Precious Fruit from Destruction by Early Frosts." *American Farmer* 6 (July 2, 1824): 113–14.

Brookshaw, George. *The Horticultural Repository.* 2 vols. London, 1823.

———. *Pomona Brittanica.* 2 vols. London, 1817.

Brosten, Dennis, and Brenda Simmonds. "Crops Gone." *Agrochemical Age,* May 1989, 6–7, 28–29.

Bruce, Philip Alexander. *Economic History of Virginia in the Seventeenth Century.* 2 vols. New York, 1896.

———. *The Social Life of Virginia in the Seventeenth Century.* 2 vols. Williamstown, Mass., 1907.

Byram, H. P. "Description of Three Fine Western Apples." *Horticulturist* 2 (1848): 19.

Byrd, William. "History of the Dividing Line betwixt Virginia and North Carolina Run in the Year of Our Lord 1728," and "A Progress to the Mines." *The Prose Works of William Byrd of Westover.* Ed. Louis B. Wright. Cambridge, Mass., 1966.

———. "Letters of the Byrd Family, William Byrd to Mr. Warner in England," July 1729. *Virginia Magazine of History and Biography* 36 (April 1928): 117–23.

———. *Natural History of Virginia.* 1737. Ed. and trans. Richard Beatty and William Mulloy. Richmond, 1940.

———. "Occaneechee Island," July 1702. *William and Mary Quarterly,* 1st ser., 11 (1902): 122.

———. *The Secret Diary of William Byrd of Westover, 1709–1712.* Ed. Louis B. Wright and Marion Tinling. Richmond, 1941.

Capron, J. W. "Planting Trees." *American Farmer* 6, no. 31 (Oct. 22, 1824): 243–44.

Carter, Landon. *The Diary of Landon Carter of Sabine Hall, 1752–1778.* Ed. Jack P. Greene. 2 vols. Charlottesville, 1965.

Castiglioni, Luigi. *Viaggio: Travels in the United States of North America, 1785–87.* Ed. and trans. Antonio Rice. Syracuse, N.Y., 1983.

Catesby, Mark. *The Natural History of Carolina, Florida, and the Bahama Islands.* 2 vols. London, 1731.

Chastellux, François Jean, marquis de. *Travels in North America in the Years 1780, 1781, and 1782.* Ed. Howard Rice, Jr. Chapel Hill, N.C., 1963.

"Cincinnatus." "Currants." *American Farmer* 4, no. 14 (June 28, 1822): 106.

Clinton, DeWitt. "Extracts from *American Agriculture and Botany.*" *American Farmer* 1, no. 14 (July 2, 1819): 108–9.

Cobbett, William. *The American Gardener.* London, 1821.

———. "List of Fruits." *American Farmer* 4, no. 47 (Feb. 28, 1823): 385–86.

Cocke, John Hartwell. "On Peach Trees." *American Farmer* 1, no. 44 (Jan. 28, 1820): 350.

Coles, S. W. *The American Fruit Book.* Boston, 1849.

Coles, Walter. "On the Culture of Potatoes, and the Insect in the Root of Peach Trees." *American Farmer* 3, no. 17 (July 20, 1821): 134.

Collin, Nicholas. "Remarks on the Great Damage Done to Apple Trees by Erroneous Pruning." Philadelphia Society for Promoting Agriculture, *Memoirs* 3 (1814): 200–202.

Condit, Henry J. "Fig History in the New World." *Agricultural History* 11, no. 2 (Apr. 1957): 19–24.

Coxe, William. "The Gloucester White, Taliafero, or Robertson Apple." Philadelphia Society for Promoting Agriculture, *Memoirs* 4 (1818): 50–51.

———. "On Orchards." Philadelphia Society for Promoting Agriculture, *Memoirs* 1 (1808): 217–26.

———. *A View of the Cultivation of Fruit Trees, and the Management of Orchards and Cider.* Philadelphia, 1817.

Coyner, Martin Boyd. "John Hartwell Cocke of Bremo. Agriculture and Slavery in the Ante-Bellum South." Ph.D. dissertation, University of Virginia, 1961.

Crèvecoeur, Michel Guillaume St. John de [Hector St. John de]. *Letters from an American Farmer.* London, 1782. Rept. New York, 1963.

Crosby, Alfred W. *Ecological Imperialism: The Biological Expansion of Europe, 900–1900.* Cambridge, Mass., 1985.

Dalmasso, Giovanni. *Uve da tavola.* Milan, 1946.

Darlington, William, ed. *Memorials of John Bartram and Humphrey Marshall.* Philadelphia, 1849.

Darrow, G. M. *The Strawberry.* New York, 1966.

Dirr, Jeffrey. "Most Common Weeds in Orchards in Virginia." In Southern Weed Science Society, *Research Report,* 39th annual meeting, Nashville, Jan. 20–22, 1986, 145.

Downing, Andrew Jackson. *The Fruits and Fruit Trees of America.* 9th ed. New York, 1849.

———. *The Fruits and Fruit Trees of America.* 2d rev. and corr. ed. by Charles Downing. New York, 1900.

Drake, C. R., M. J. Weaver, A. P. Elliot, and S. A. Tolin. *Diseases of Grapes and Their Control in Virginia.* Blacksburg, Va., 1984.

Duchesne, Antoine. *Histoire naturelle des fraisiers.* Paris, 1766.

———. "Natural History of Strawberries." Trans. provided by Stephen Wilhelm, University of California, Davis.

Dufour, John James. *The American Vine Dresser's Guide.* Cincinnati, 1826.

Duhamel Du Monceau, Henri Louis. *Traité des arbres fruitiers.* 2 vols. Paris, 1768.

Dutton, Joan Parry. *Plants of Colonial Williamsburg.* Williamsburg, Va., 1979.

Eddis, William. *Letters from America.* Ed. Aubrey C. Land. Cambridge, Mass., 1969.

Elmore, C. D. "Weed Survey, Southern States." In Southern Weed Science Society, *Research Report,* 39th annual meeting, Nashville, Jan. 20–22, 1986, 155.

Eppler, Alexander. "The Cornelian Cherry Dogwood." *Pomona* 22 (Winter 1988): 47–49.

Falconer, Thomas. "Soap Suds as a Manure." *American Farmer* 4, no. 13 (June 21, 1822): 100.

Fithian, Philip Vickers. *Journal and Letters of Philip Vickers Fithian: A Plantation Tutor of the Old Dominion, 1773–1774.* Ed. Hunter Dickinson Farish. Williamsburg, Va., 1957.

Fitz, James. *Southern Apple and Peach Culturist.* Richmond, 1872.

Fitzhugh, William. "Letters of William Fitzhugh." *Magazine of Virginia History and Biography* 1, no. 4 (April 1894): 391–410.

Fleischmann, Charles L. *Grapes of America.* N.p., 1867.

Fletcher, Stevenson Whitcomb. *A History of Fruit Growing in Virginia.* Staunton, Va., 1932.

——. *Pennsylvania Agriculture and Country Life.* Harrisburg, Pa., 1950.

——. *The Strawberry in North America.* New York, 1917.

Forest, Elizabeth Kellam de. *The Gardens and Grounds at Mount Vernon.* Mount Vernon, Va., 1982.

Forsyth, William. *A Treatise on the Culture and Management of Fruit Trees.* Ed. William Cobbett. Philadelphia, 1802; 2d ed., New York, 1803.

From Seed to Flower: Philadelphia, 1681–1876, a Horticultural Point of View. Philadelphia, 1976.

Galet, Pierre. *Cépages et vignobles de France.* 4 vols. Montpelier, France, 1958–64.

Gallesio, Giorgio. *Pomona italiana.* 4 vols. Pisa, 1817.

Gardiner, John, and David Hepburn. *The American Gardener.* Washington, D.C., 1804.

Garrigues, Edward. "Some Observations on Fruit Trees." Philadelphia Society for Promoting Agriculture, *Memoirs* 2 (1811): 183–85.

Gibbes, W. S. "The Vine." *American Farmer* 5, no. 16 (July 11, 1823): 124.

Glover, Thomas. "An Account of Virginia." Royal Society, *Philosophical Transactions* 2 (June 20, 1676; rept. Oxford, 1904).

Goodwin, Lucia. "Fruits from Mazzei." Trans. of letters from Philip Mazzei to Jefferson dealing with fruit trees and grapes. Sept. 1983. Monticello Research Department, Thomas Jefferson Memorial Foundation, Charlottesville, Va.

——. *Italians in the Monticello Orchard.* Keepsake for anniversary dinner, Apr. 12, 1982. Thomas Jefferson Memorial Foundation, Charlottesville, Va.

Gordon, Col. James. "Journal of Col. James Gordon." *William and Mary Quarterly,* 1st ser., 9 (Jan. 1903): 195–205.

Hackney, John. "Culture of the Peach Tree." *American Farmer* 6, no. 10 (May 28, 1824): 75.

Hammond, N. "Soft Soap, Undiluted, an Excellent Cleanser of Fruit Trees." *American Farmer* 6, no. 51 (Mar. 11, 1825): 402–3.

Harper, R. G. "Address before the Maryland Agricultural Society, November 25, 1824." *American Farmer* 6, no. 38 (Dec. 10, 1824): 297.

Harvill, A. M., Ted R. Bradley, and Charles E. Stevens. *Atlas of the Virginia Flora.* Farmville, Va., 1981.

Hatch, Peter J. "Thomas Jefferson, Citizen Genet, and the Fuji Apple." *Pomona* 24 (Oct. 1991): 13–16.

Hazan, Victor. *Italian Wines.* New York, 1982.

Hazard, Ebenezer. "The Journal of Ebenezer Hazard in Virginia, 1777." Ed. Fred Shelley. *Virginia Magazine of History and Biography* 62, no. 4 (Oct. 1954): 403–50.

Hedrick, Ulysses P. *The Cherries of New York.* Albany, 1915.

——. *The Grapes of New York.* Albany, 1908.

——. *A History of Horticulture in America to 1860.* New York, 1950.

——. *The Peaches of New York.* Albany, 1914.

——. *The Pears of New York.* Albany, 1921.

——. *The Plums of New York.* Albany, 1911.

Hench, Atcheson L. "The Name 'Albemarle Pippin.'" *Magazine of Albemarle History* 14 (1954): 21–25.

Henrey, Blanche. *British Botanical and Horticultural Literature before 1800.* 3 vols. London, 1975.

Hold, Cheryl. "Mount Clare Orchard Floral Analysis." Research report for the Baltimore Center for Archaeology, Baltimore, n.d.

Hooker, William. *Pomona Londinensis.* London, 1818.

Hooper, E. J. *Hooper's Western Fruit Book.* Cincinnati, 1857.

Horsfall, Frank. "Pine Mouse Invasion." American Society for Horticultural Science, *Proceedings* 85 (Nov. 1964): 22–24.

Hortus Third: A Concise Dictionary of Plants Cultivated in the United States and Canada. New York, 1976.

Insect and Mite Pests of Apple and Peach in Virginia. Blacksburg, Va., 1973.

Jackson, Donald, ed. *The Diaries of George Washington.* 6 vols. Charlottesville, Va., 1976–79.

Jacocks, Jonathan H. "On the Use of Juniper Rails." *American Farmer* 4, no. 2 (Apr. 5, 1822): 10.

Janson, H. Frederic. "William Coxe: A Survey of His Life and Work." In William Coxe, *A View of the Cultivation of Fruit Trees and Management of Orchards and Cider.* Rept. Rockton, Ontario, 1976. Pp. i–xxiv.

Jefferson, Thomas. *Notes on the State of Virginia.* Trenton, N.J. 1803. Ed. William Peden. Chapel Hill, N.C., 1955.

Johnson, Stephen William. *Rural Economy*. New Brunswick, N.J., 1805.

Jones, Hugh. *The Present State of Virginia*. London, 1724. Ed. Richard L. Morton. Chapel Hill, N.C., 1956.

Joyce, John. "Virginia in 1785: Letter from John Joyce to Robert Dicksen (Mar. 24, 1785)." *Virginia Magazine of History and Biography* 23, no. 4 (1915): 407–14.

Kalm, Peter. *Travels in North America*. 2 vols. Ed. and trans. Adolph Benson. New York, 1937.

Keith, G. W. "Scab of Apples." In *Plant Diseases* (Yearbook of Agriculture). Washington, D.C., 1953. Pp. 646–52.

Kelso, William. "A Report on the Archaeological Excavations at Monticello, Charlottesville, Virginia, 1979–1981." Research report for Thomas Jefferson Memorial Foundation, Charlottesville, Va., 1982.

Kenrick, William. *The New American Orchardist*. Boston, 1845.

Knight, Thomas. *A Treatise on the Culture of the Apple and Pear*. London, 1814.

Langley, Batty. *Pomona; or, The Fruit-Garden Illustrated*. London, 1729.

La Rochefoucauld-Liancourt, Duc de. *Travels through the United States of North America . . . in the Years 1795, 1796, 1797*. English trans., London, 1799.

Laudrum, Abner. "Fruit Trees, Grafting, etc." *American Farmer* 4, no. 34 (Nov. 15, 1822): 268–69.

Lawson, John. *The History of Carolina*, 1714. Ed. Francis Latham Harris. Richmond, 1937.

Leach, Charles. "Colonial Berries: Small Fruits Adapted to American Agriculture." Research report for the National Colonial Farm, Accokeek, Md., 1977.

Leach, William Elferd. "Note on the Insect [*Aphis lanigera*]." Horticultural Society of London, *Transactions* 3 (1819): 60.

Lee, Lucinda. *Journal of a Young Lady of Virginia, 1782*. Stratford, Va., 1974.

Leighton, Ann. *American Gardens in the Eighteenth Century: "For Use or Delight."* Boston, 1976.

Loudon, J. C. *An Encyclopædia of Gardening*. London, 1825.

McGann, Martin. "Apple Cultivars in the Lower Hudson Valley prior to 1860." Research report for Sleepy Hollow Restorations, Tarrytown, N.Y., 1987.

McGrew, John R. "The 'Alexander' Grape." *American Wine Society Journal* 8, no. 2 (1976): 19–21.

——. "Some Untold Episodes in the History of Virginia Grapes and Wine." *American Wine Society Journal* 18, no. 3 (1986): 82–85.

McMahon, Bernard. *The American Gardener's Calendar*. Philadelphia, 1806.

Malone, Dumas. *Jefferson the President, 1805–1809*. Boston, 1974.

Manks, Dorothy S. "John Adlum." Introduction to John Adlum. *A Memoir on the Cultivation of the Vine in America, and the Best Mode of Making Wine*. Rept. Hopewell, N.J., 1971.

——. "Some Early American Horticultural Writers and Their Works: 1. John Adlum and William Cobbett." *Huntia* 2 (Oct. 15, 1965): 66–110.

Martin, Alice A. *All about Apples*. Boston, 1976.

Martin, Peter. *The Pleasure Gardens of Virginia, from Jamestown to Jefferson*. Princeton, N.J., 1991.

Martin, Samuel. Letter on "Peach Trees." *American Farmer* 3, no. 38 (Dec. 14, 1821): 302.

Matlack, Timothy. "On Peach Trees." Philadelphia Society for Promoting Agriculture, *Memoirs* 1 (1808): 273–79.

——. "On the Cultivation of the Vine." *American Farmer* 6, no. 42 (Jan. 7, 1825): 329, reprinted from Philadelphia Society for Promoting Agriculture, *Memoirs* 4 (1818).

Maxwell, Hu. "The Use and Abuse of Forests by the Virginia Indians." *William and Mary Quarterly*, 2d ser., 19 (Oct. 1910): 73–91.

Mayo, William, ed. "Virginia Council Journals, 1726–1753." *Virginia Magazine of History and Biography* 32 (Jan. 1954): 56.

Mease, James. "Account of the Virginia Cyder Apple." Philadelphia Society for Promoting Agriculture, *Memoirs* 4 (1818): 49–51.

——, ed. A. F. M. Willich. *Domestic Encyclopedia*. 1st American ed. 5 vols. Philadelphia, 1803–4.

Michaux, François André. "Travels to the West of the Alleghany Mountains, 1805." In *Early Western Travels*. Ed. Reuben Gold Thwaites. Cleveland, 1904.

Michel, Francis Louis. "Report of the Journey of Francis Louis Michel, from Berne, Switzerland, to Virginia, October 2, 1701, to December 1, 1702." Ed. and trans. William J. Hinke. *Virginia Magazine of History and Biography* 24 (1916): 1–43, 113–41, 275–303.

Miller, Philip. *The Gardener's Dictionary*. 8th ed. London, 1768.

Mitchell, Samuel L. "Letter to David Hosack, M.D., on the Improvement of Orchards, Apples, and Cider." *American Farmer* 6, no. 29 (Oct. 28, 1824): 226.

——. "On the Insects Which Injure Plums and Cherries." *American Farmer* 6, no. 23 (Aug. 27, 1824): 183.

Molon, Girolamo. *Ampelografia*. Milan, 1906.

Morison, Samuel Eliot, and Henry Steele Commager. *The Growth of the American Republic*. New York, 1950.

Morrison, A. J., ed. *Travels in Virginia in Revolutionary Times*. Lynchburg, Va., 1922.

Mosley, Sir Oswald. "On the *Aphis lanigera*, or American Blight." Horticultural Society of London, *Transactions* 3 (1819): 54–60.

Muse, Dr. Joseph. "Address to Agricultural Society of Annapolis." *American Farmer* 1, no. 16 (July 2, 1819): 124–25.

Nichols, Lew. "Rating the Golden Oldies for Cider." *Pomona* 20 (Spring 1987): 57.

Niemcewicz, Julian Ursyn. *Under Their Vine and Fig Tree: Travels through America in 1797–1799, 1805.* Ed. and trans. Mitchie J. E. Budka. Elizabeth City, N.J., 1965.

Noelden, George Henry. "Some Further Observations on the Method of Ringing Fruit Trees." Horticultural Society of London, *Transactions* 1 (1815): 382.

Noël Hume, Mrs. Ivor. *Food.* Williamsburg, Va., 1978.

Otey, W. W. "The Best Varieties for a Commercial Orchard." Virginia State Horticultural Society, *Report*, Dec. 2, 3, 1902, 174.

Otterbacher, A. G., and R. M. Skirvin. "Derivation of the Binomial *Fragaria × ananassa* for the Cultivated Strawberry." *Hortscience* 8 (Dec. 1988): 637–39.

P. L. "Concerning Fruit Trees." *American Farmer* 3, no. 58 (Mar. 8, 1822): 400.

Parkinson, John. *Paradisi in sole paradisus terrestris.* London, 1629. Rept. New York, 1974.

Parkinson, Richard. *A Tour in America in 1798, 1799, and 1800.* London, 1805.

Peattie, Donald. *A Natural History of Trees of Eastern North America.* 2d ed. New York, 1966.

Peters, Richard. "Herbage and Shrubs Spontaneously Produced, after Forest Timber Burnt, by Firing the Woods." Philadelphia Society for Promoting Agriculture, *Memoirs* 1 (1808): 237–39.

———. "On Orchards." Philadelphia Society for Promoting Agriculture, *Memoirs* 1 (1808): 217–27.

———. "On Peach Trees." Philadelphia Society for Promoting Agriculture, *Memoirs* 1 (1808): 15–24, 183–86.

———. "On the Injurious Effects of Clover to Orchards." Philadelphia Society for Promoting Agriculture, *Memoirs* 1 (1808): 119–23.

———. "On Tough Sod, Star of Bethlehem, and Blue Bottle." Philadelphia Society for Promoting Agriculture, *Memoirs* 2 (1811): 178–82.

———. "Remarks." Philadelphia Society for Promoting Agriculture, *Memoirs* 2 (1811): 103–4.

Peterson, Merrill, ed. *Visitors to Monticello.* Charlottesville, Va., 1989.

Phillips, Henry. "Figs." *American Farmer* 4, no. 24 (Sept. 6, 1822): 189–90.

———. "Strawberries." *American Farmer* 4, no. 33 (Nov. 8, 1822): 357.

Phillips, William. "On Peach Trees." Philadelphia Society for Promoting Agriculture, *Memoirs* 2 (1811): 12–16.

Pickering, Thomas. "Some Account of the Virginia Crab Apple." Philadelphia Society for Promoting Agriculture, *Memoirs* 3 (1814): 392–94.

Pinney, Thomas. *A History of Wine in America.* Berkeley, Calif., 1989.

"Pomona." "Cider." *American Farmer* 4, no. 30 (Oct. 18, 1822): 237.

Powel, John Hare. "On the Cultivation of Peach Trees and Drying of Fruits." *American Farmer* 6, no. 51 (Mar. 11, 1825): 401–2.

Preston, Samuel. "On Fruit and Fruit Trees." Philadelphia Society for Promoting Agriculture, *Memoirs* 2 (1811): 79–88.

Prince, William Robert. *The Pomological Manual.* 2 vols. New York, 1832.

———. *A Treatise on the Vine.* New York, 1830.

Pryor, Elizabeth B. "Orchard Fruits of the Colonial Chesapeake." Research report no. 14 for the National Colonial Farm, Accokeek, Md., n.d.

Ragan, W. H., ed. *Nomenclature of the Apple.* Washington, D.C., 1905.

Randall, Harry S. *The Life of Thomas Jefferson.* 3 vols. New York, 1858.

Randolph, John, Jr. ["A Citizen of Virginia"]. *A Treatise on Gardening.* Ed. Marjorie Fleming Warner. Rept. Richmond, 1924.

Randolph, Mary. *The Virginia House-wife.* Ed. Karen Hess. Columbia, S.C., 1984.

Randolph, Thomas Mann. "Transactions of the Agricultural Society of Albemarle, Copy of a Letter from Col. Thomas M. Randolph (Read May 10, 1824)." *American Farmer* 6, no. 7 (June 18, 1824): 98.

Raphael, Sandra. *An Oak Spring Pomona.* Upperville, Va., 1990.

———. *An Oak Spring Sylva.* Upperville, Va., 1989.

Richter, P. L. "Description of Coxe's 'A View of the Cultivation of Fruit Trees of America.'" In manuscript of 2d ed. of William Coxe, "A View of the Cultivation of Fruit Trees," vi–vii, National Agricultural Library, Beltsville, Md. Published in *Science* 44, no. 1123 (July 14, 1916).

Roach, F. A. *The Cultivated Fruits of Britain.* London, 1985.

Robbins, Christine Chapman. *David Hosack, Citizen of New York.* Philadelphia, 1964.

Roberts, Algernon. "Extirpation of Wild Garlic." Philadelphia Society for Promoting Agriculture, *Memoirs* 2 (1811): 120–21.

Robinson, Jancis. *Vines, Grapes, and Wine.* New York, 1986.

Rouché, Berton. "One Hundred Thousand Varieties." *New Yorker*, Aug. 11, 1975, 33–40.

Rovasenda, Giuseppe dei Conti di. *Saggio di ampelografia universala.* Milan, 1877.

"Rusticus." "Planting Apple Orchards." *American Farmer* 6, no. 48 (Feb. 18, 1825): 380.

The Saga of a City: Lynchburg, Virginia, 1776–1936. Lynchburg, Va., 1936.

Sale, Edith Tunis. *Historic Gardens of Virginia.* Rev. ed. Richmond, 1930.

Sarudy, Barbara Wells. "Eighteenth-Century Gardens of the Chesapeake." *Journal of Garden History* 9 (July–Sept., 1989).

Sawyer, L. "Scuppernong Grapes." *American Farmer* 4, no. 37 (Dec. 6, 1822): 295–96.

Say, Thomas. "On the Peach Tree Insect." *American Farmer* 6, no. 41 (Dec. 31, 1824): 334–35.

Silsbee, Nathaniel, "Pruning Fruit Trees." *American Farmer* 6, no. 49 (Feb. 25, 1825): 391–92.

Skinner, John. "Culpable Neglect of Fruit Trees." *American Farmer* 4, no. 16 (July 9, 1824): 121.

Smith, Margaret Bayard. *The First Forty Years of Washington Society*. Ed. Gaillard Hunt. New York, 1906.

——. "Recollections of a Visit to Monticello." *Richmond Enquirer*, Jan. 18, 1823.

Sowerby, E. Millicent. *Catalogue of the Library of Thomas Jefferson*. 5 vols. Washington, D.C., 1959.

Spooner, John Jones. "A Topographical Description of Prince George County, 1793." *Tyler's Quarterly Magazine* 5, no. 1 (July 1923): 1–11.

Springer, C. "Raul's Gennetting Apple." *Horticulturist* 2 (1848): 147.

Spurrier, John. *The Practical Farmer*. Wilmington, Del., 1793.

Stanton, Lucia. "Correspondence." Correspondence of Jefferson, Jean David, and L. Girardin compiled and translated for Thomas Jefferson Memorial Foundation, Charlottesville, Va., 1985.

——. "Grapes from Italy." Research report for Thomas Jefferson Memorial Foundation, Charlottesville, Va., 1983.

——. "Interim Compilation of Documents on Fencing, etc." Research report for Thomas Jefferson Memorial Foundation, Charlottesville, Va., 1988.

——. "Plants from Lewis and Clark Grown by Jefferson at Monticello." Research report for Thomas Jefferson Memorial Foundation, Dec. 1, 1988.

Stetson, Sarah Patee. "American Garden Books Transplanted and Native, before 1807." *William and Mary Quarterly* 3d ser., 3 (July 1946): 343–69.

Stipp, David. "Apple of Our Eye Could Soon Have 'Made in Japan' Tag." *Wall Street Journal*, Oct. 25, 1989.

Strachey, William. *Historie of Travaile in Virginia Brittania*. Ed. Louis B. Wright and Virginia Freund. London, 1953.

Sturtevant, Edward Lewis. *Notes on Edible Plants*. Ed. U. P. Hedrick (as *Sturtevant's Edible Plants of the World*). New York, 1972.

Swem, E. G., ed. *Brothers of the Spade: Correspondence of Peter Collinson of London and of John Custis of Williamsburg, Virginia, 1734–1746*. Barre, Mass., 1957.

Tayloe, John. "On Virginia Husbandry." Philadelphia Society for Promoting Agriculture, *Memoirs* 2 (1811): 102.

[Taylor, John] "A Citizen of Virginia." *Arator* (Being a Series of Agricultural Essays, Practical and Political). Georgetown, D.C., 1813.

Thomas, Evan, Jr. "On the Preservation of Peach Trees." *American Farmer* 6, no. 5 (Apr. 23, 1824): 37.

Thomas, John J. *The American Fruit Culturist*. New York. 1867.

Tinling, Marion, ed. *The Correspondence of the Three William Byrds of Westover, Virginia 1664–1776*. 2 vols. Charlottesville, Va., 1977.

Treville Lawrence, R. de, III, ed. *Jefferson and Wine: Model of Moderation*. 2d ed., The Plains, Va., 1989.

Trinci, Cosimo. *L'agricoltore sperimentato*. Venice, 1768.

Triolo, Victor A. "The Probable Origin of the Synonym Janet ('Ralls')." *Pomona* 14 (March 1991): 30–36, and (Oct. 1991): 3–11.

Troubetzkoy, Ulrich. "Big Business from Little Apples." *Virginia Cavalcade*, Autumn 1960, 23–26.

True, Rodney H. "Some Neglected Botanical Results of the Lewis and Clark Expedition." American Philosophical Society, *Proceedings* 67 (1928): 1–19.

Tyler, Lynn Gardiner, ed. *Narratives of Early Virginia, 1606–1625*. New York, 1946.

Van Alsteyn, Edward. "Care of Apple Orchards." Virginia State Horticultural Society, *Report*, Nov. 20, 21, 1900, 17.

Van Deman, H. E. "Modern Apple Culture." Virginia State Horticultural Society, *Report*, Nov. 20, 21, 1900, 108–13.

"Veritas." "Orchards." *American Farmer* 3, no. 24 (Sept. 7, 1821): 191.

Viala, Pierre. *Traité général d'ampélographie*. 7 vols. Paris, 1909–10.

W. G. C. "Queries on Barking Fruit Trees." *American Farmer* 4, no. 13 (June 21, 1822): 101.

Wardlaw, Georgia Dickinson. "Young Victoria Had Voice Sweet as Virginia Bird." *Richmond Times-Dispatch*, Mar. 5, 1961.

Wellington, Mr. "Ringing Fruit Trees." *American Farmer* 6, no. 14 (June 25, 1824): 111.

Wellington, Richard. *Vinifera or European Grapes in New York*. New York State Agricultural Experiment Station, circular no. 101. Geneva, N.Y., 1934.

White, William. *Gardening for the South*. New York, 1859.

Wilhelm, Stephen, and James E. Sagen. *A History of the Strawberry*. Berkeley, Calif., 1972.

Willis, J. "A Wash for Fruit Trees." *American Farmer* 3, no. 11 (June 7, 1822): 84.

Woodburn, Elisabeth. "Books Published from 1861–1920." In U. P. Hedrick, *A History of Horticulture in America to 1860*. Rept. Portland, Oreg., 1988.

Worth, James. "An Account of the Insect So Destructive to the Peach Tree." *American Farmer* 6, no. 42 (Dec. 31, 1824): 325.

——. "Observations on Insects with a View to Arrest Their Destructive Ravages." *American Farmer* 4, no. 49 (Feb. 28, 1823): 394–96.

——. "On the Hessian Fly." *American Farmer* 3, no. 24 (Sept. 7, 1821): 187–90.

——. "On the Insects Which Injure Plums." *American Farmer* 6, no. 23 (Aug. 27, 1823): 183.

——. "Some Observations on the Disease of the Morello Cherry, and Management of Trees." *American Farmer* 3, no. 43 (Jan. 18, 1822): 342.

——. "Strawberries." *American Farmer* 5, no. 24 (Sept. 3, 1823): 190.

Wynkoop, Henry, "Account of a Crab Apple Orchard." Philadelphia Society for Promoting Agriculture, *Memoirs* 3 (1814): 189–94.

——. "On Cyder Making." Philadelphia Society for Promoting Agriculture, *Memoirs* 3 (1814): 45–46.

Credits

Preston Bell (drawing by): fig. 7

Colonial Williamsburg Foundation: fig. 8

Betty Carter Fort: fig. 16

The Henry E. Huntington Library: fig. 4

The Historical Society of Pennsylvania: fig. 93

Skip Johns (photo by): figs. 17, 19, 20, 24, 43, 44, 64, 65, 80, 90, 94, 100, 102, 103, 111; plates 12, 19, 26, 32, 43, 45, 49

Library of Congress, Rare Book and Special Collections Division: fig. 5

Margherita Marchione, Salvatori Center for Mazzei Studies: fig. 92

Massachusetts Historical Society: figs. 27, 28 (N-127/K094b), 29 (N-127/K094b), 30, 33, 34, 35 (N-234/K169i), 36, 42 (N-273/K000), 91 (N-127/K094b)

The Mount Vernon Ladies' Association: fig. 9

National Agricultural Library, Special Collections: figs. 45, 95, 97, 98, 101, 104, 109; plates 1, 4, 5, 6, 7, 8, 9, 13, 14, 15, 16, 17, 18, 20, 22, 23, 24, 25, 27, 28, 29, 30, 31, 33, 34, 35, 36, 37, 38, 39, 40, 42, 44, 46, 47, 48

National Portrait Gallery, London: fig. 14

Suzanne Norton (drawing by): fig. 9

The State Museum of Pennsylvania, Pennsylvania Historical and Museum Commission: fig. 96

Leonard Phillips (photo by): second preface figure and text fig. 21

Lucia Stanton (drawing by): fig. 6

Thomas Jefferson Memorial Foundation: preface figures and text. figs. 3 (gift of Mr. and Mrs. Carl Smith and Mr. and Mrs. T. Eugene Worrell), 6, 17, 19, 20, 21, 24, 43, 44, 64, 65, 66, 80, 90, 94, 100, 102, 103, 111, 114; plates 2, 3, 10, 11, 12, 19, 21, 26, 32, 41, 43, 45, 49

University of Virginia Library, Special Collections Department, Thomas Jefferson Papers: figs. 31, 35

University of Virginia Library, Special Collections Department: figs. 40, 52, 61, 63, 69, 73, 75, 77, 79, 85, 106, 107, 108, 115, 116, 117

Virginia State Horticultural Society: figs. 37, 47

Washington and Lee University, Lexington, Va., Washington/Custis/Lee Collection: fig. 22

Yale University, Benjamin Franklin Papers, Beinecke Rare Book Room and Manuscript Library: fig. 32

Index

Note: An italicized page number refers to an illustration on that page.

Abercrombie, John, 24
Adams, John, 94, 131
Adams, Thomas, 133
Adlum, John, 131, 135, 146, 148, 158; and Alexander grape, 137, 152; letter from Jefferson, quoted, 138; *A Memoir on the Cultivation of the Vine in America, and the Best Mode of Making Wine*, 139, 145, 154
Agricultural Society of Albemarle, 39
Agricultural Society of Annapolis, 83
Alexander, James, 135, 152
Almond, bitter, 125, 126; as grown by Jefferson, 125; Lady, 126; *Prunus dulcis* var. *amara*, 125; *Prunus dulcis* var. *dulcis*, 125; sweet, 125, 126
"American Farmer," 119–20; on apple orchards, 59; and cherry, 95, 96; and currant, 176; on early fruit growers, 14; *An Epitome of Mr. Forsyth's Treatise on the Culture and Management of Fruit Trees*, 23–24; and fig, 163–64; and gooseberry, 178; and nectarine, 122; and peach, 86, 87; and pear, 101–2; and plum, 109, 111; on pruning, 34; and quince, 128; and raspberry, 179
American Farmer, 6, 64, 139, 154, 176; on American orchards, 33; on cherry, 96; essay by Bolling in, 143; essay by Cocke in, 18; letters in, quoted, 25; on pests, 35, 36, 37, 38, 84, 111; and strawberry, 172; on weeds, 39; writing by Adlum in, 145, 152; writing by Phillips in, 164
American Philosophical Society, 145
American Pomological Society, 69
Anbury, Thomas, 29
Anthracnose, 146, 152
Antill, Edward, 143, 148, 149, 152; "Essay on the Cultivation of the Vine, and the Making of Wine, Suited to the Different Climates in North-America," 145
Apple: Bellflower, 63; Calville Blanc d' Hiver, 66, 76; Carthouse, 19, 62, 63; Cherokee Wilding, 19; Cherry Cheeks, 19; Clarke Pearmain, 49, 62, 66, 76; culture, 66; "Detroit large white," 76; Detroit Red, 76; Early Harvest, 49, 63, 66, 76, 77; English Codling, 61, 62, 77, 77; Esopus Spitzenburg, 59, 73, 74; —, as grown by Jefferson, 39, 41, 48, 53; Father Abraham, 19, 62, 63, 64; Fuji, 9, 70; Gloucester White, 62; Golden Pippin, 62; Golden Russet, 61, 62; Golden Wilding, 19, 49, 66, 77; Harvey, 61; Hereford Red Streak, 62; Hewes Crab, 5, 19, 62, 74, 75; —, as grown by Jefferson, 39, 41, 49, 59, 65, 66; "Iron wilding," 77; Juniting, 61; Leathercoat, 61; Limbertwig, 19, 62, 63; Lowrey, 62; "Mammoth," 77; Maryland Red Streak, 17; Medlar Russetin, 77; Milam, 62, 63; Newtown Pippin (Albemarle Pippin), 26, 60, 62, 63, 66, 71; —, compared with Ralls Genet, 70; —, in England, 72–73; —, as grown by Jefferson, 39, 41, 42, 46, 53, 59; —, history of, 5, 9; Nonpareil, 62; Ortley, 76; "Ox-eye striped," 77; pests of, 66–69; Pilot, 62; Pomme Gris, 78; Pryor's Red, 19, 62, 63; Ralls Genet, 9, 62, 63, 69, 70; Red June, 19; Red Streak, 61, 62; Rhode Island Greening, 5; Roxbury Russet, 5, 66; Royal Pearmain, 62; Russetins, 78; Shacklehills, 19; Sheepnose, 63; Spice, 63; Summer Pearmain, 61; Taliaferro, 9, 19, 62, 65, 66, 75–76; —, as grown by Jefferson, 39, 41, 53, 59; Vandevere, 62; Virginia Greening, 19, 63; Virginia Spice, 19; Virginia White, 5, 62, 78; White, 62, 66; White Bellflower, 76; White Calville, 76; Winesap, 62, 63; Winter Cheese, 19; Winter Pearmain, 61; Yellow Bellflower, 62
Apple mill and press, 65
Apple scab, 68
Appleton, Thomas, 135, 158
Apricot: Angelic, 51; Angelica, 50, 121; Black, 119; Brussels, 119, 121; Davis's Clingstone, 119; Early, 119; Green, 119; as grown by Jefferson, 117; Large Early, 119, 121; Late, 119; Melon, 48, 117, 121; Moor Park, 51, 117, 119, 120; Newington, 119; Peach, 49, 50, 51, 117, 120–21; pests of, 119–20; Roman, 119
Armstrong, John, 39, 49, 76, 77, 112

Bacon, Edmund, 9, 29, 30, 51, 65, 66
Bailey, L. H., 69; and apple, 59, 63, 64; on pests, 35; and quince, 127, 128; and strawberry, 169, 170
Bailey, Robert, 27, 49, 111
Bailey, Samuel, nursery of, 62–63, 70
Balyal, Abraham, 45, 48, 86, 91
Banister, John, 80, 83, 122; *Natural History*, 13
Barclay, James, 55
Barton, Benjamin, 83, 85; on pests, 36
Bartram, John, 35, 80, 109, 111, 119; and apple growers, 72; fertilization system of, 32; and nectarine, 122; and peach, 83; and weeds, 39
Bartram, John, Jr., 167, 176, 180; and fig, 163, 164; nursery of, 172, 173, 178
Bartram, Moses, 83
Bartram, William, 83; and fig, 163; and grape, 154, 158, 160; and strawberry, 170
Beach, S. A., 74; *The Apples of New York*, 70, 75
Berkeley, William, 61, 127, 139, 142
Berry: squares, 7, 132, 133, 175, 178, 180; varieties at Monticello, 180; *see also* Currant; Gooseberry; Raspberry; Strawberry
Beverley, Robert, 111, 122, 139, 143, 152, 178; and apple, 62; and currant, 176; and fig, 163; and grape, 142; *The History and Present State of Virginia*, 13; and peach, 80, 83; and plum, 109; and raspberry, 179; and strawberry, 170
Bitter rot, 68
Black knot, 96
Black rot, 35, 131, 146, 149, 151, 152
Blair, Archibald, 18

Bolling, James, 68

Bolling, Robert, 139, 145, 148, 152; "Essay on the Utility of Vine Planting in Virginia," 143; "Sketch of Vine Culture for Pennsylvania, Maryland, Virginia, and the Carolinas," 143, 145

Booth, William, nursery of, 63, 75, 87, 124, 126

Broadnax, John, 97

Brookshaw, George, 165; *The Horticultural Repository*, 165; *Pomona Brittanica*, 179

Bruce, Philip, 29, 64

Byrd, William, 81, 93, 111, 139, 152, 178; and almond, 125; and cherry, 94–95; and cider, 64, 78; and currant, 176; and grape, 142; *Natural History*, 61, 100, 119; and nectarine, 122; and pear, 101; and plum, 109, 110; and quince, 128; and raspberry, 179; and strawberry, 171

Carolina parrot, 69

Carroll, Charles, 39, 101, 119, 122

Carter, Charles, 139, 142

Carter, Landon, 33, 75, 114, 139, 142; and cherry, 95; and currant, 176; and fig, 164; and gooseberry, 178; and peach, 81; and plum, 110–11; and strawberry, 171, 172

Carter, Mrs. Robert, 119

Castiglioni, Luigi, 19, 55, 80, 81, 109

Cate (slave of Jefferson), 81

Catesby, Mark, *The Natural History of Carolina, Florida, and the Bahama Islands*, 69

Cedar-apple rust, 68

Chastellux, marquis de, 60–61

Chelsea Physic Garden, 20

Cherry: August, 97; Black Heart, 93, 94, 95, 96, 97; Bleeding Heart, 95, 97; "Broadnax," 97; Carnation, 95, 96, 97; —, at Monticello, 41, 53; —, uses of, 93; Cornelian, 97; Early Richmond, 98; Kentish, 95, 96, 98; "May," 98; May Duke, 15, 95, 96, 98, 99; —, at Monticello, 41; —, uses of, 93; at Monticello, 94; Morello, 95, 96, 97–98; as ornamental, 93–94; Ox Heart, 15, 95; pests of, 96; preservation, 94, 95; propagation, 96; *Prunus avium*, 7; "Tuckahoe grey heart," 98; uses of, 94–95; White Heart, 95, 98–99

Cherry leaf spot, 96

Cider, 59–61, 64–66

Clifford, George, 169, 173

Clinton, DeWitt, 35, 36

Cobbett, William, 14, 22, 23, 83, 152; *The American Gardener*, 23; and apricot, 119; on fences, 27, 29; and fig, 164; and gooseberry, 178; on irrigation, 32; and nectarine, 122; and peach, 85; on pests, 35, 38; and plum, 109; on pruning, 82; and raspberry, 179; and strawberry, 173; on weeds, 39

Cocke, Ann Barraud, 18

Cocke, Elizabeth, 110, 112

Cocke, John Hartwell, 15, 17–19, 31, 33, 85, 97; and almond, 125; and apple, 19, 71, 74, 77; and apricot, 119, 120; and cherry, 98; and currant, 176; and fig, 161, 164; fruit garden of, 8, 14, 19; and Fruit Tree Association, 18; and gooseberry, 178; and grape, 138; Lower Bremo, 18; and nectarine, 122, 124; and peach, 87; and pear, 100, 101, 105, 106; and plum, 110, 111, 112, 113, 115; and quince, 128; Recess cottage, 18, 19; treating peach borer, 18, 84; Upper Bremo, 17, 18, 19

Codling moth, 36

Colden, Cadwallader, 62

Coles, Isaac, 27, 45, 104; and cherry, 96, 98; and fig, 161; and peach, 86

Coles, Walter, 84, 88

Collinson, Michael, 72

Collinson, Peter, 109, 176; and apple, 72; and apricot, 119; and nectarine, 122; and peach, 80, 85; on pests, 35, 36; and plum, 111; on plum curculio, 120; on strawberry, 171

Cooper, Joseph, 5, 110, 113

Coulter, Thomas, 84

Coxe, William, 31, 33, 84; and apple, 71, 74; and apricot, 121; and cherry, 97–98; on fire blight, 102; and nectarine, 122, 124; and peach, 85, 87, 88, 90, 91; and pear, 101, 102, 106; on pests, 36, 68, 69; and plum, 109, 112, 113, 115–16; on pruning, 34; and quince, 127, 128; *A View of the Cultivation of Fruit Trees*, 6, 18, 36, 103

Crabgrass, 38

Crèvecoeur, Hector St. John de, 35

Cultivation, 32–33

Curculio, *see* Plum curculio

Currant: Champagne, 176; culture of, 179; as grown by Jefferson, 175–76; "Lewis' Fragrant," 176, 180; Red Dutch, 176; *Ribes aureum*, 180; *Ribes odoratum*, 176, 180; *Ribes sativum*, 176, 180; White Dutch, 176, 180

Custis, John, 31, 32, 111; and currant, 176; and fig, 166; and gooseberry, 178; and peach, 85; on pests, 36; and plum, 109; and strawberry, 171

David, Jean, 131, 137–38

Dean, Samuel, *New England Farmer*, 171

Deer, 68–69

Dickson, Robert, 31

Divers, George, 49, 100, 172, 174; and almond, 126; and apple, 73, 74; and raspberry, 176, 178

Domestic Encyclopedia, 84, 119, 145, 152, 158, 171

Downing, Andrew Jackson, 1, 3, 39, 161; and almond, 126; and apple, 64, 71, 74, 78; and apricot, 120, 121; and cherry, 97, 98; and currant, 180; and fig, 166; *Fruits and Fruit Trees of America*, 1, 2, 87; and grape, 154, 155; and nectarine, 124; and peach, 83, 86, 88, 91, 92; and pear, 102, 103, 104, 106; and plum, 110, 112, 113, 115, 116; on plum curculio, 111; and raspberry, 180; *Treatise on the Theory and Practice of Landscape Gardening*, 1

Downing, Charles, 105

Downy mildew, 131, 146, 151

Drayton, William, 110, 113, 161, 165

Duchesne, Antoine, 169; *Histoire naturelle des fraisiers*, 169; and strawberry, 171, 172

Dufour, John James, 131, 145, 152, 154, 158; *The American Vine Dresser's Guide*, 135; vine-training systems, 148

Duhamel Du Monceau, Henri Louis, *Traité des arbres fruitiers*, 76

Durand of Dauphiné, 64

Eddis, William, 13

Elgin Botanic Gardens, 171

Ellicott, George, 96

Eppes, Francis, 46, 49, 66

Eppes, John Wayles, 135, 180

Estave, Andrew, 139, 142–43, 152

Evans, Lewis, 66

Faris, William, 164, 176

Farm Book, 32, 49

Fences, 6, 27, 28, 29

Fig, 161, 163, 165; Angelique, 48, 166; Brown Ischia, 163; Brunswick, 163; culture, 164; in history, 163; Marseilles, 41, 48, 165–66; White, 162, 166

Fire blight, 35, 67, 68, 100, 102

Fithian, Philip Vickers, 19, 119; and fig, 164; and gooseberry, 178; and nectarine, 122; and peach, 81; and strawberry, 171

Fitz, James, 33, 60, 69, 75, 76; *Southern Apple and Peach Culturist*, 6, 66

Fitzhugh, William, 29, 61, 109

Fletcher, S. W., 35, 170

Florence Botanical Garden, 135, 158

Flyspeck, 36, 68

Forsyth, William, 38, 95; and apricot, 119; and currant, 176; "Forsyth's Composition," 22, 33; and pear, 102; and plum, 112, 116; pruning techniques of, 33, 34; and quince, 127; treating peach borer, 84; *Treatise on the Culture and Management of Fruit Trees*, 14, 18, 22, 23, 26, 34

Franklin, Benjamin, 72, 124, 133

Freeman, John, 51

Frézier, Amedée François, 169, 173

Fruit garden, 14–15

Fruit spot, 68

Fruit varieties, 39, 41

Gallesio, Giorgio, 90, 91, 121, 157

Garden Book, 6, 25, 43, 52, 54, 73; and berries, 179; on cherry, 93; fruit names in, 42; and grape, 132, 134, 135; recipe in, 175; records of plantings in, 10, 51; and strawberry, 167

Geismar, Major von, 134

Genet, Edmund Charles, 69, 70

Gerard, John, 170

Giannini, Antonio, 27, 44, 45, 46, 48; and Monticello vineyard, 134, 135

Gilmer, George, 98

Girardin, Louis Hue, 138

Glover, Thomas, 176; and apple, 61; and apricot, 119; and cherry, 95; and fig, 163; and gooseberry, 177; and grape, 140; and pear, 101; and plum, 109

Gooseberry, 177, 178; culture, 179; Houghton, 178

Grape: "Abrostine Red," 158; "Abrostine White," 158; Aleatico, 158; Alexander, 135, 139, 152, 153, 154; —, as grown by Jefferson, 137, 138; "Black cluster," 154; Black Hamburg, 154; Bland, 158; Catawba, 139, 147, 151; Chasselas Dorè, 154; Chasselas Rosè, 154; Cornichon Blanc, 156; culture, 144–52; Fox, 140; Furmint, 158; Galletta, 157; growing in Virginia, 139–44; "Lachrima Christi," 158; Luglienga, 157; "Malaga," 154–55; Mammolo Toscano, 158; at Monticello, 132–39; Morgiano, 158; "Muscadine," 155; Muscat Blanc, 155; Muscat of Alexandria, 157; Norton's Seedling, 160; Norton's Virginia, 159; pests of, 140, 149, 151; "Piedmont Malmsey," 157; "Purple Syrian," 160; Red Hamburg, 157; Regina, 157; Sangiovese, 158; Scuppernong, 139, 160; Seralamanna, 157; "Smyrna," 157–58; "Tokay," 158; training and pruning, 148–49; Trebbiano, 158; *Vitis labrusca*, 131; *Vitis rotundifolia*, 131; *Vitis vinifera*, 131, 137, 138, 142, 144; —, at Colle, 134; —, at Monticello, 135; —, pests of, 140, 146; —, wine from, 141; *Vitis vulpina*, 134, 141; White Frontinac, 155

Gray, Asa, 108

Gray, Francis Calley, 64–65

Great George (slave of Jefferson), 48

Grove, William Hugh, 31; and apricot, 119; and grape, 140; and peach, 80–81, 82; and raspberry, 179; and strawberry, 171

Hackley, Harriet, 126

Hall, Francis, 55

Hamilton, William, 27, 161

Hariot, Thomas, 170

Hawkins, Benjamin, 135, 146, 154

Hedrick, U. P., 38, 113; and apple, 71, 78; and apricot, 119; and cherry, 94, 97, 98; and gooseberry, 178; and grape, 140; *The Grapes of New York*, 154; and nectarine, 122; and peach, 81, 82, 86, 88, 90; and pear, 102, 103; *The Pears of New York*, 102; on pests, 35; and plum, 114

Hepburn, Alexander, 50, 51, 89, 135; and apricot, 120, 121; nursery of, 24, 86; and plum, 116

Hooker, William J., 59

Hooper, E. J., 75

Hooper, William, 29

Horticultural Society of London, 73, 177

Horticulture, origins of American, 5–6

Hosack, David, 103, 171

Isaac (slave of Jefferson), 27

Jackson, James, 49, 91

James River Garden Club, *Historic Gardens of Virginia*, 164

Jardin des Plantes, 38

Jefferson, Martha, 34, 35, 81

Jefferson, Peter, 42

Jefferson, Thomas, 3; on American viticulture, 138–39; and apple, 75; and cherry, 97; and cidermaking, 65–66, 74; comparing European and American fruit trees, 46, 48; on cultivation, 32; directions for planting, 31–32; and fig, 164, 165; fruit garden and kitchen garden, 7; fruit library of, 20–24; and fruit variety collection, 39–40; influence on horticulture, 9; on Mazzei's viticultural experiments, 134; *Notes on the State of Virginia*, 38, 42, 111; nurseries of, 24–25; orchard chart, 1811, 51–52, 53; orchard plan, 1778, 44, 45, 46; orchard plan, 1783, 46; orchard plan, 1811, 54; ornamental farm plan, 3; and peach, 86–87; and pear, 100, 103; on pests, 34–35; as planter, 6–10; on planting, 31–32; on propagation, 26–27; on pruning, 33; "Revisal of my Fruit, 1783," 46, 47; on staking, 32; and strawberry, 167, 172; and vineyard plan, 135; on weeds, 38–39; and wine, 131; writing on fruit cultivation, 9–10

Johnson, S. W., 131, 146, 148, 149; grape training, 149; *Rural Economy*, 145

Johnson, William, 138

Jones, Hugh, 95, 96; *The Present State of Virginia*, 142

Josslyn, John, *New England Rarities*, 39

Joyce, John, 127

Jupiter (slave of Jefferson), 65

Kalm, Peter, 20, 29, 39, 61, 68; and cherry, 94; and pear, 102; and raspberry, 179

Kenrick, William, 39, 64, 75; and apple, 70; and apricot, 121; and fig, 166; and peach, 83; and pear, 104, 105, 106; and strawberry, 173

Knight, Thomas, 100

Landreth nursery, 63, 88, 103, 110, 121, 124

Langley, Batty, 14, 19, 112; and apricot, 117, 121; and cherry, 95; and currant, 176; and nectarine, 124; *New Principles of Gardening*, 20; and

Langley, Batty (*cont.*)
  plum, 115, 116; *Pomona: or, The Fruit-Garden Illustrated*, 20, 21; and strawberry, 170
La Rochefoucauld-Liancourt, duc de, 82, 86
Lawson, John, 139; and apple, 77; and apricot, 119; and gooseberry, 178; *History of Carolina*, 13; and nectarine, 122; and peach, 79; and pear, 101; and plum, 109; and quince, 127–28; and raspberry, 179; and strawberry, 171
Leaf blight, 36, 68
Legaux, Peter, 131, 137, 145, 148, 154; as source of grape vines, 135, 152
Lewis, Meriwether, 24, 49, 180
Lewis, Nicholas, 32
Lewis and Clark expedition, 24, 175
London Horticultural Society, 103, 179
Loudon, J. C., 157; *Encyclopædia of Gardening*, 55

Madison, James, 48, 131
Madison, James (Reverend), 46, 134
Main, Thomas: nursery of, 24, 27, 49; —, apples from, 73; —, grapes from, 135, 154–55, 157; —, peaches from, 86, 88, 91
Malesherbes, Chrétien-Guillaume de Lamoignon de, 134, 144
Maryland Gazette and Baltimore General Advertiser, 59, 63
Mason, George, 85, 86, 91, 94, 97, 134
Matlack, Timothy, 32, 103, 116, 117; and apricot, 120; and grape, 135, 145, 160; letter from Jefferson, quoted, 6; "On the Cultivation of the Vine," quoted, 144; and peach, 86, 87, 88, 91; and pear, 102, 105–6; and plum, 113; as source of fruit trees, 51
Mayo, William, 81, 86
Mazzei, Philip, 9, *133*, 139, 152; and almond, 126; and apricot, 117, 120, 121; and grape, 132–34, 157–58; influence on Jefferson, 42, 44; and peach, 86, 89, 90, 91, 92; and plum, 115, 116; and raspberry, 178; as source for fruit varieties, 49, 50, 51; as source for vines, 135; and strawberry, 172; and viticulture, 131, 134, 143, 144, 146
McMahon, A., nursery, 176, 180
McMahon, Bernard, 23, 131, 145; *American Gardener's Calendar*, 24, 25, 83, 87, 145, 178; and apricot, 121; and currant, 175, 180; and fig, 163; and gooseberry, 180; and grape, 137, 152, 154, 155, 157; —, training system for, 148, 149; nursery of, 75, 172, 173, 178; and plum, 109, 111; on pruning, 34; and raspberry, 180; and staking transplants, 32; and strawberry, 167, 171, 174; and traditional fruit garden, 14
Mease, James, 74, 75, 145, 152, 171, 178
Menefie, George, 61, 95
Meriwether, Nicholas, 45, 71, 105
Meriwether, William, 49, 51, 86, 88, 121
Mice, 68–69
Michaux, François André, 14
Michel, Francis Louis, 13, 61–62, 95, 101, 109
Miller, Philip, 24, 25, 32, 112; and almond, 125; and cherry, 93, 95, 98; and currant, 176; and fig, 163, 165; *Gardener's Dictionary*, 16, 20, 22, 163, 169; and grape, 152, 154; on mobby, 80–81; and nectarine, 124; and peach, 88, 90; and plum, 111, 113, 115, 116; and quince, 127; and raspberry, 179; and strawberry, 172; and traditional fruit garden, 14
Monroe, James, 131, 138, 172
Monticello: as *ferme ornée*, 1; fruit garden, 7, 8, 9–10, 14–15; nurseries, 24–25; orchard plans, 44–46, 48, *50*, 53, *54*; site, 30–31; southeastern slope, *30*; viticulture at, 131
Moore, Gershom, 70

Morgan, Patrick, 27, 45
Morris, Robert Hunter, 91

Nectarine: Elruge, 122; Fairchild's Early, 122; Franklin, 122; as grown by Jefferson, 122; "Kaskaskia soft," 122; Newington, 122; "plumb," 122; Red Roman, 49, 122, 124; Yellow Roman, 49, 122, 124
North orchard, 7, 30, 46, 48, 49; and cider, 66; and Clarke Pearmain, 76; and Hewes Crab, 74; number of trees planted in, 53, 65
Norton, Daniel N., 160
Notes on the State of Virginia, 38, 42, 111
Nurseries, 24–25, 46, 51

Oldmixon, John, 81; *The British Empire in America*, 88
Orr, Henry, 164

Parent, Etienne, 134
Parkinson, John, 24, 101; and almond, 125; and cherry, 95, 97–98; and fig, 165; and peach, 91; and pear, 101; and plum, 110, 113, 114, 115; and quince, 127; and raspberry, 178–79; and strawberry, 167, 170
Parkinson, Richard, 13, 14, 29, 39, 64; and apple, 71; and apricot, 119; and cherry, 97; and currant, 176; and gooseberry, 178; and nectarine, 122, 127; and pear, 102; on pests, 68; and plum, 109, 112, 116; and raspberry, 179
Peach: Alberges, 49, 50, 51, 90; Algiers Yellow, 90; Apple, 51, 86, 90–91; bloody, 89; Breast of Venus (Poppa di Venere), 39, 49, 50, 51, 86, 89–90; Catherine, 85; culture, 79–80, 83–85; "General Jackson's," 91; Green Nutmeg, 39, 49, 85, 86, 91; Heath Cling, 39, 85, 86, 87, 88; Indian Blood Cling, 86, 88–89; Jefferson's collection of, 86–87; "Lady's favorite," 91; Large Yellow Pineapple, 88; Lemon Cling, 26, 39, 88; Maddelena, 86, 91; Magdalen, 51; "Magdalene," 91; Malta, 91; "Mammoth," 91; Morris's Red Rareripe, 86, 91; Morris's White Rareripe, 39, 91; "October," 49, 91, 92; Oldmixon Cling, 39, 86, 88; Oldmixon Free, 39, 86, 88; "Plumb," 91; Portugal, 85, 91; propagation, 85–86; Red Rareripe, 39; Sanguinole, 88; San Jacopo, 91; St. James, 51; "soft," 91–92; Teton de Venus, 89; uses of, 81–82; Vaga Loggia, 39, 49, 51, 86, 92
Peach borer, 18, 35, 83, 84
Peach scab, 36
Peach yellows, 35, 83
Peale, Charles Willson, 38, 39, 51
Pear: Bergamot, 101; Beurré Gris, 41, 49, *103*, *104*; Bon Chretiens, 101; Crassane, 41, 48, *104*, 105; Holt's Sugar, 101; Jargonelle, 101; Kieffer, 100; May, 101; Meriwether, 105; pests of, *37*, 102; Pound, 101; Rousselet, 103; Royal, 41, 48, 105; St. Germaine, 48, 101, *105*, 106; Seckel, 41, 51, 102, 103–4; "Sugar," 106; Virgouleuse, 41, 48, *106*; Warden, 101
Penn, Thomas, 152
Penn, William, 80
Pennsylvania Horticultural Society, 102
Pests, 29, 34–38, 83–84, 96; *see also* Apple scab; Bitter rot; Black knot; Black rot; Carolina parrot; Cedar-apple rust; Cherry leaf spot; Codling moth; Deer; Downy mildew; Fire blight; Flyspeck; Fruit spot; Leaf blight; Mice; Peach borer; Peach scab; Peach yellows; Phylloxera; Plum curculio; Powdery mildew; Quince rust; Tent caterpillar; Woolly aphid
Peters, Richard, 25, 37, 38, 83, 84–85, 102
Peyton, Bernard, 160
Philadelphia Society for Promoting Agriculture, *Memoirs*, 6, 9, 37, 74, 84

Philadelphia Society for the Promotion of Viticulture, 137

Phylloxera, 35, 131, 141, *151*, 152

Pickering, Thomas, 74

Pierce, Jane, 163

Pinney, Thomas, 139; *History of Wine in America*, 131–32

Planting, 31–32

Plum: Apricot, 113; Black, 109; Blue Imperatrice, *114*; Boccon del Re, 116; Brignole, 49, 110, 113; Chickasaw, 5, 41, *107*, 108, 111–12; Cooper's Large, 110, 113; Damson, 108, 109, 110, 111, 114–15; Drap d' Or, 108, 115; "Florida," 107, 115; Green Gage, 41, 48, 108, 109, *110*, 112; —, grafting of, 111; as grown by Jefferson, 108; Horse, 107, 115; Imperatrice, 115; Imperial, 110; Large white sweet, 115; Magnum Bonum, 48, 108, 110, 112–13; Mirabelle, 51, *115*; Murrey, 109; Muscle, 111, 115; Myrobolan, 108, 111; native, 108–9; Orleans, 110, 115–16; Prune, 108, 110; Red Imperial, 116; Regina, 51, 116; Royal, 116; St. Julien, 111

Plum curculio, 35, 83, 109, 111, 119–20

Poison ivy, 38

Poplar Forest, 32, 70, 78, 167

Powdery mildew, 96, 131, 146, 151, 152, 179

Prato, Giovannini da, 44, 137

Preston, Samuel, 38

Prestwould, 15, 31

Prince, Benjamin, 71, 77, 125, 178; nursery of, 18, 64, 78, 110, 176

Prince, Robert, nursery of, 160

Prince, William Robert, 94, 97, 154

Prince, William, Jr., 5, 31, 120; and cherry, 98; and plum, 110

Prince, William, Sr.: and cherry, 97; nursery of, 8, 15, 24, 122; —, apples from, 63, 73, 76; —, apricots from, 117, 119, 120, 121; —, broadside, 4; —, nectarines from, 124; —, order to, 48; —, peaches from, 85, 86, 87, 88, 90, 91; —, pears from, 101, 104; —, plums from, 110, 112–13, 116; —, strawberries from, 174; and plum, 115

Propagation, 6, 26–27

Pruning, 33–34, *144*, *150*

Quince: Barbary, 127, 128; Brunswick, 127, 128; Portugal, 127; Portugal Apple, 127, *128*

Quince rust, 68

Rafinesque, Constantine, *American Manual of Grape Vines and the Method of Making Wine*, 154

Ralls, Caleb, 69, 70

Randolph, Anne Cary, 171

Randolph, Jane Nicholas, 19, 82

Randolph, John, 171, 176; *Treatise*, 179

Randolph, Martha, 65, 178

Randolph, Mary, *Virginia House-wife*, 95, 111, 127

Randolph, Thomas Jefferson, 19, 29, 82, 96

Randolph, Thomas Mann, 27, 49, 65, 83, 172; letter from Jefferson, quoted, 81–82; letter to Jefferson, quoted, 30; and peach, 85; on weeds, 39

Raspberry: Antwerp, 41, 178, 180; culture of, 179; "Monthly," 176; Red Antwerp, 176, 179; White Antwerp, 176, 179

Rea, John, 97, 112

Reibelt, J. P., 27

Richardson, Richard, 135

Richter, P. L., 36, 68

Ronaldson, James, 180

Rush, Benjamin, 64

Say, Thomas, 84

Schoepf, Johann David, 13

Shadwell, 68

Short, William, 86

Skinner, John, 25, 38, 179

Skipwith, Jean, 15, 22, 97; and apple, 71, 74; and currant, 176; and fig, 164; and nectarine, 122, 124; and peach, 85; and plum, 112

Skipwith, Peyton, 15, 31, 104

Smith, John, 7, 39, 61, 139, 140; and fig, 163; and plum, 109

Smith, Margaret Bayard, 161, 164, 178, 180

Smith, William, 97, 98; nursery of: apples from, 62, 71, 74, 78; —, advertisement for, *63*; —, cherries from, 96; —, peaches from, 85; —, pears from, 101; —, plums from, 110, 112, 115

Sorsby, Thomas, 15, 78; nursery of, 62, 71, 74, 85

Southern Planter, 33, 71, 84, 85

Spooner, John James, 19

Spotswood, Alexander, 139, 152

Spruel, George E., 160

Spurrier, John, *Practical Farmer*, 66

Staking, 32

Stevenson, Andrew, 73

Stockton, Frank, 55

Strachey, William, 109, 140

Stratchan and Maury nursery, 62, 70, 75, 101

Strawberry, 167, 169; Alpine, 167, 171, 172, 173; Capiton, 167; Chili, 167, 170, 171, *173*; culture, 171–72; Hautboy, 167, 170, 171; Hudson, 41, 171, 174; Pine, 169, 171; Scarlet, 167, 169, 171; Wood, 167, *168*, 171

Submural beds, 7, 161

Taliaferro, Richard, 45, 75

Tasker, Benjamin, Jr., 152

Tayloe, John, 66, 164

Taylor, James, 73, 86, 91, 122

Taylor, John, 66, 68–69; *Arator*, 61

Tent caterpillar, 36, 68

Thomas, John Jay, 64, 71, 111

Thornton, William, 137, 161

Thöuin, André, 38

Threlkeld, John, 51, 86, 117, 120, 121

Tilton, James, 83, 84

Trist, Nicholas, 82

Trist, Virginia, 55

Tucker, St. George, *15*, 19, 31, 33; and almond, 125; and apple, 71; and apricot, 117, 119; and cherry, 97, 98; fruit garden of, 8, 14, 15–16; and nectarine, 122, 124; and peach, 85, 88; and pear, 101; and plum, 110, 111, 112, 113, 115; and quince, 128

United States Department of Agriculture, *Nomenclature of the Apple*, 59–60

University of Virginia, 18

Ursula (slave of Jefferson), 65

Vineyards, Monticello, 131, *132*; espalier system, *150*; plan, *133*, *136*

Virginia Almanac, 15

Virginia Company, 95

Virginia Fruit Tree Association, 64

Virginia Gazette, 22, 142, 143; advertisements in, 14, 19, 59, 74, 81, 117; —, nursery, 119

Virginia State Horticultural Society, *Report*, 60, 72

Walker, James, 45, 97

Walker, Thomas, 71–72

Walten, Philip, 63, 110, 124

Warren, Richard, 119, 122

Washington, George, 22, 31, 32, 33, 131, 139; and almond, 125; and apple, 71; and apricot, 117, 119; and cherry, 93, 97; "cherry walk," 16; and currant, 176; and fences, 29; fruit garden of, 8, 14, 16, 17; and gooseberry, 178; and grape, 143–44; Langley's influence on, 20; letter from Mazzei, quoted, 133–34; Mount Vernon, 16–17, 20; and nectarine, 122, 124; nursery of, 25; and peach, 79, 85, 88, 91; and pear, 100, 101, 106; and plum, 111, 112, 115; and quince, 128

Weather Memorandum Book, 10, 135

Weeds, 38–39

White, William, 66, 81, 83, 96, 111; and fig, 165; and plum, 111

Williams, Edward, "Treatise of the Vine," 140

Woolly aphid, 69

Wormley [Hughes] (slave of Jefferson), 29, 164

Worth, James, 36, 96

Worthington, James, 172

Wynkoop, Henry, 33, 65, 75

Wythe, George, 15, 117, 122, 134